SHONEN JUMP MANGA

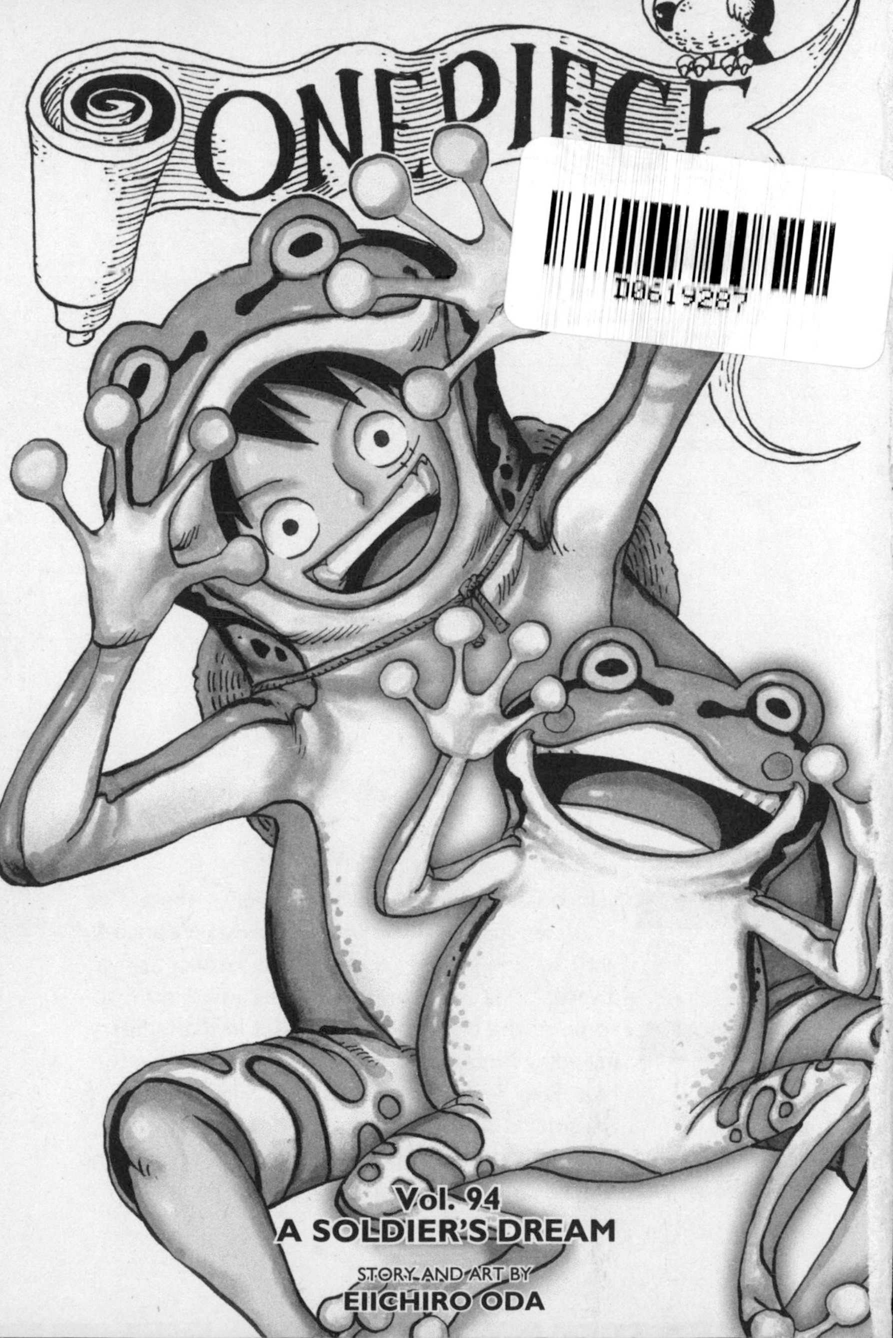
ONE PIECE

Vol. 94

A SOLDIER'S DREAM

STORY AND ART BY

EIICHIRO ODA

尾田栄一郎

Apparently, snails won't travel over their own trails because they hate the sliminess of it. **What gives?!!**

-Eiichiro Oda, 2019

Eiichiro Oda began his manga career at the age of 17, when his one-shot cowboy manga **Wanted!** won second place in the coveted Tezuka manga awards. Oda went on to work as an assistant to some of the biggest manga artists in the industry, including Nobuhiro Watsuki, before winning the Hop Step Award for new artists. His pirate adventure **One Piece**, which debuted in **Weekly Shonen Jump** in 1997, quickly became one of the most popular manga in Japan.

The story of ONE PIECE 1»94

Characters

The Straw Hat Crew

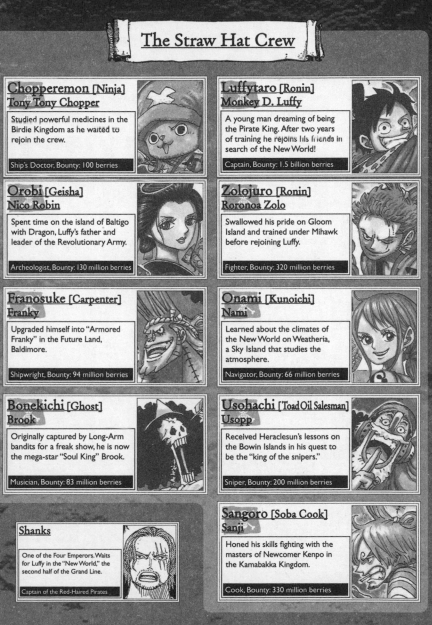

Chopperemon [Ninja]
Tony Tony Chopper

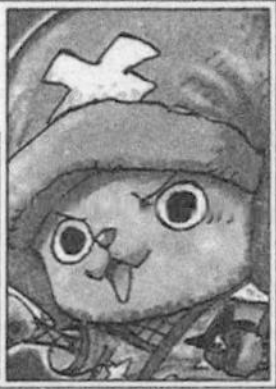

Studied powerful medicines in the Birdie Kingdom as he waited to rejoin the crew.

Ship's Doctor, Bounty: 100 berries

Luffytaro [Ronin]
Monkey D. Luffy

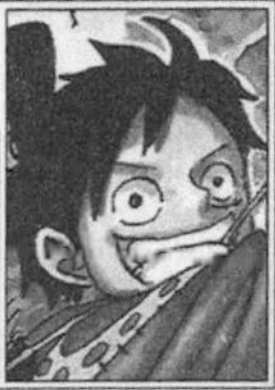

A young man dreaming of being the Pirate King. After two years of training he rejoins his friends in search of the New World!

Captain, Bounty: 1.5 billion berries

Orobi [Geisha]
Nico Robin

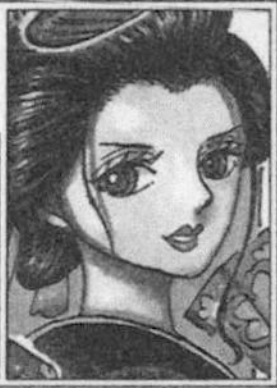

Spent time on the island of Baltigo with Dragon, Luffy's father and leader of the Revolutionary Army.

Archeologist, Bounty: 130 million berries

Zolojuro [Ronin]
Roronoa Zolo

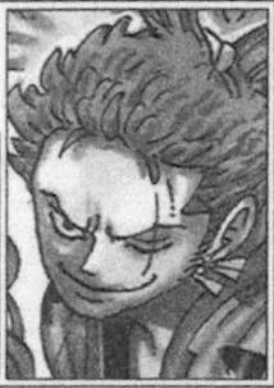

Swallowed his pride on Gloom Island and trained under Mihawk before rejoining Luffy.

Fighter, Bounty: 320 million berries

Franosuke [Carpenter]
Franky

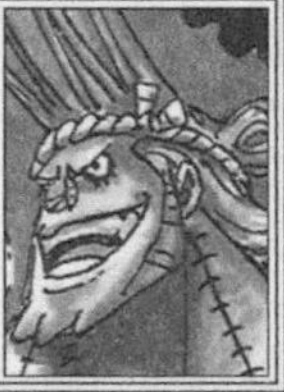

Upgraded himself into "Armored Franky" in the Future Land, Baldimore.

Shipwright, Bounty: 94 million berries

Onami [Kunoichi]
Nami

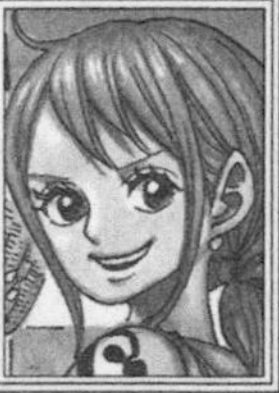

Learned about the climates of the New World on Weatheria, a Sky Island that studies the atmosphere.

Navigator, Bounty: 66 million berries

Bonekichi [Ghost]
Brook

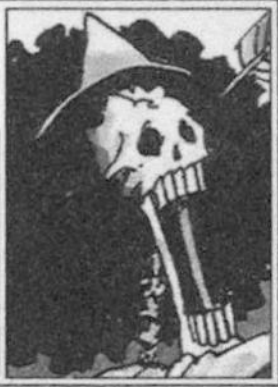

Originally captured by Long-Arm bandits for a freak show, he is now the mega-star "Soul King" Brook.

Musician, Bounty: 83 million berries

Usohachi [Toad Oil Salesman]
Usopp

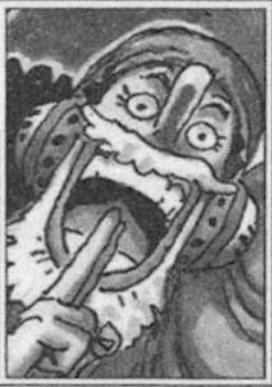

Received Heraclesun's lessons on the Bowin Islands in his quest to be the "king of the snipers."

Sniper, Bounty: 200 million berries

Shanks

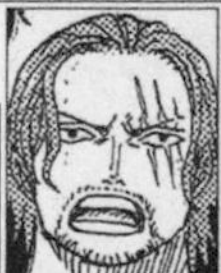

One of the Four Emperors. Waits for Luffy in the "New World," the second half of the Grand Line.

Captain of the Red-Haired Pirates

Sangoro [Soba Cook]
Sanji

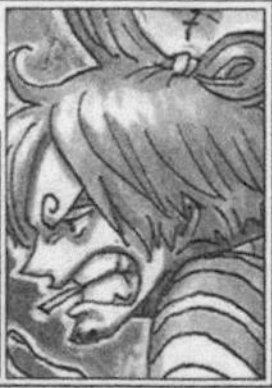

Honed his skills fighting with the masters of Newcomer Kenpo in the Kamabakka Kingdom.

Cook, Bounty: 330 million berries

Ninja-Pirate-Mink-Samurai Alliance

Characters

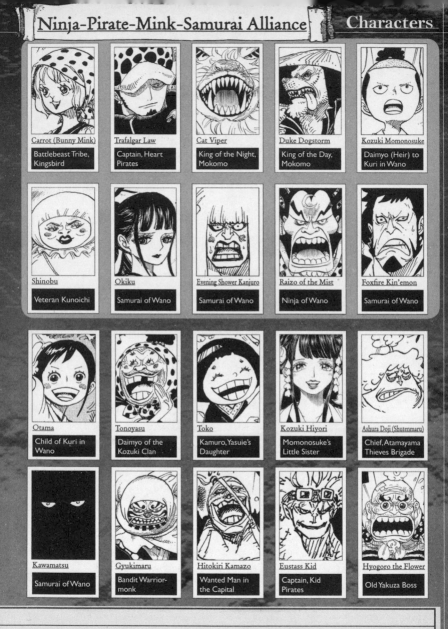

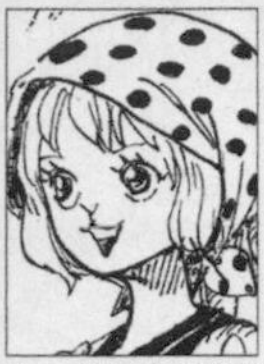
Carrot (Bunny Mink)
Battlebeast Tribe, Kingsbird

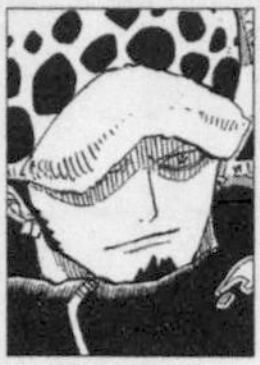
Trafalgar Law
Captain, Heart Pirates

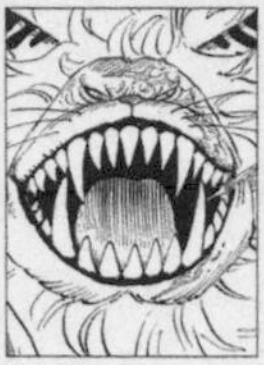
Cat Viper
King of the Night, Mokomo

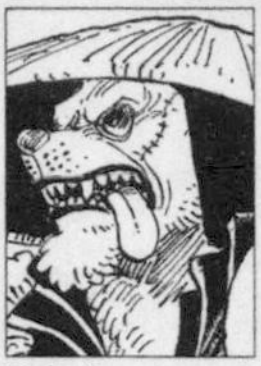
Duke Dogstorm
King of the Day, Mokomo

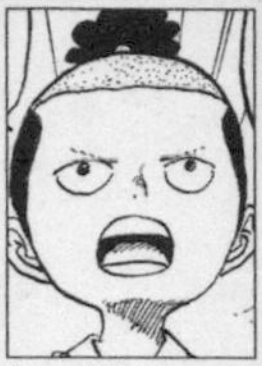
Kozuki Momonosuke
Daimyo (Heir) to Kuri in Wano

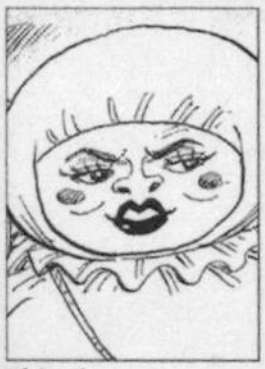
Shinobu
Veteran Kunoichi

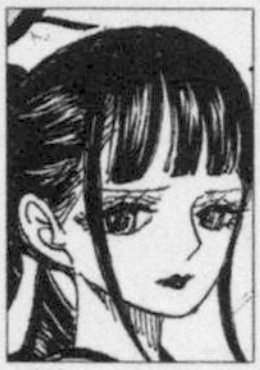
Okiku
Samurai of Wano

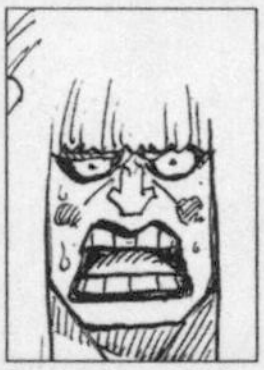
Evening Shower Kanjuro
Samurai of Wano

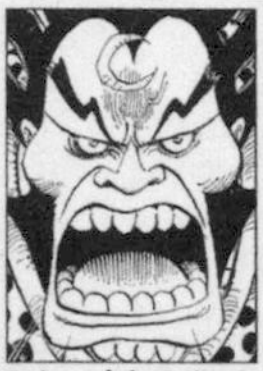
Raizo of the Mist
Ninja of Wano

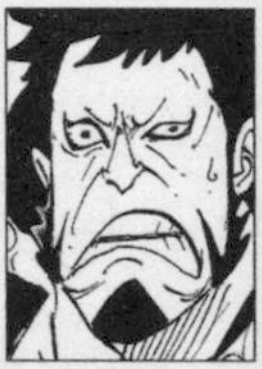
Foxfire Kin'emon
Samurai of Wano

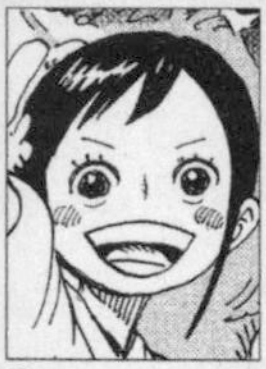
Otama
Child of Kuri in Wano

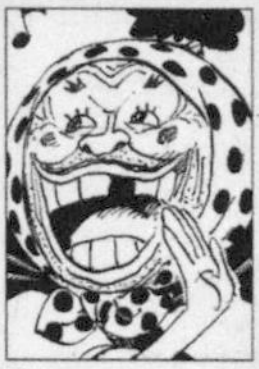
Tonoyasu
Daimyo of the Kozuki Clan

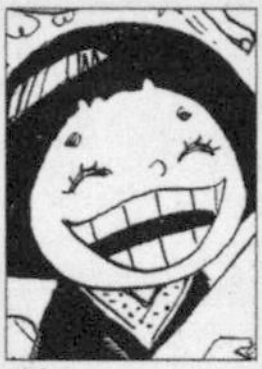
Toko
Kamuro, Yasuie's Daughter

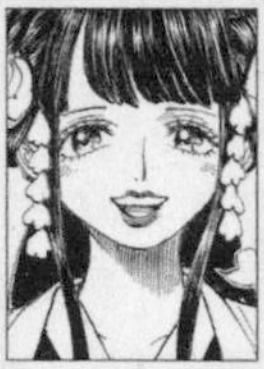
Kozuki Hiyori
Momonosuke's Little Sister

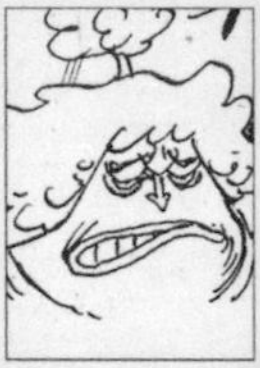
Ashura Doji (Shutenmaru)
Chief, Atamayama Thieves Brigade

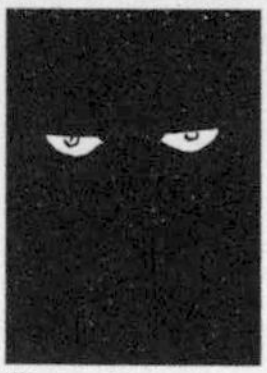
Kawamatsu
Samurai of Wano

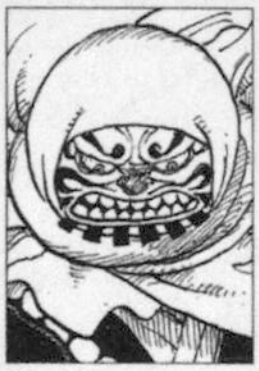
Gyukimaru
Bandit Warrior-monk

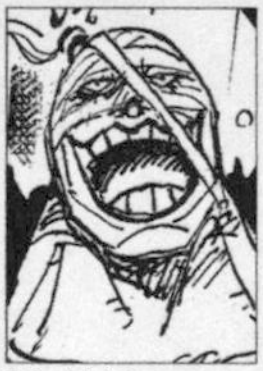
Hitokiri Kamazo
Wanted Man in the Capital

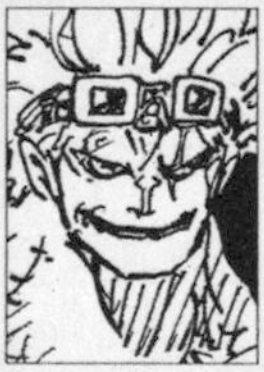
Eustass Kid
Captain, Kid Pirates

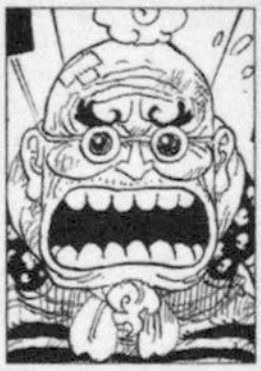
Hyogoro the Flower
Old Yakuza Boss

As the group works to collect info, free Luffy and gather more allies, Kaido's side learns about the raid plan. A former daimyo with the Kozuki Clan, Yasuie realizes the danger and gives up his life to pretend to take responsibility, sending the plan back to square one. Kin'emon and company mourn his death, but there are still many problems to be solved before the raid...

The story of ONE PIECE 1»94

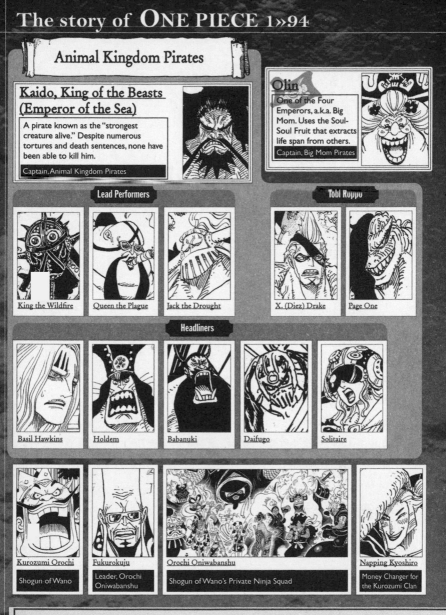

Animal Kingdom Pirates

Kaido, King of the Beasts (Emperor of the Sea)

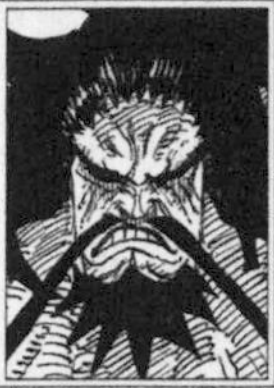

A pirate known as the "strongest creature alive." Despite numerous tortures and death sentences, none have been able to kill him.

Captain, Animal Kingdom Pirates

Olin

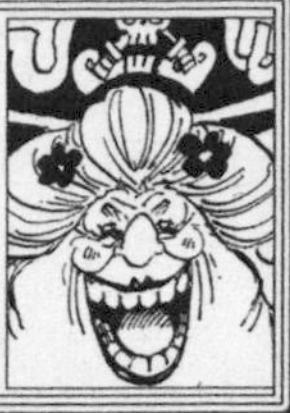

One of the Four Emperors, a.k.a. Big Mom. Uses the Soul-Soul Fruit that extracts life span from others.

Captain, Big Mom Pirates

Lead Performers

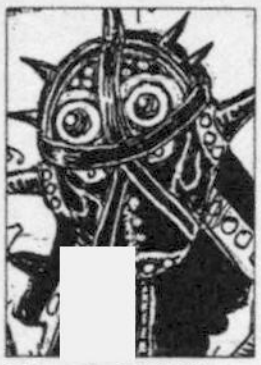

King the Wildfire

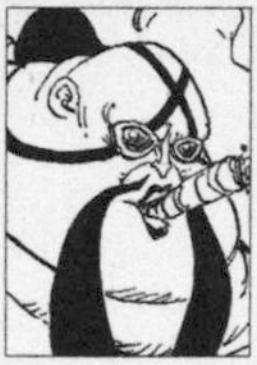

Queen the Plague

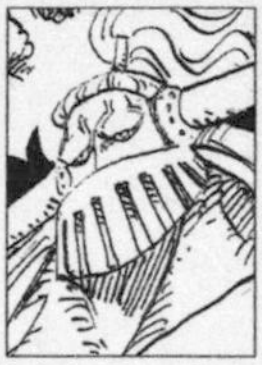

Jack the Drought

Tobi Roppo

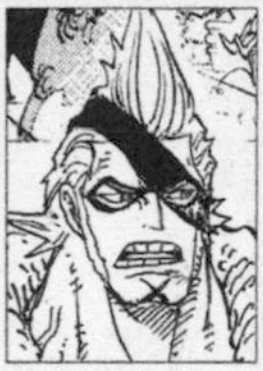

X. (Diez) Drake

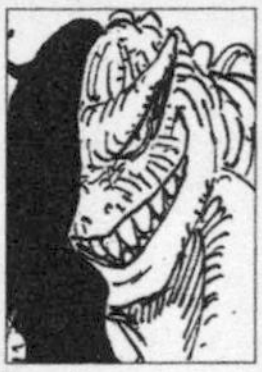

Page One

Headliners

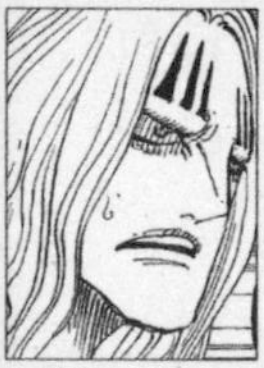

Basil Hawkins

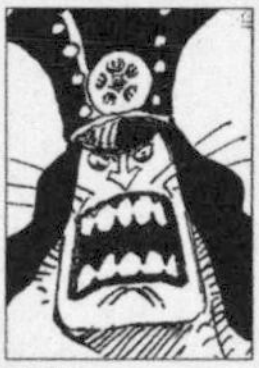

Holdem

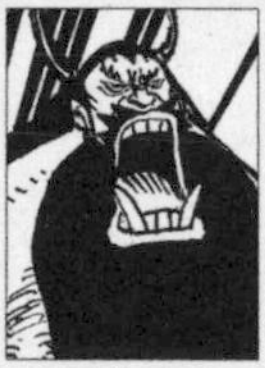

Babanuki

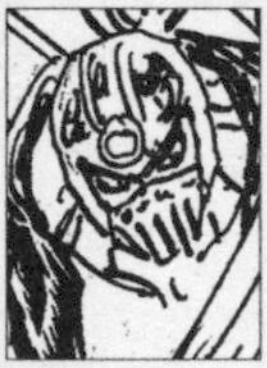

Daifugo

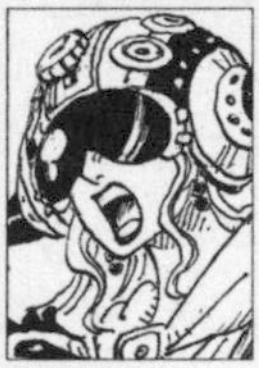

Solitaire

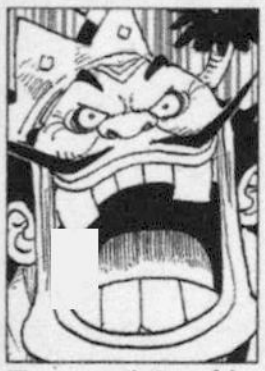

Kurozumi Orochi

Shogun of Wano

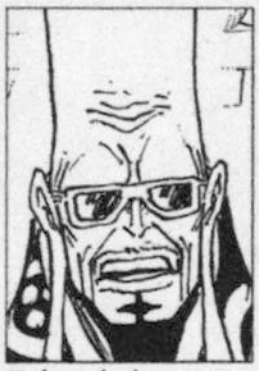

Fukurokuju

Leader, Orochi Oniwabanshu

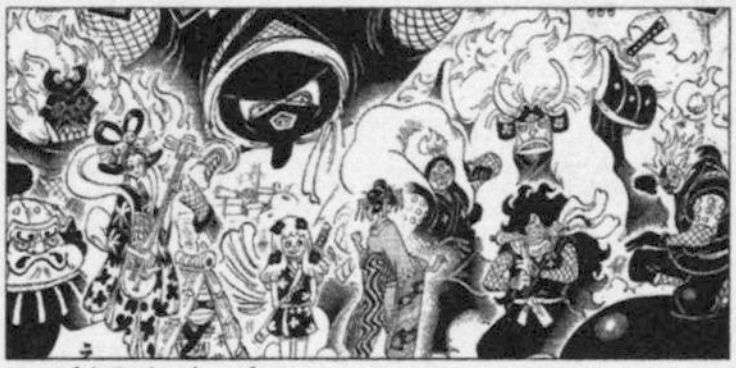

Orochi Oniwabanshu

Shogun of Wano's Private Ninja Squad

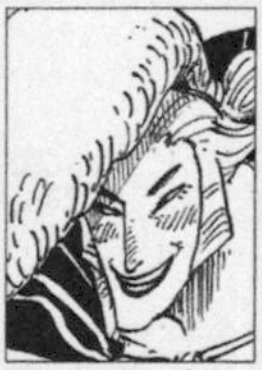

Napping Kyoshiro

Money Changer for the Kurozumi Clan

Story

After two years of hard training, the Straw Hat pirates are back together, first at the Sabaody Archipelago and then through Fish-Man Island to their next stage: the New World!!

Luffy and crew disembark on Wano for the purpose of defeating Kaido, one of the Four Emperors. They begin to recruit allies for a raid in two weeks' time, but Kaido's sudden appearance leads to Luffy's defeat. Luffy is sent to the excavation labor camp while the rest of the crew is spotted by Kaido's underlings and have to go on the run!

WANO ONE PIECE

Vol. 94
A SOLDIER'S DREAM

CONTENTS

Chapter 943:
SMILE

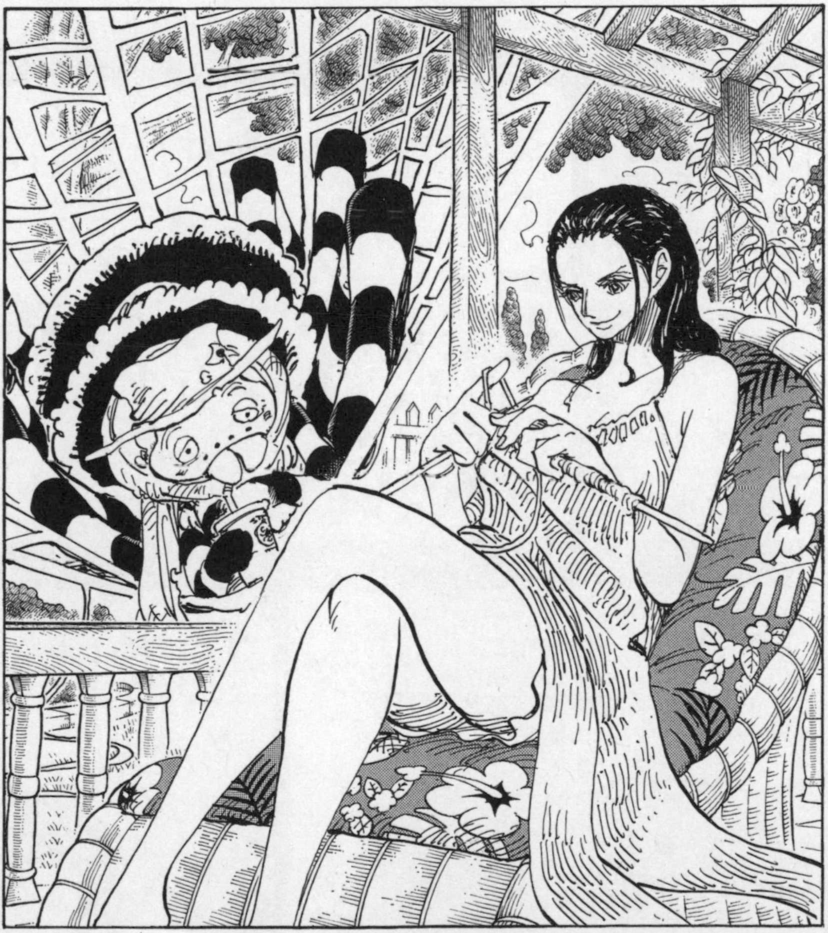

REQUEST: "ROBIN KNITTING WITH TARANTULA THREAD" BY NODA SKYWALKER

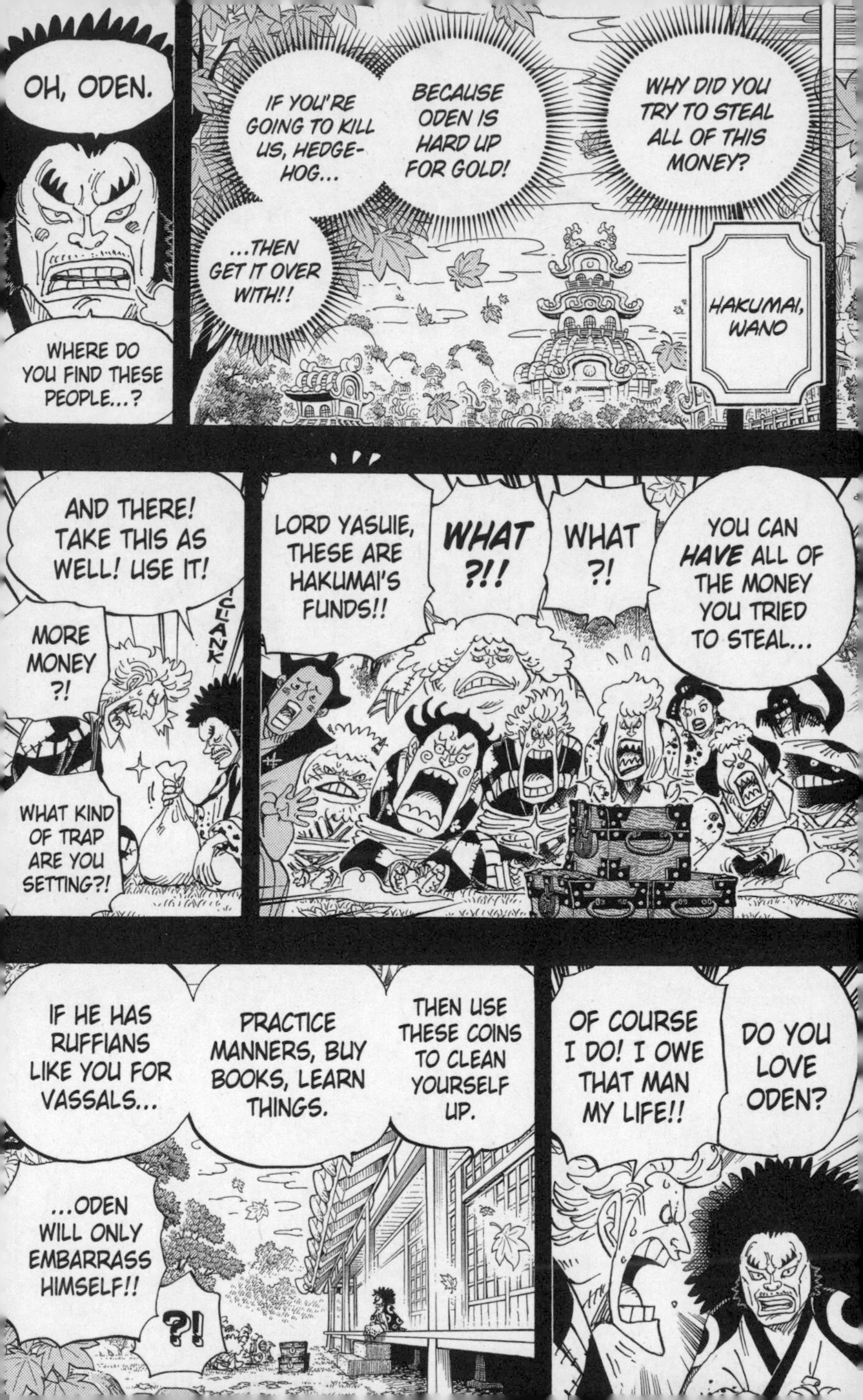
WHY DID YOU TRY TO STEAL ALL OF THIS MONEY?
HAKUMAI, WANO
BECAUSE ODEN IS HARD UP FOR GOLD!
IF YOU'RE GOING TO KILL US, HEDGE-HOG...
...THEN GET IT OVER WITH!!
OH, ODEN.
WHERE DO YOU FIND THESE PEOPLE...?
YOU CAN HAVE ALL OF THE MONEY YOU TRIED TO STEAL...
WHAT ?!
WHAT ?!!
LORD YASUIE, THESE ARE HAKUMAI'S FUNDS!!
AND THERE! TAKE THIS AS WELL! USE IT!
CLANK
MORE MONEY ?!
WHAT KIND OF TRAP ARE YOU SETTING?!
DO YOU LOVE ODEN?
OF COURSE I DO! I OWE THAT MAN MY LIFE!!
THEN USE THESE COINS TO CLEAN YOURSELF UP.
PRACTICE MANNERS, BUY BOOKS, LEARN THINGS.
IF HE HAS RUFFIANS LIKE YOU FOR VASSALS...
...ODEN WILL ONLY EMBARRASS HIMSELF!!
?!

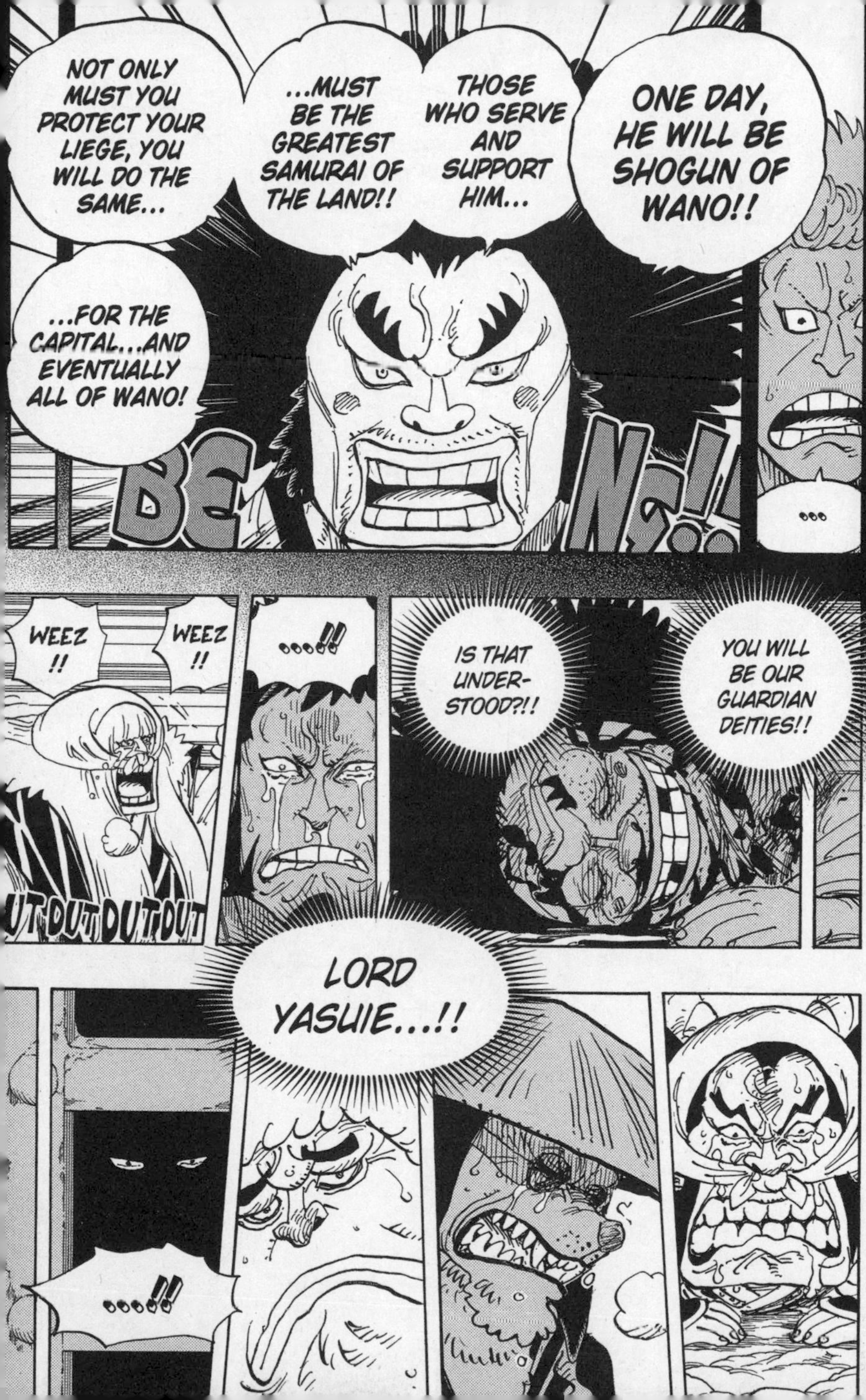
ONE DAY, HE WILL BE SHOGUN OF WANO!!
THOSE WHO SERVE AND SUPPORT HIM...
...MUST BE THE GREATEST SAMURAI OF THE LAND!!
NOT ONLY MUST YOU PROTECT YOUR LIEGE, YOU WILL DO THE SAME...
...FOR THE CAPITAL...AND EVENTUALLY ALL OF WANO!
BENG!!
...
YOU WILL BE OUR GUARDIAN DEITIES!!
IS THAT UNDERSTOOD?!!
...!!
WEEZ !!
WEEZ !!
DUT DUT DUT DUT
LORD YASUIE...!!
...!!

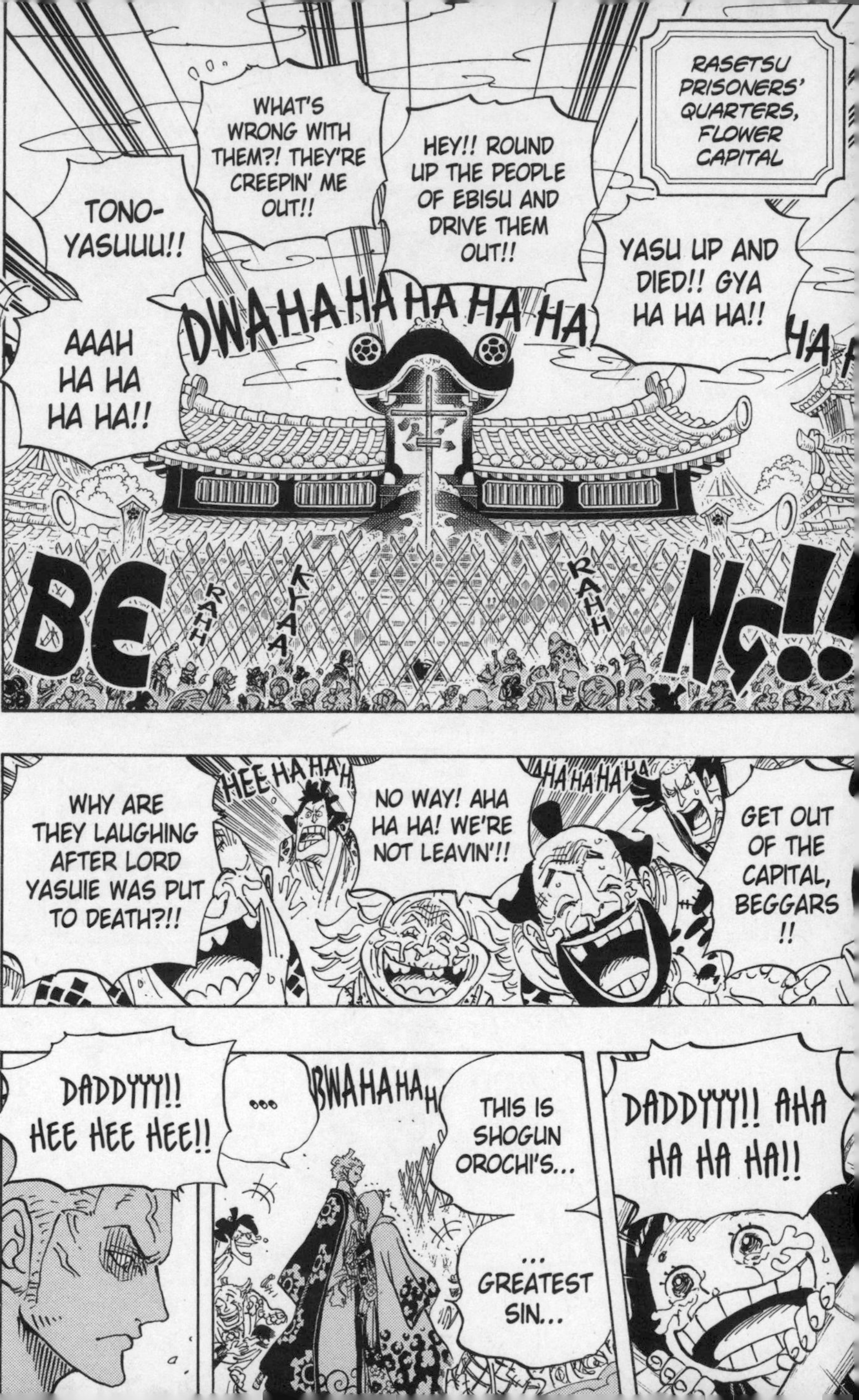
RASETSU PRISONERS' QUARTERS, FLOWER CAPITAL
YASU UP AND DIED!! GYA HA HA HA!!
HA
HEY!! ROUND UP THE PEOPLE OF EBISU AND DRIVE THEM OUT!!
WHAT'S WRONG WITH THEM?! THEY'RE CREEPIN' ME OUT!!
TONO-YASUUU!!
DWAHAHAHAHAHAHA
AAAH HA HA HA HA!!
BE
NG!!
RAHH
KYAA
RAHH
GET OUT OF THE CAPITAL, BEGGARS!!
AHAHAHAHA
NO WAY! AHA HA HA! WE'RE NOT LEAVIN'!!
HEE HAHAHA
WHY ARE THEY LAUGHING AFTER LORD YASUIE WAS PUT TO DEATH?!!
DADDYYY!! AHA HA HA HA!!
THIS IS SHOGUN OROCHI'S...
... GREATEST SIN...
BWAHAHAHA
...
DADDYYY!! HEE HEE HEE!!

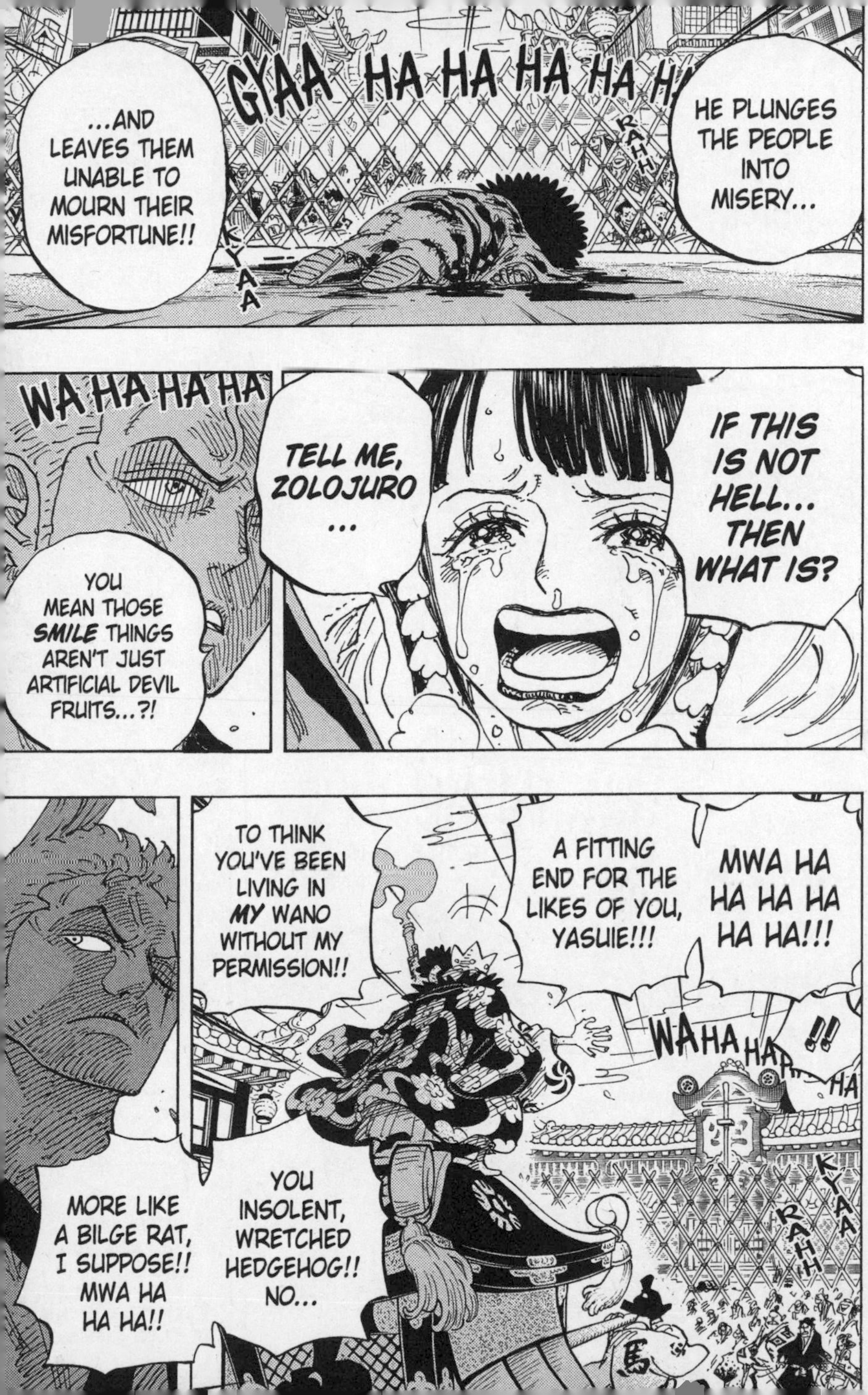
HE PLUNGES THE PEOPLE INTO MISERY...
GYAA HA HA HA HA HA
RAHH
KYAA
...AND LEAVES THEM UNABLE TO MOURN THEIR MISFORTUNE!!
IF THIS IS NOT HELL... THEN WHAT IS?
TELL ME, ZOLOJURO ...
WA HA HA HA
YOU MEAN THOSE SMILE THINGS AREN'T JUST ARTIFICIAL DEVIL FRUITS...?!
MWA HA HA HA HA HA HA!!!
A FITTING END FOR THE LIKES OF YOU, YASUIE!!!
TO THINK YOU'VE BEEN LIVING IN MY WANO WITHOUT MY PERMISSION!!
WAHAHA HA HA!!
KYAA
RAHH
YOU INSOLENT, WRETCHED HEDGEHOG!! NO...
MORE LIKE A BILGE RAT, I SUPPOSE!! MWA HA HA HA!!

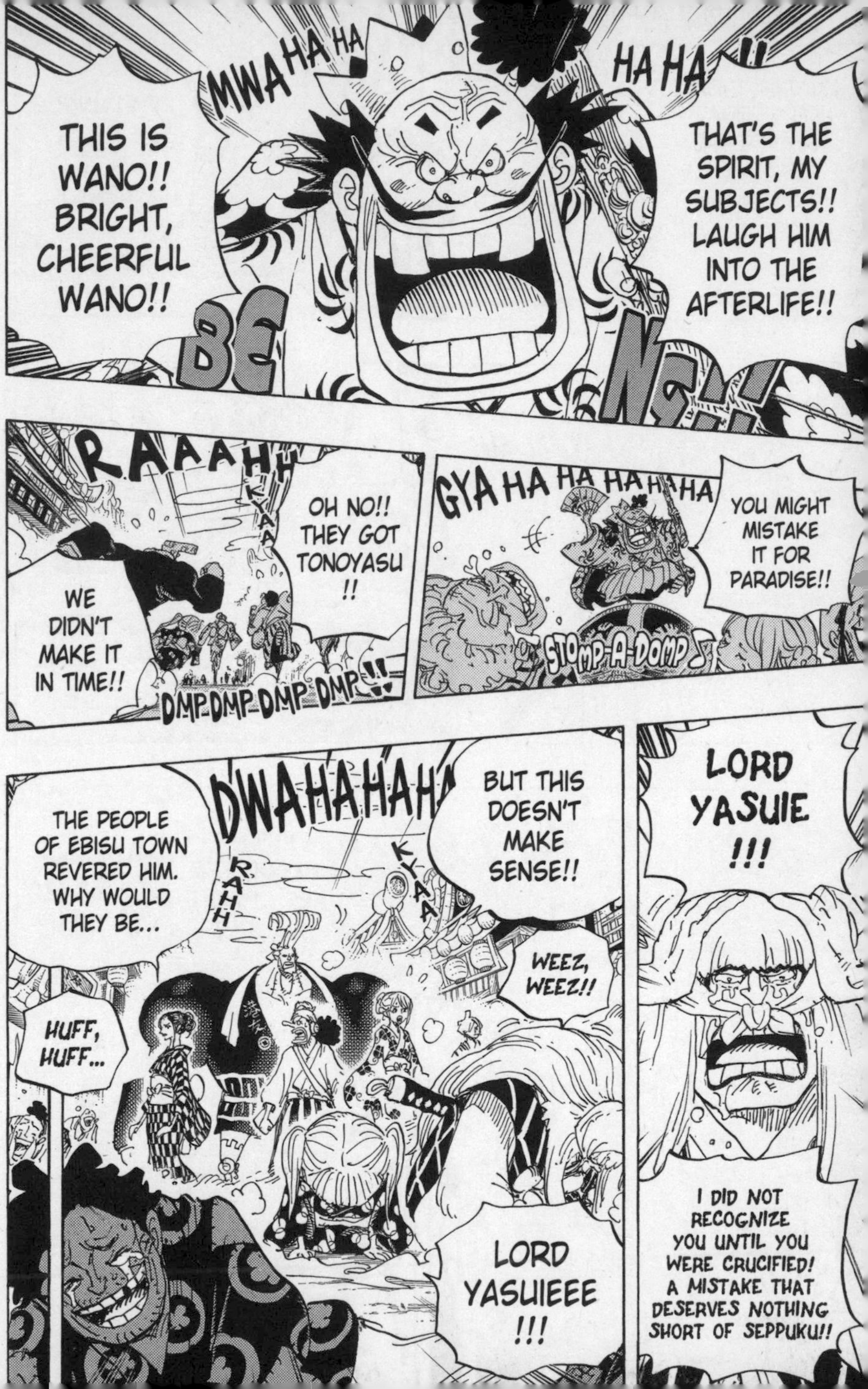
MWA HA HA HA HA HA!!
THAT'S THE SPIRIT, MY SUBJECTS!! LAUGH HIM INTO THE AFTERLIFE!!
THIS IS WANO!! BRIGHT, CHEERFUL WANO!!
BE-NGH!!
GYA HA HA HA HA HA HA
YOU MIGHT MISTAKE IT FOR PARADISE!!
STOMP-A-DOMP
RAAAHH
KYAA
OH NO!! THEY GOT TONOYASU!!
WE DIDN'T MAKE IT IN TIME!!
DMP DMP DMP DMP!!
LORD YASUIE!!!
I DID NOT RECOGNIZE YOU UNTIL YOU WERE CRUCIFIED! A MISTAKE THAT DESERVES NOTHING SHORT OF SEPPUKU!!
BUT THIS DOESN'T MAKE SENSE!!
DWAHAHAHAHA
THE PEOPLE OF EBISU TOWN REVERED HIM. WHY WOULD THEY BE...
KYAA
RAHH
WEEZ, WEEZ!!
HUFF, HUFF...
LORD YASUIEEE!!!

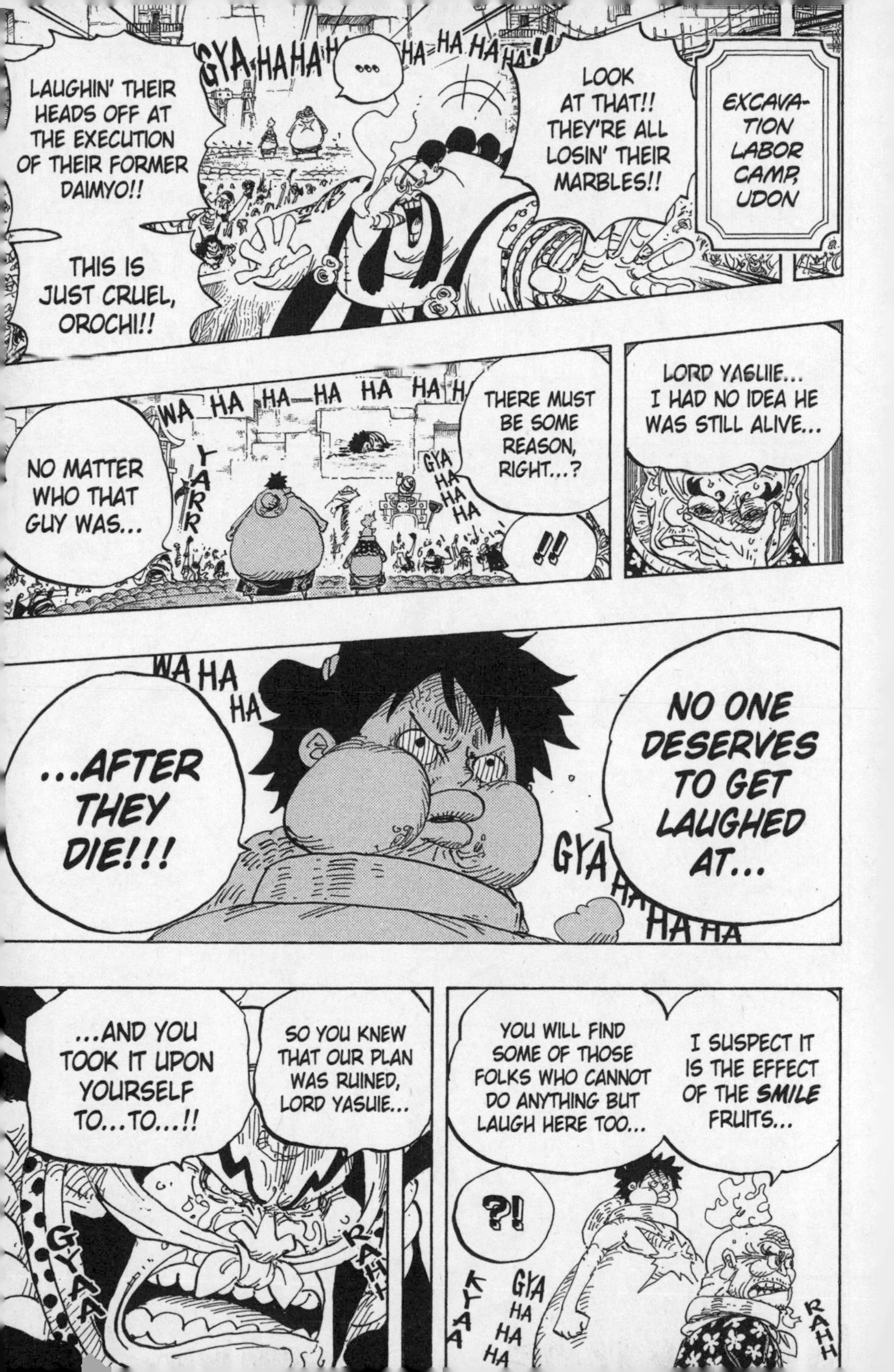
EXCAVATION LABOR CAMP, UDON
LOOK AT THAT!! THEY'RE ALL LOSIN' THEIR MARBLES!!
GYA HAHA HA HA HA HA HA!!
...
LAUGHIN' THEIR HEADS OFF AT THE EXECUTION OF THEIR FORMER DAIMYO!!
THIS IS JUST CRUEL, OROCHI!!
LORD YASUIE... I HAD NO IDEA HE WAS STILL ALIVE...
THERE MUST BE SOME REASON, RIGHT...?
!!
WA HA HA HA HA HA H
GYA HA HA HA HA
YARR
NO MATTER WHO THAT GUY WAS...
NO ONE DESERVES TO GET LAUGHED AT...
GYA HA HA HA
WA HA HA
...AFTER THEY DIE!!!
I SUSPECT IT IS THE EFFECT OF THE SMILE FRUITS...
YOU WILL FIND SOME OF THOSE FOLKS WHO CANNOT DO ANYTHING BUT LAUGH HERE TOO...
RAHH
?!
GYA HA HA HA
KYAA
SO YOU KNEW THAT OUR PLAN WAS RUINED, LORD YASUIE...
...AND YOU TOOK IT UPON YOURSELF TO...TO...!!
RAHH
GYAA

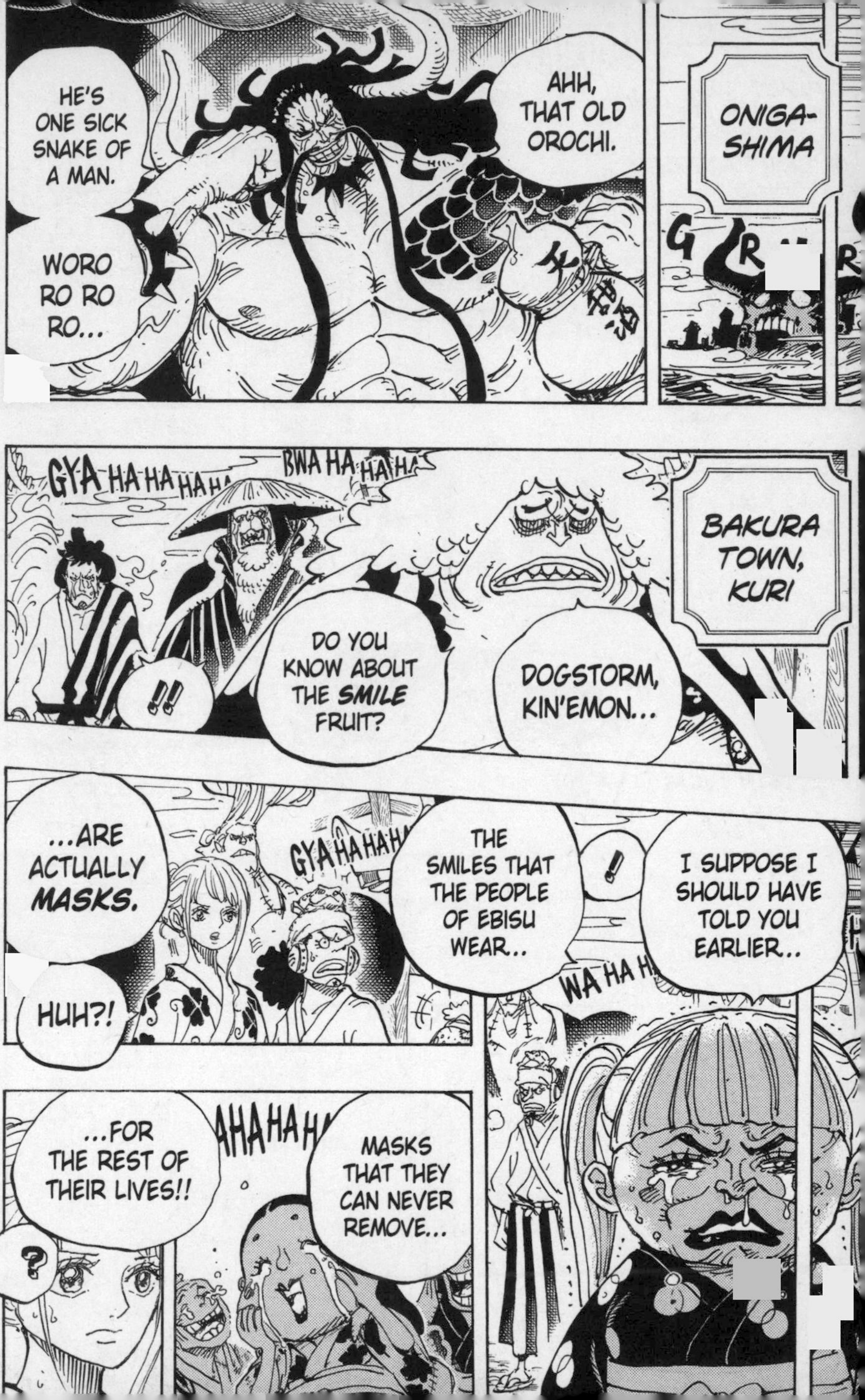
ONIGA-SHIMA
AHH, THAT OLD OROCHI.
HE'S ONE SICK SNAKE OF A MAN.
WORORO RO RO...
BAKURA TOWN, KURI
BWA HA HA HA
GYA HA HA HA HA
DOGSTORM, KIN'EMON...
DO YOU KNOW ABOUT THE *SMILE* FRUIT?
!!
I SUPPOSE I SHOULD HAVE TOLD YOU EARLIER...
!
THE SMILES THAT THE PEOPLE OF EBISU WEAR...
WA HA HA
...ARE ACTUALLY *MASKS.*
GYAHAHAHA
HUH?!
MASKS THAT THEY CAN NEVER REMOVE...
AHAHAHA
...FOR THE REST OF THEIR LIVES!!
?

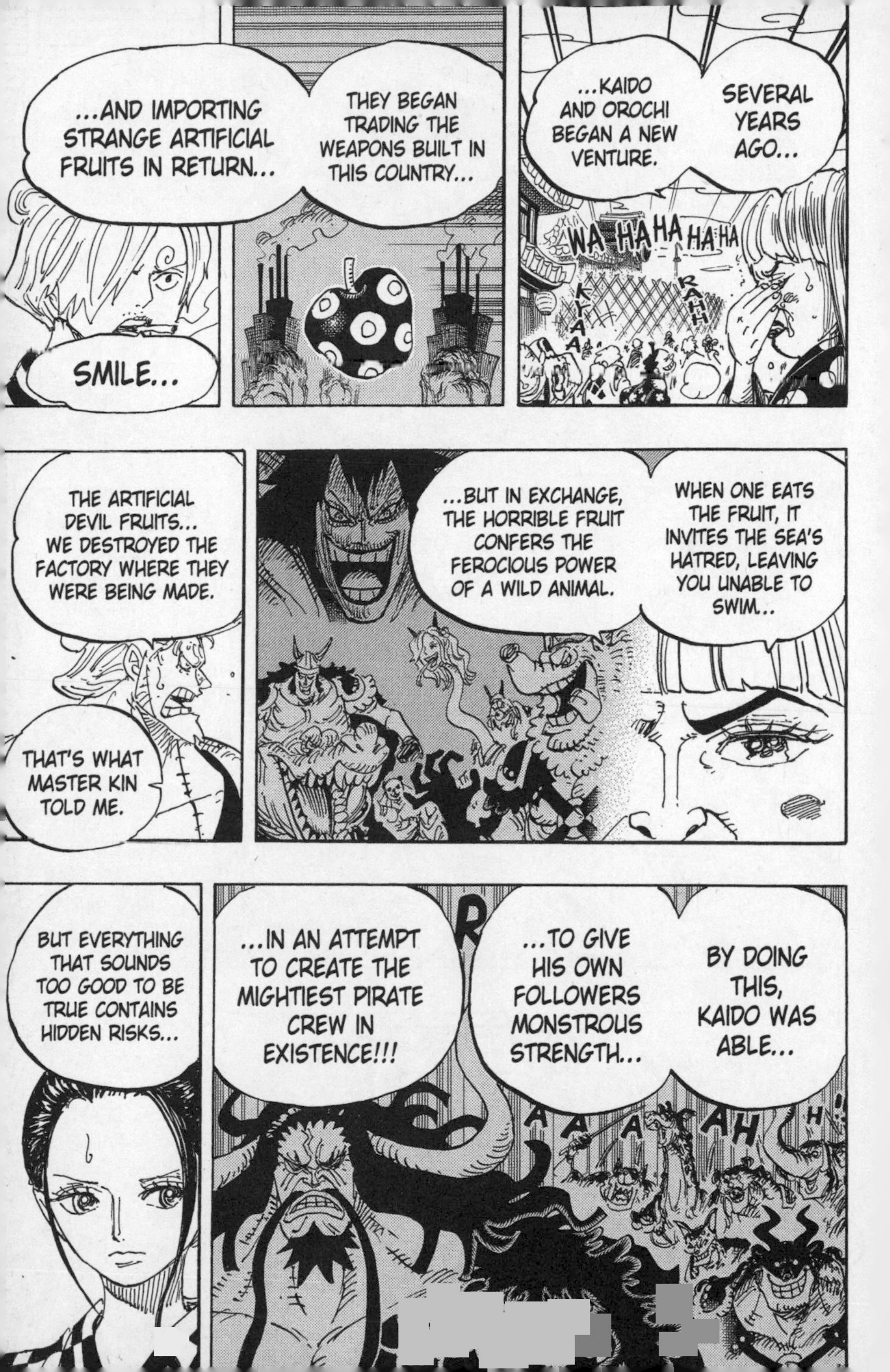
SEVERAL YEARS AGO...
...KAIDO AND OROCHI BEGAN A NEW VENTURE.
WA HA HA HA HA HA
RAHH
KYAA
THEY BEGAN TRADING THE WEAPONS BUILT IN THIS COUNTRY...
...AND IMPORTING STRANGE ARTIFICIAL FRUITS IN RETURN...
SMILE...
WHEN ONE EATS THE FRUIT, IT INVITES THE SEA'S HATRED, LEAVING YOU UNABLE TO SWIM...
...BUT IN EXCHANGE, THE HORRIBLE FRUIT CONFERS THE FEROCIOUS POWER OF A WILD ANIMAL.
THE ARTIFICIAL DEVIL FRUITS... WE DESTROYED THE FACTORY WHERE THEY WERE BEING MADE.
THAT'S WHAT MASTER KIN TOLD ME.
BY DOING THIS, KAIDO WAS ABLE...
...TO GIVE HIS OWN FOLLOWERS MONSTROUS STRENGTH...
...IN AN ATTEMPT TO CREATE THE MIGHTIEST PIRATE CREW IN EXISTENCE!!!
R
AAAAH
BUT EVERYTHING THAT SOUNDS TOO GOOD TO BE TRUE CONTAINS HIDDEN RISKS...

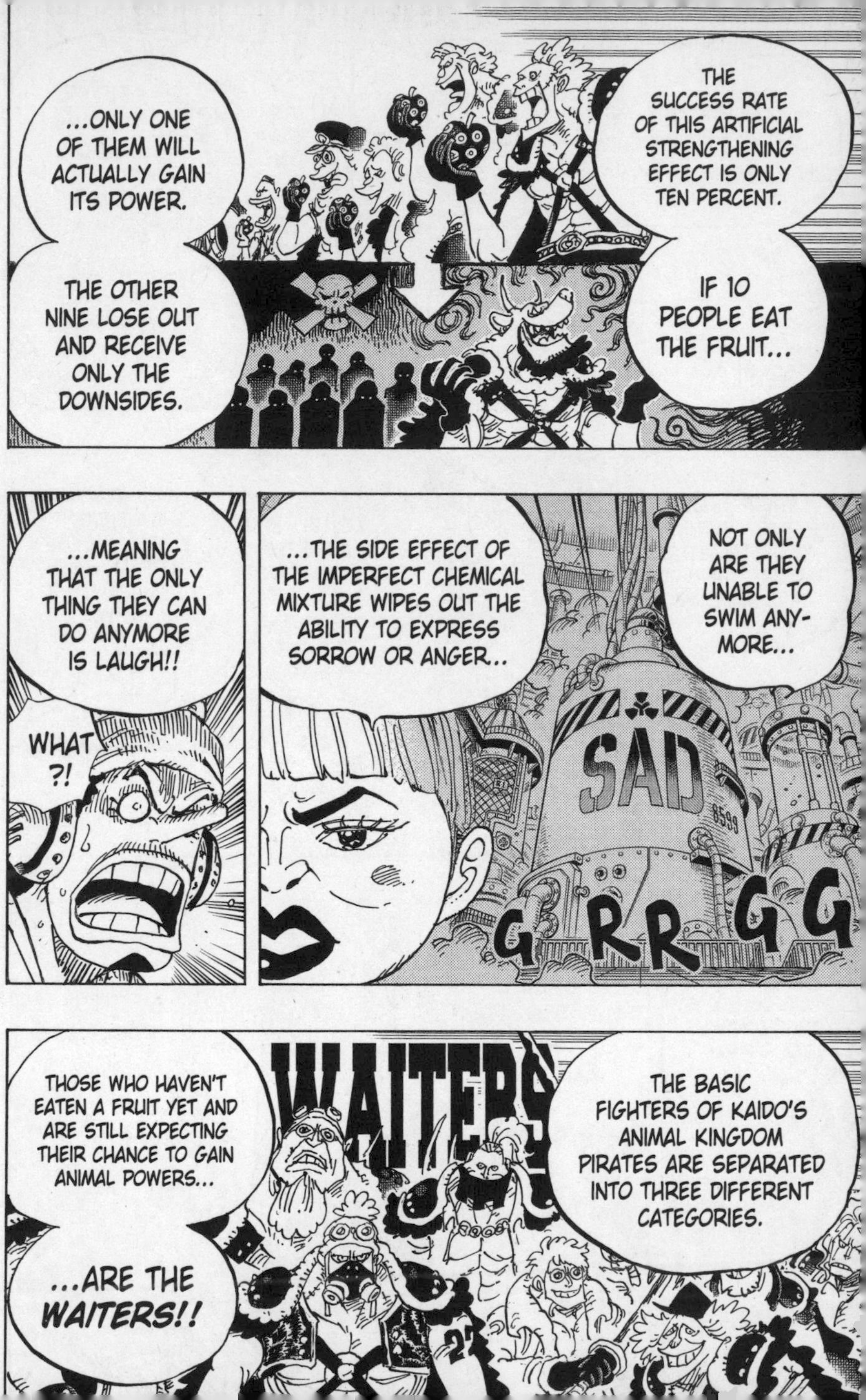
THE SUCCESS RATE OF THIS ARTIFICIAL STRENGTHENING EFFECT IS ONLY TEN PERCENT.
IF 10 PEOPLE EAT THE FRUIT...
...ONLY ONE OF THEM WILL ACTUALLY GAIN ITS POWER.
THE OTHER NINE LOSE OUT AND RECEIVE ONLY THE DOWNSIDES.
NOT ONLY ARE THEY UNABLE TO SWIM ANY-MORE...
...THE SIDE EFFECT OF THE IMPERFECT CHEMICAL MIXTURE WIPES OUT THE ABILITY TO EXPRESS SORROW OR ANGER...
SAD
8599
GRRGG
...MEANING THAT THE ONLY THING THEY CAN DO ANYMORE IS LAUGH!!
WHAT ?!
THE BASIC FIGHTERS OF KAIDO'S ANIMAL KINGDOM PIRATES ARE SEPARATED INTO THREE DIFFERENT CATEGORIES.
WAITERS
THOSE WHO HAVEN'T EATEN A FRUIT YET AND ARE STILL EXPECTING THEIR CHANCE TO GAIN ANIMAL POWERS...
...ARE THE WAITERS!!

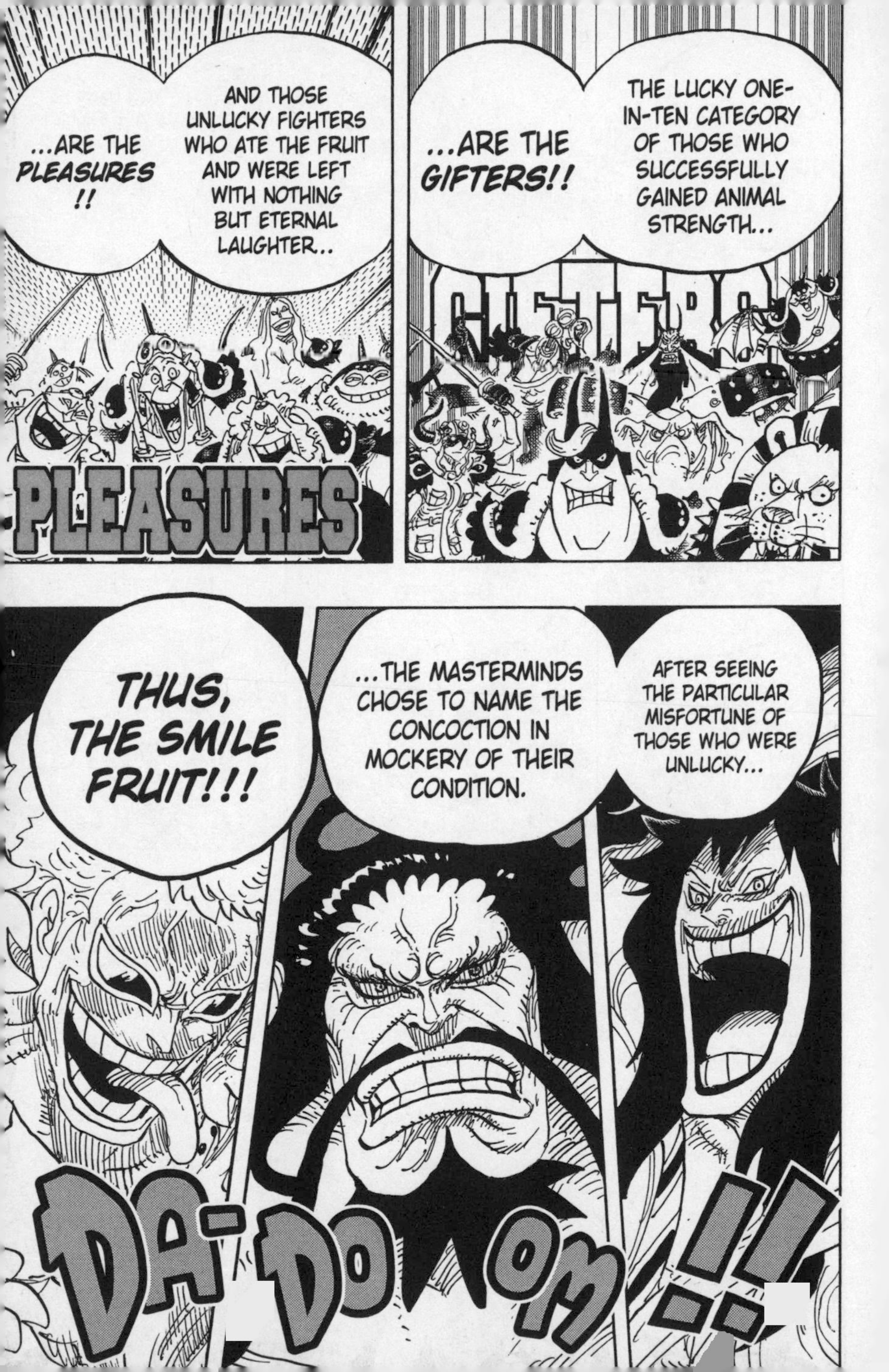
THE LUCKY ONE-IN-TEN CATEGORY OF THOSE WHO SUCCESSFULLY GAINED ANIMAL STRENGTH...
...ARE THE GIFTERS!!
AND THOSE UNLUCKY FIGHTERS WHO ATE THE FRUIT AND WERE LEFT WITH NOTHING BUT ETERNAL LAUGHTER...
...ARE THE PLEASURES!!
PLEASURES
AFTER SEEING THE PARTICULAR MISFORTUNE OF THOSE WHO WERE UNLUCKY...
...THE MASTERMINDS CHOSE TO NAME THE CONCOCTION IN MOCKERY OF THEIR CONDITION.
THUS, THE SMILE FRUIT!!!
DA-DOOM..!!

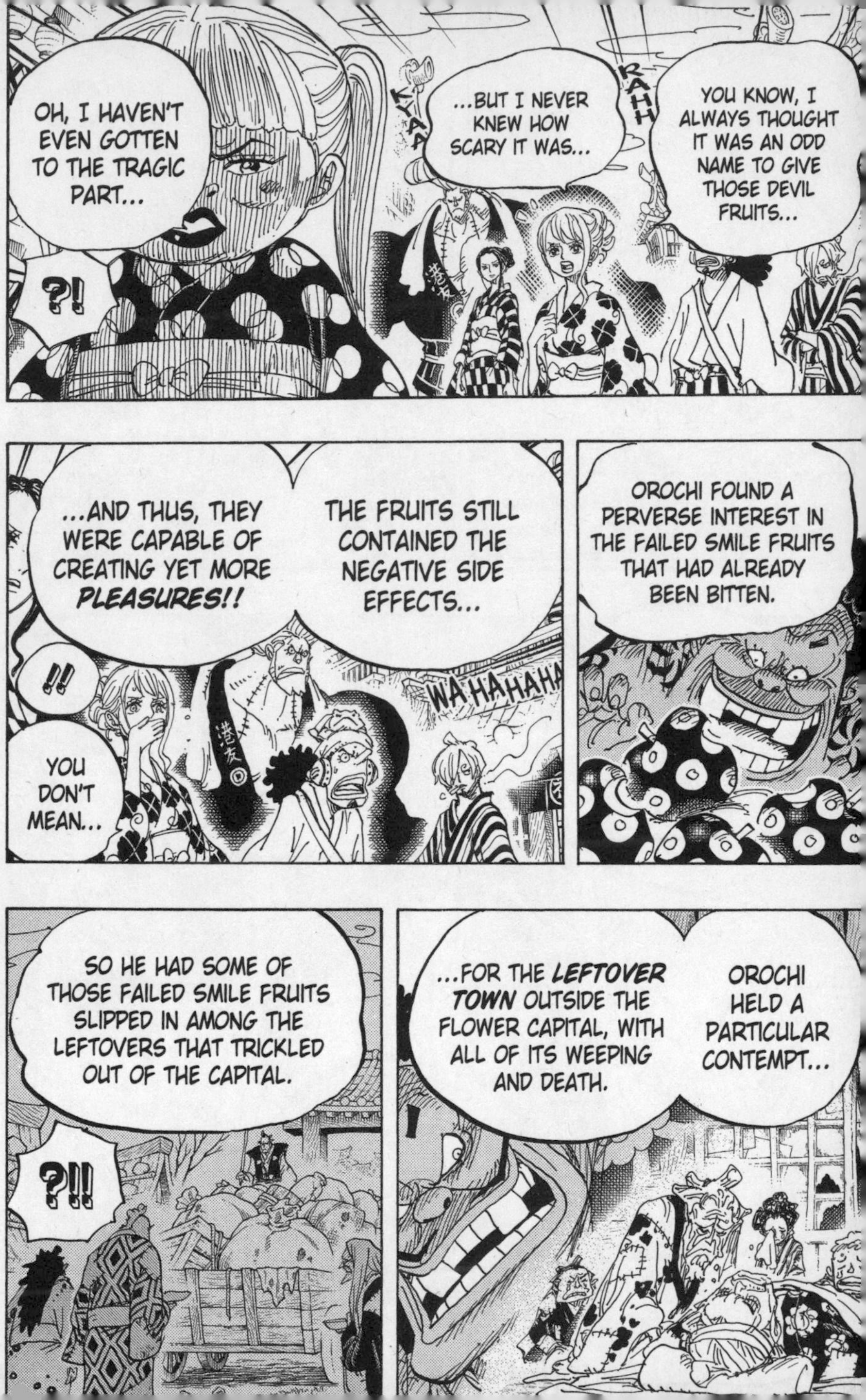
YOU KNOW, I ALWAYS THOUGHT IT WAS AN ODD NAME TO GIVE THOSE DEVIL FRUITS...
RAHH
...BUT I NEVER KNEW HOW SCARY IT WAS...
KYAA
OH, I HAVEN'T EVEN GOTTEN TO THE TRAGIC PART...
?!
OROCHI FOUND A PERVERSE INTEREST IN THE FAILED SMILE FRUITS THAT HAD ALREADY BEEN BITTEN.
THE FRUITS STILL CONTAINED THE NEGATIVE SIDE EFFECTS...
...AND THUS, THEY WERE CAPABLE OF CREATING YET MORE *PLEASURES!!*
WA HA HAHA
!!
YOU DON'T MEAN...
OROCHI HELD A PARTICULAR CONTEMPT...
...FOR THE *LEFTOVER TOWN* OUTSIDE THE FLOWER CAPITAL, WITH ALL OF ITS WEEPING AND DEATH.
SO HE HAD SOME OF THOSE FAILED SMILE FRUITS SLIPPED IN AMONG THE LEFTOVERS THAT TRICKLED OUT OF THE CAPITAL.
?!!

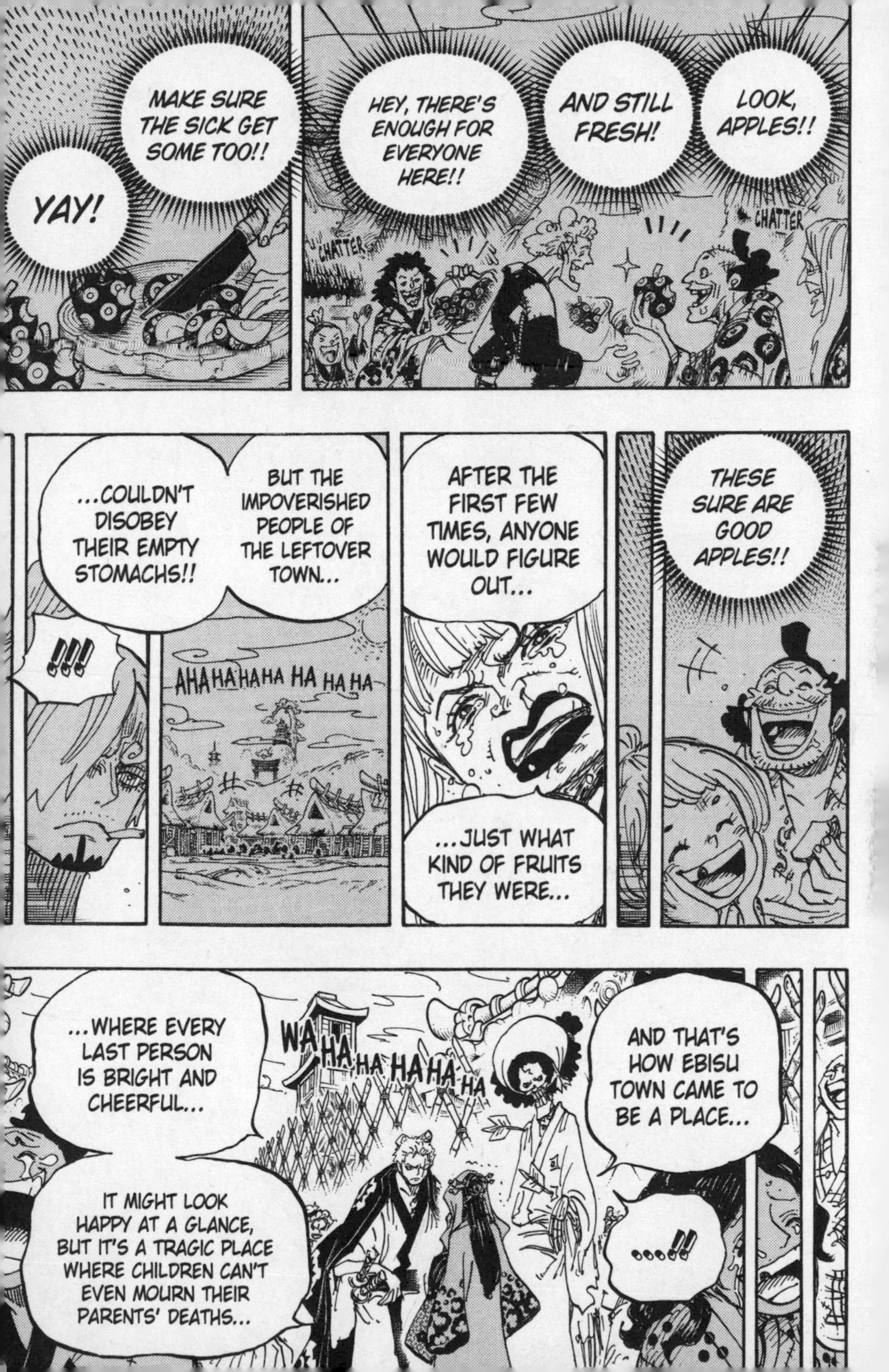
LOOK, APPLES!!
CHATTER
AND STILL FRESH!
HEY, THERE'S ENOUGH FOR EVERYONE HERE!!
CHATTER
MAKE SURE THE SICK GET SOME TOO!!
YAY!
THESE SURE ARE GOOD APPLES!!
AFTER THE FIRST FEW TIMES, ANYONE WOULD FIGURE OUT...
...JUST WHAT KIND OF FRUITS THEY WERE...
BUT THE IMPOVERISHED PEOPLE OF THE LEFTOVER TOWN...
AHAHAHAHA HA HA HA
...COULDN'T DISOBEY THEIR EMPTY STOMACHS!!
!!!
AND THAT'S HOW EBISU TOWN CAME TO BE A PLACE...
WAHAHAHA HAHAHA HA
...WHERE EVERY LAST PERSON IS BRIGHT AND CHEERFUL...
....!!
IT MIGHT LOOK HAPPY AT A GLANCE, BUT IT'S A TRAGIC PLACE WHERE CHILDREN CAN'T EVEN MOURN THEIR PARENTS' DEATHS...

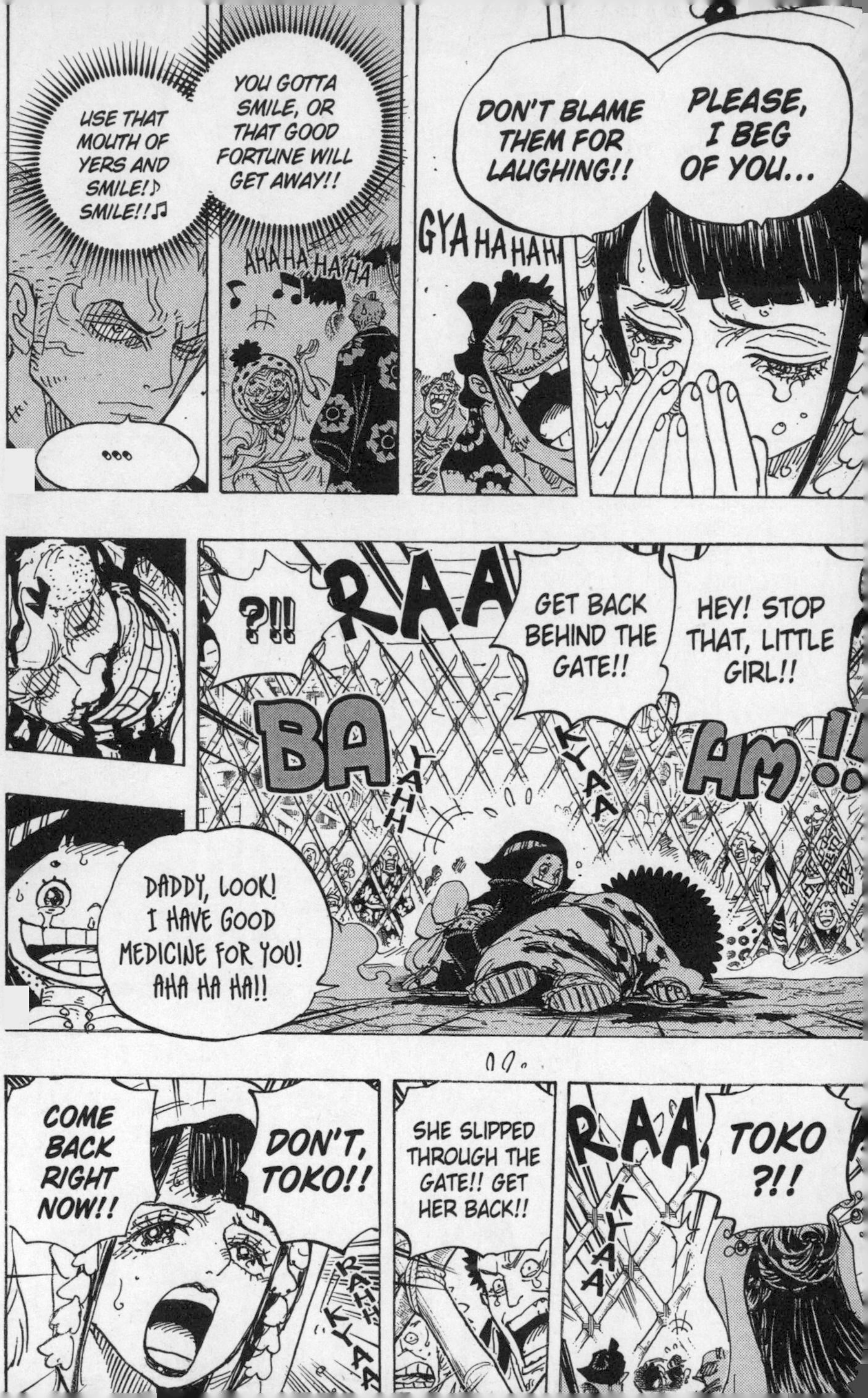
PLEASE, I BEG OF YOU...
DON'T BLAME THEM FOR LAUGHING!!
GYA HA HA HA
AHA HA HA HA
YOU GOTTA SMILE, OR THAT GOOD FORTUNE WILL GET AWAY!!
USE THAT MOUTH OF YERS AND SMILE!♪ SMILE!!♫
...
HEY! STOP THAT, LITTLE GIRL!!
GET BACK BEHIND THE GATE!!
RAA
?!!
BA
AM!!
KYAA
YAHHH
DADDY, LOOK! I HAVE GOOD MEDICINE FOR YOU! AHA HA HA!!
TOKO ?!!
RAA
KYAA
SHE SLIPPED THROUGH THE GATE!! GET HER BACK!!
DON'T, TOKO!!
COME BACK RIGHT NOW!!
KYAA

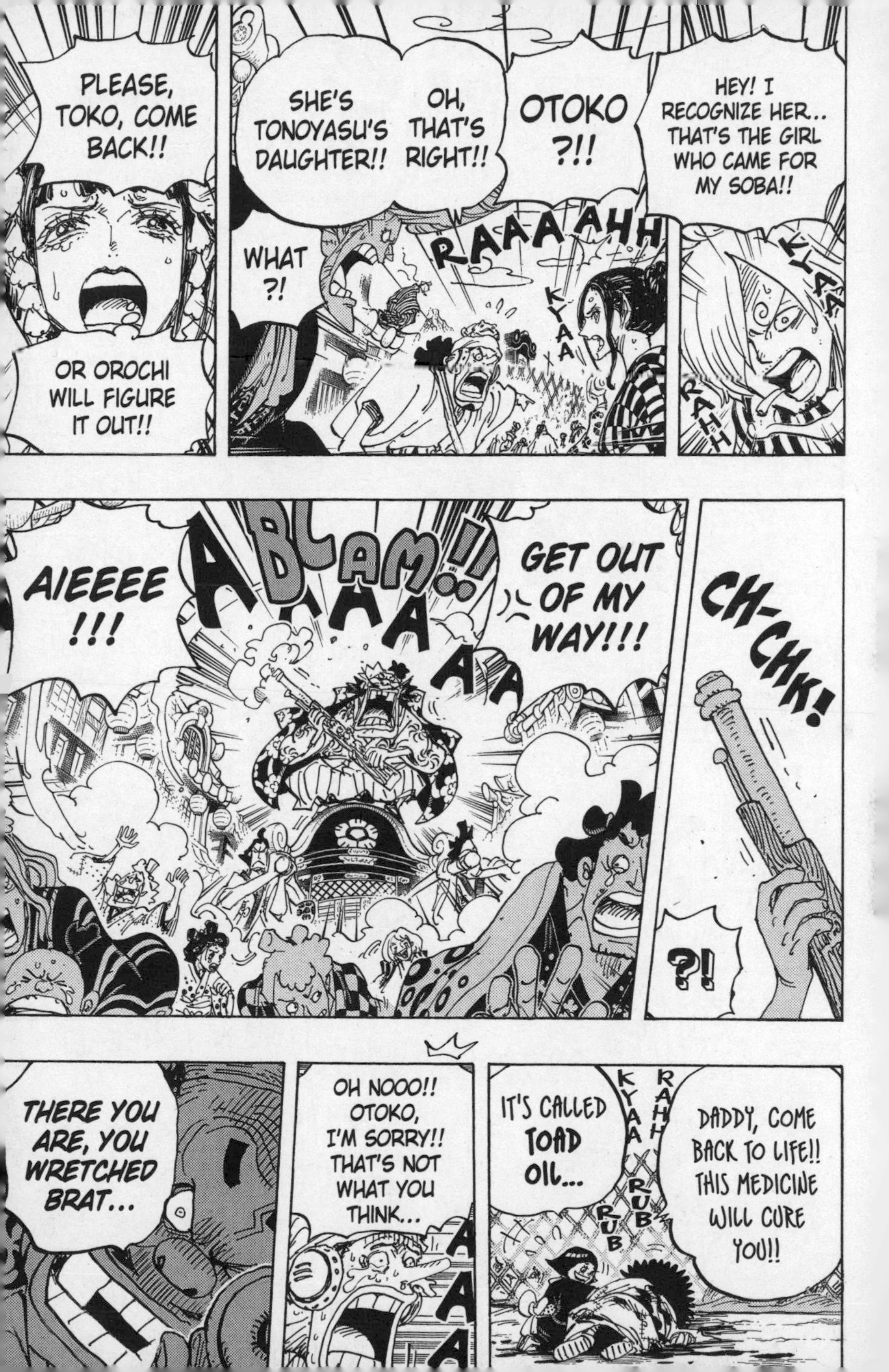
HEY! I RECOGNIZE HER.. THAT'S THE GIRL WHO CAME FOR MY SOBA!!
KYAA
RAHH
OTOKO ?!!
OH, THAT'S RIGHT!!
SHE'S TONOYASU'S DAUGHTER!!
RAAAAAHH
KYAA
WHAT ?!
PLEASE, TOKO, COME BACK!!
OR OROCHI WILL FIGURE IT OUT!!
CH-CHK!
?!
GET OUT OF MY WAY!!!
BLAM!!
AAAAAA
AIEEEE !!!
DADDY, COME BACK TO LIFE!! THIS MEDICINE WILL CURE YOU!!
RAHH
KYAA
RUB
RUB
IT'S CALLED TOAD OIL...
OH NOOO!! OTOKO, I'M SORRY!! THAT'S NOT WHAT YOU THINK...
AAA
THERE YOU ARE, YOU WRETCHED BRAT...

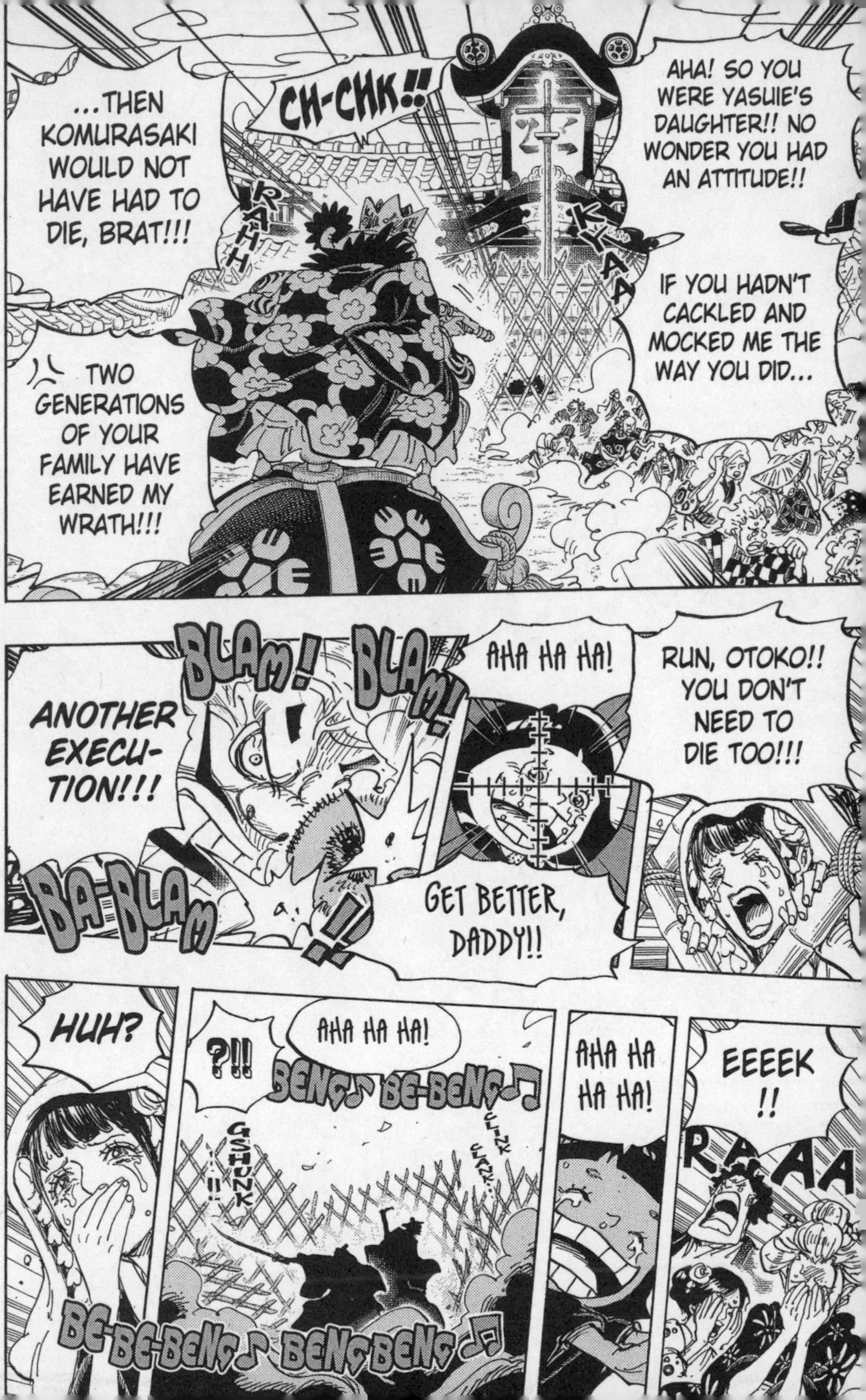
AHA! SO YOU WERE YASUIE'S DAUGHTER!! NO WONDER YOU HAD AN ATTITUDE!!
IF YOU HADN'T CACKLED AND MOCKED ME THE WAY YOU DID...
CH-CHK!!
KYAA
RAHHH
...THEN KOMURASAKI WOULD NOT HAVE HAD TO DIE, BRAT!!!
TWO GENERATIONS OF YOUR FAMILY HAVE EARNED MY WRATH!!!
RUN, OTOKO!! YOU DON'T NEED TO DIE TOO!!!
AHA HA HA!
GET BETTER, DADDY!!
BLAM! BLAM!
!!
ANOTHER EXECUTION!!!
BA-BLAM
EEEEK !!
RAAA
AHA HA HA HA!
AHA HA HA!
?!!
BENG♪ BE-BENG♫
CLINK CLANK...
GSHUNK
!!
BE-BE-BENG♪ BENG BENG♫
HUH?

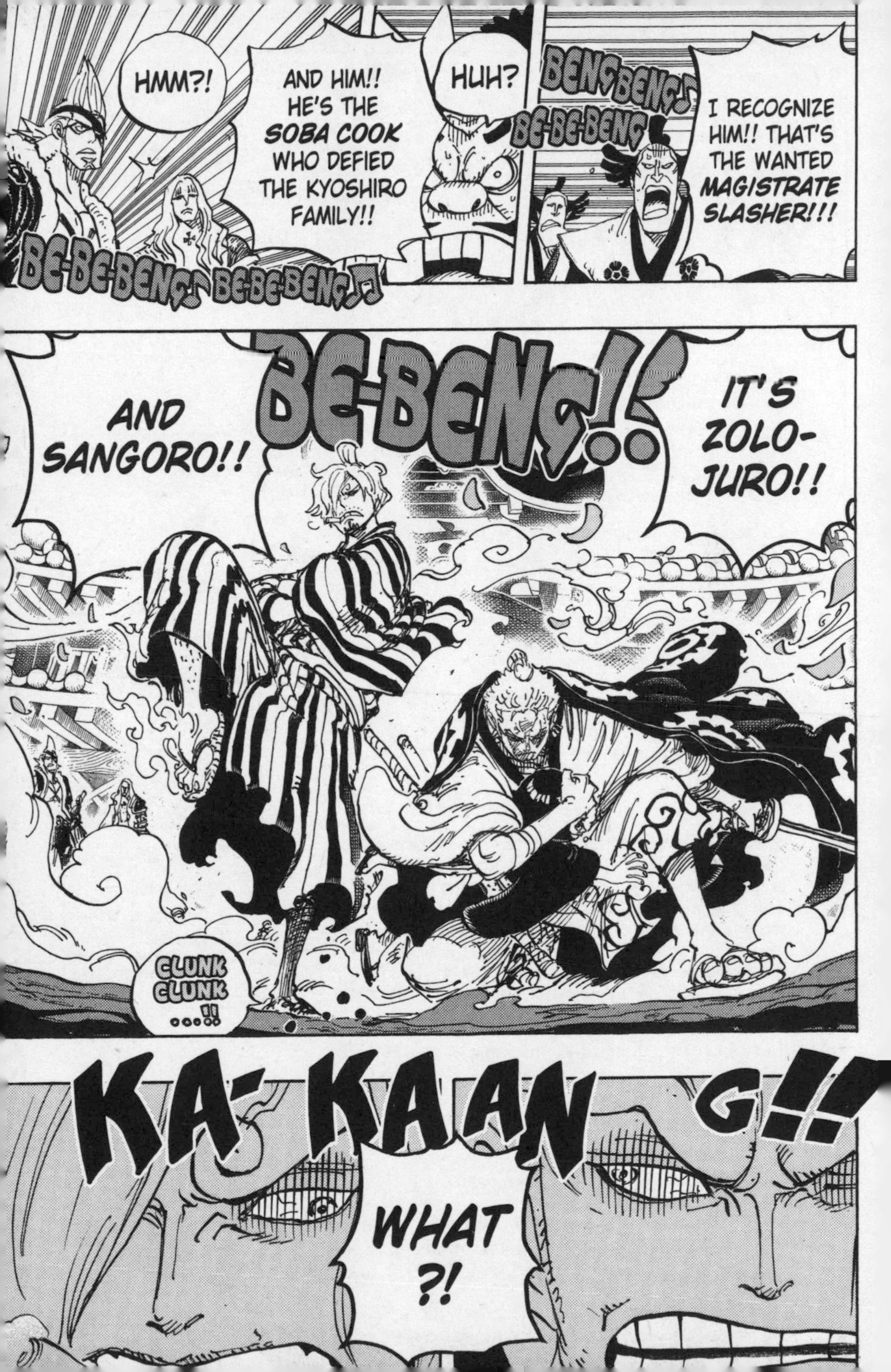
BENG BENG♪
BE-BE-BENG
I RECOGNIZE HIM!! THAT'S THE WANTED MAGISTRATE SLASHER!!!
HUH?
AND HIM!! HE'S THE SOBA COOK WHO DEFIED THE KYOSHIRO FAMILY!!
HMM?!
BE-BE-BENG♪ BE-BE-BENG♪
IT'S ZOLO-JURO!!
BE-BENG!!
AND SANGORO!!
CLUNK CLUNK ...!!
KA-KAAANG!!
WHAT ?!

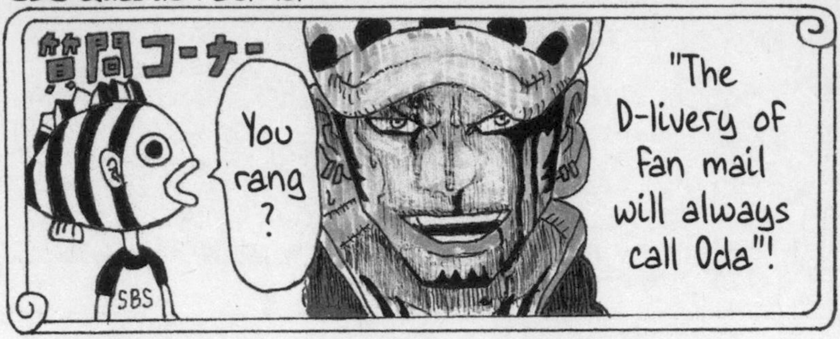
質問コーナー
"The D-livery of fan mail will always call Oda"!
You rang?
SBS

(Masamichi Kobayashi, Gunma)

Q: I'm starting the SBS!

--Normal Is Best

A: Whoa!! It's so normal!! You can't get more normal!!
I wasn't expecting this.

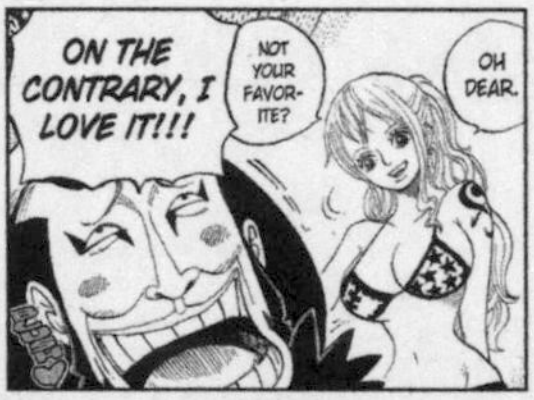
OH DEAR.
NOT YOUR FAVORITE?
ON THE CONTRARY, I LOVE IT!!!

Q: Odacchi! You're not supposed to tie breast-bands around your head as a disguise!

--Takataka

A: Huh? Oh, come now! Wa ha ha ha! You joker, you! Wa ha ha ha ha!! Wa ha ha ha ha ha...huh? I hear police sirens...

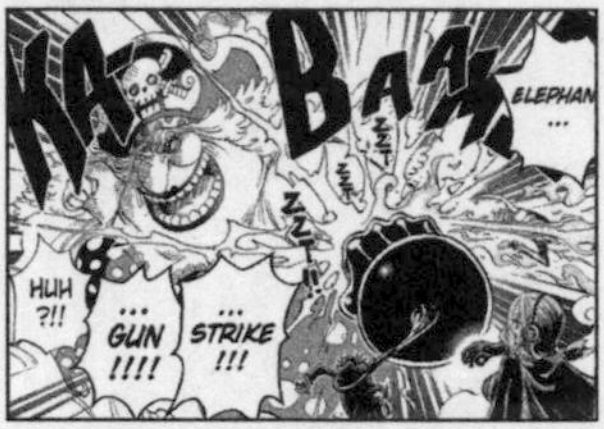
KA BAAM
ELEPHAN...
...STRIKE!!!
...GUN!!!!
HUH?!!

Q: I have a very important announcement, Oda Sensei. On page 23 of volume 87, isn't Sanji kicking Big Mom? What happened to the Sanji who wouldn't kick a woman?!

--Momotaro Hunter

A: Actually, I got several letters pointing this out. You're wrong! In that scene, Big Mom is throwing a punch at Reiju, and Luffy and Sanji are trying to block it. But how can you stop a punch from Big Mom just by standing there? You can't! So he had to kick just to neutralize the force of her fist! That's a defensive act, and not kicking a woman! Sanji's ironclad oath hasn't been broken!!

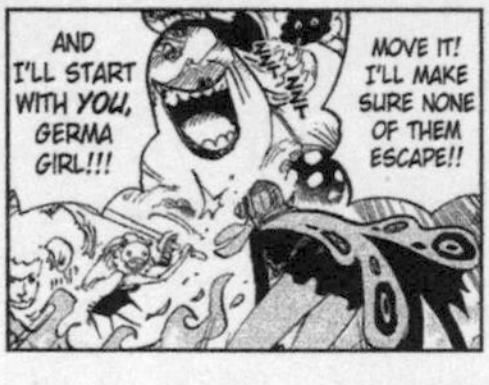
MOVE IT! I'LL MAKE SURE NONE OF THEM ESCAPE!!
AND I'LL START WITH YOU, GERMA GIRL!!!

Q: I just have one thing to say to Sanji.

"If it's a mixed bath already, you don't need to use your stealth function!!"

--Toshiy

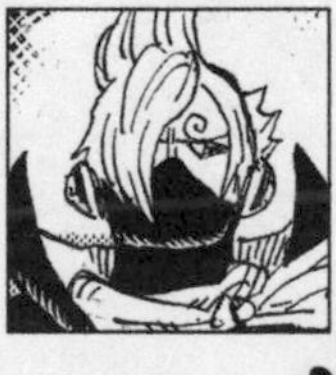

A: Well, Sanji? Did you hear that?

Sanji: Toshiy, don't you know that it's not acceptable to ogle a naked woman, just because the bath happens to be mixed-use?! But if I go invisible, I can ogle all I...

A: Stop right there, Sanji!!
Peeping at women is a crime, young boys!! C'mon, it's SBS time!

Chapter 944: PARTNER

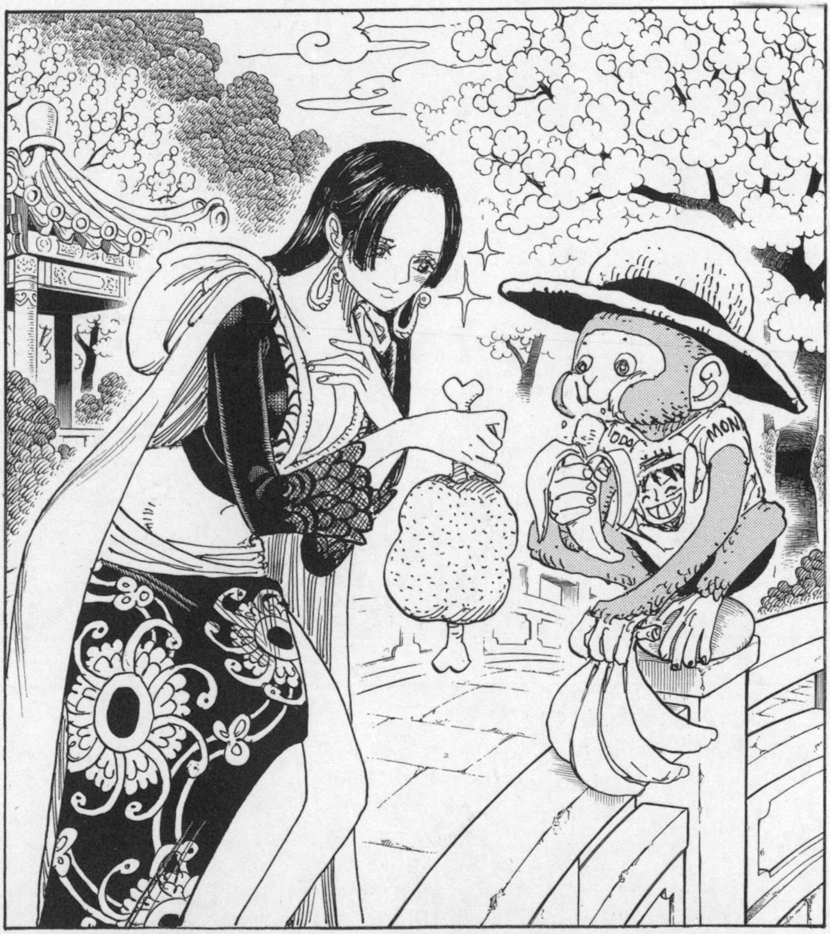

REQUEST: "HANCOCK BLUSHING AFTER PUTTING A STRAW HAT ON A YOUNG MONKEY (WEARING A LUFFY T-SHIRT)" BY ONANTURE

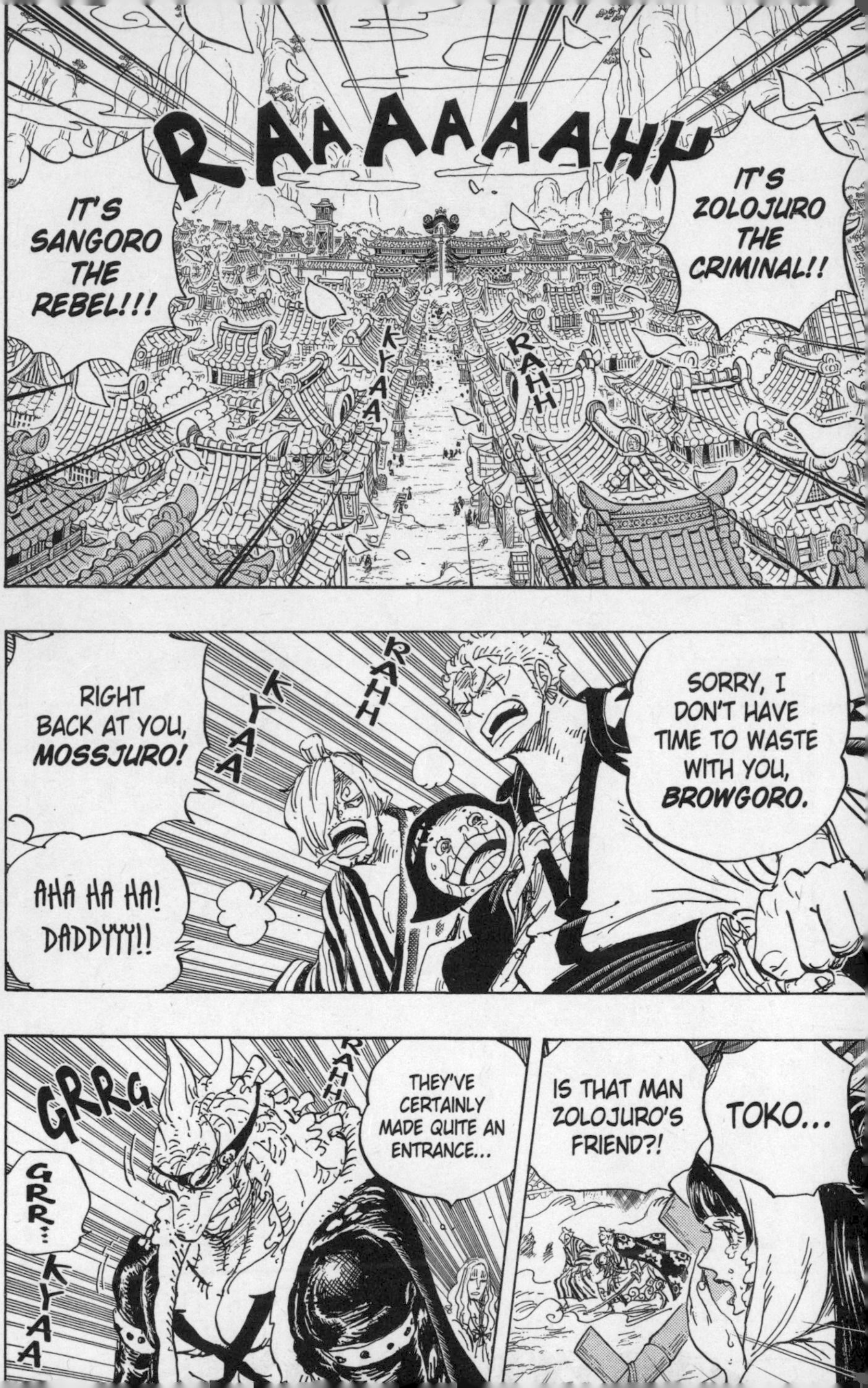
IT'S ZOLOJURO THE CRIMINAL!!
RAAAAAAHH
IT'S SANGORO THE REBEL!!!
RAHH
KYAA
SORRY, I DON'T HAVE TIME TO WASTE WITH YOU, BROWGORO.
RAHH
KYAA
RIGHT BACK AT YOU, MOSSJURO!
AHA HA HA! DADDYYY!!
TOKO...
IS THAT MAN ZOLOJURO'S FRIEND?!
THEY'VE CERTAINLY MADE QUITE AN ENTRANCE...
RAHH
GRRG
GRR...
KYAA

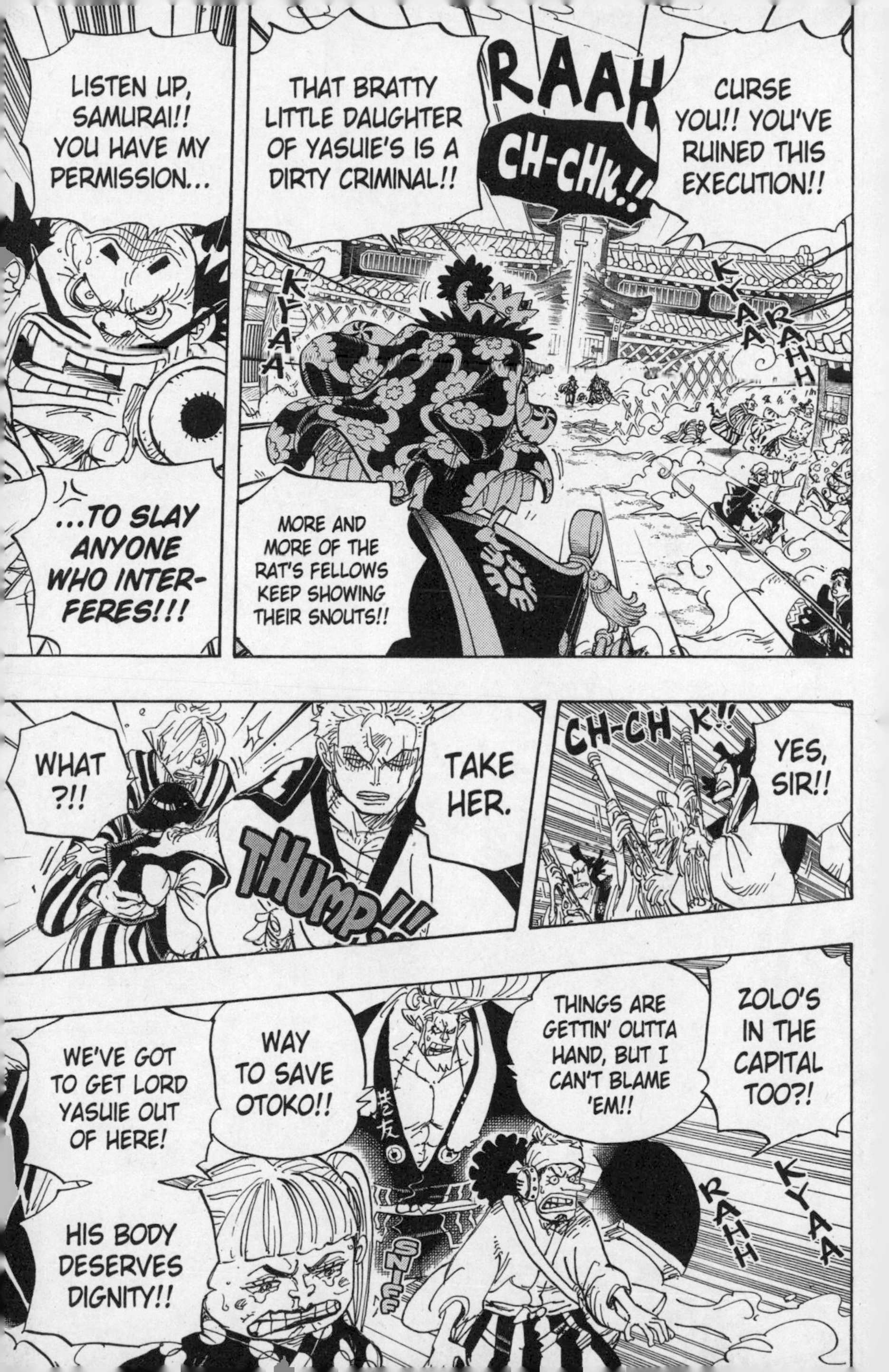
CURSE YOU!! YOU'VE RUINED THIS EXECUTION!!
RAAH
CH-CHK!!
THAT BRATTY LITTLE DAUGHTER OF YASUIE'S IS A DIRTY CRIMINAL!!
KYAARAHH
KYAA
MORE AND MORE OF THE RAT'S FELLOWS KEEP SHOWING THEIR SNOUTS!!
LISTEN UP, SAMURAI!! YOU HAVE MY PERMISSION...
...TO SLAY ANYONE WHO INTERFERES!!!
YES, SIR!!
CH-CHK!!
TAKE HER.
THUMP!!
WHAT?!!
ZOLO'S IN THE CAPITAL TOO?!
THINGS ARE GETTIN' OUTTA HAND, BUT I CAN'T BLAME 'EM!!
KYAA
RAHH
WAY TO SAVE OTOKO!!
SNIFF
WE'VE GOT TO GET LORD YASUIE OUT OF HERE!
HIS BODY DESERVES DIGNITY!!

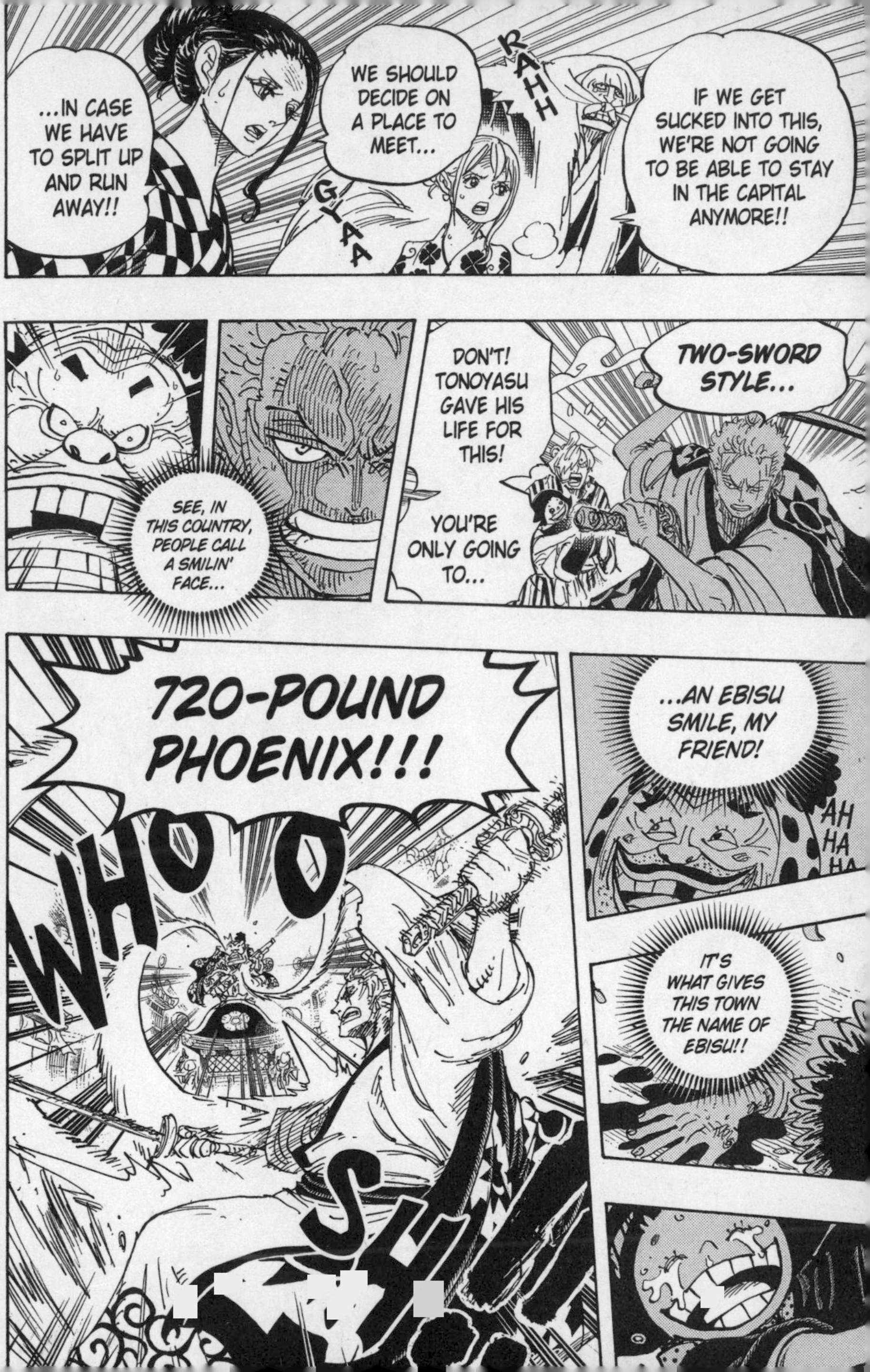
IF WE GET SUCKED INTO THIS, WE'RE NOT GOING TO BE ABLE TO STAY IN THE CAPITAL ANYMORE!!
RAHH
WE SHOULD DECIDE ON A PLACE TO MEET...
GYAA
...IN CASE WE HAVE TO SPLIT UP AND RUN AWAY!!
TWO-SWORD STYLE...
DON'T! TONOYASU GAVE HIS LIFE FOR THIS!
YOU'RE ONLY GOING TO...
SEE, IN THIS COUNTRY, PEOPLE CALL A SMILIN' FACE...
...AN EBISU SMILE, MY FRIEND!
AH HA HA
IT'S WHAT GIVES THIS TOWN THE NAME OF EBISU!!
720-POUND PHOENIX!!!
WHOOO
SH

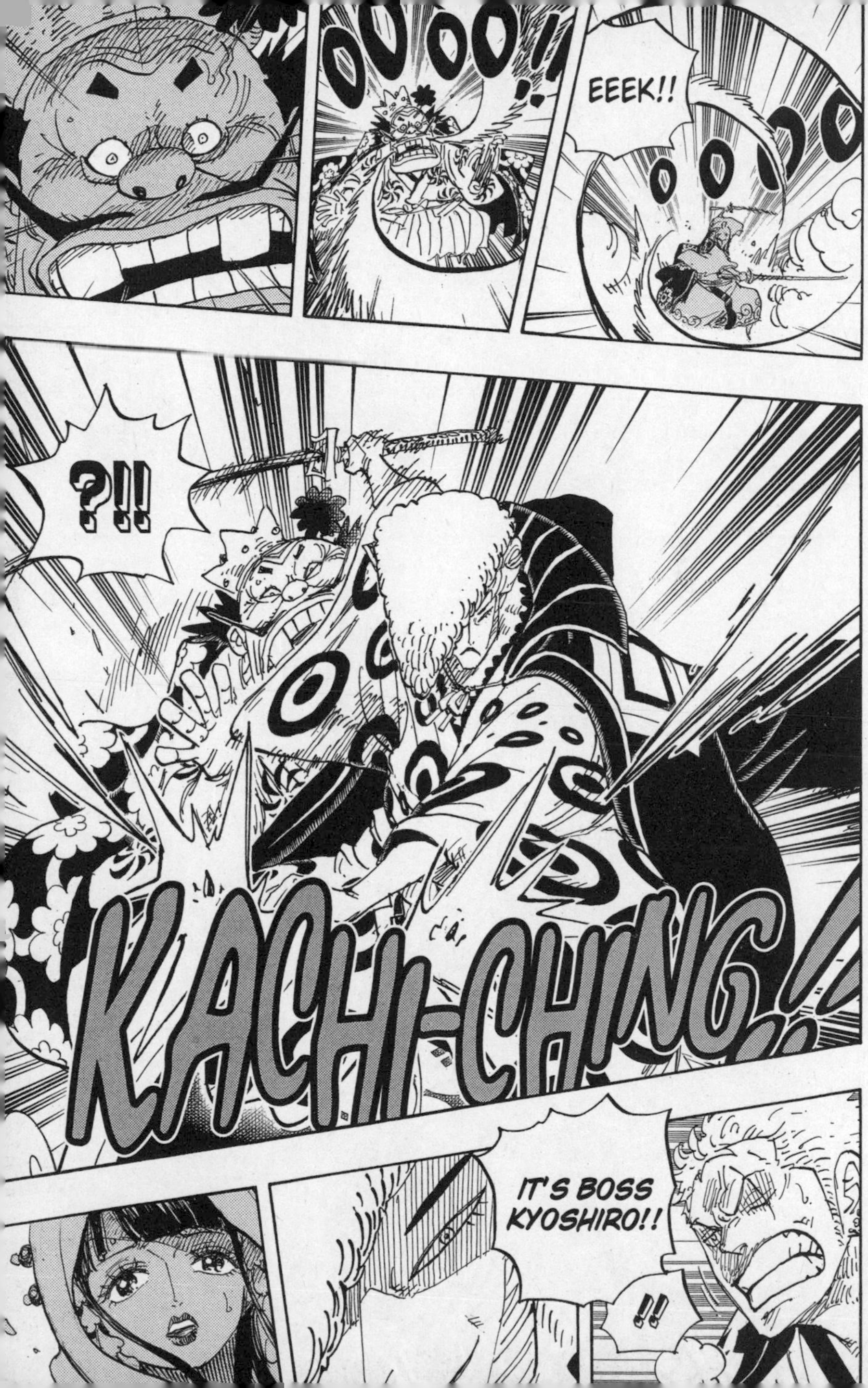
EEEK!!
OOOO!!
?!!
KACHI-CHING!!
IT'S BOSS KYOSHIRO!!
!!

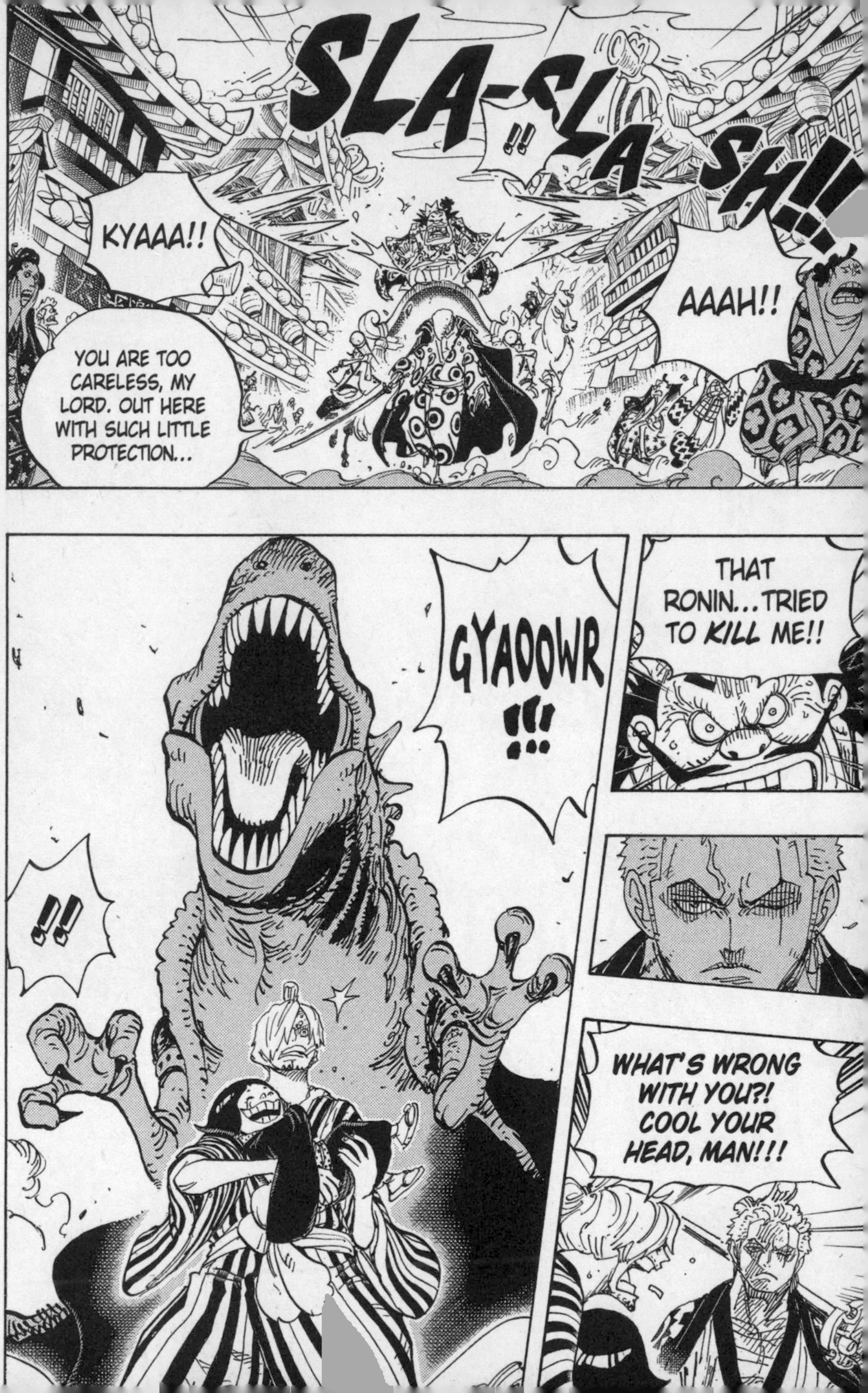
SLA-SLA-SH!!!
!!
AAAH!!
KYAAA!!
YOU ARE TOO CARELESS, MY LORD. OUT HERE WITH SUCH LITTLE PROTECTION...
THAT RONIN...TRIED TO KILL ME!!
WHAT'S WRONG WITH YOU?! COOL YOUR HEAD, MAN!!!
GYAOOWR!!!
!!

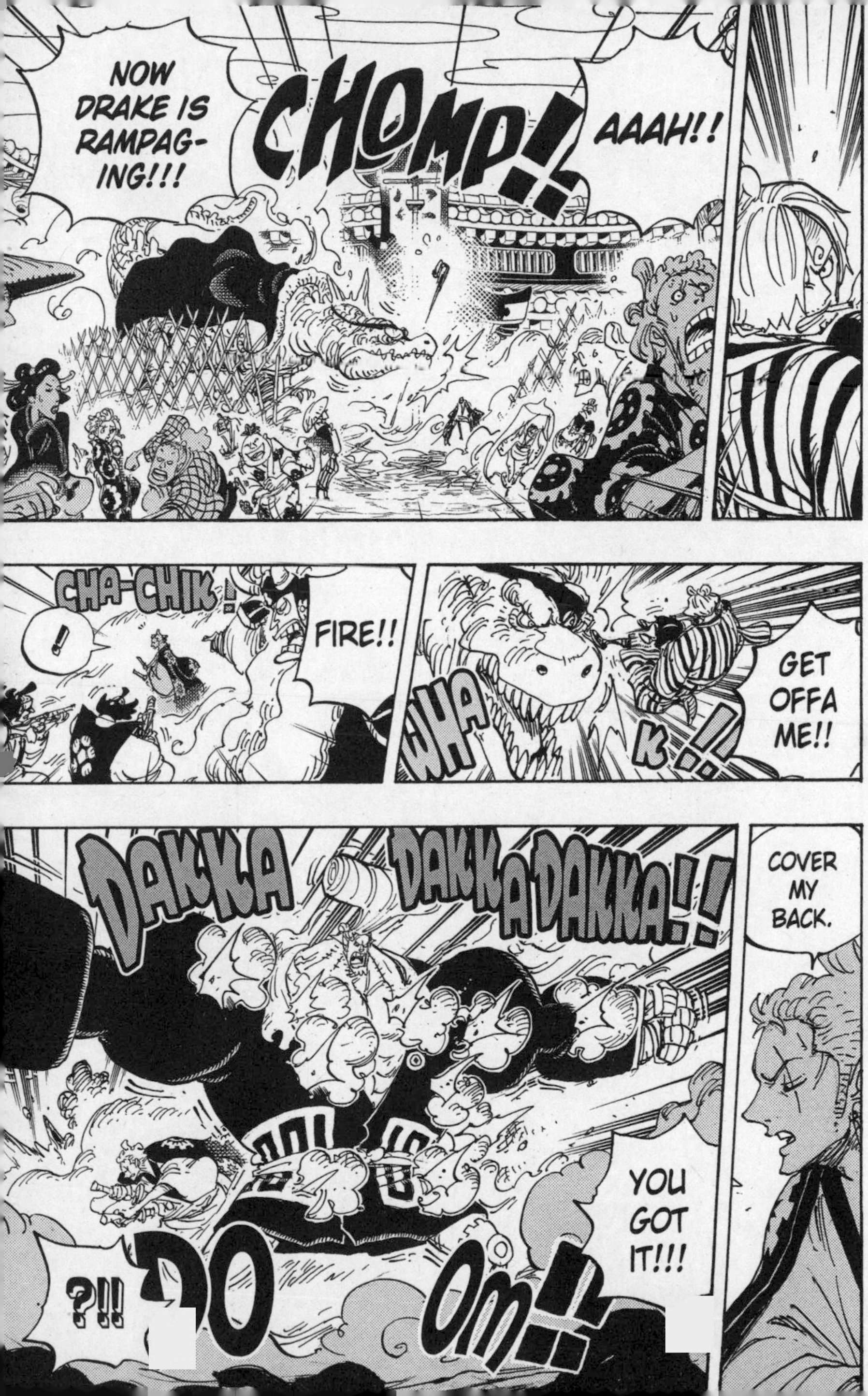
AAAH!!
CHOMP!!
NOW DRAKE IS RAMPAGING!!!
GET OFFA ME!!
WHAK!!
FIRE!!
CHA-CHIK!
!
COVER MY BACK.
DAKKA DAKKA DAKKA!!
YOU GOT IT!!!
DOOM!!
?!!

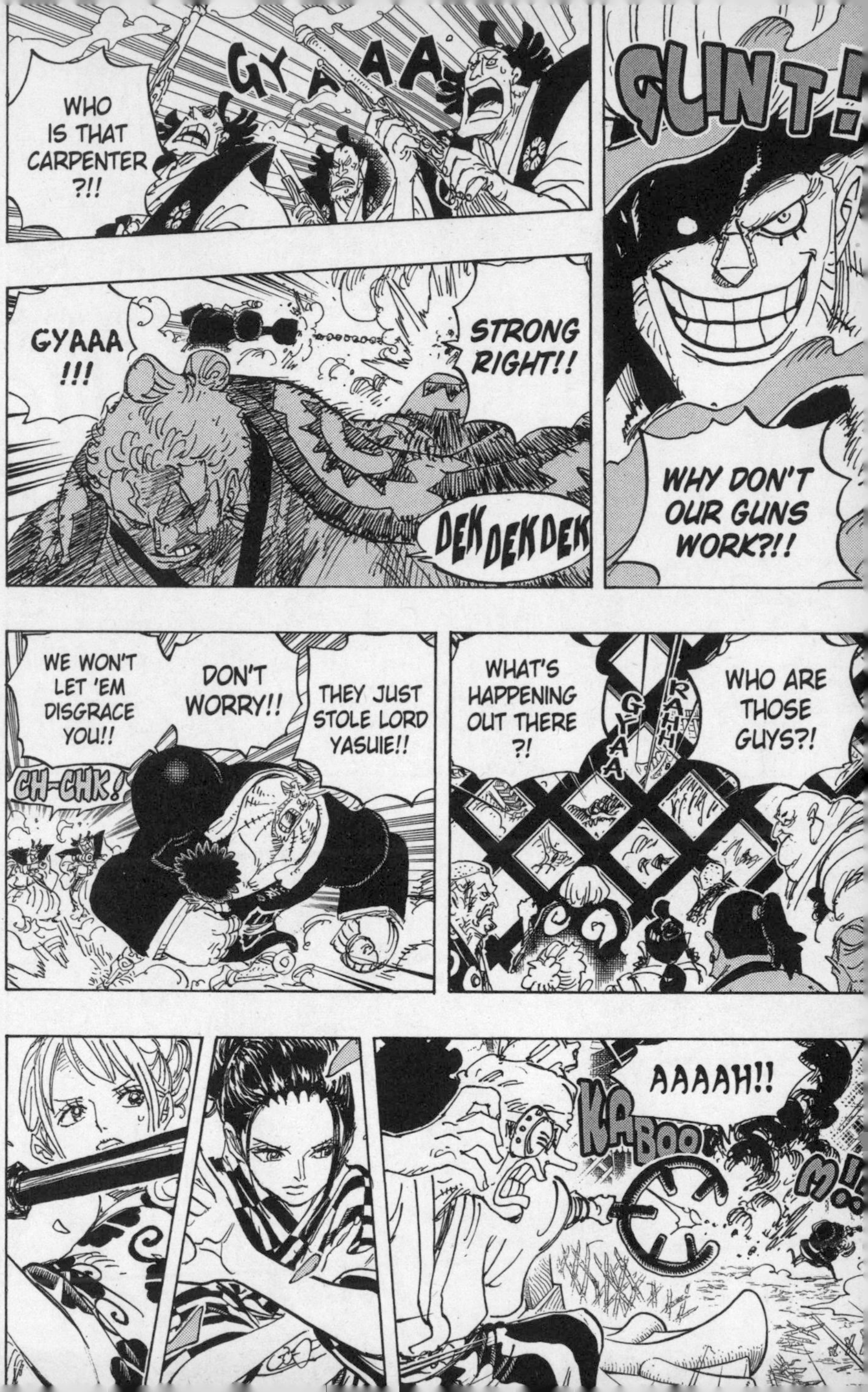
GLINT!!
WHY DON'T OUR GUNS WORK?!!
GYAAA
WHO IS THAT CARPENTER ?!!
STRONG RIGHT!!
GYAAA !!!
DEK DEK DEK
WHO ARE THOSE GUYS?!
RAHH
GYAAA
WHAT'S HAPPENING OUT THERE ?!
THEY JUST STOLE LORD YASUIE!!
DON'T WORRY!!
WE WON'T LET 'EM DISGRACE YOU!!
CH-CHK!
AAAAH!!
KABOOM!!

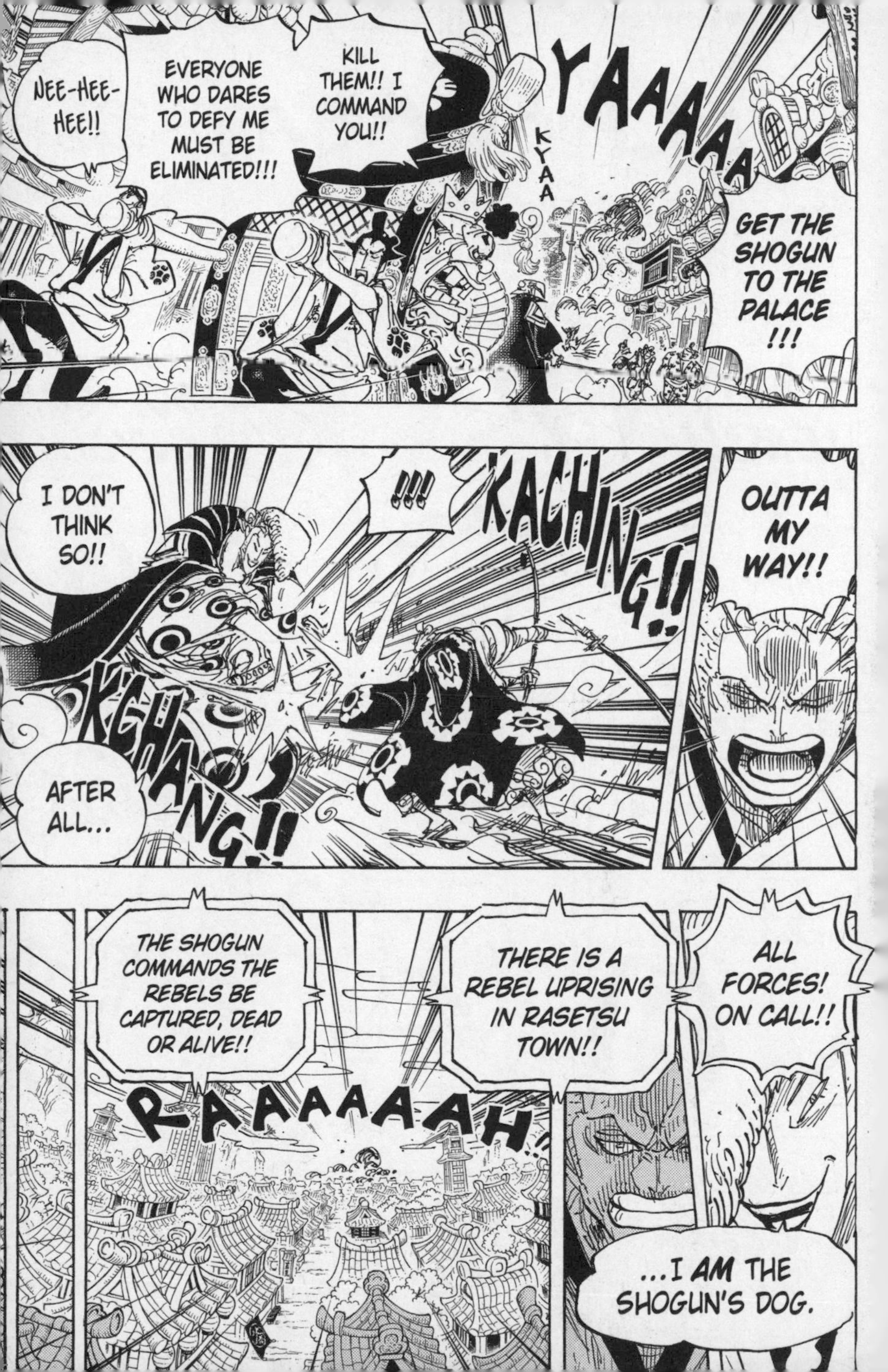
YAAAAAA
KYAA
GET THE SHOGUN TO THE PALACE!!!
KILL THEM!! I COMMAND YOU!!
EVERYONE WHO DARES TO DEFY ME MUST BE ELIMINATED!!!
NEE-HEE-HEE!!
OUTTA MY WAY!!
KACHING!!
!!!
I DON'T THINK SO!!
KCHANG!!
AFTER ALL...
ALL FORCES! ON CALL!!
...I AM THE SHOGUN'S DOG.
THERE IS A REBEL UPRISING IN RASETSU TOWN!!
THE SHOGUN COMMANDS THE REBELS BE CAPTURED, DEAD OR ALIVE!!
RAAAAAAH!!

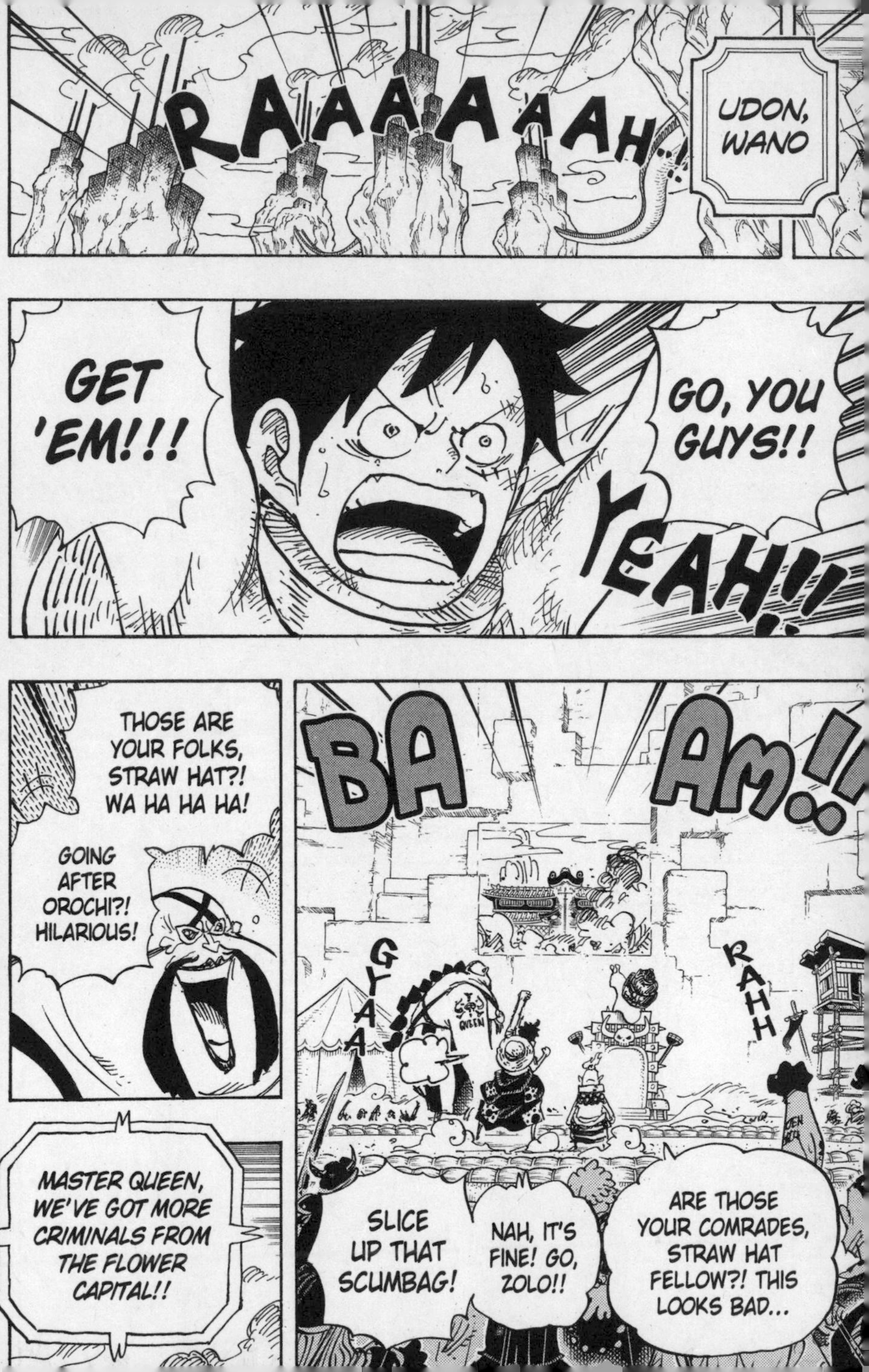
UDON, WANO
RAAAAAH..!!
GO, YOU GUYS!!
YEAH!!
GET 'EM!!!
BA AM..!!
RAHH
GYAAA
ARE THOSE YOUR COMRADES, STRAW HAT FELLOW?! THIS LOOKS BAD...
NAH, IT'S FINE! GO, ZOLO!!
SLICE UP THAT SCUMBAG!
THOSE ARE YOUR FOLKS, STRAW HAT?! WA HA HA HA!
GOING AFTER OROCHI?! HILARIOUS!
MASTER QUEEN, WE'VE GOT MORE CRIMINALS FROM THE FLOWER CAPITAL!!

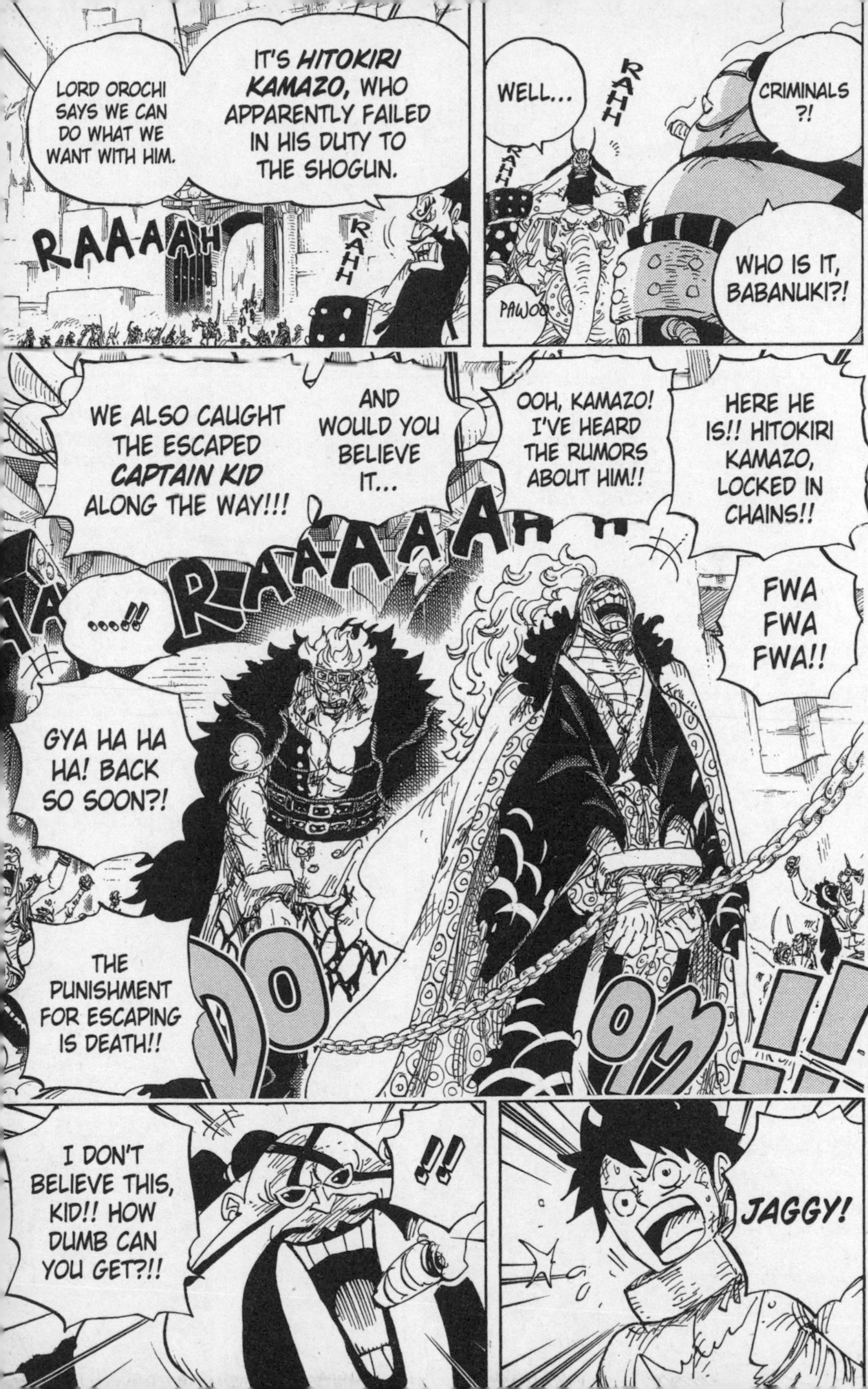
CRIMINALS ?!
RAHH
WELL...
RAHH
WHO IS IT, BABANUKI?!
PAWOO
IT'S *HITOKIRI KAMAZO,* WHO APPARENTLY FAILED IN HIS DUTY TO THE SHOGUN.
LORD OROCHI SAYS WE CAN DO WHAT WE WANT WITH HIM.
RAHH
RAAAAH
HERE HE IS!! HITOKIRI KAMAZO, LOCKED IN CHAINS!!
OOH, KAMAZO! I'VE HEARD THE RUMORS ABOUT HIM!!
AND WOULD YOU BELIEVE IT...
WE ALSO CAUGHT THE ESCAPED *CAPTAIN KID* ALONG THE WAY!!!
RAAAAAAR
FWA FWA FWA!!
...!!
GYA HA HA HA! BACK SO SOON?!
THE PUNISHMENT FOR ESCAPING IS DEATH!!
DOOM!!
JAGGY!
!!
I DON'T BELIEVE THIS, KID!! HOW DUMB CAN YOU GET?!!

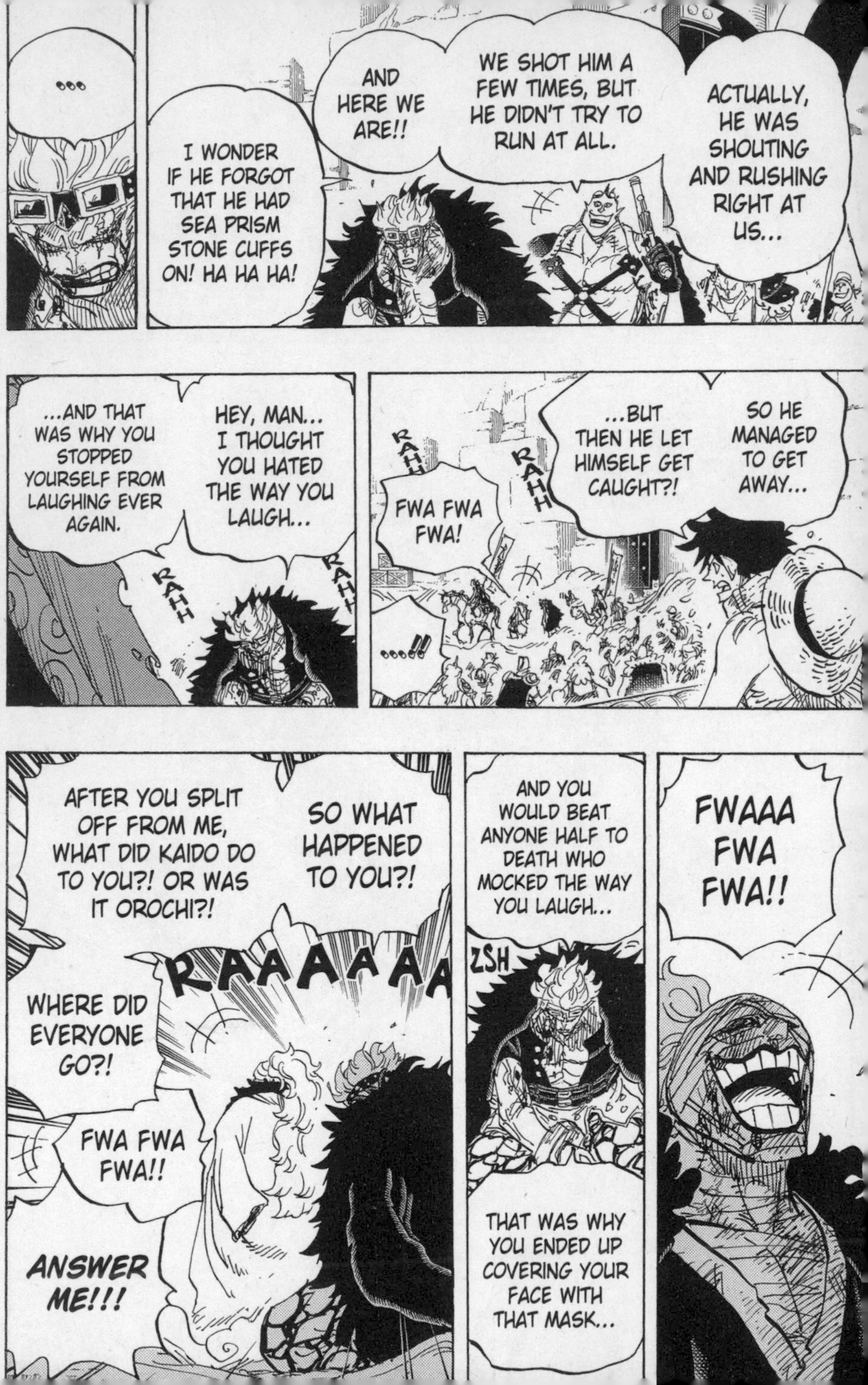
ACTUALLY, HE WAS SHOUTING AND RUSHING RIGHT AT US...
WE SHOT HIM A FEW TIMES, BUT HE DIDN'T TRY TO RUN AT ALL.
AND HERE WE ARE!!
I WONDER IF HE FORGOT THAT HE HAD SEA PRISM STONE CUFFS ON! HA HA HA!
...
SO HE MANAGED TO GET AWAY...
...BUT THEN HE LET HIMSELF GET CAUGHT?!
RAHH
FWA FWA FWA!
RAHH
....!!
HEY, MAN... I THOUGHT YOU HATED THE WAY YOU LAUGH...
...AND THAT WAS WHY YOU STOPPED YOURSELF FROM LAUGHING EVER AGAIN.
RAHH
RAHH
FWAAA FWA FWA!!
AND YOU WOULD BEAT ANYONE HALF TO DEATH WHO MOCKED THE WAY YOU LAUGH...
ZSH
THAT WAS WHY YOU ENDED UP COVERING YOUR FACE WITH THAT MASK...
SO WHAT HAPPENED TO YOU?!
AFTER YOU SPLIT OFF FROM ME, WHAT DID KAIDO DO TO YOU?! OR WAS IT OROCHI?!
RAAAAAA
WHERE DID EVERYONE GO?!
FWA FWA FWA!!
ANSWER ME!!!

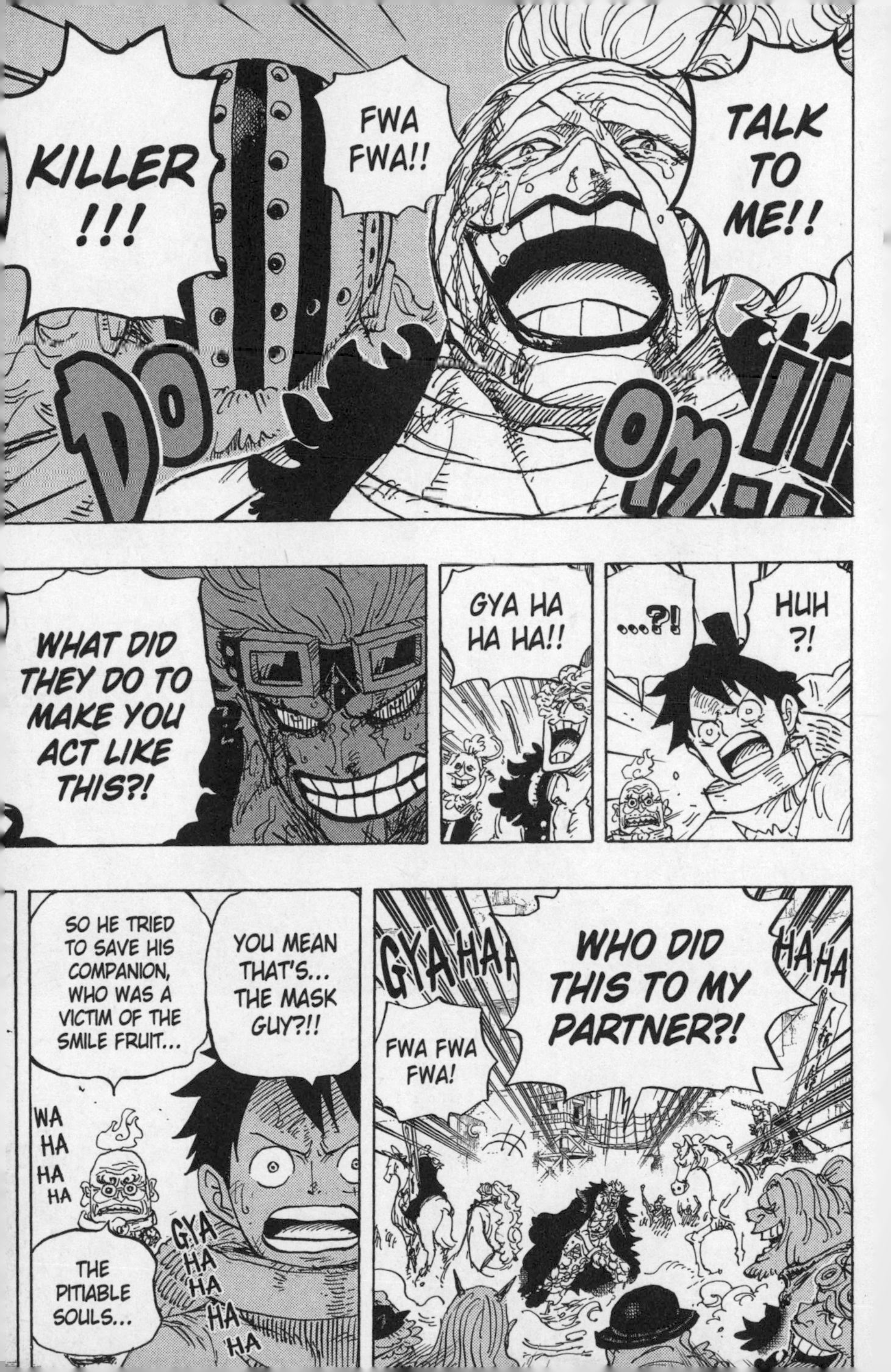
TALK TO ME!!
FWA FWA!!
KILLER!!!
DOOM!!
HUH?!
...?!
GYA HA HA HA!!
WHAT DID THEY DO TO MAKE YOU ACT LIKE THIS?!
HA HA HA
WHO DID THIS TO MY PARTNER?!
GYAHAHA
FWA FWA FWA!
YOU MEAN THAT'S... THE MASK GUY?!!
SO HE TRIED TO SAVE HIS COMPANION, WHO WAS A VICTIM OF THE SMILE FRUIT...
WA HA HA HA HA
GYA HA HA HA HA HA
THE PITIABLE SOULS...

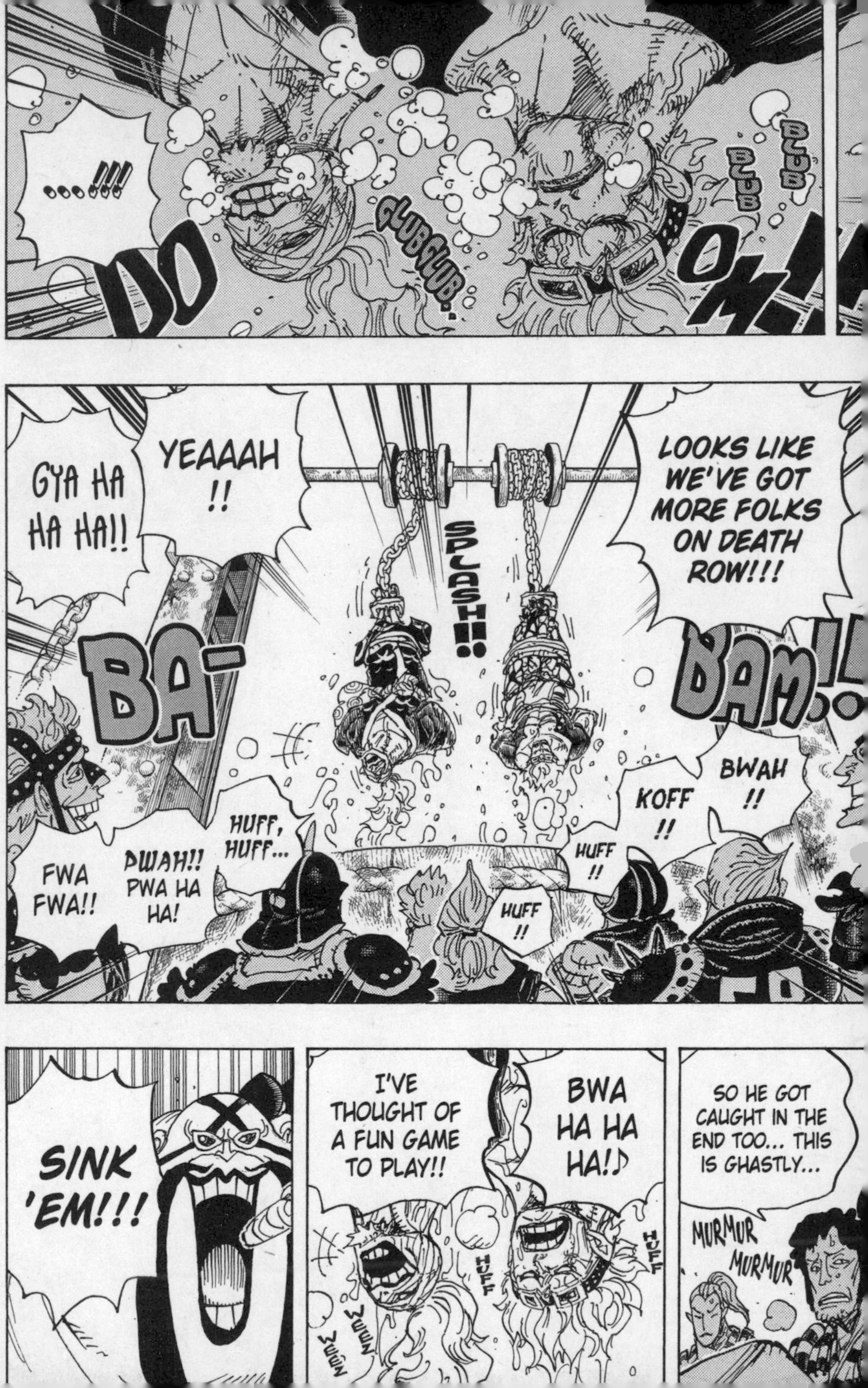
BLUB
BLUB
OH!!
GLUBGLUB...
DO
...!!!
LOOKS LIKE WE'VE GOT MORE FOLKS ON DEATH ROW!!!
BAM!!
BWAH !!
KOFF !!
HUFF !!
HUFF !!
SPLASH!!
HUFF, HUFF...
YEAAAH !!
GYA HA HA HA!!
BA-
PWAH!! PWA HA HA!
FWA FWA!!
SO HE GOT CAUGHT IN THE END TOO... THIS IS GHASTLY...
MURMUR
MURMUR
BWA HA HA HA!♪
I'VE THOUGHT OF A FUN GAME TO PLAY!!
HUFF
HUFF
WEEN
WEEN
SINK 'EM!!!

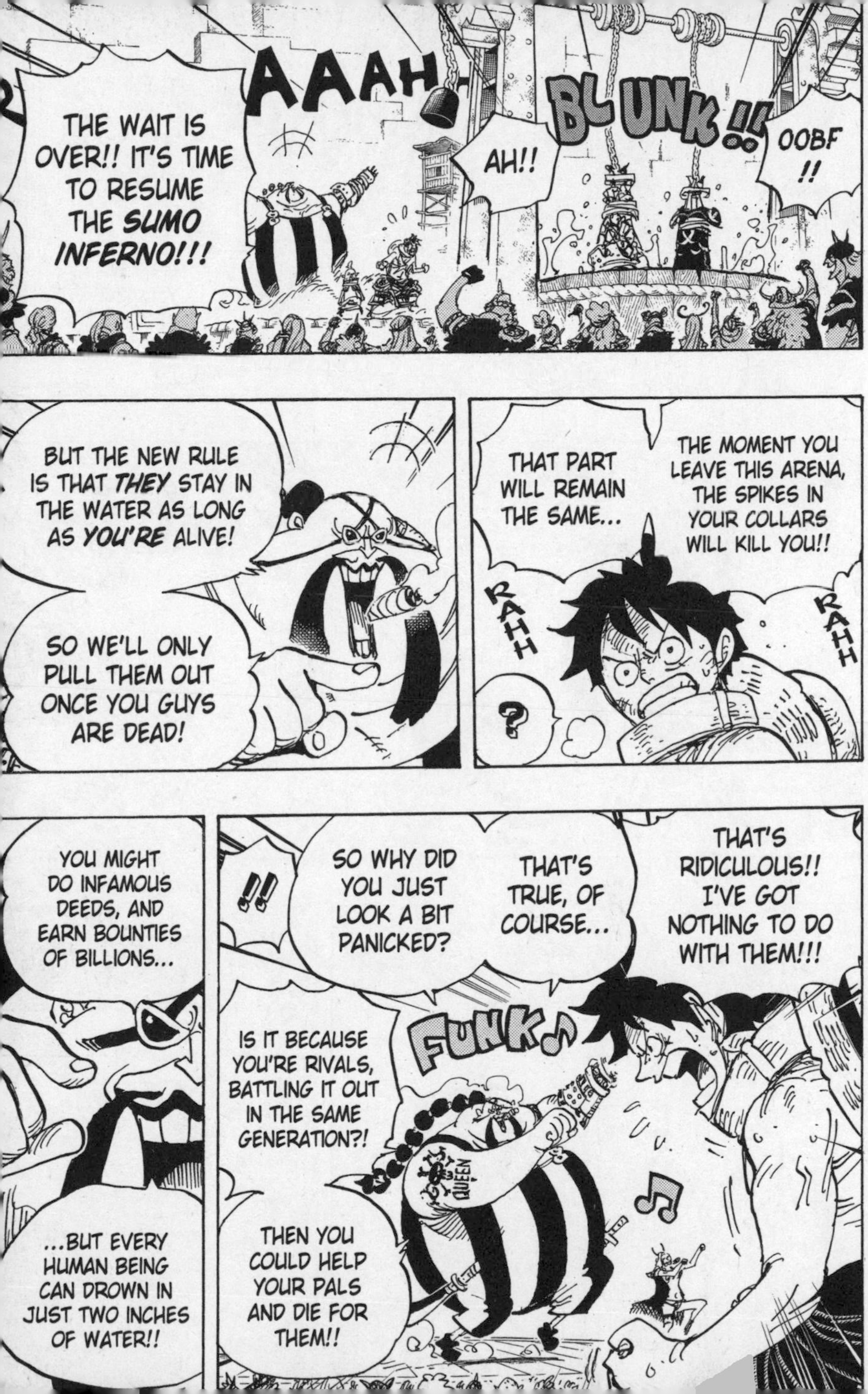
THE WAIT IS OVER!! IT'S TIME TO RESUME THE *SUMO INFERNO!!!*
AAAAH
AH!!
BLUNK!!
OOBF !!
BUT THE NEW RULE IS THAT *THEY* STAY IN THE WATER AS LONG AS *YOU'RE* ALIVE!
SO WE'LL ONLY PULL THEM OUT ONCE YOU GUYS ARE DEAD!
THAT PART WILL REMAIN THE SAME...
THE MOMENT YOU LEAVE THIS ARENA, THE SPIKES IN YOUR COLLARS WILL KILL YOU!!
RAHH
RAHH
?
YOU MIGHT DO INFAMOUS DEEDS, AND EARN BOUNTIES OF BILLIONS...
...BUT EVERY HUMAN BEING CAN DROWN IN JUST TWO INCHES OF WATER!!
!!
SO WHY DID YOU JUST LOOK A BIT PANICKED?
THAT'S TRUE, OF COURSE...
THAT'S RIDICULOUS!! I'VE GOT NOTHING TO DO WITH THEM!!!
FUNK♪
IS IT BECAUSE YOU'RE RIVALS, BATTLING IT OUT IN THE SAME GENERATION?!
THEN YOU COULD HELP YOUR PALS AND DIE FOR THEM!!
QUEEN

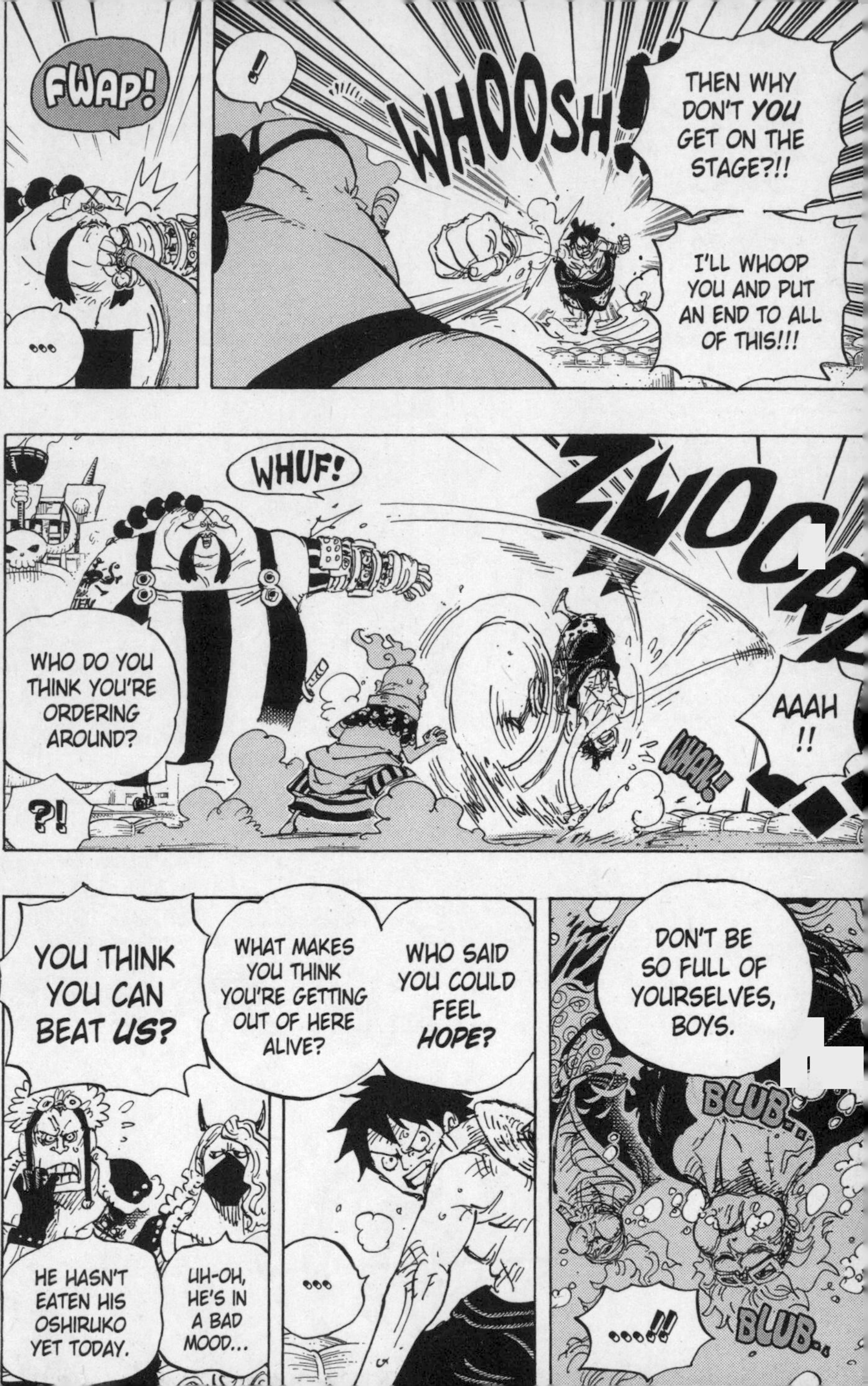
THEN WHY DON'T YOU GET ON THE STAGE?!!
WHOOSH!
I'LL WHOOP YOU AND PUT AN END TO ALL OF THIS!!!
!
FWAP!
...
AAAH !!
WHUF!
WHAK!
WHO DO YOU THINK YOU'RE ORDERING AROUND?
?!
DON'T BE SO FULL OF YOURSELVES, BOYS.
BLUB..
BLUB..
...!!
WHO SAID YOU COULD FEEL HOPE?
WHAT MAKES YOU THINK YOU'RE GETTING OUT OF HERE ALIVE?
YOU THINK YOU CAN BEAT US?
...
UH-OH, HE'S IN A BAD MOOD...
HE HASN'T EATEN HIS OSHIRUKO YET TODAY.

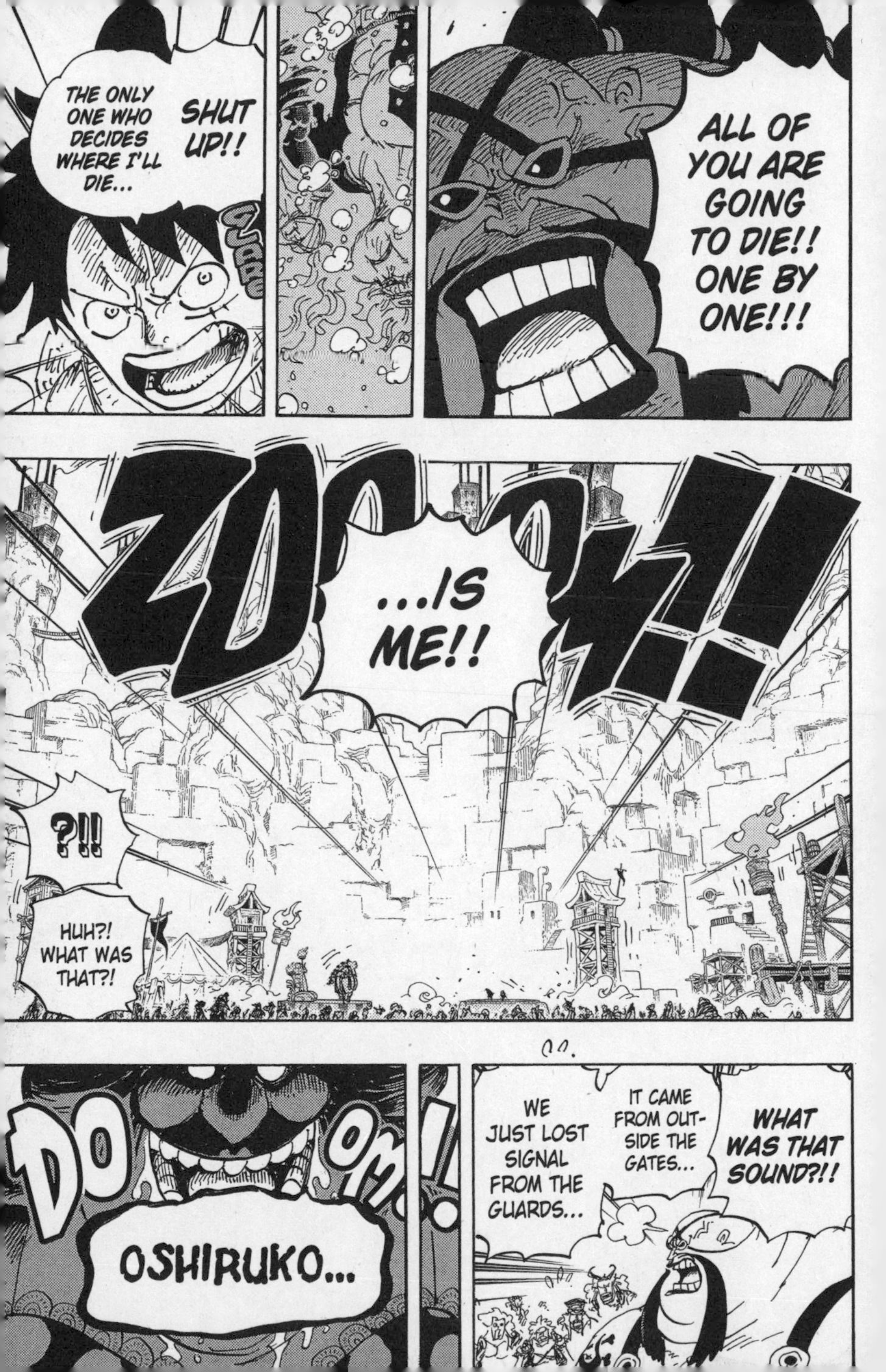
ALL OF YOU ARE GOING TO DIE!! ONE BY ONE!!!
SHUT UP!!
THE ONLY ONE WHO DECIDES WHERE I'LL DIE...
...IS ME!!
?!!
HUH?! WHAT WAS THAT?!
WHAT WAS THAT SOUND?!!
IT CAME FROM OUT-SIDE THE GATES...
WE JUST LOST SIGNAL FROM THE GUARDS...
OSHIRUKO...

Chapter 945: OLIN

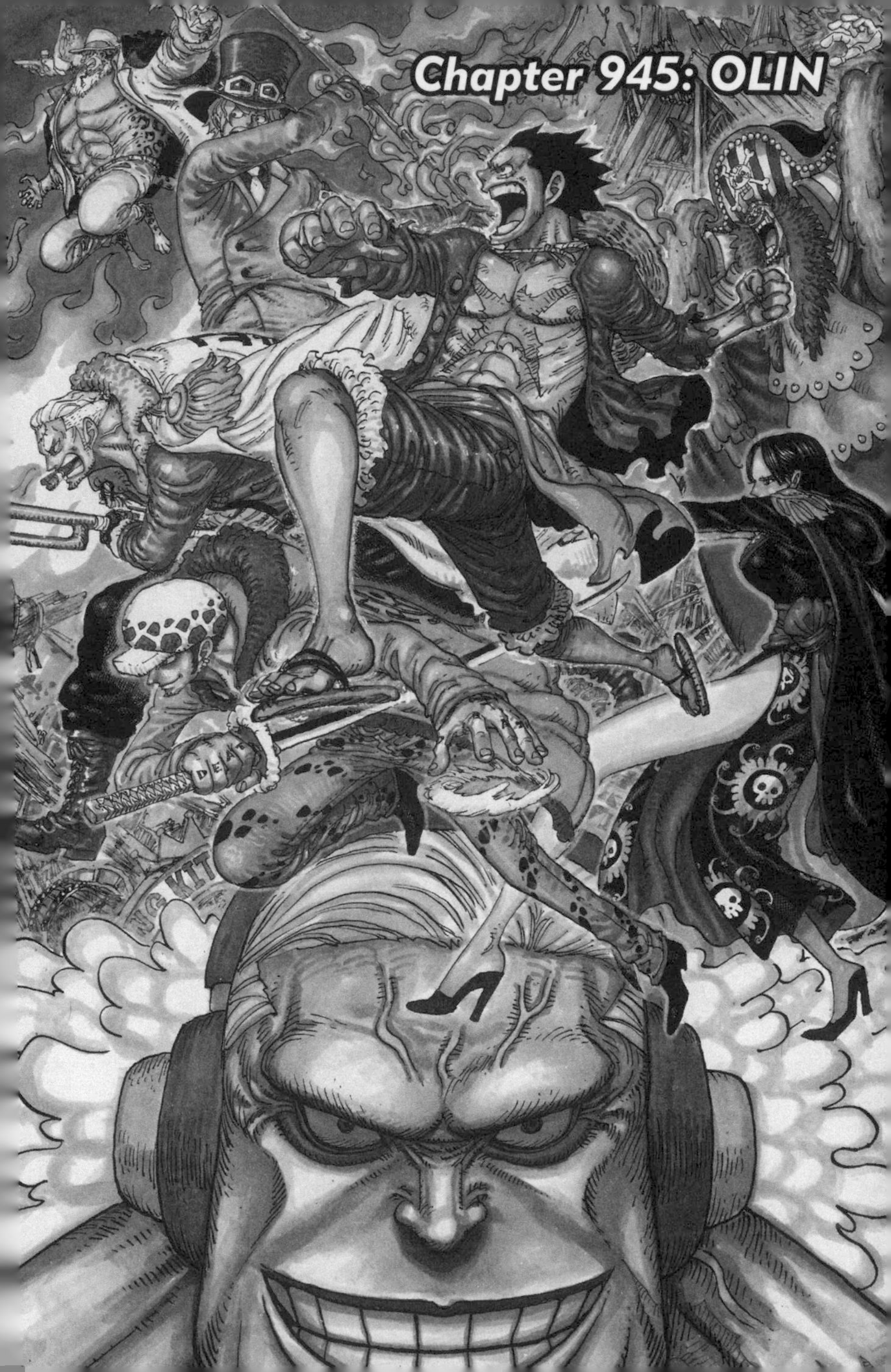

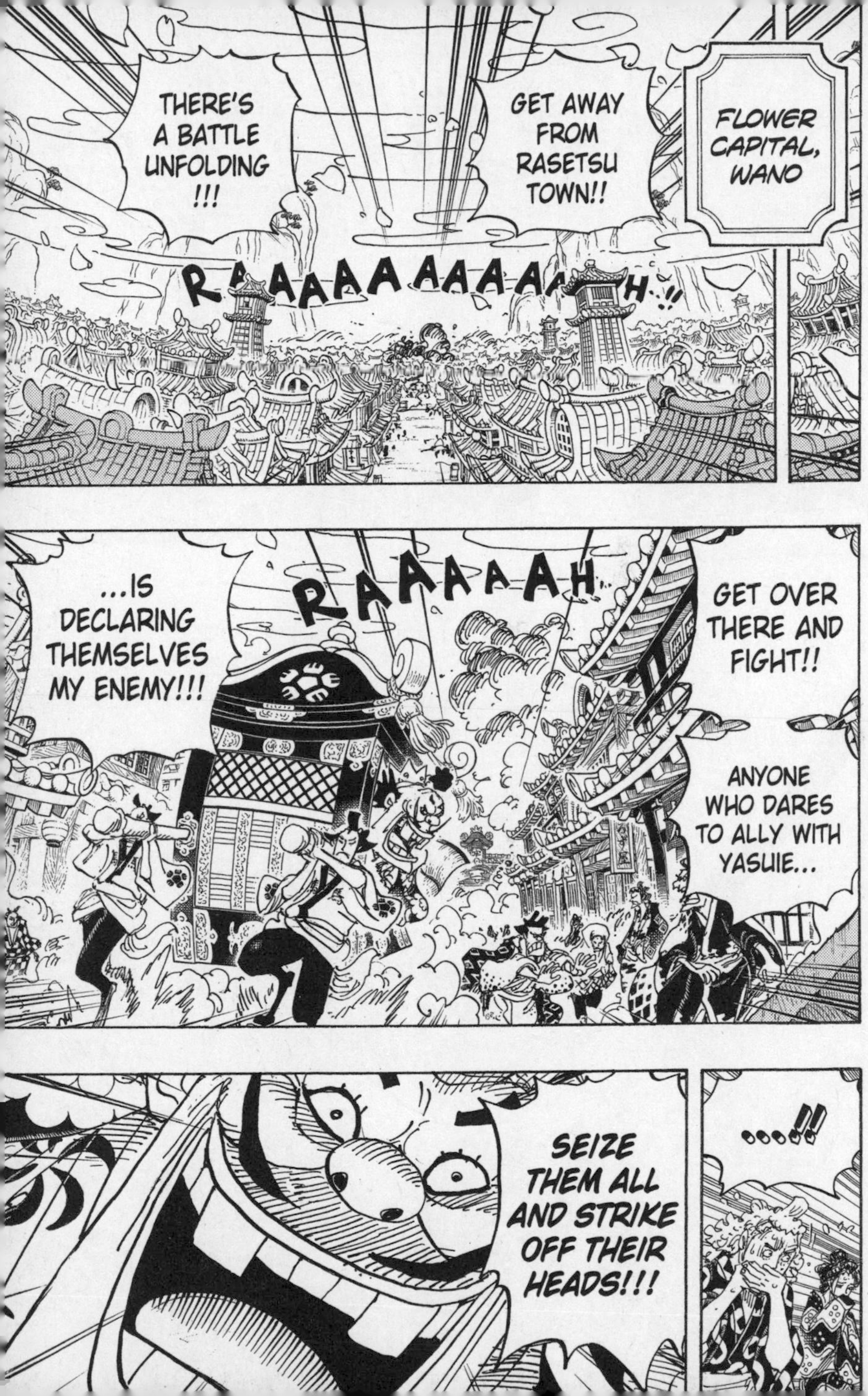
FLOWER CAPITAL, WANO
GET AWAY FROM RASETSU TOWN!!
THERE'S A BATTLE UNFOLDING!!!
RAAAAAAAAAAAH!!
GET OVER THERE AND FIGHT!!
ANYONE WHO DARES TO ALLY WITH YASUIE...
RAAAAAH
...IS DECLARING THEMSELVES MY ENEMY!!!
....!!
SEIZE THEM ALL AND STRIKE OFF THEIR HEADS!!!

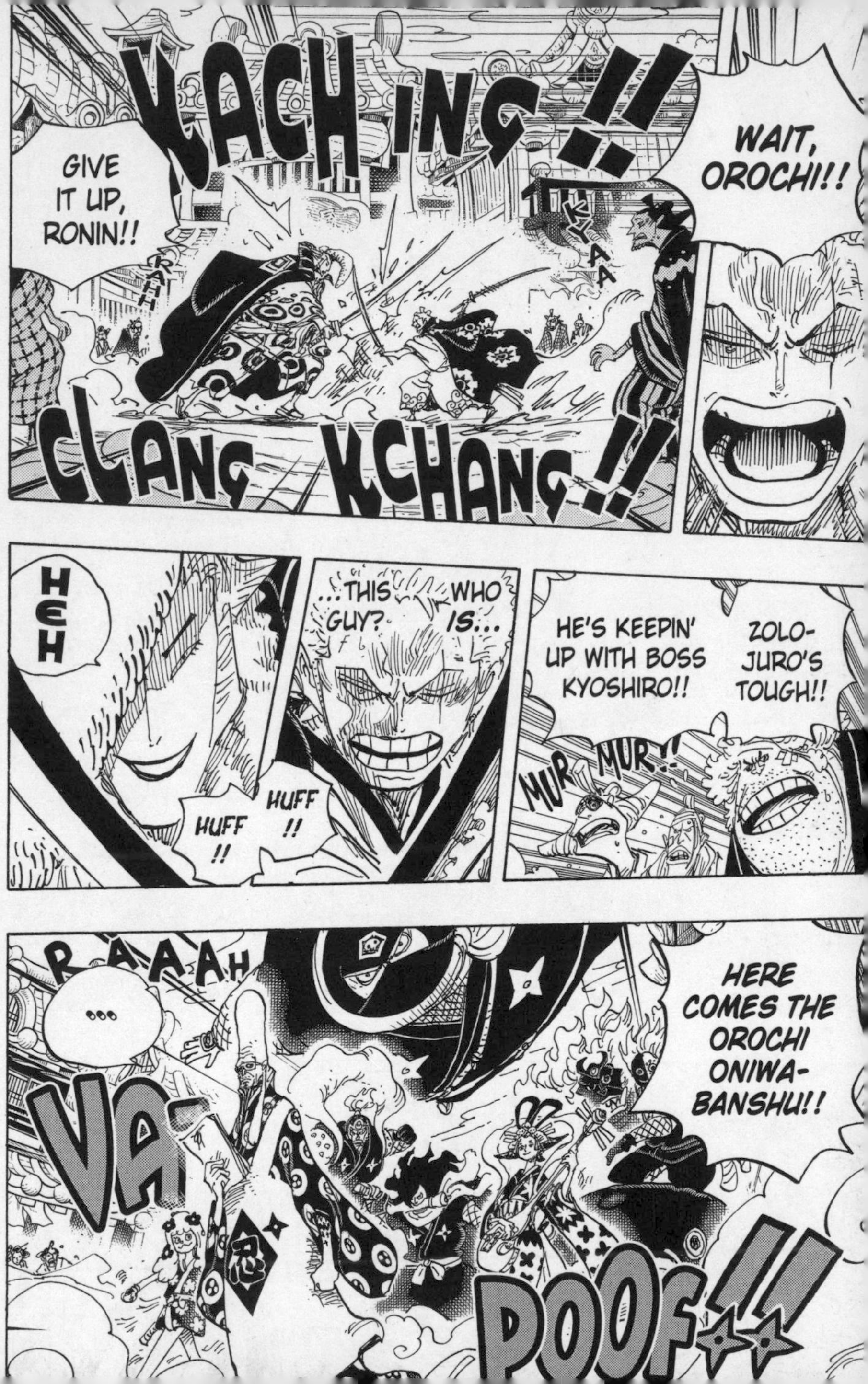
WAIT, OROCHI!!
KYAA
KACHING!!
GIVE IT UP, RONIN!!
RAHH
KCHANG!!
CLANG
ZOLO-JURO'S TOUGH!!
HE'S KEEPIN' UP WITH BOSS KYOSHIRO!!
MUR MUR!!
WHO IS... ...THIS GUY?
HUFF!!
HUFF!!
HEH
HERE COMES THE OROCHI ONIWA-BANSHU!!
RAAAH
...
VA-
POOF!!

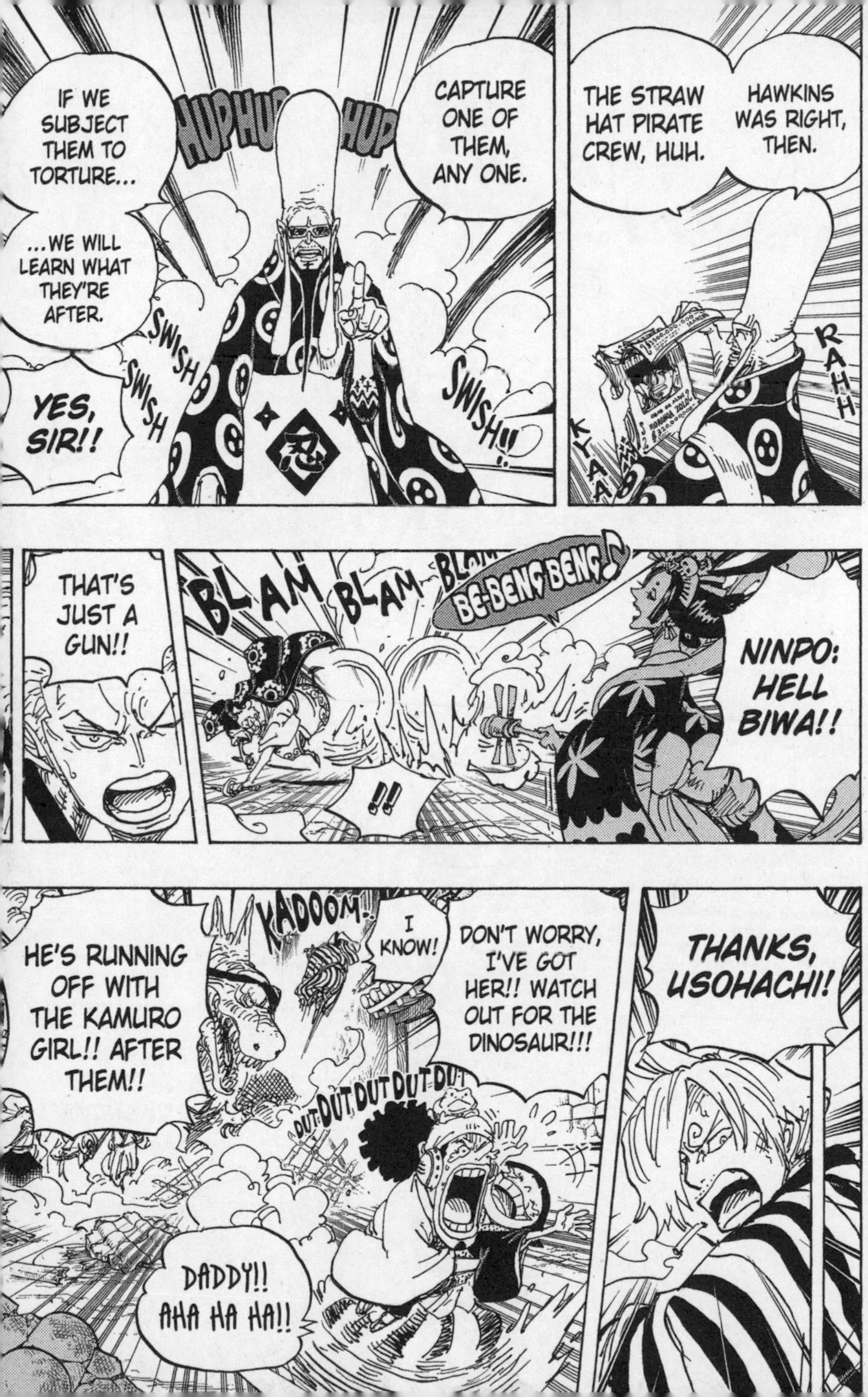
HAWKINS WAS RIGHT, THEN.
THE STRAW HAT PIRATE CREW, HUH.
RAHH
KYAA
CAPTURE ONE OF THEM, ANY ONE.
HUP HUP HUP
IF WE SUBJECT THEM TO TORTURE...
...WE WILL LEARN WHAT THEY'RE AFTER.
SWISH!!
SWISH
SWISH
YES, SIR!!
BE-BENG BENG♪
NINPO: HELL BIWA!!
BLAM BLAM BLAM
!!
THAT'S JUST A GUN!!
THANKS, USOHACHI!
DON'T WORRY, I'VE GOT HER!! WATCH OUT FOR THE DINOSAUR!!!
I KNOW!
KADOOM
HE'S RUNNING OFF WITH THE KAMURO GIRL!! AFTER THEM!!
DUT DUT DUT DUT DUT
DADDY!! AHA HA HA!!

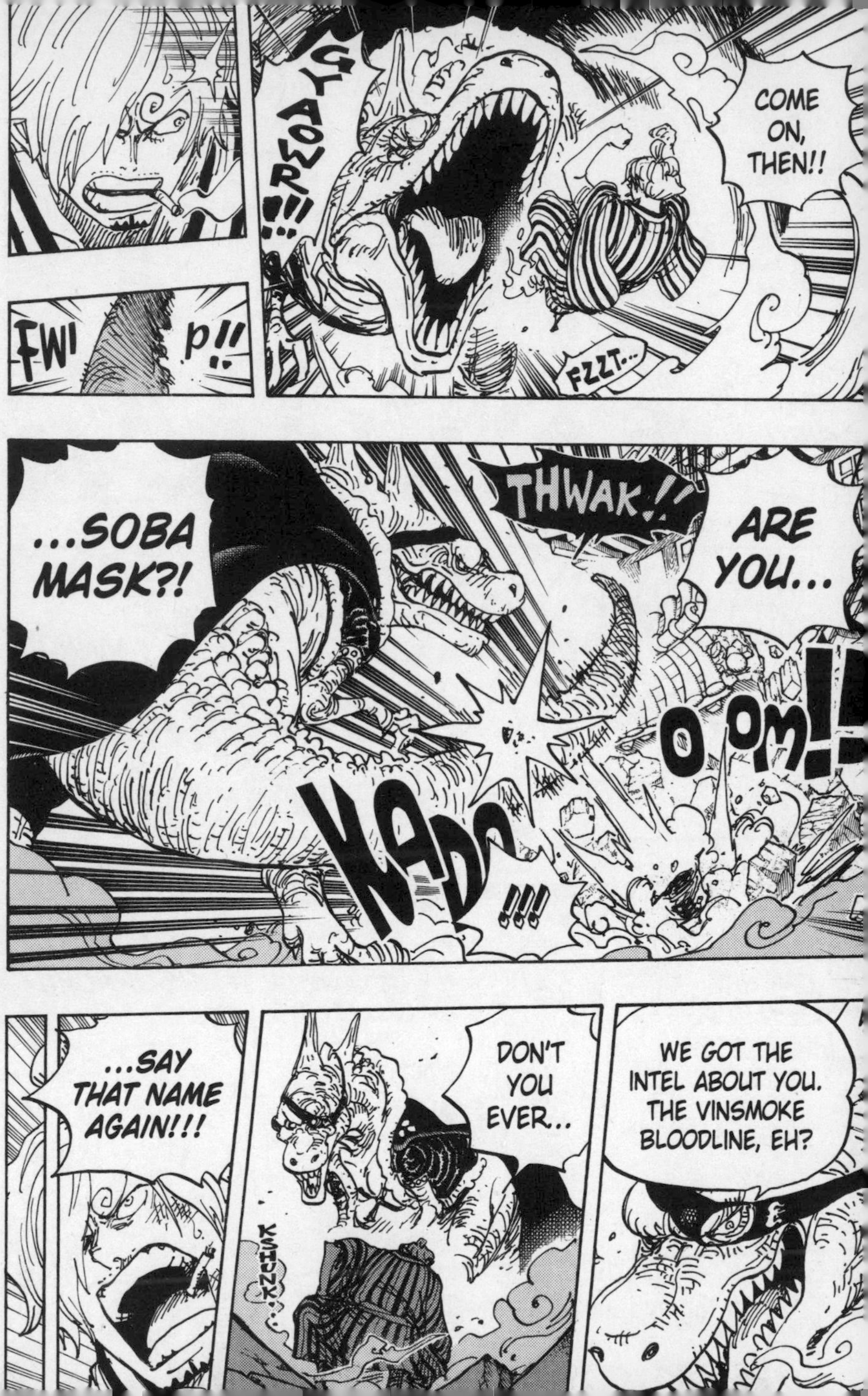
COME ON, THEN!!
GYAOWR!!...
FZZT...
FWIP!!
ARE YOU...
THWAK!!
...SOBA MASK?!
OOM!!
KADO!!!
WE GOT THE INTEL ABOUT YOU. THE VINSMOKE BLOODLINE, EH?
DON'T YOU EVER...
KSHUNK...
...SAY THAT NAME AGAIN!!!

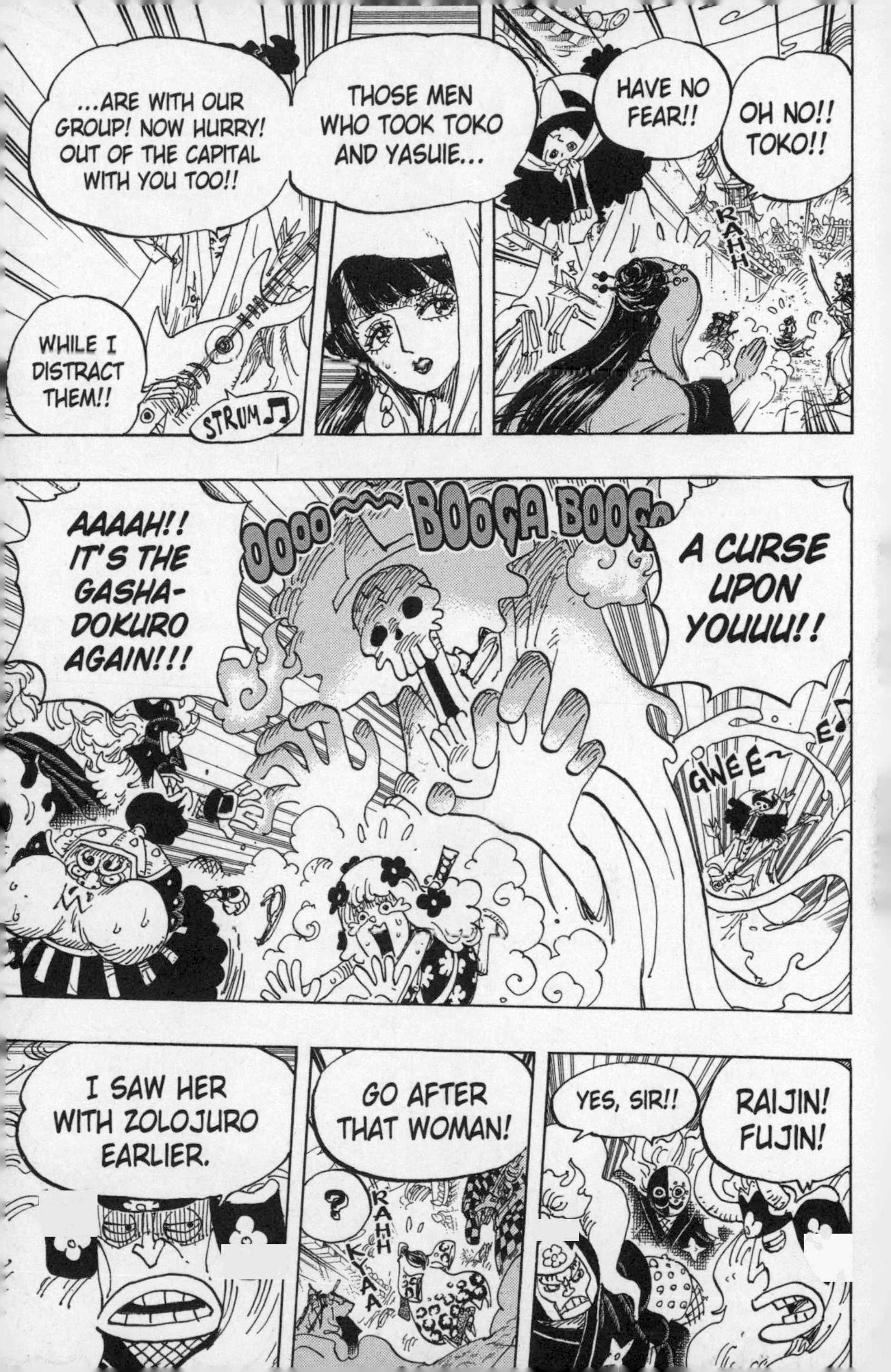
OH NO!! TOKO!!
HAVE NO FEAR!!
RAHH
THOSE MEN WHO TOOK TOKO AND YASUIE...
...ARE WITH OUR GROUP! NOW HURRY! OUT OF THE CAPITAL WITH YOU TOO!!
WHILE I DISTRACT THEM!!
STRUM♫
A CURSE UPON YOUUU!!
OOOO~~ BOOGA BOO
GWEE~E♪
AAAAH!! IT'S THE GASHA-DOKURO AGAIN!!!
RAIJIN! FUJIN!
YES, SIR!!
GO AFTER THAT WOMAN!
RAHH
?
KYAA
I SAW HER WITH ZOLOJURO EARLIER.

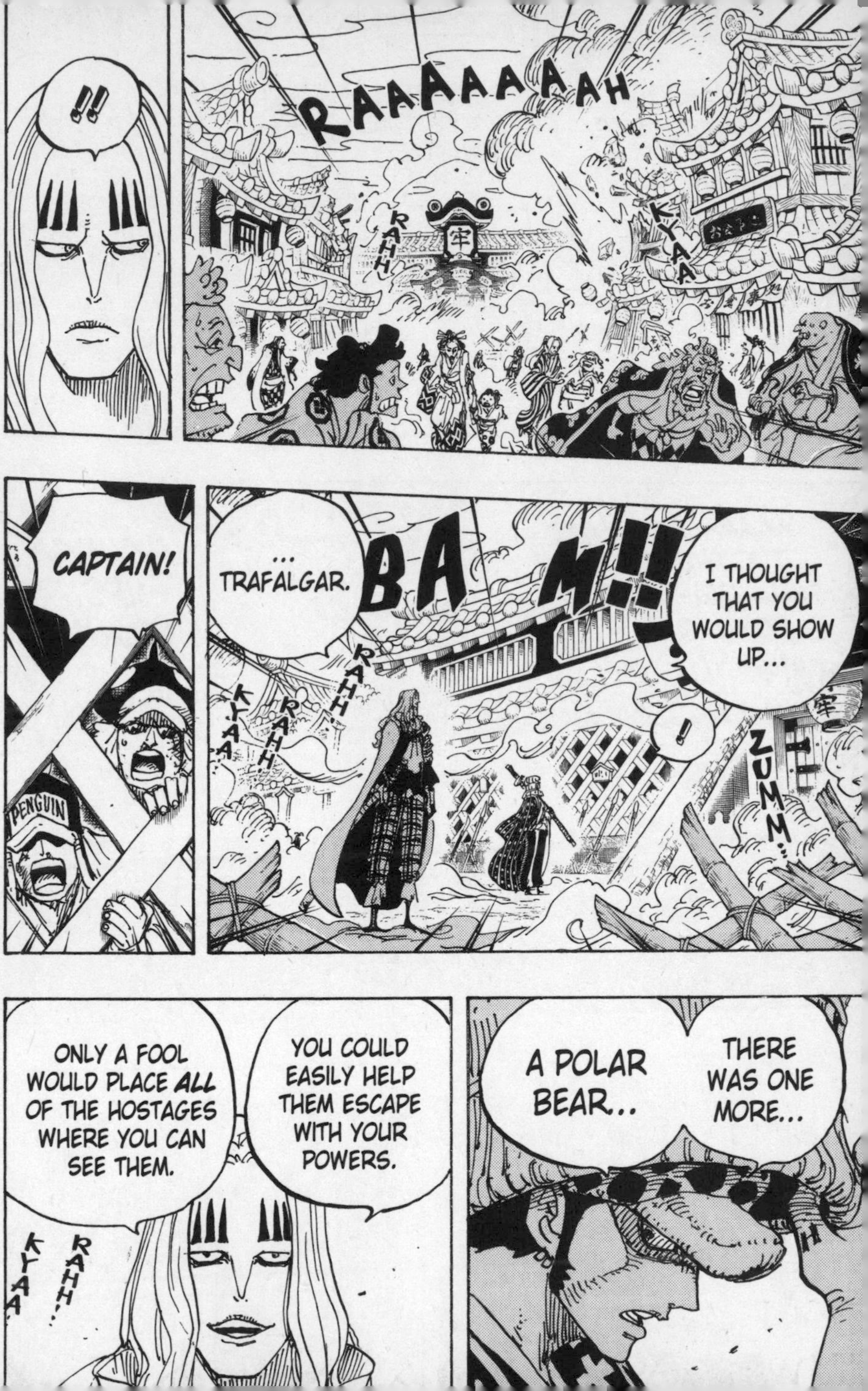
RAAAAAAAAH
RAHH
KYAA
!!
I THOUGHT THAT YOU WOULD SHOW UP...
BAM!!
... TRAFALGAR.
RAHH.
!
ZUMM...
RAHH
KYAA
CAPTAIN!
PENGUIN
THERE WAS ONE MORE...
A POLAR BEAR...
YOU COULD EASILY HELP THEM ESCAPE WITH YOUR POWERS.
ONLY A FOOL WOULD PLACE ALL OF THE HOSTAGES WHERE YOU CAN SEE THEM.
RAHH!
KYAA

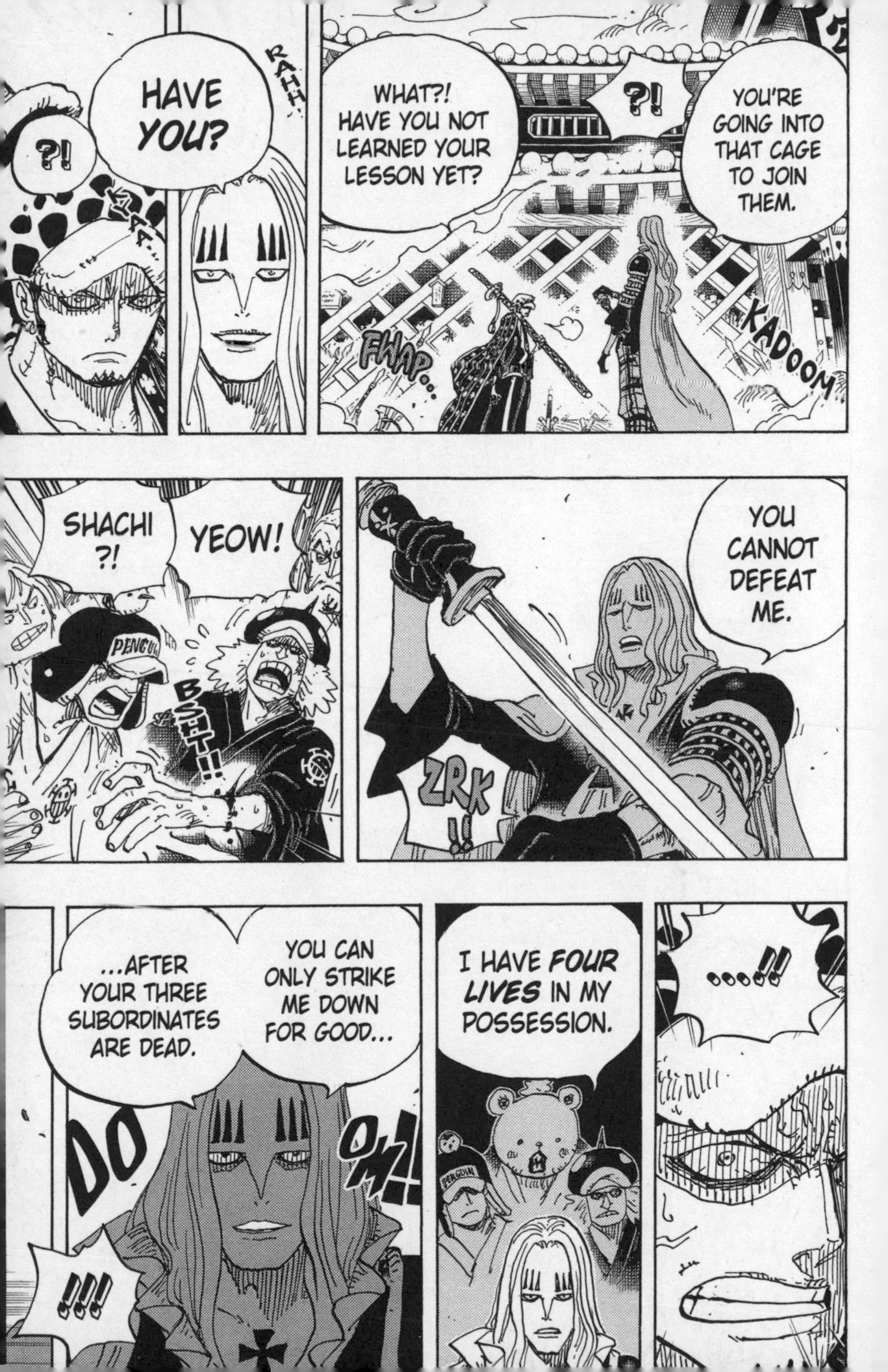
YOU'RE GOING INTO THAT CAGE TO JOIN THEM.
?!
WHAT?! HAVE YOU NOT LEARNED YOUR LESSON YET?
KADOOM
FWAP...
RAHH
HAVE *YOU?*
?!
YOU CANNOT DEFEAT ME.
ZRK!!
YEOW!
SHACHI ?!
BSHT!!
...!!
I HAVE *FOUR LIVES* IN MY POSSESSION.
YOU CAN ONLY STRIKE ME DOWN FOR GOOD...
...AFTER YOUR THREE SUBORDINATES ARE DEAD.
DOOM!!
!!!

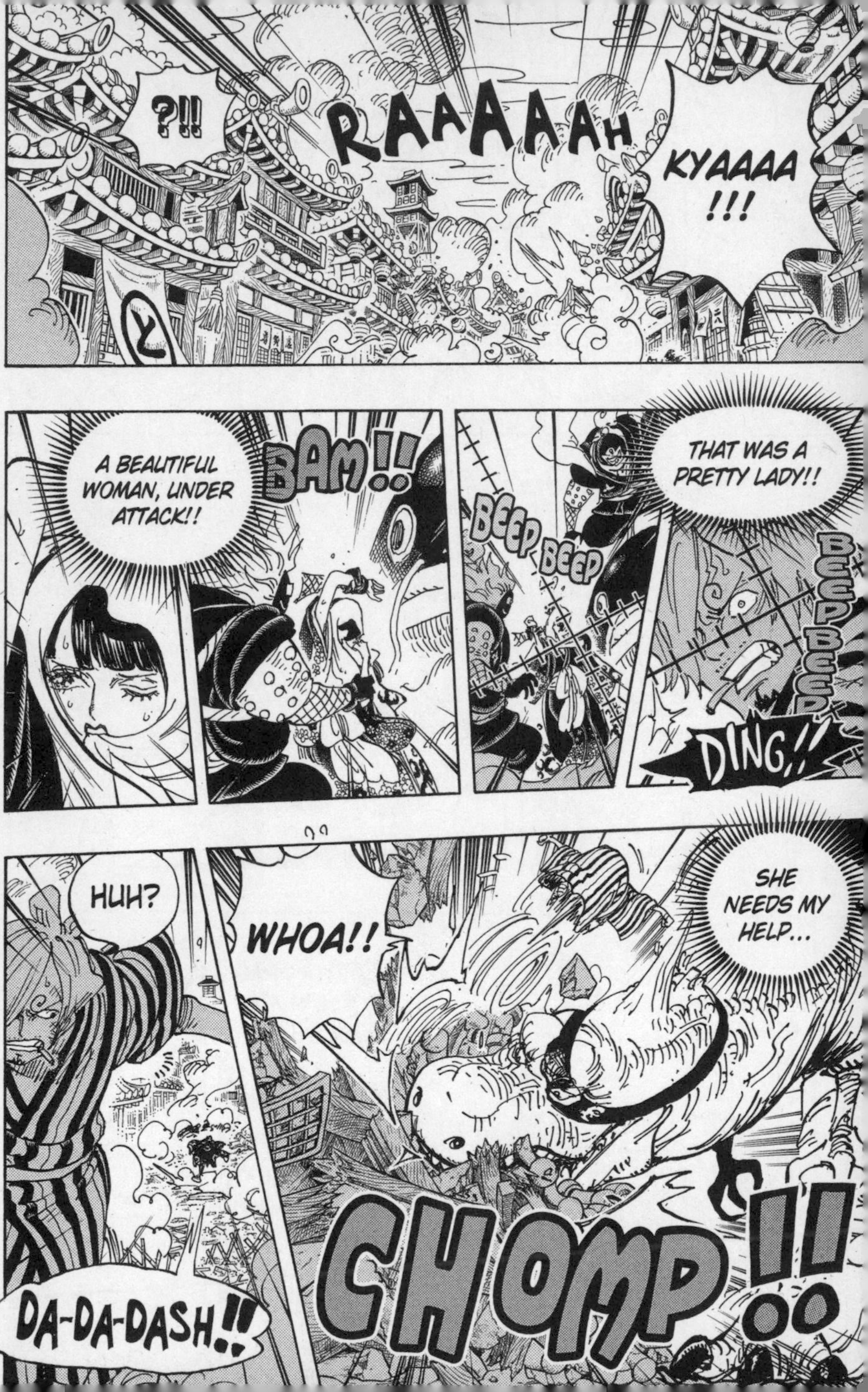
KYAAAA !!!
RAAAAAH
?!!
THAT WAS A PRETTY LADY!!
BEEP BEEP
DING!!
BEEP BEEP
BAM!!
A BEAUTIFUL WOMAN, UNDER ATTACK!!
SHE NEEDS MY HELP...
CHOMP!!
WHOA!!
HUH?
DA-DA-DASH!!

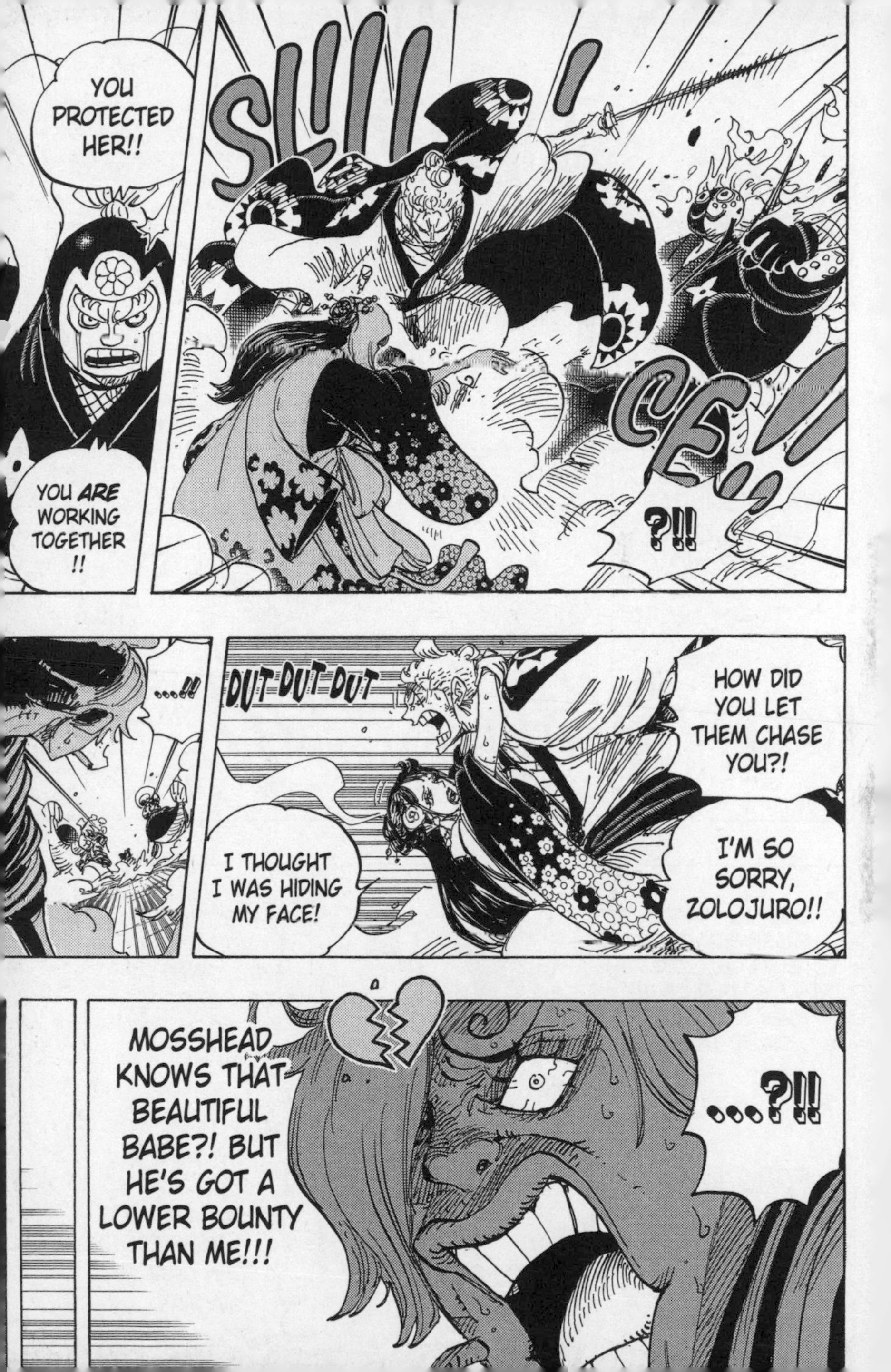
SLI
CE!!
?!!
YOU PROTECTED HER!!
YOU ARE WORKING TOGETHER !!
HOW DID YOU LET THEM CHASE YOU?!
DUT DUT DUT
I'M SO SORRY, ZOLOJURO!!
I THOUGHT I WAS HIDING MY FACE!
...!!
...?!!
MOSSHEAD KNOWS THAT BEAUTIFUL BABE?! BUT HE'S GOT A LOWER BOUNTY THAN ME!!!

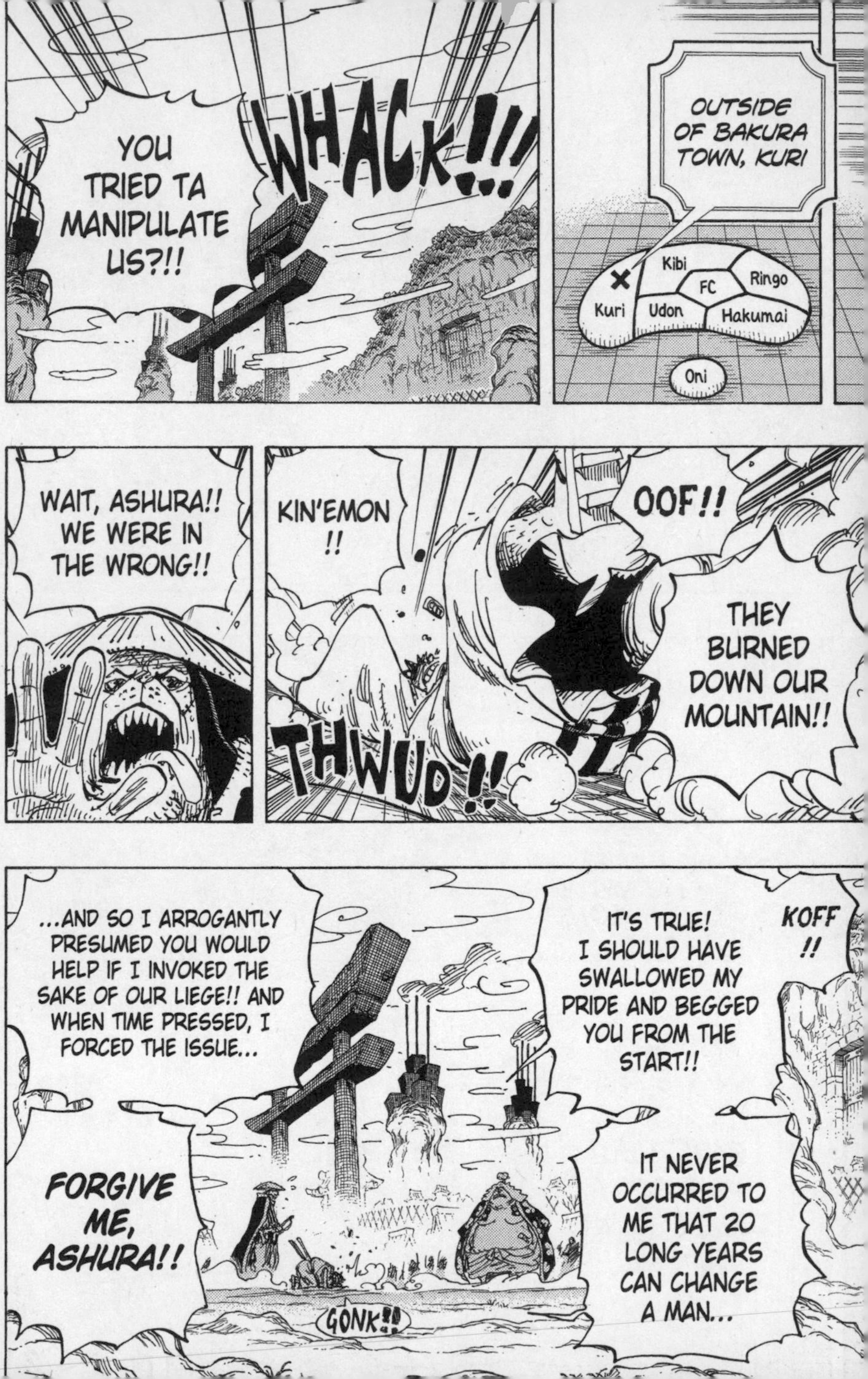
OUTSIDE OF BAKURA TOWN, KURI
Kibi
Ringo
FC
Kuri
Udon
Hakumai
Oni
WHACK!!!
YOU TRIED TA MANIPULATE US?!!
OOF!!
THEY BURNED DOWN OUR MOUNTAIN!!
KIN'EMON!!
THWUD!!
WAIT, ASHURA!! WE WERE IN THE WRONG!!
KOFF!!
IT'S TRUE! I SHOULD HAVE SWALLOWED MY PRIDE AND BEGGED YOU FROM THE START!!
...AND SO I ARROGANTLY PRESUMED YOU WOULD HELP IF I INVOKED THE SAKE OF OUR LIEGE!! AND WHEN TIME PRESSED, I FORCED THE ISSUE...
IT NEVER OCCURRED TO ME THAT 20 LONG YEARS CAN CHANGE A MAN...
FORGIVE ME, ASHURA!!
GONK!!

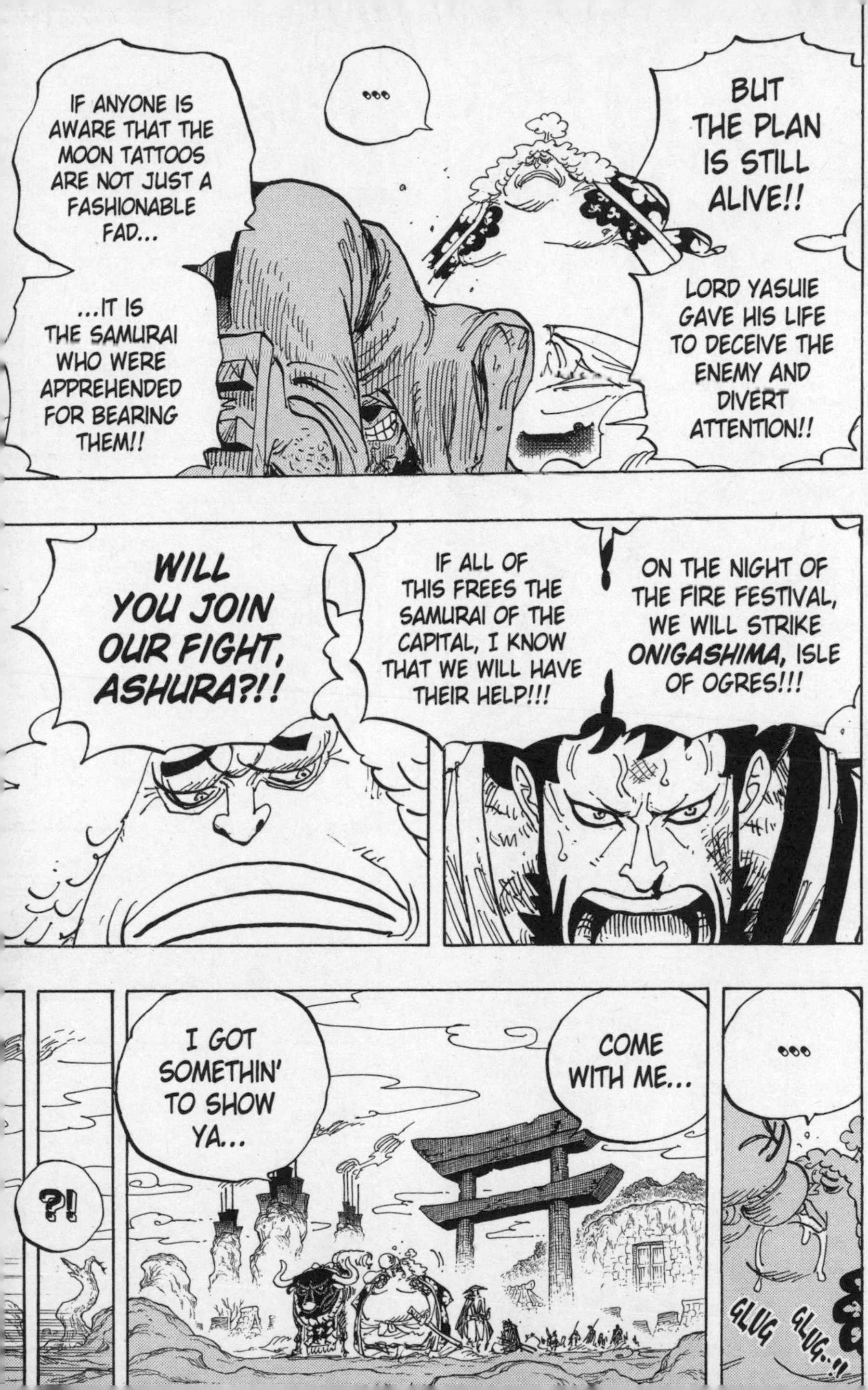
BUT THE PLAN IS STILL ALIVE!!
LORD YASUIE GAVE HIS LIFE TO DECEIVE THE ENEMY AND DIVERT ATTENTION!!
...
IF ANYONE IS AWARE THAT THE MOON TATTOOS ARE NOT JUST A FASHIONABLE FAD...
...IT IS THE SAMURAI WHO WERE APPREHENDED FOR BEARING THEM!!
ON THE NIGHT OF THE FIRE FESTIVAL, WE WILL STRIKE ONIGASHIMA, ISLE OF OGRES!!!
IF ALL OF THIS FREES THE SAMURAI OF THE CAPITAL, I KNOW THAT WE WILL HAVE THEIR HELP!!!
WILL YOU JOIN OUR FIGHT, ASHURA?!!
...
GLUG GLUG..!!
COME WITH ME...
I GOT SOMETHIN' TO SHOW YA...
?!

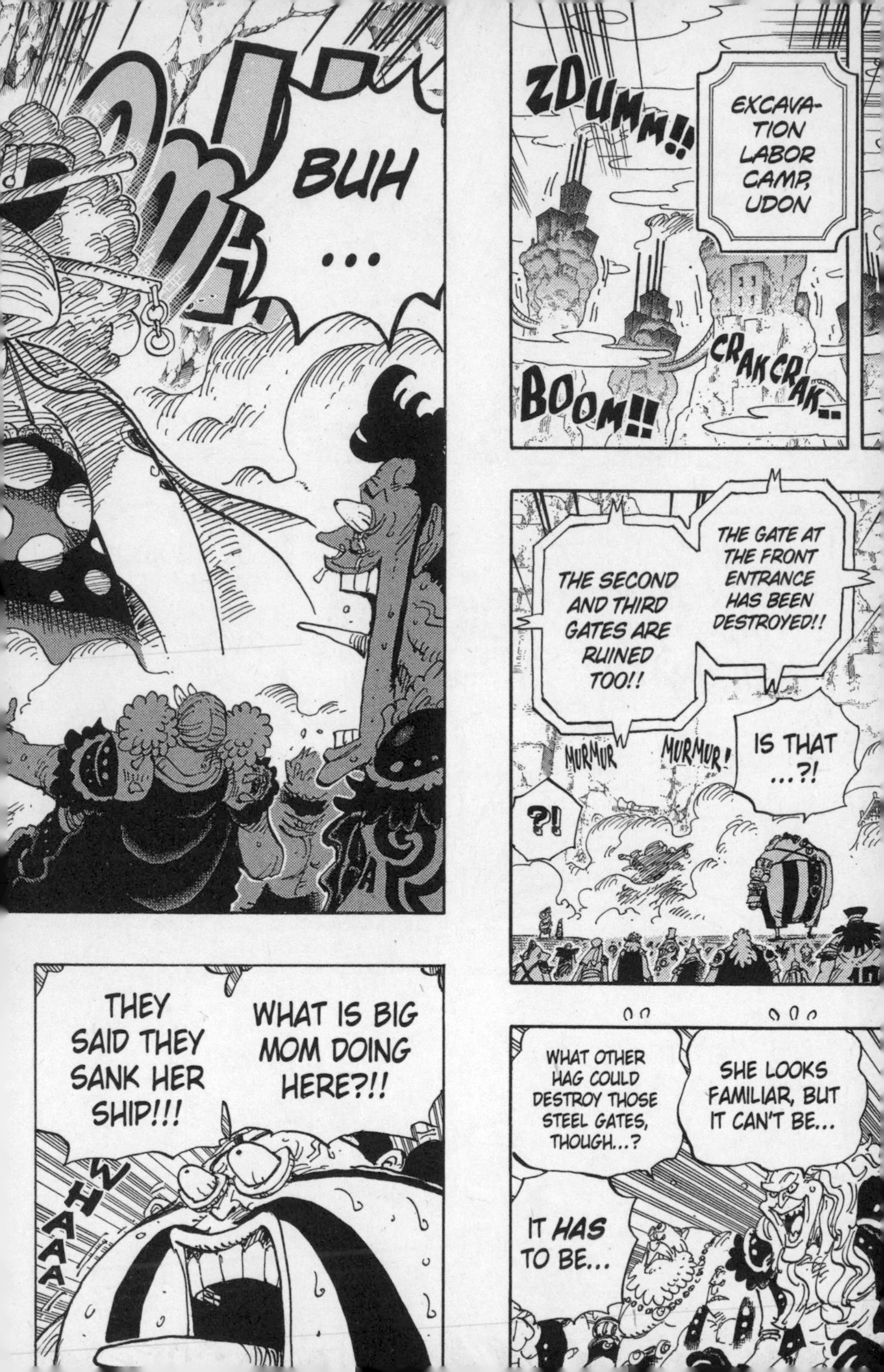
ZDUMM!!
EXCAVATION LABOR CAMP, UDON
CRAKCRAK...
BOOM!!
THE GATE AT THE FRONT ENTRANCE HAS BEEN DESTROYED!!
THE SECOND AND THIRD GATES ARE RUINED TOO!!
IS THAT ...?!
MURMUR!
MURMUR
?!
BUH
...
SHE LOOKS FAMILIAR, BUT IT CAN'T BE...
WHAT OTHER HAG COULD DESTROY THOSE STEEL GATES, THOUGH...?
IT *HAS* TO BE...
WHAT IS BIG MOM DOING HERE?!!
THEY SAID THEY SANK HER SHIP!!!
WHAAAA

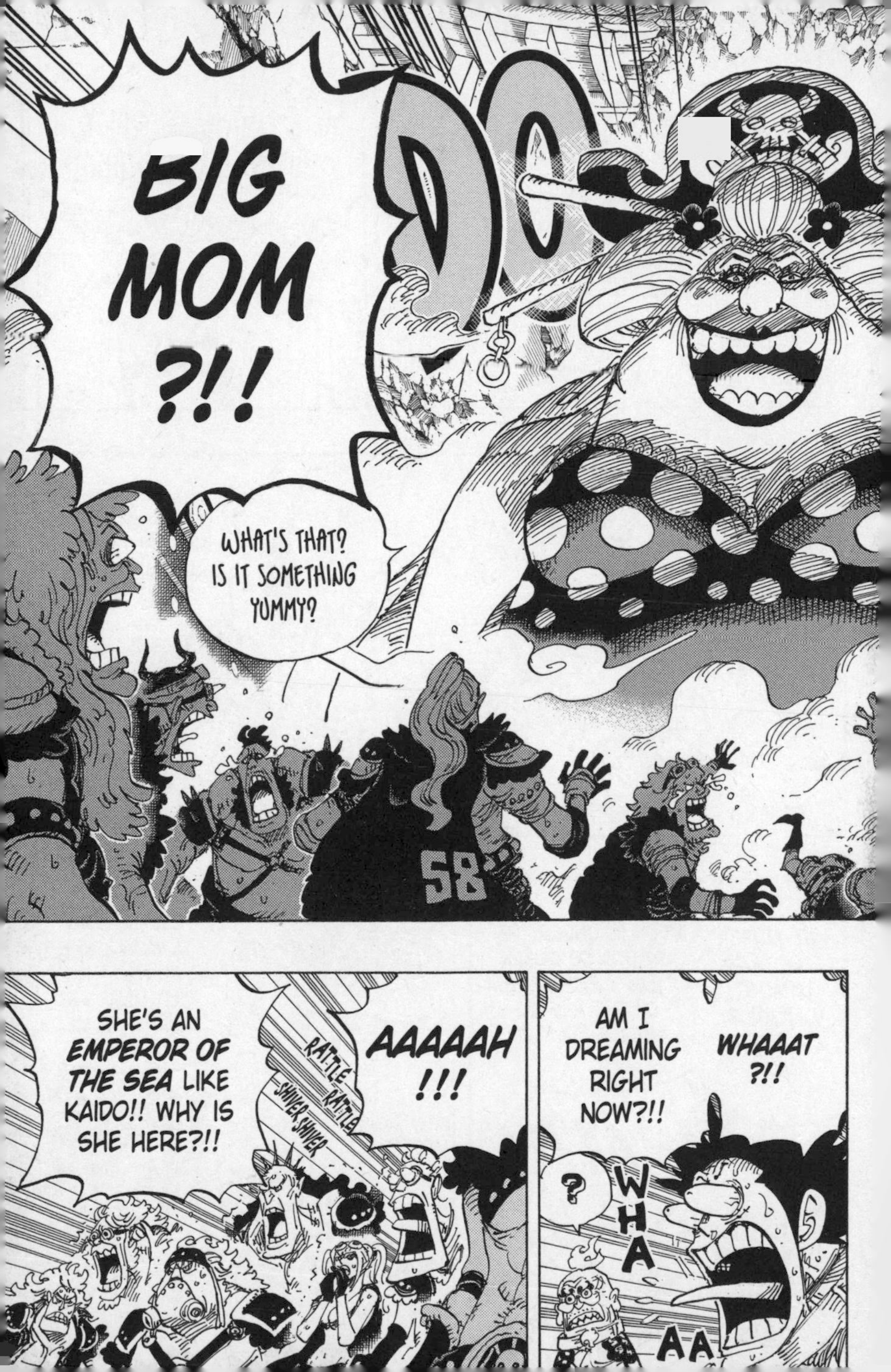

BIG MOM ?!!
WHAT'S THAT? IS IT SOMETHING YUMMY?
WHAAAT ?!!
AM I DREAMING RIGHT NOW?!!
?
WHA
A
AA
AAAAAH !!!
RATTLE RATTLE
SHIVER SHIVER
SHE'S AN EMPEROR OF THE SEA LIKE KAIDO!! WHY IS SHE HERE?!!

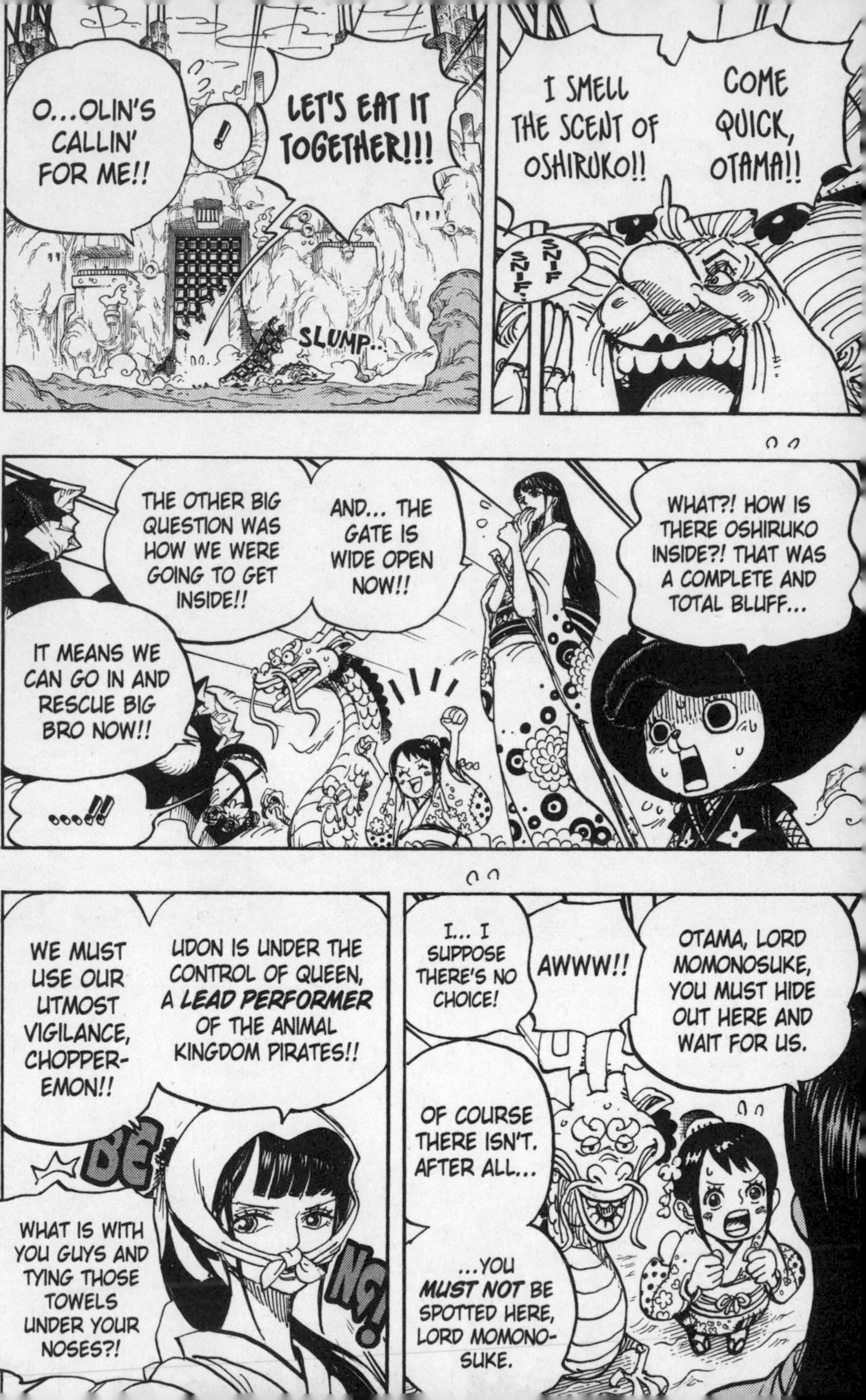
COME QUICK, OTAMA!!
I SMELL THE SCENT OF OSHIRUKO!!
SNIF SNIF
LET'S EAT IT TOGETHER!!!
!
O...OLIN'S CALLIN' FOR ME!!
SLUMP...
WHAT?! HOW IS THERE OSHIRUKO INSIDE?! THAT WAS A COMPLETE AND TOTAL BLUFF...
AND... THE GATE IS WIDE OPEN NOW!!
THE OTHER BIG QUESTION WAS HOW WE WERE GOING TO GET INSIDE!!
IT MEANS WE CAN GO IN AND RESCUE BIG BRO NOW!!
...!!
OTAMA, LORD MOMONOSUKE, YOU MUST HIDE OUT HERE AND WAIT FOR US.
AWWW!!
I... I SUPPOSE THERE'S NO CHOICE!
OF COURSE THERE ISN'T. AFTER ALL...
...YOU MUST NOT BE SPOTTED HERE, LORD MOMONOSUKE.
UDON IS UNDER THE CONTROL OF QUEEN, A LEAD PERFORMER OF THE ANIMAL KINGDOM PIRATES!!
WE MUST USE OUR UTMOST VIGILANCE, CHOPPER-EMON!!
BENG!
WHAT IS WITH YOU GUYS AND TYING THOSE TOWELS UNDER YOUR NOSES?!

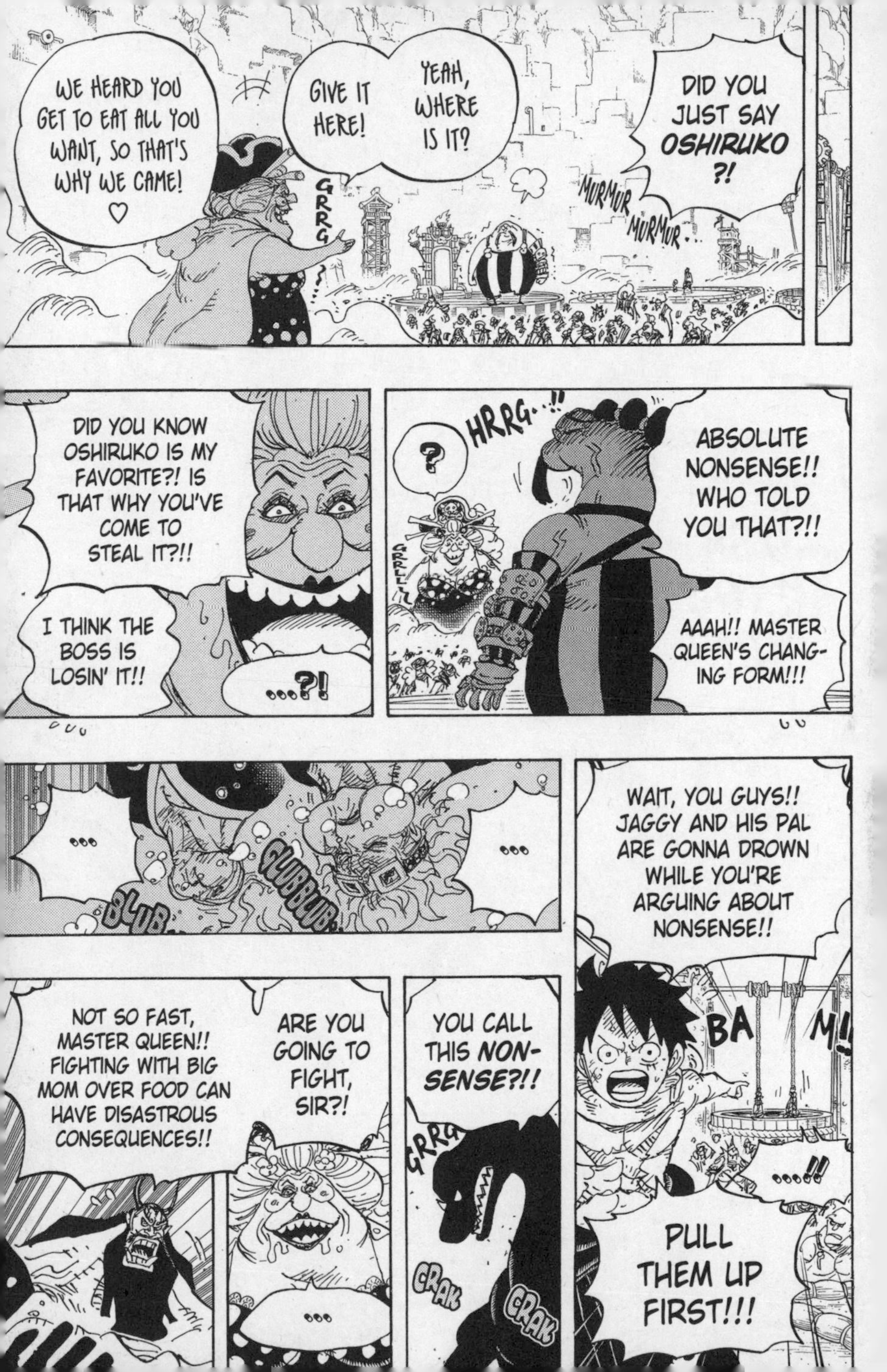
DID YOU JUST SAY OSHIRUKO?!
MURMUR MURMUR...
YEAH, WHERE IS IT?
GIVE IT HERE!
GRRG
WE HEARD YOU GET TO EAT ALL YOU WANT, SO THAT'S WHY WE CAME! ♡
HRRG..!!
?
ABSOLUTE NONSENSE!! WHO TOLD YOU THAT?!!
AAAH!! MASTER QUEEN'S CHANGING FORM!!!
DID YOU KNOW OSHIRUKO IS MY FAVORITE?! IS THAT WHY YOU'VE COME TO STEAL IT?!!
I THINK THE BOSS IS LOSIN' IT!!
...?!
WAIT, YOU GUYS!! JAGGY AND HIS PAL ARE GONNA DROWN WHILE YOU'RE ARGUING ABOUT NONSENSE!!
BAM!!
...!!
PULL THEM UP FIRST!!!
...
GLUBGLUB
BLUB
...
YOU CALL THIS NONSENSE?!!
GRRRG
CRAK
CRAK
ARE YOU GOING TO FIGHT, SIR?!
...
NOT SO FAST, MASTER QUEEN!! FIGHTING WITH BIG MOM OVER FOOD CAN HAVE DISASTROUS CONSEQUENCES!!

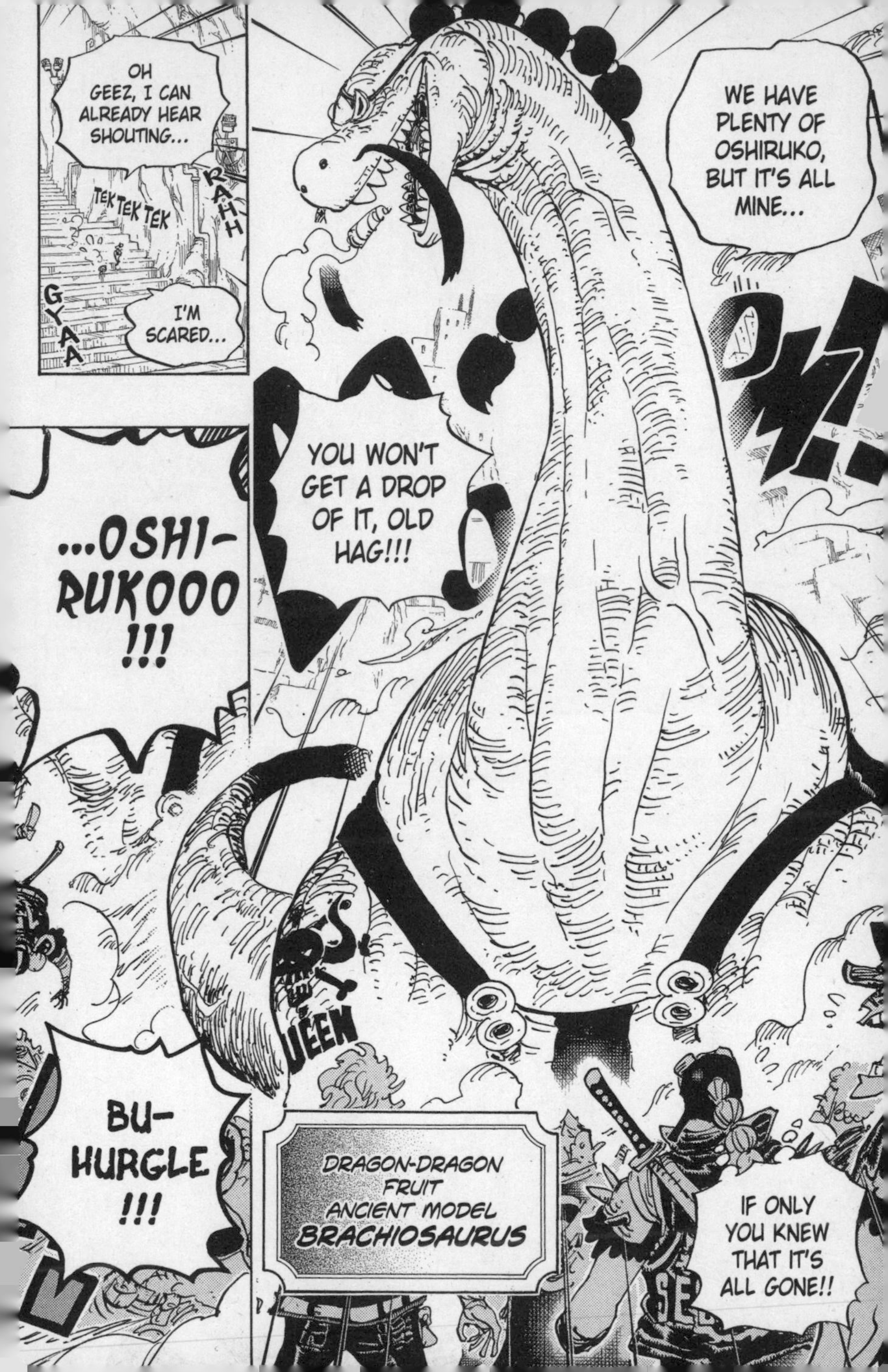
WE HAVE PLENTY OF OSHIRUKO, BUT IT'S ALL MINE...
YOU WON'T GET A DROP OF IT, OLD HAG!!!
DRAGON-DRAGON FRUIT ANCIENT MODEL BRACHIOSAURUS
IF ONLY YOU KNEW THAT IT'S ALL GONE!!
OH GEEZ, I CAN ALREADY HEAR SHOUTING...
TEK TEK TEK
RAHH
GYAA
I'M SCARED...
...OSHI-RUKOOO!!!
BU-HURGLE!!!

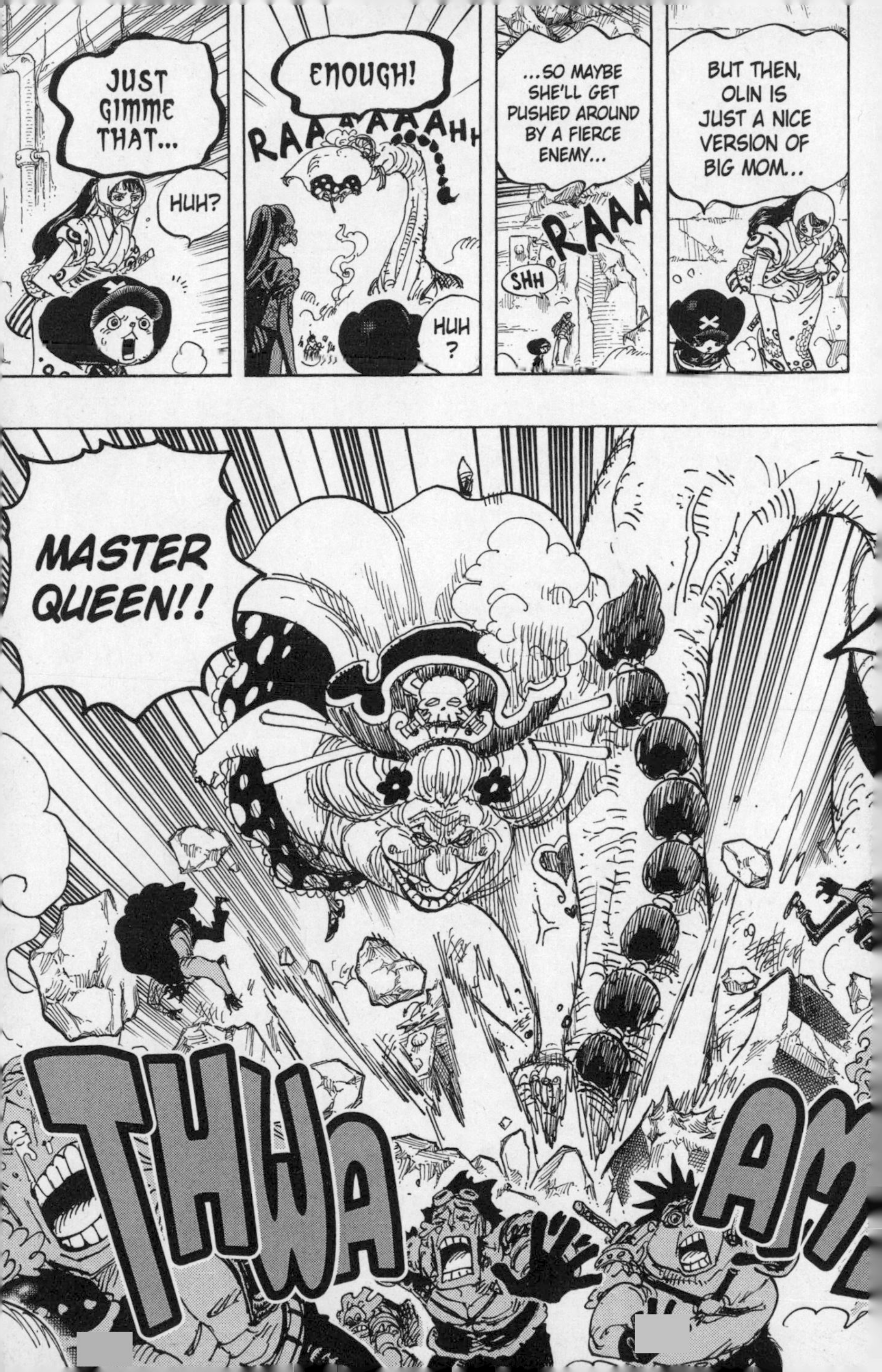
BUT THEN, OLIN IS JUST A NICE VERSION OF BIG MOM...
...SO MAYBE SHE'LL GET PUSHED AROUND BY A FIERCE ENEMY...
RAAA
SHH
ENOUGH!
RAAAAAAAHH
HUH?
JUST GIMME THAT...
HUH?
MASTER QUEEN!!
THWA
AM

SO THIS IS THE SBS QUESTION SEGMENT, HUH?

DON'T TEAR THE PAGE!!!

(Bouvardia, Tokyo)

Q: We all know that the naming pattern of the Navy admirals is a color plus an animal in Japanese. I'm imagining that there must be some kind of deliberating body within the Navy that determines the admiral names. Could the man in charge of this body actually be the legendary Vice Admiral Namingheim? I mean, it has to be, right...?!

--Iroha

A: Y...yes!! How did you know about him? There are other Navy members who have nicknames like that, not just the admirals, but they're all named by him!! ➡

I'm gonna name the hell outta ya!

Vice Admiral Nay Mingheim

Q: Chapter 943... I'm stunned!!! (Beng!!) Is that Izo?! The 16th division commander of the Whitebeard Pirates was formerly one of the Akazaya Nine? Whoa... Was Kozuki Oden the former 16th division commander?!

--420 Land

A: Whoa... That's a very small detail you've picked up on. That's the flashback scene where a young Kin'emon and cohorts get captured. There certainly are nine of them present, but what should be Okiku looks a bit...different? Izo, by the way, is one of the Whitebeard division captains who showed up in the Paramount War. He wears traditional Japanese clothing and does resemble that character. Also, there's that note in volume 82, chapter 820, that a number of Wano people were on Whitebeard's ship too. All of this will be made clearer in time, so just sit back and read. You'll figure it out!

OKAY, SO... ODEN, DOG AND CAT WERE ON WHITEBEARD'S SHIP, THEN...

!!!

?!

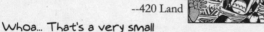

Chapter 946:
QUEEN VS. OLIN

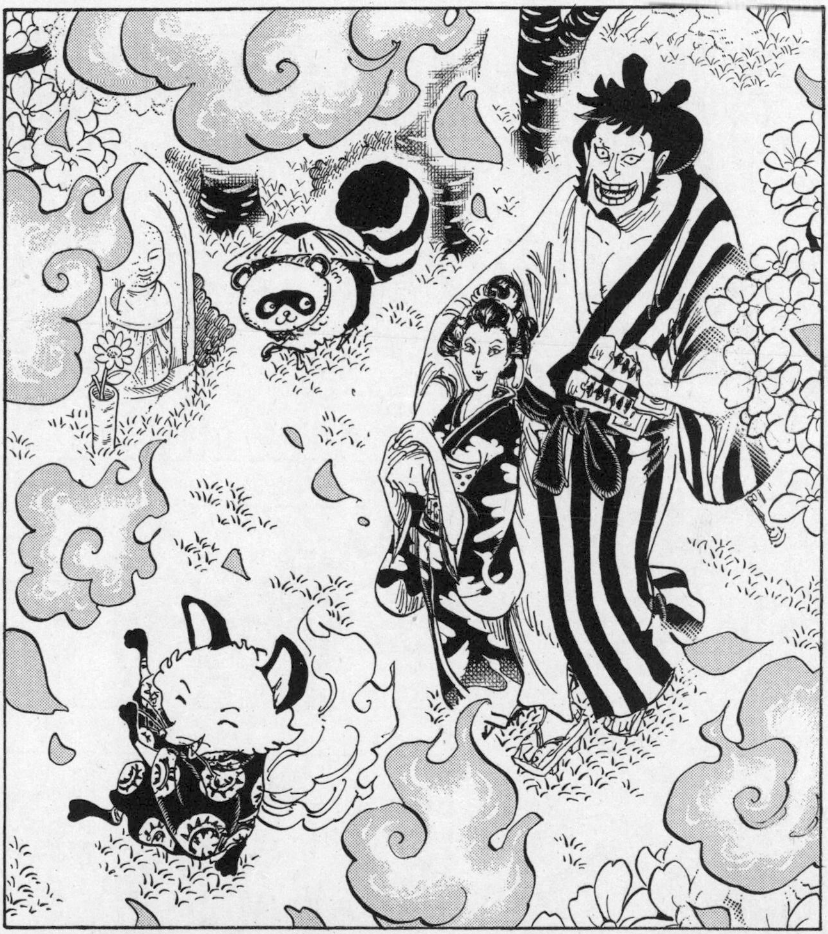

REQUEST: "KIN'EMON AND OTSURU ON A NIGHTTIME DATE BY FOXFIRE-LIGHT" BY HONEYLICKER

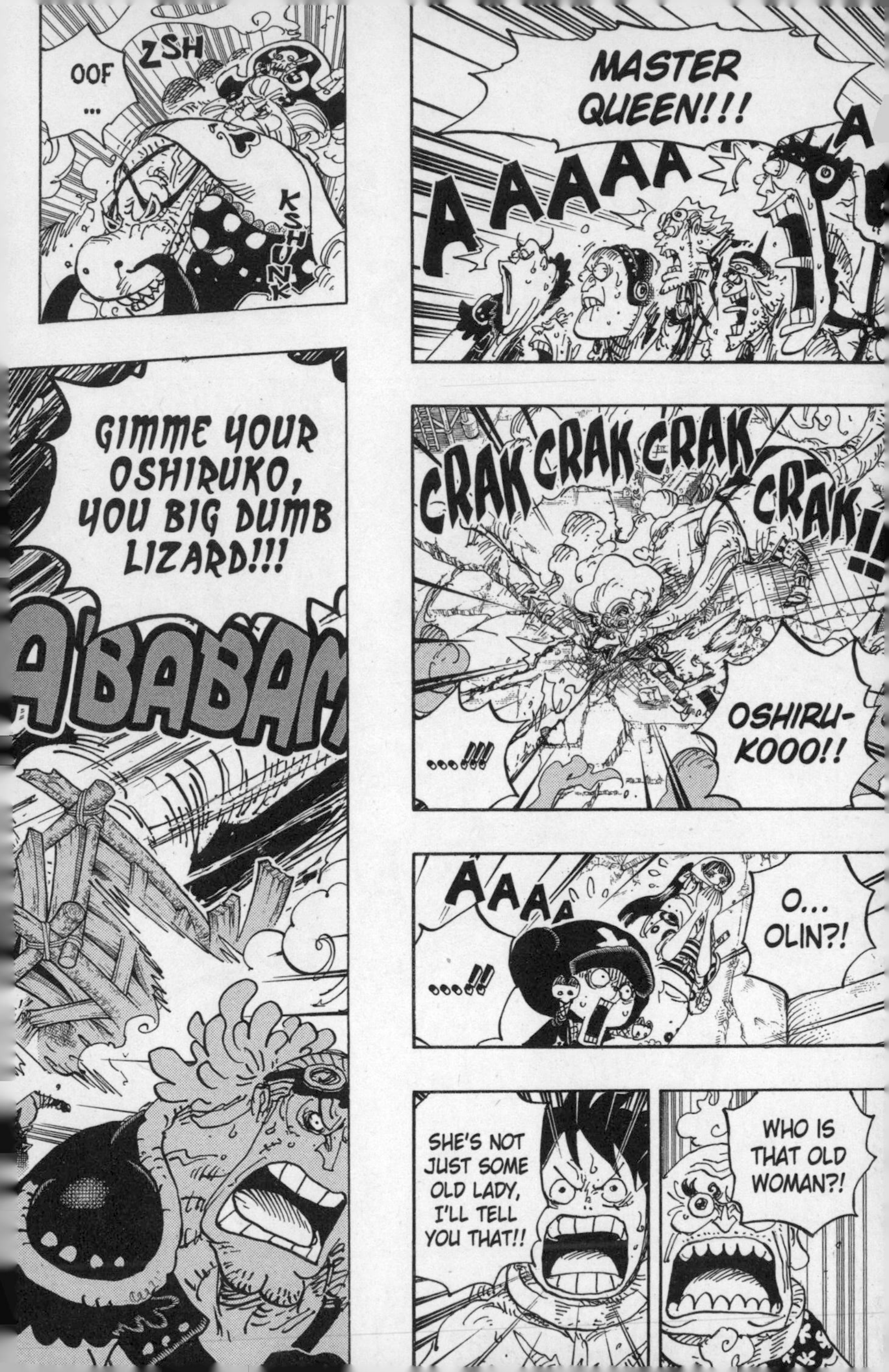
MASTER QUEEN!!!
AAAAAA A
ZSH
OOF ...
KSHUNK
CRAK CRAK CRAK CRAK!!
OSHIRU-KOOO!!
...!!!
AAAA
O... OLIN?!
...!!
WHO IS THAT OLD WOMAN?!
SHE'S NOT JUST SOME OLD LADY, I'LL TELL YOU THAT!!
GIMME YOUR OSHIRUKO, YOU BIG DUMB LIZARD!!!
BABAM

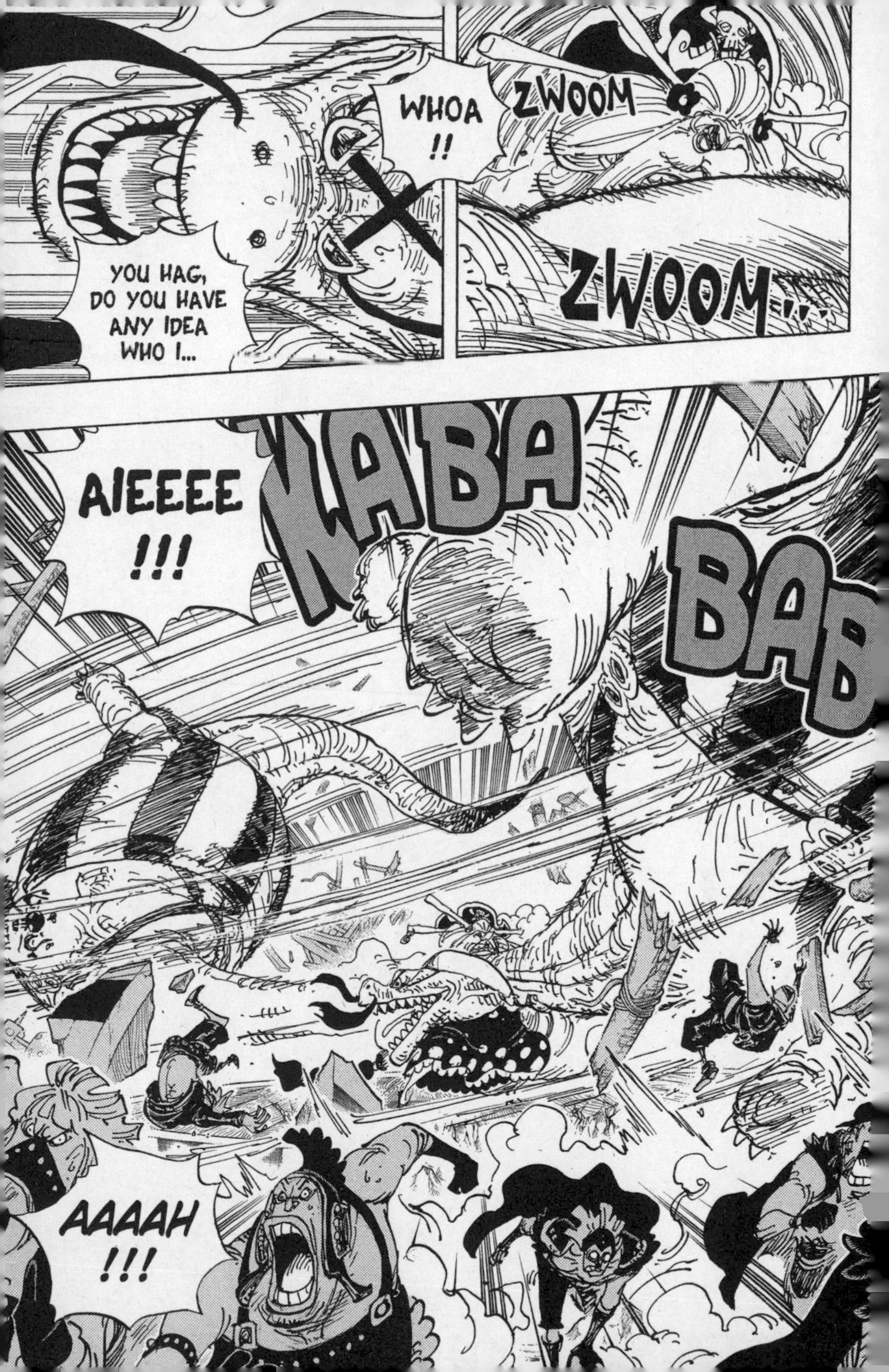
ZWOOM
ZWOOM...
WHOA !!
YOU HAG, DO YOU HAVE ANY IDEA WHO I...
KABA
BAB
AIEEEE !!!
AAAAH !!!

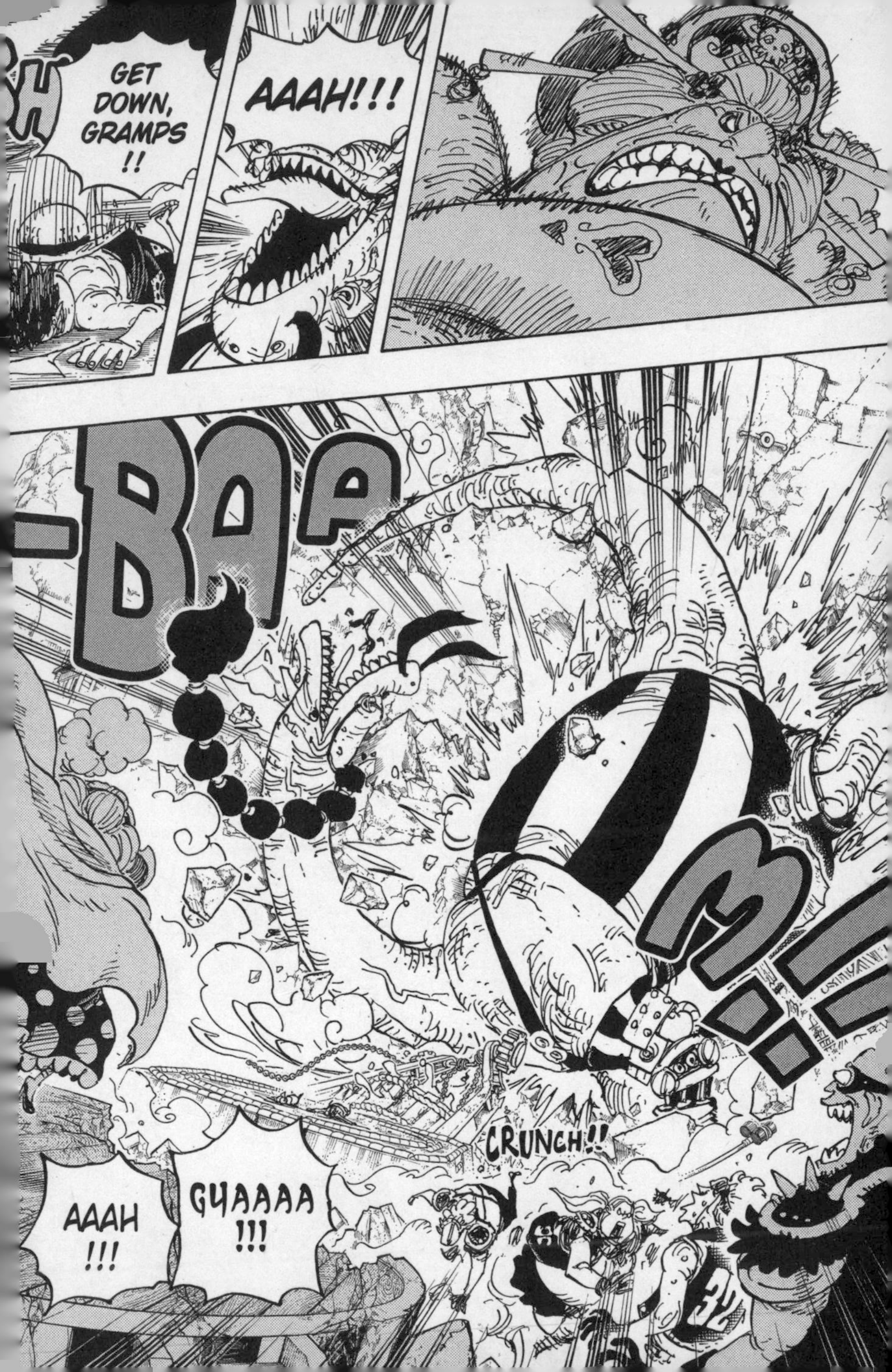
AAAH!!!
GET DOWN, GRAMPS!!
CRUNCH!!
GUAAAA!!!
AAAH!!!

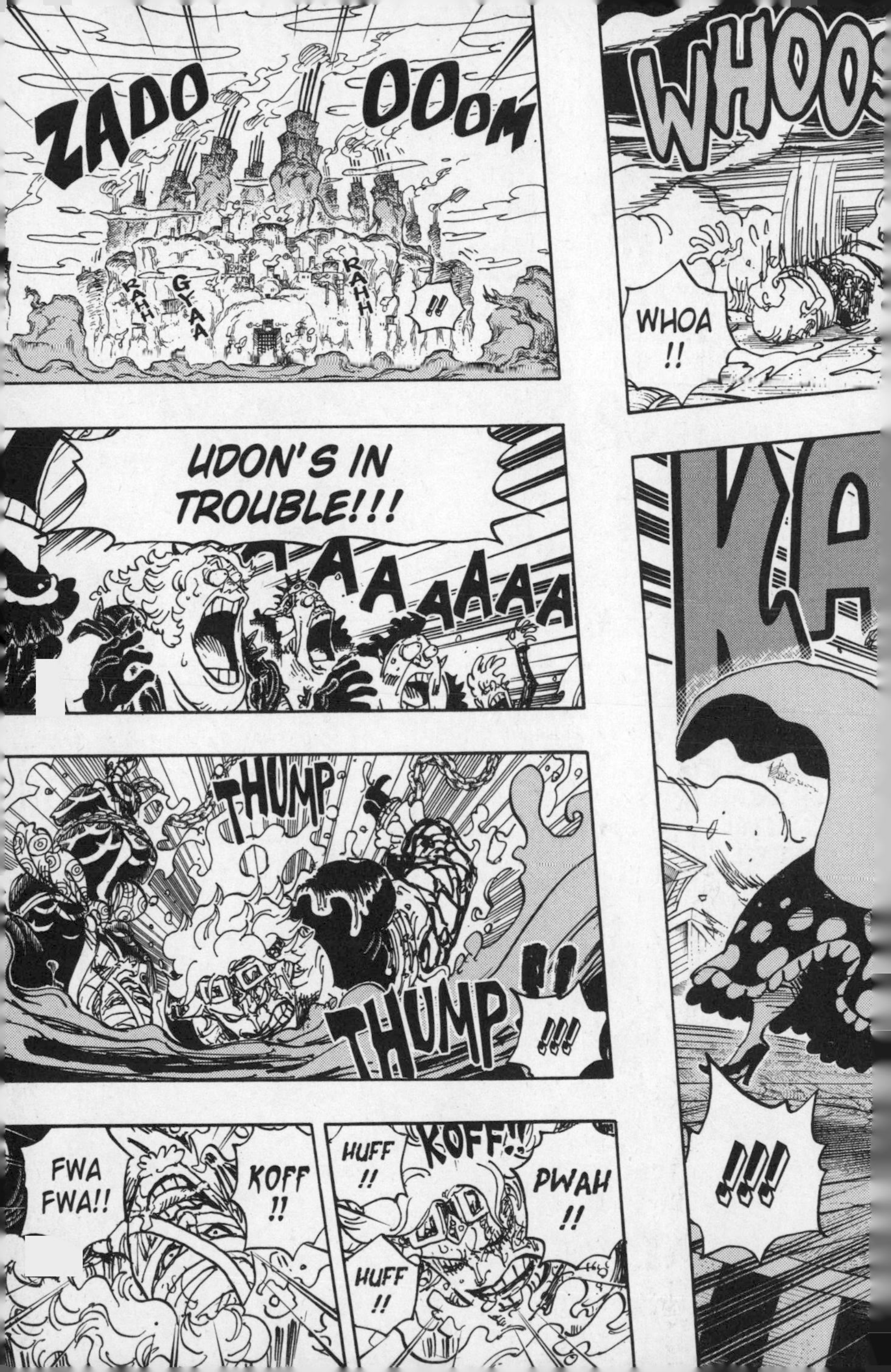
WHOOS
WHOA !!
KA
!!!
ZADO OOOM
RAHH
GYAA
RAHH
!!
UDON'S IN TROUBLE!!!
AAAAAA
THUMP
THUMP !!
!!!
KOFF!!
PWAH !!
HUFF !!
HUFF !!
KOFF !!
FWA FWA!!

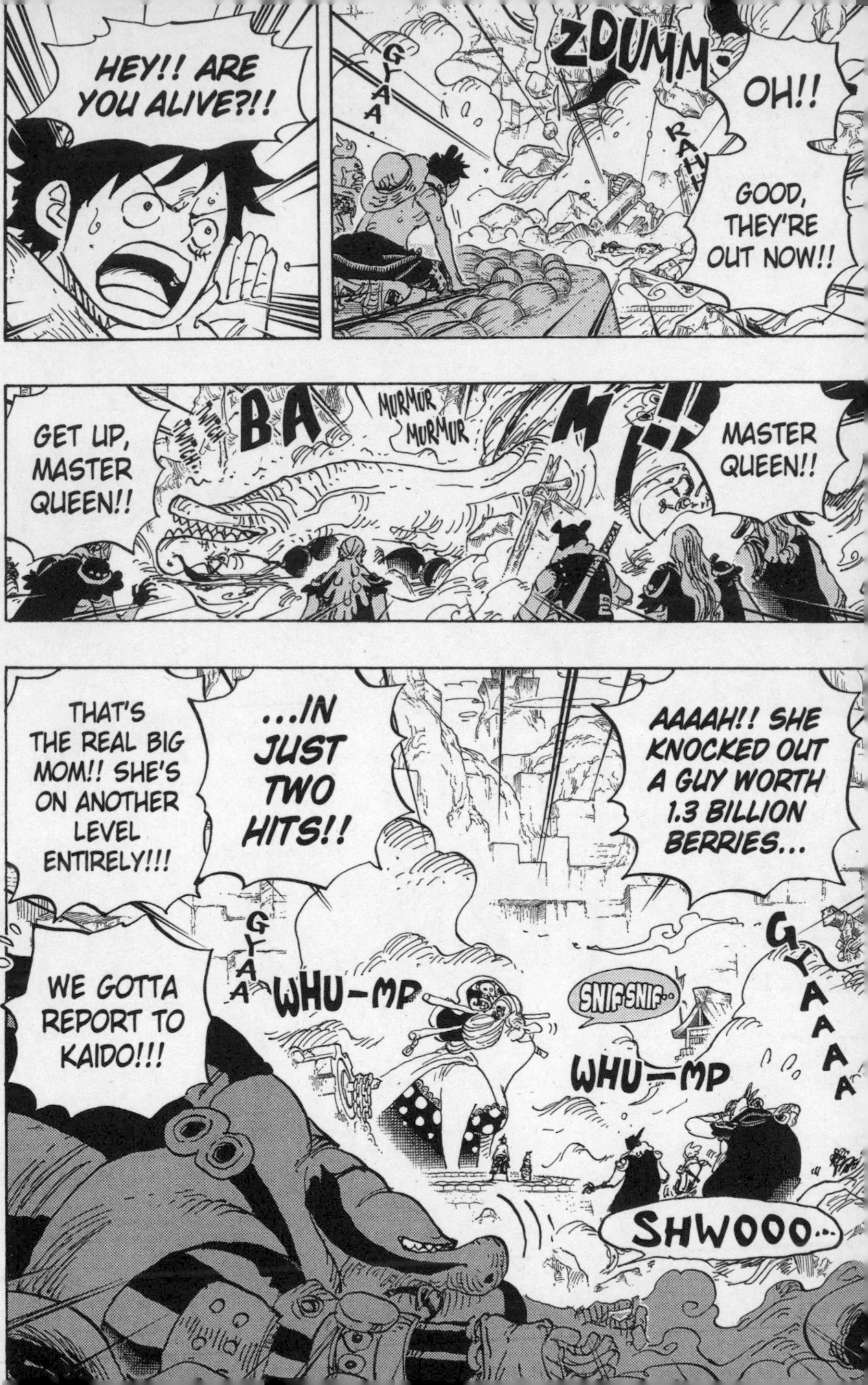
ZDUMM
OH!!
GOOD, THEY'RE OUT NOW!!
RAH!
GYAA
HEY!! ARE YOU ALIVE?!!
MASTER QUEEN!!
BAM!!
MURMUR MURMUR
TWITCH TWITCH
GET UP, MASTER QUEEN!!
AAAAH!! SHE KNOCKED OUT A GUY WORTH 1.3 BILLION BERRIES...
...IN JUST TWO HITS!!
THAT'S THE REAL BIG MOM!! SHE'S ON ANOTHER LEVEL ENTIRELY!!!
GYAAAAA
SNIF SNIF
WHU-MP
WHU-MP
GYAA
WE GOTTA REPORT TO KAIDO!!!
SHWOOO...

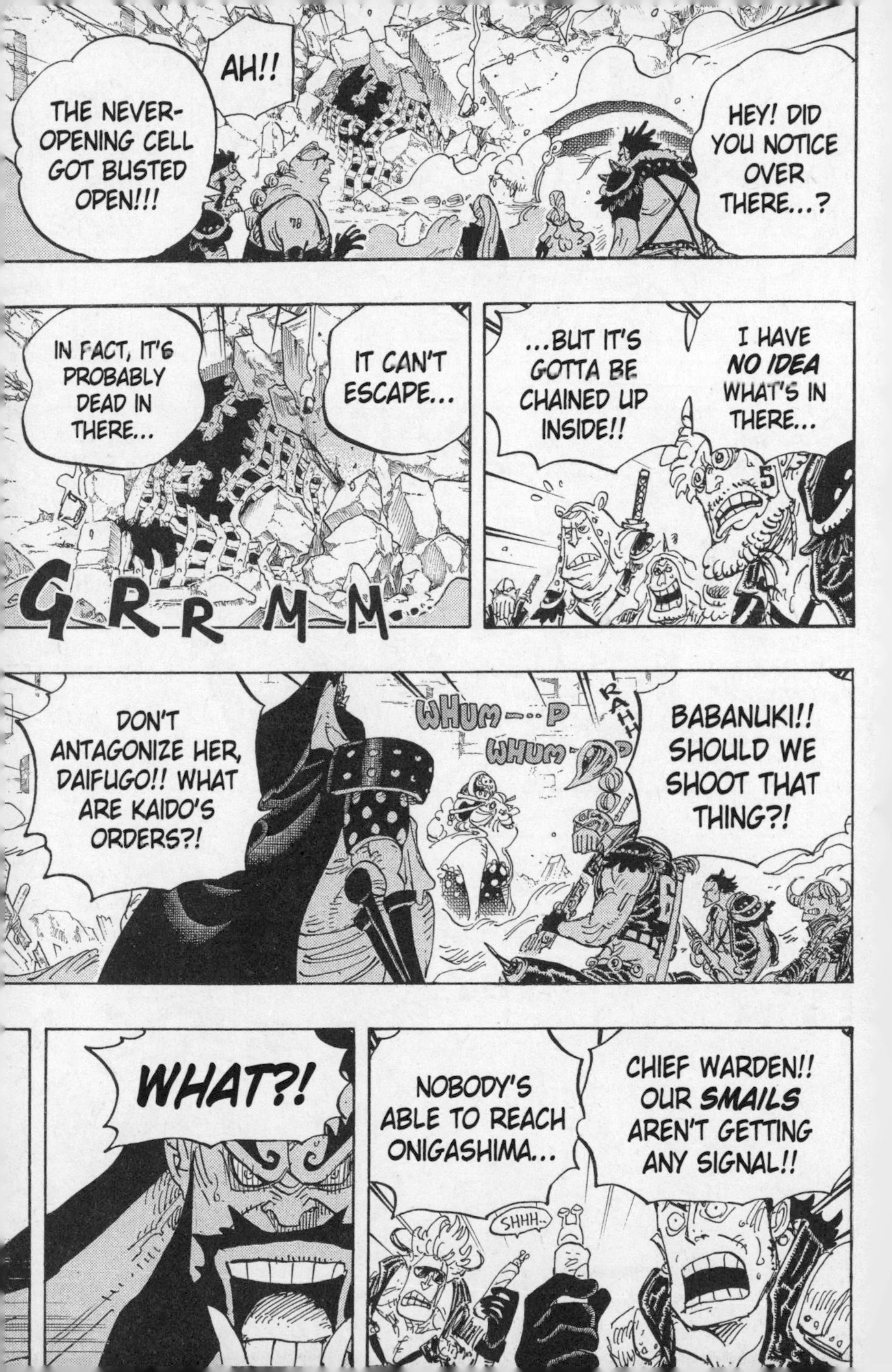
HEY! DID YOU NOTICE OVER THERE...?
AH!!
THE NEVER-OPENING CELL GOT BUSTED OPEN!!!
I HAVE *NO IDEA* WHAT'S IN THERE...
...BUT IT'S GOTTA BE CHAINED UP INSIDE!!
IT CAN'T ESCAPE...
IN FACT, IT'S PROBABLY DEAD IN THERE...
GRRMM
BABANUKI!! SHOULD WE SHOOT THAT THING?!
RAHH
WHUM---P
WHUMP
DON'T ANTAGONIZE HER, DAIFUGO!! WHAT ARE KAIDO'S ORDERS?!
CHIEF WARDEN!! OUR *SMAILS* AREN'T GETTING ANY SIGNAL!!
NOBODY'S ABLE TO REACH ONIGASHIMA...
SHHH..
WHAT?!

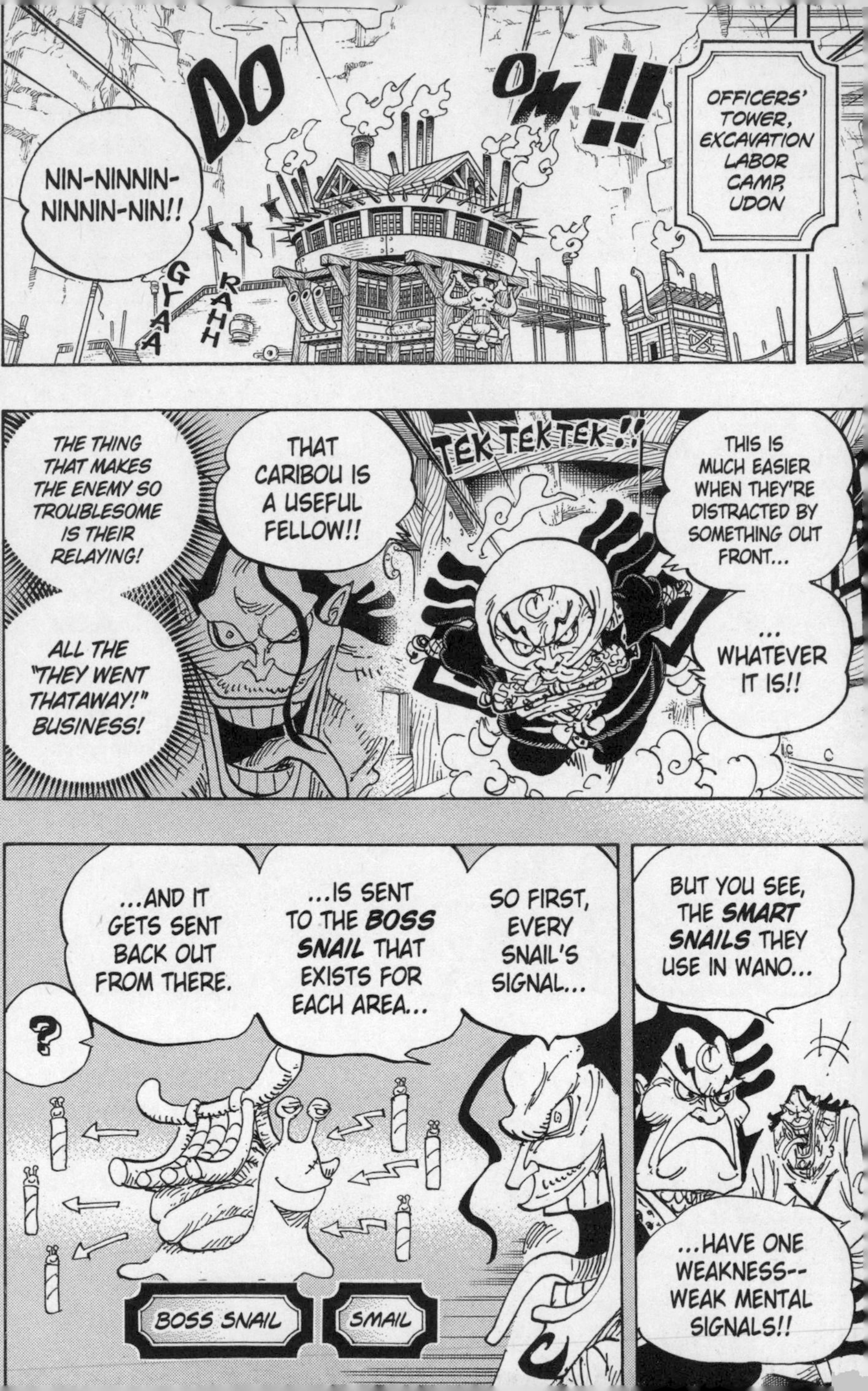

OFFICERS' TOWER, EXCAVATION LABOR CAMP, UDON
DO OM!!
NIN-NINNIN-NINNIN-NIN!!
RAHH
GYAAA
THIS IS MUCH EASIER WHEN THEY'RE DISTRACTED BY SOMETHING OUT FRONT...
... WHATEVER IT IS!!
TEK TEKTEK!!
THAT CARIBOU IS A USEFUL FELLOW!!
THE THING THAT MAKES THE ENEMY SO TROUBLESOME IS THEIR RELAYING!
ALL THE "THEY WENT THATAWAY!" BUSINESS!
BUT YOU SEE, THE **SMART SNAILS** THEY USE IN WANO...
...HAVE ONE WEAKNESS-- WEAK MENTAL SIGNALS!!
SO FIRST, EVERY SNAIL'S SIGNAL...
...IS SENT TO THE **BOSS SNAIL** THAT EXISTS FOR EACH AREA...
...AND IT GETS SENT BACK OUT FROM THERE.
?
SMAIL
BOSS SNAIL

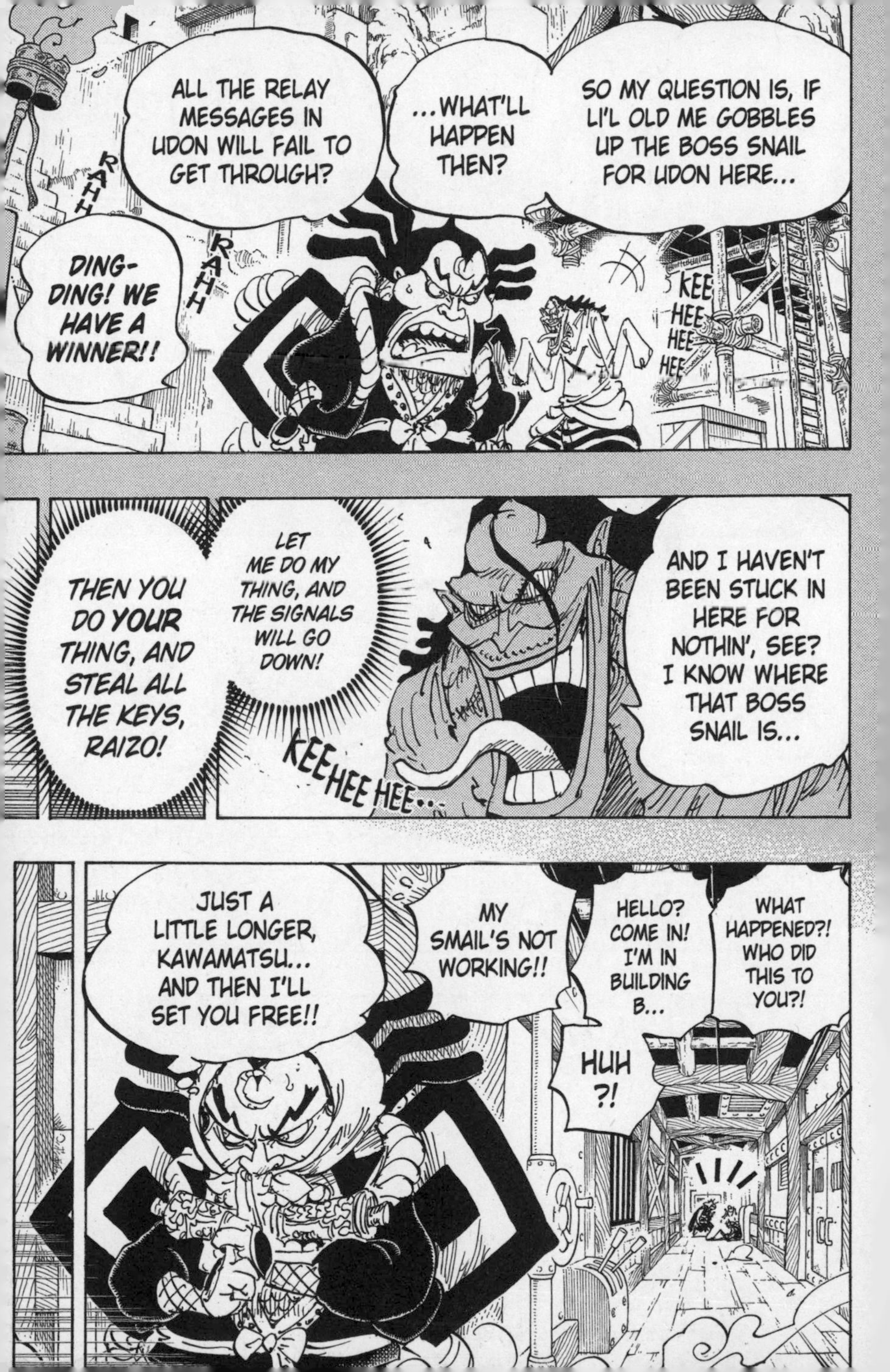
SO MY QUESTION IS, IF LI'L OLD ME GOBBLES UP THE BOSS SNAIL FOR UDON HERE...
...WHAT'LL HAPPEN THEN?
ALL THE RELAY MESSAGES IN UDON WILL FAIL TO GET THROUGH?
KEE HEE HEE HEE
RAHH RAHH
DING-DING! WE HAVE A WINNER!!
AND I HAVEN'T BEEN STUCK IN HERE FOR NOTHIN', SEE? I KNOW WHERE THAT BOSS SNAIL IS...
LET ME DO MY THING, AND THE SIGNALS WILL GO DOWN!
KEEHEE HEE...
THEN YOU DO YOUR THING, AND STEAL ALL THE KEYS, RAIZO!
WHAT HAPPENED?! WHO DID THIS TO YOU?!
HELLO? COME IN! I'M IN BUILDING B...
MY SMAIL'S NOT WORKING!!
HUH?!
JUST A LITTLE LONGER, KAWAMATSU... AND THEN I'LL SET YOU FREE!!

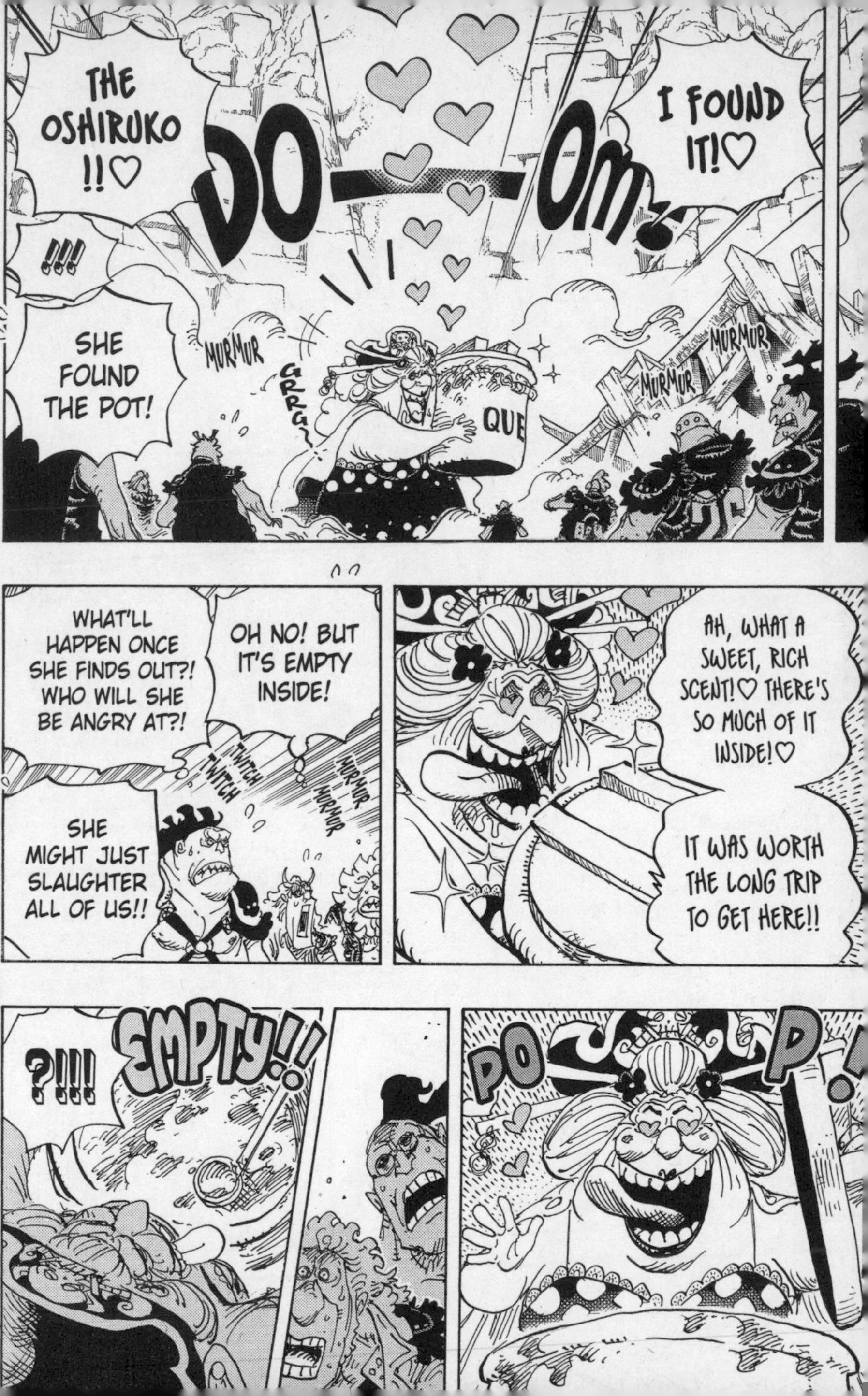
I FOUND IT!♡
DO--OM
THE OSHIRUKO!!♡
!!!
MURMUR
MURMUR
MURMUR
QUE
GRRG
SHE FOUND THE POT!
AH, WHAT A SWEET, RICH SCENT!♡ THERE'S SO MUCH OF IT INSIDE!♡
IT WAS WORTH THE LONG TRIP TO GET HERE!!
OH NO! BUT IT'S EMPTY INSIDE!
WHAT'LL HAPPEN ONCE SHE FINDS OUT?! WHO WILL SHE BE ANGRY AT?!
MURMUR MURMUR
TWITCH TWITCH
SHE MIGHT JUST SLAUGHTER ALL OF US!!
PO P!
EMPTY!!
?!!!

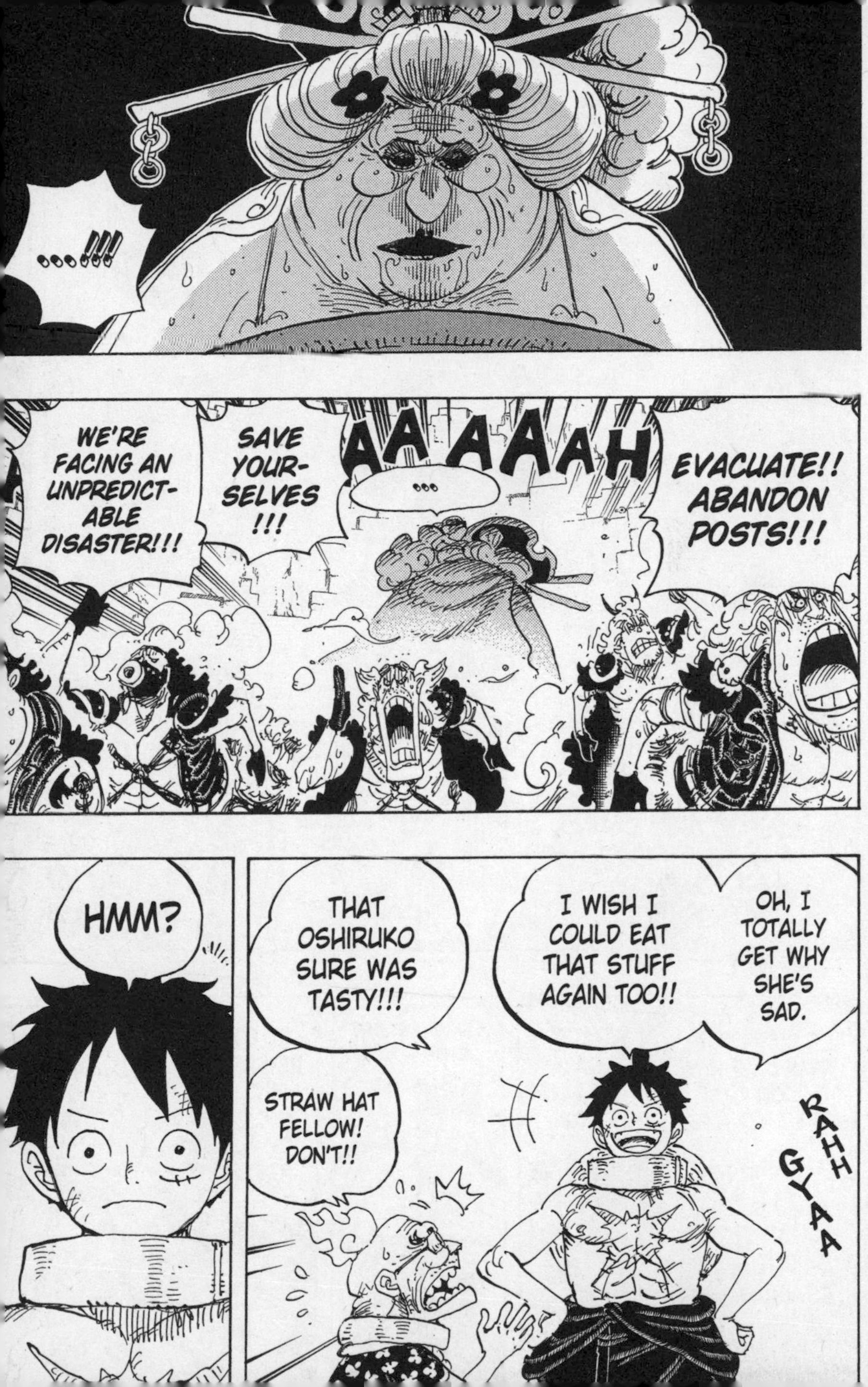
...!!!
EVACUATE!! ABANDON POSTS!!!
AAAAAH
...
SAVE YOUR-SELVES!!!
WE'RE FACING AN UNPREDICT-ABLE DISASTER!!!
OH, I TOTALLY GET WHY SHE'S SAD.
I WISH I COULD EAT THAT STUFF AGAIN TOO!!
THAT OSHIRUKO SURE WAS TASTY!!!
RAHH GYAA
STRAW HAT FELLOW! DON'T!!
HMM?

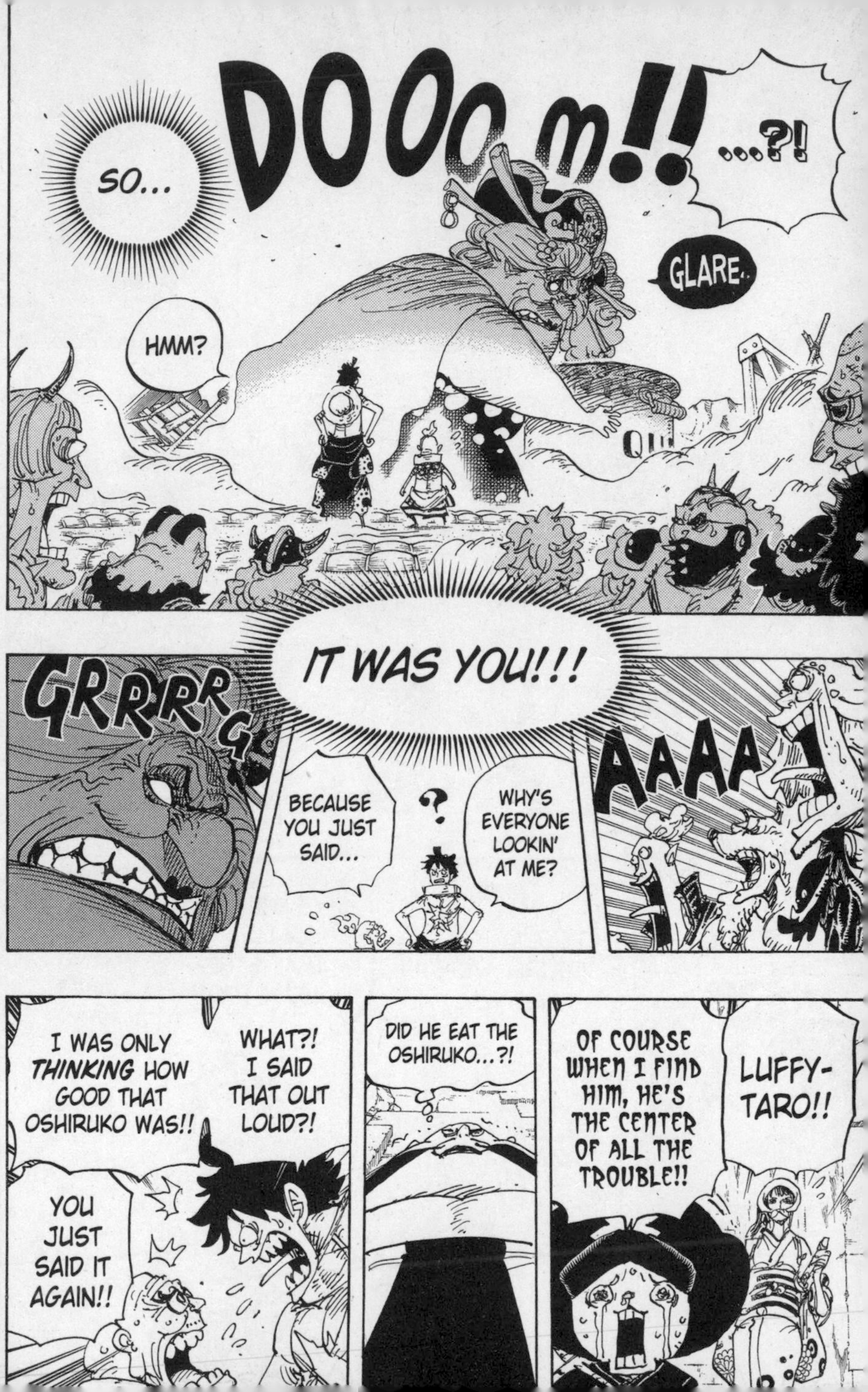
...?!
DOOOm!!
SO...
GLARE
HMM?
IT WAS YOU!!!
AAAA
WHY'S EVERYONE LOOKIN' AT ME?
?
BECAUSE YOU JUST SAID...
GRRRRG
LUFFY-TARO!!
OF COURSE WHEN I FIND HIM, HE'S THE CENTER OF ALL THE TROUBLE!!
DID HE EAT THE OSHIRUKO...?!
WHAT?! I SAID THAT OUT LOUD?!
I WAS ONLY *THINKING* HOW GOOD THAT OSHIRUKO WAS!!
YOU JUST SAID IT AGAIN!!

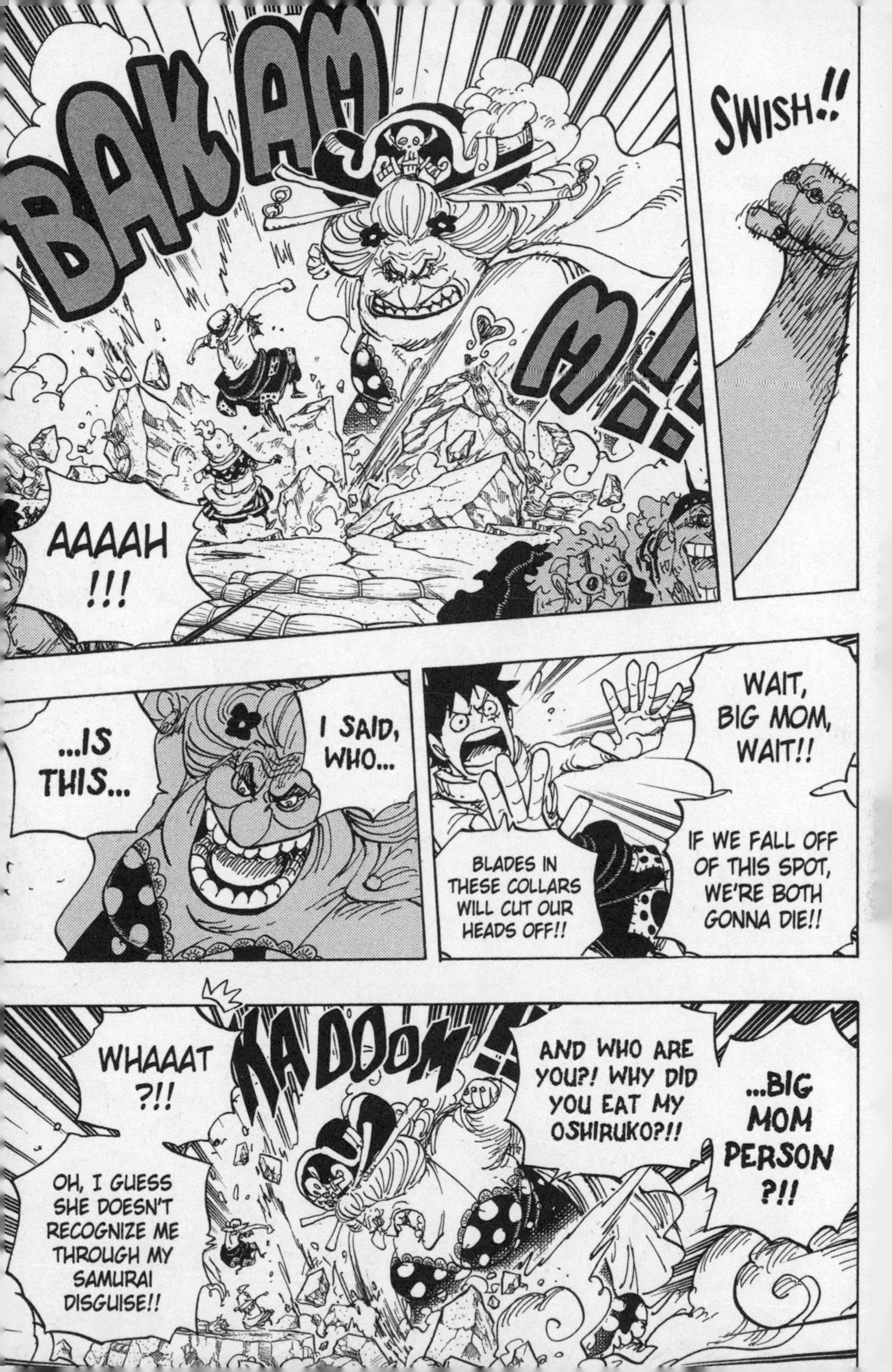
SWISH!!
BAKAMM!!
AAAAH !!!
WAIT, BIG MOM, WAIT!!
IF WE FALL OFF OF THIS SPOT, WE'RE BOTH GONNA DIE!!
BLADES IN THESE COLLARS WILL CUT OUR HEADS OFF!!
I SAID, WHO...
...IS THIS...
...BIG MOM PERSON ?!!
AND WHO ARE YOU?! WHY DID YOU EAT MY OSHIRUKO?!!
KADOOM!!
WHAAAT ?!!
OH, I GUESS SHE DOESN'T RECOGNIZE ME THROUGH MY SAMURAI DISGUISE!!

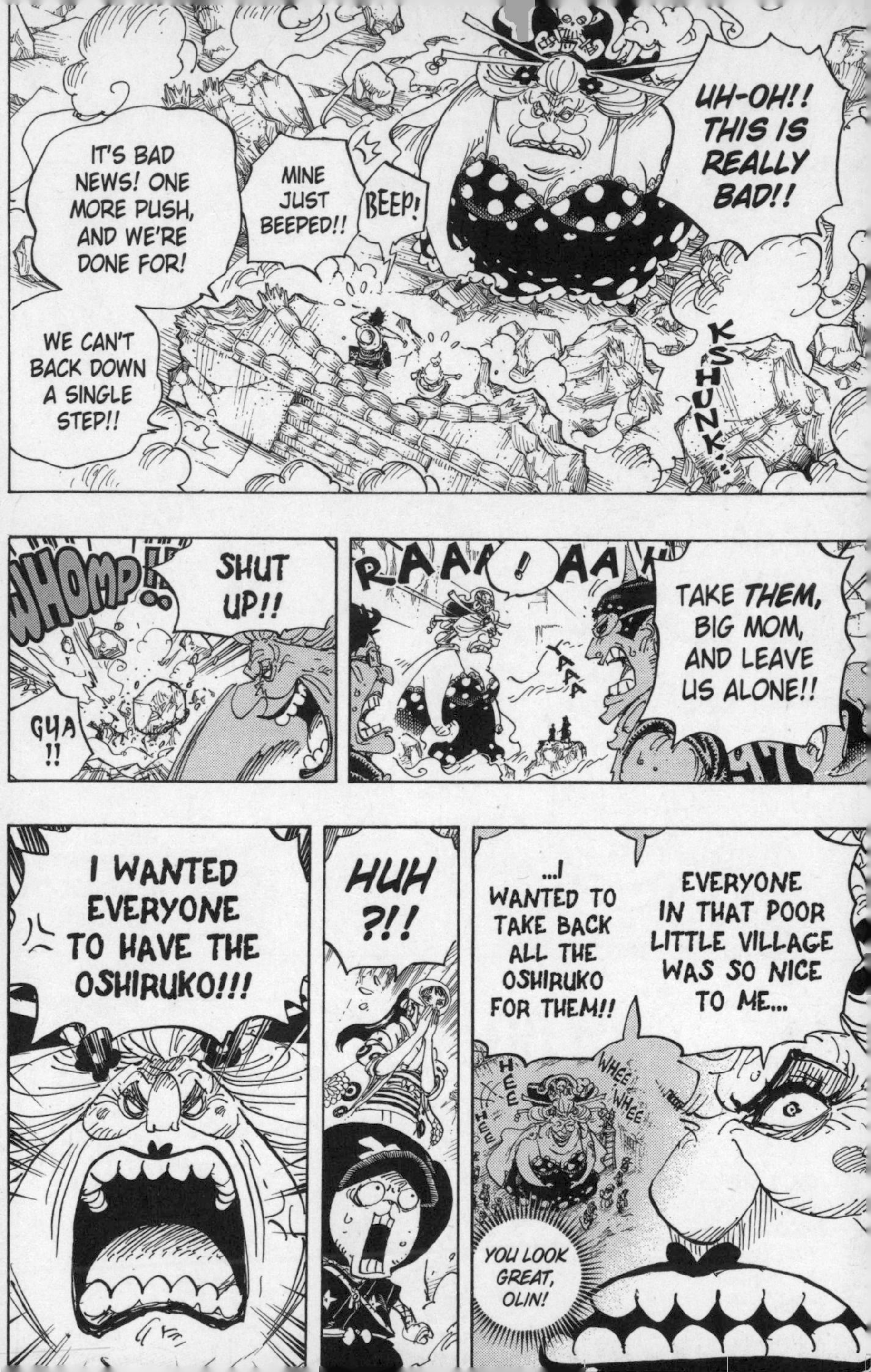
UH-OH!! THIS IS REALLY BAD!!
KSHUNK...
BEEP!
MINE JUST BEEPED!!
IT'S BAD NEWS! ONE MORE PUSH, AND WE'RE DONE FOR!
WE CAN'T BACK DOWN A SINGLE STEP!!
TAKE THEM, BIG MOM, AND LEAVE US ALONE!!
RAAA! AA
YAAA
SHUT UP!!
WHOMP!!
GYA!!
EVERYONE IN THAT POOR LITTLE VILLAGE WAS SO NICE TO ME...
...I WANTED TO TAKE BACK ALL THE OSHIRUKO FOR THEM!!
WHEE WHEE
HEE HEE
YOU LOOK GREAT, OLIN!
HUH?!!
I WANTED EVERYONE TO HAVE THE OSHIRUKO!!!

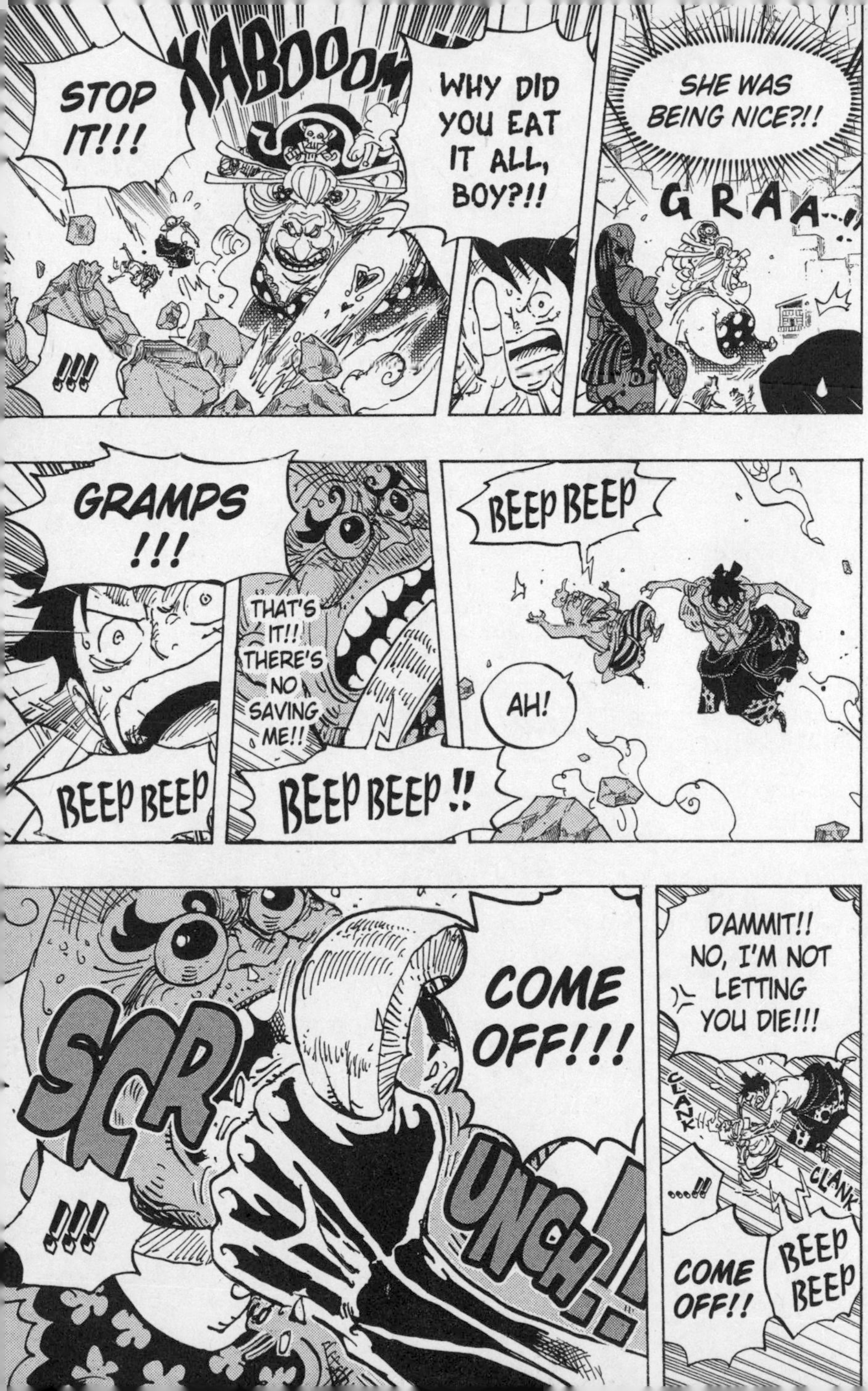
SHE WAS BEING NICE?!!
GRAA...!!
WHY DID YOU EAT IT ALL, BOY?!!
KABOOOM
STOP IT!!!
!!!
BEEP BEEP
AH!
THAT'S IT!! THERE'S NO SAVING ME!!
BEEP BEEP!!
GRAMPS!!!
BEEP BEEP
DAMMIT!! NO, I'M NOT LETTING YOU DIE!!!
CLANK
CLANK
...!!
BEEP BEEP
COME OFF!!
COME OFF!!!
SCR
UNCH..!!
!!!

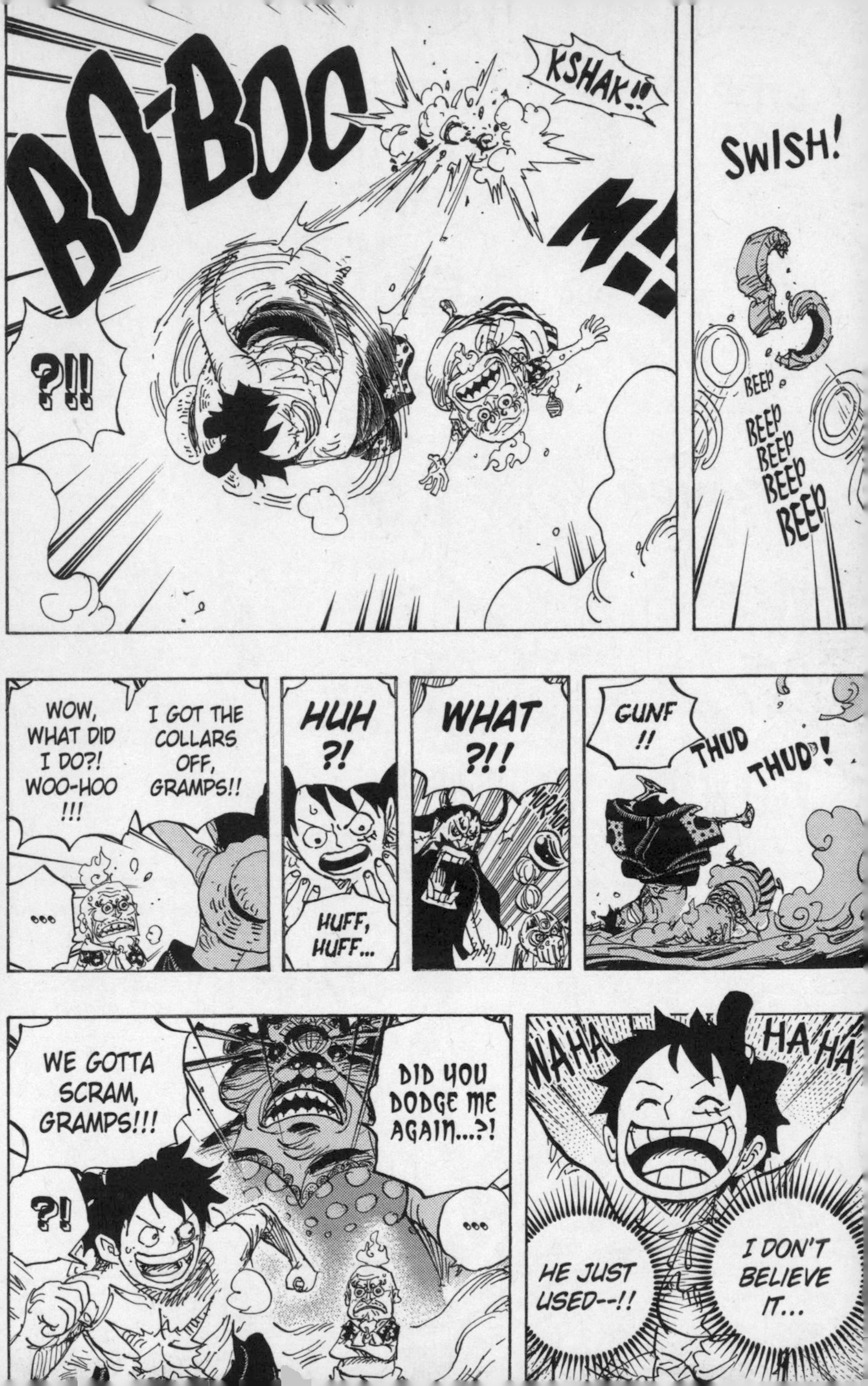
SWISH!
BEEP
BEEP BEEP BEEP BEEP
KSHAK!!
BO-BOOM!!
?!!
GUNF!!
THUD THUD!
WHAT?!!
HUH?!
HUFF, HUFF...
I GOT THE COLLARS OFF, GRAMPS!!
WOW, WHAT DID I DO?! WOO-HOO!!!
...
HA HA
WAHA
I DON'T BELIEVE IT...
HE JUST USED--!!
DID YOU DODGE ME AGAIN...?!
WE GOTTA SCRAM, GRAMPS!!!
?!
...

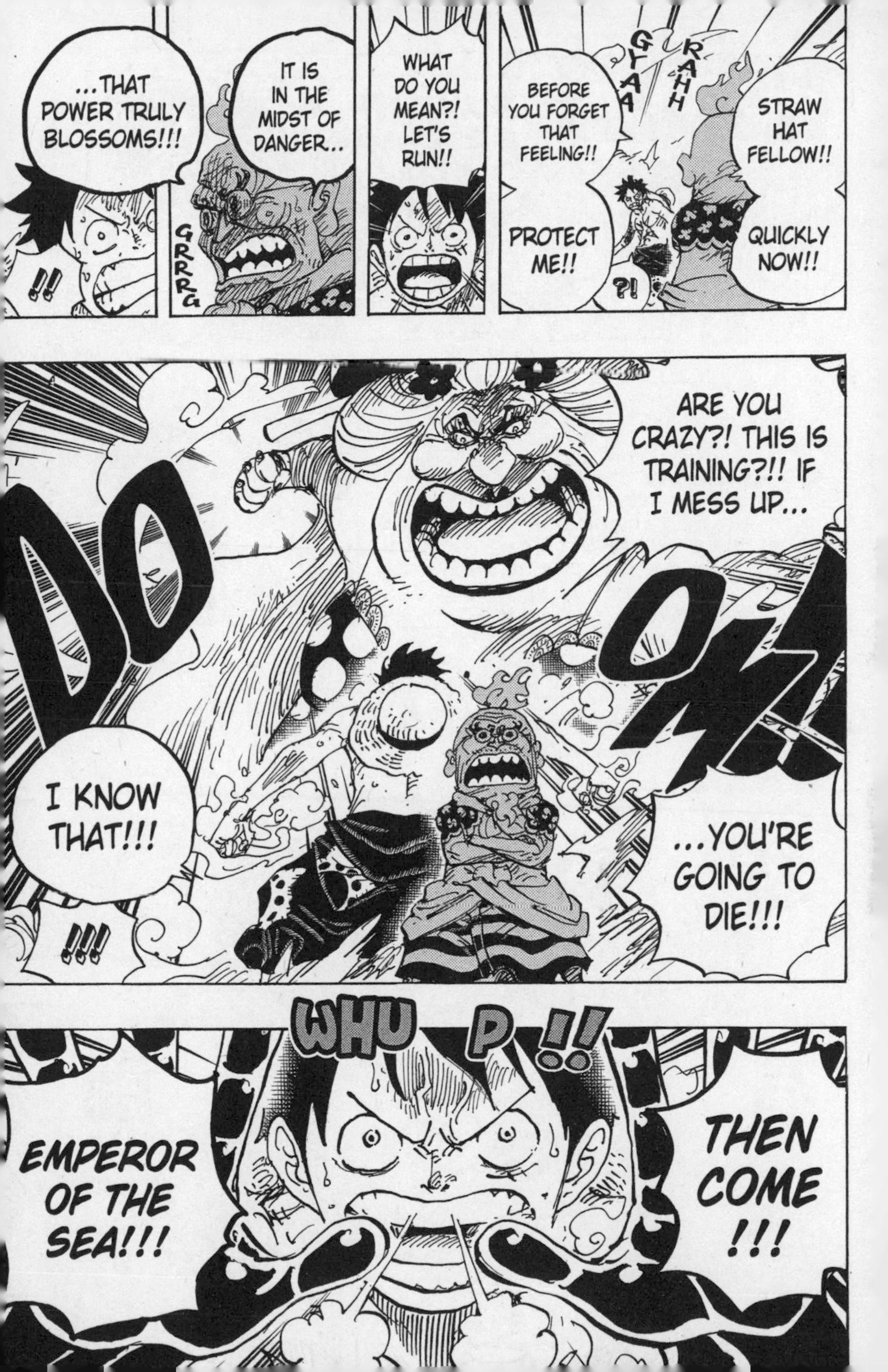
STRAW HAT FELLOW!!
QUICKLY NOW!!
RAHHH
GYAA
BEFORE YOU FORGET THAT FEELING!!
PROTECT ME!!
?!
WHAT DO YOU MEAN?! LET'S RUN!!
IT IS IN THE MIDST OF DANGER...
GRRRG
...THAT POWER TRULY BLOSSOMS!!!
!!
ARE YOU CRAZY?! THIS IS TRAINING?!! IF I MESS UP...
...YOU'RE GOING TO DIE!!!
DOOM
I KNOW THAT!!!
!!!
WHUP!!
THEN COME!!!
EMPEROR OF THE SEA!!!

SBS Question Corner

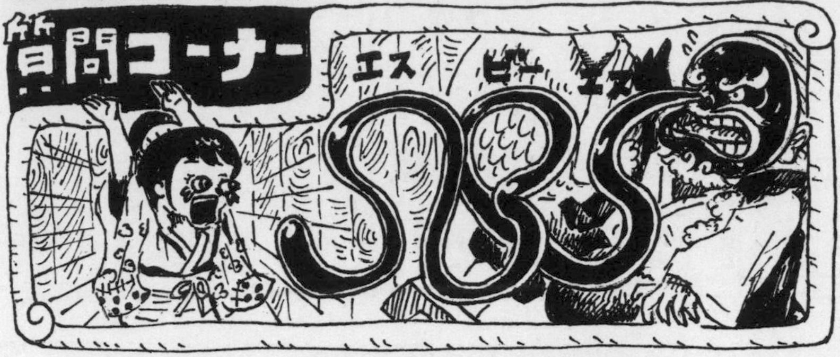
質問コーナー
エス ビー エス
SBS
(Naoki Sagawa, Ibaraki)

Q: Is it just a coincidence that Kin'emon's wife is named Otsuru, and there's also the Otsuru in the Navy?

--Ruru

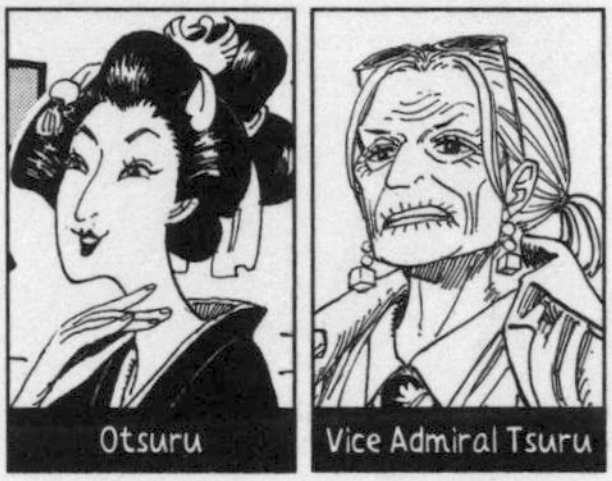
Otsuru
Vice Admiral Tsuru

A: Yeah, they're the same, aren't they? But here's the thing. Does everyone remember a shojo manga by the title of *Nana*? As a matter of fact, the two main characters are both named Nana! It's redundant! But the series is super popular and famous!! So, like...it's okay, right? And if they should meet one day, they're going to say... "Guess what, Tsuru? My name's Tsuru too."

Q: Show us Usopp at age 40 and 60!!

--Match and Takeshi

A: Okay, here!

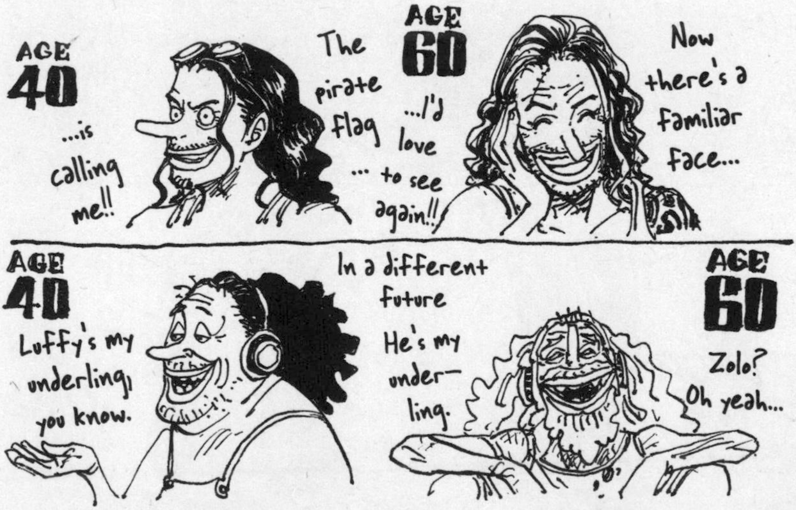
AGE 40
...is calling me!!
The pirate flag...
AGE 60
...I'd love... to see again!!
Now there's a familiar face...
AGE 40
Luffy's my underling, you know.
In a different future
He's my under-ling.
AGE 60
Zolo? Oh yeah...

Chapter 947:
QUEEN'S GAMBLE

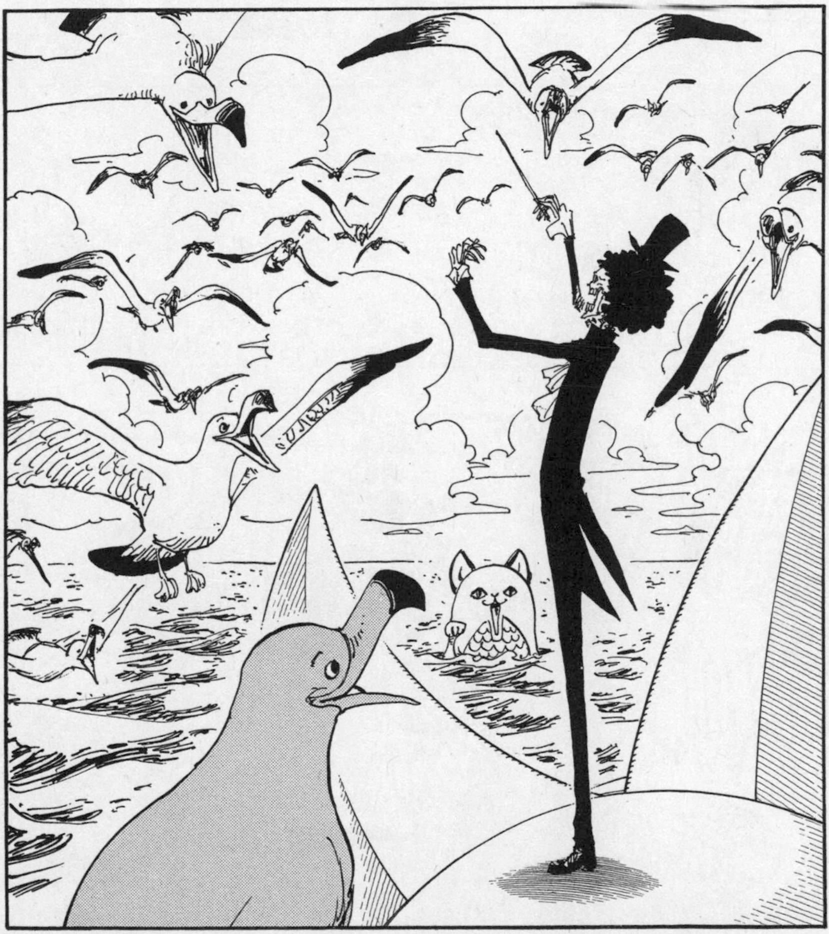

REQUEST: "BROOK CONDUCTING A CHORUS OF SEAGULLS ON THE DECK OF THE *SUNNY*" BY NODA SKYWALKER

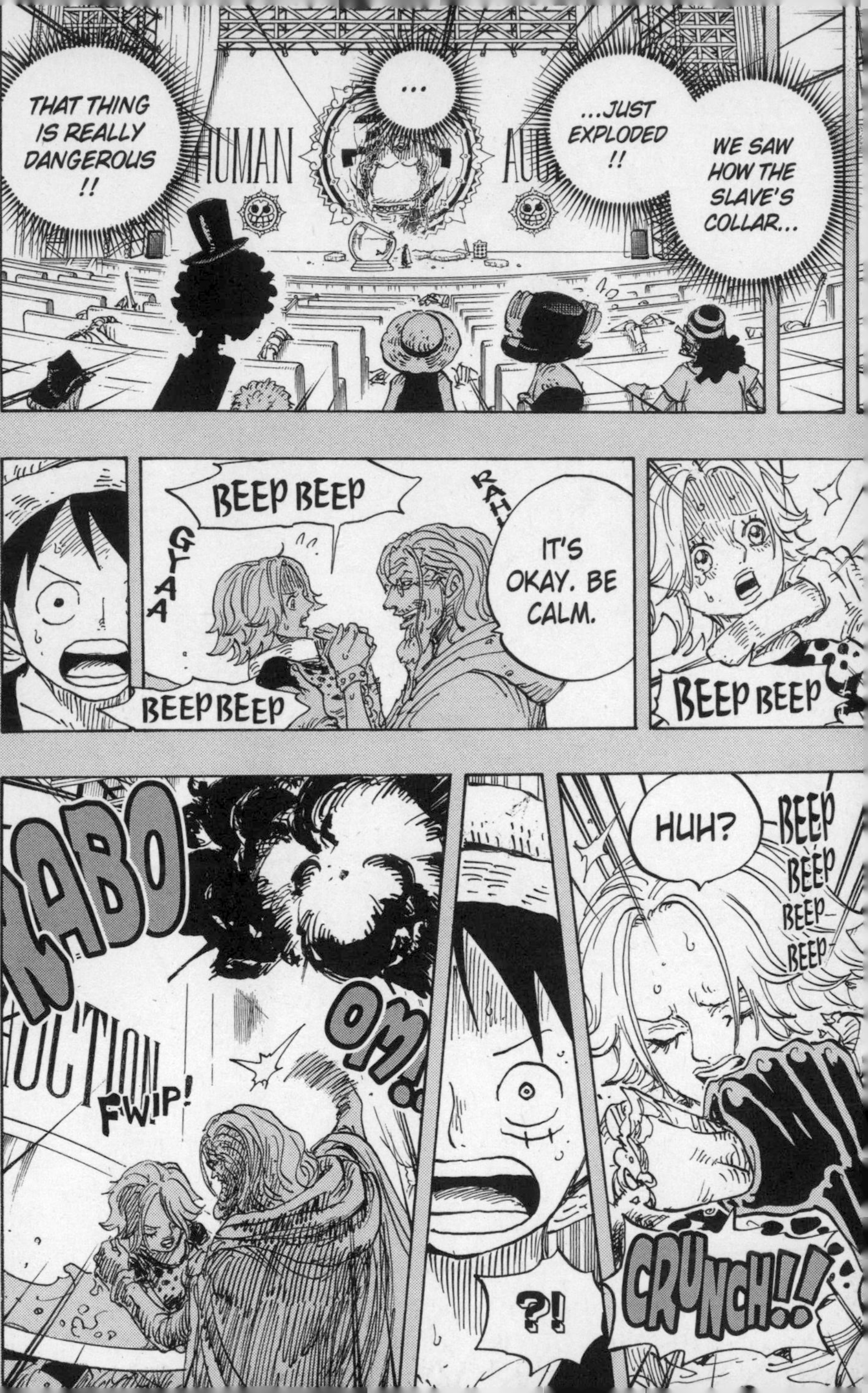
WE SAW HOW THE SLAVE'S COLLAR...
...JUST EXPLODED !!
...
THAT THING IS REALLY DANGEROUS !!
HUMAN
BEEP BEEP
IT'S OKAY. BE CALM.
BEEP BEEP
GYAA
BEEP BEEP
HUH?
BEEP BEEP BEEP BEEP
CRUNCH!!!
?!
FWIP!

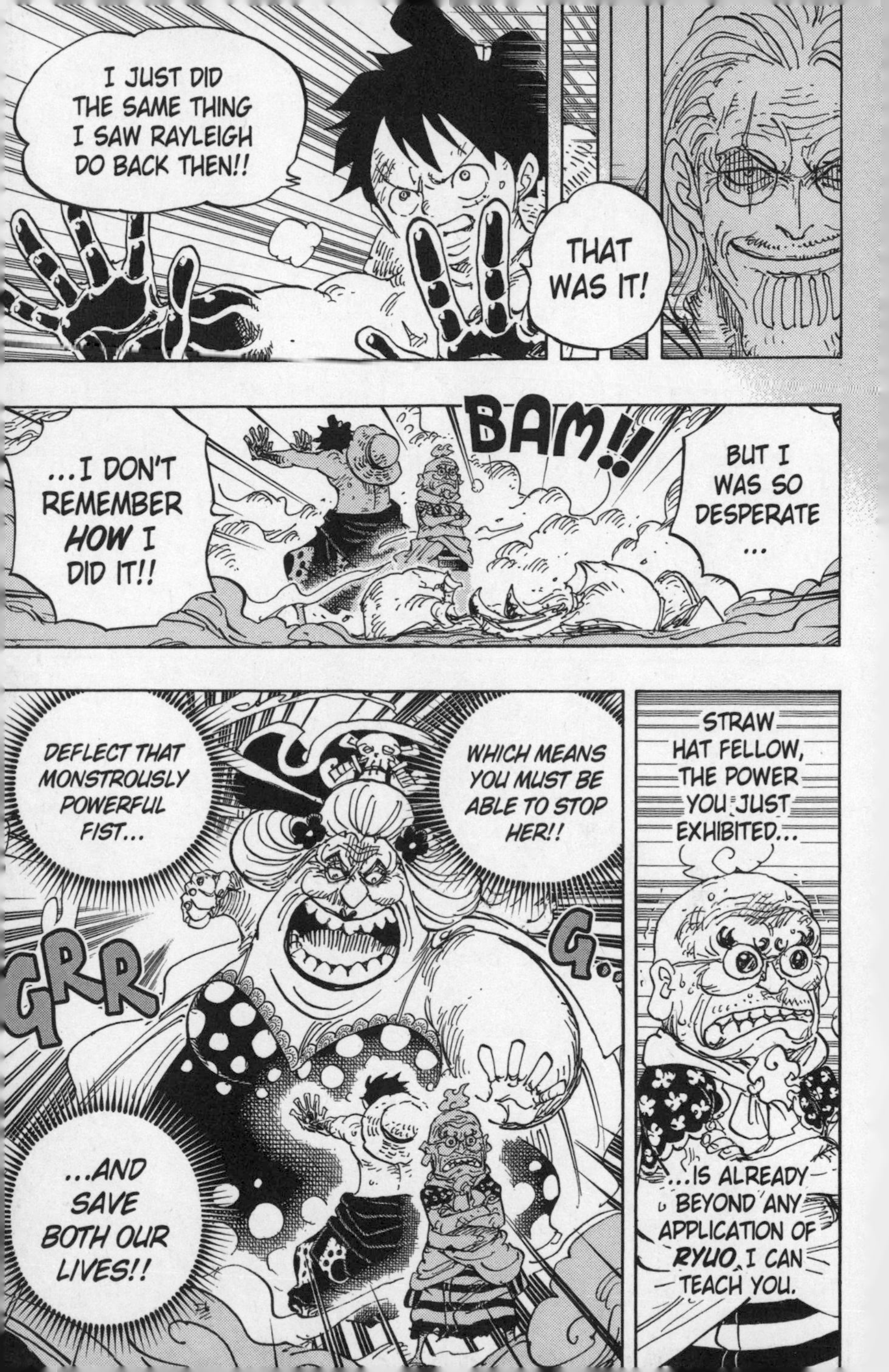
THAT WAS IT!
I JUST DID THE SAME THING I SAW RAYLEIGH DO BACK THEN!!
BUT I WAS SO DESPERATE...
BAM!!
...I DON'T REMEMBER *HOW* I DID IT!!
STRAW HAT FELLOW, THE POWER YOU JUST EXHIBITED...
...IS ALREADY BEYOND ANY APPLICATION OF *RYUO* I CAN TEACH YOU.
WHICH MEANS YOU MUST BE ABLE TO STOP HER!!
DEFLECT THAT MONSTROUSLY POWERFUL FIST...
G...
GRR
...AND SAVE BOTH OUR LIVES!!

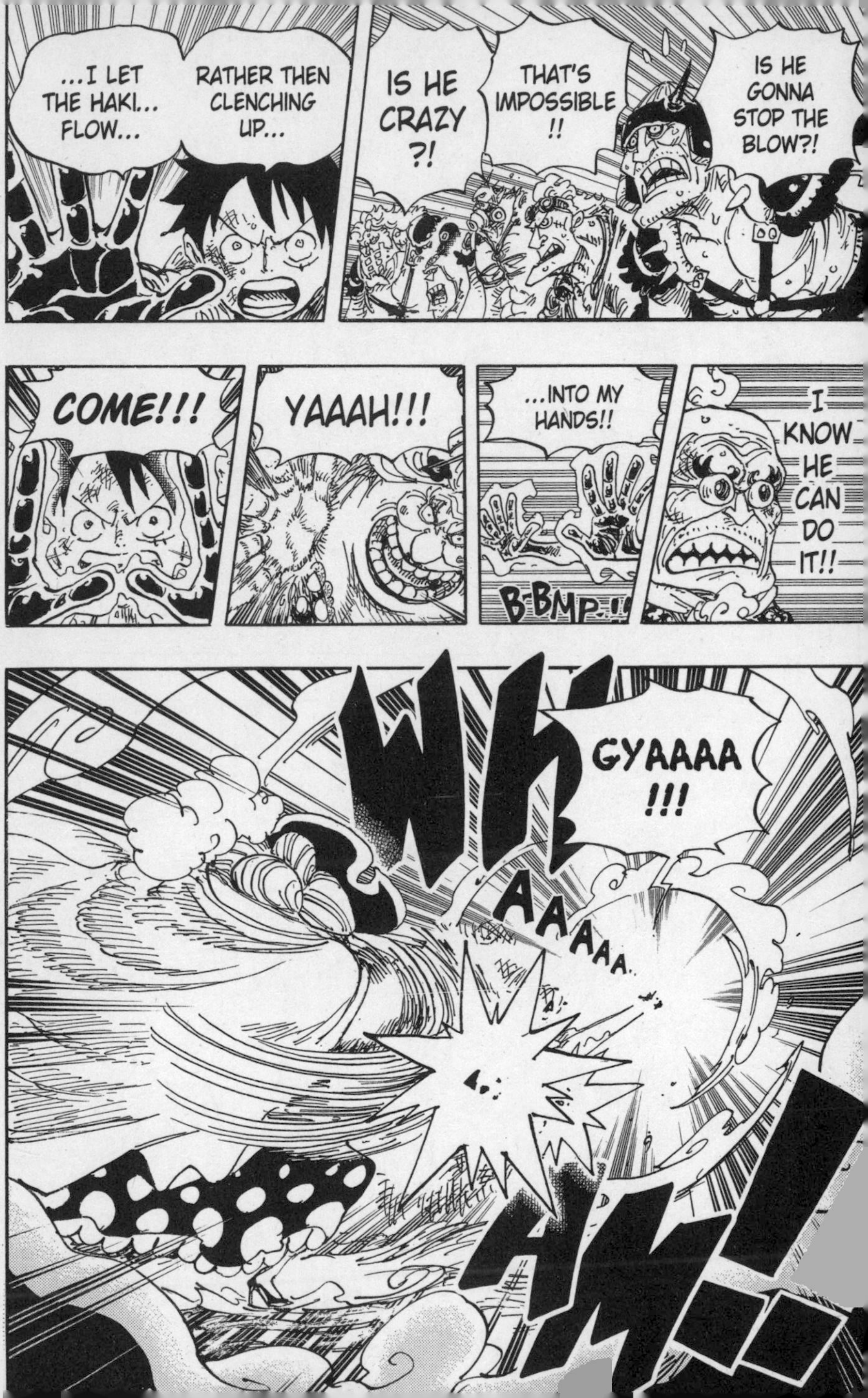
IS HE GONNA STOP THE BLOW?!
THAT'S IMPOSSIBLE !!
IS HE CRAZY ?!
RATHER THEN CLENCHING UP...
...I LET THE HAKI... FLOW...
I KNOW HE CAN DO IT!!
...INTO MY HANDS!!
B-BMP!!
YAAAH!!!
COME!!!
GYAAAA !!!
WHAAAAAAM!!

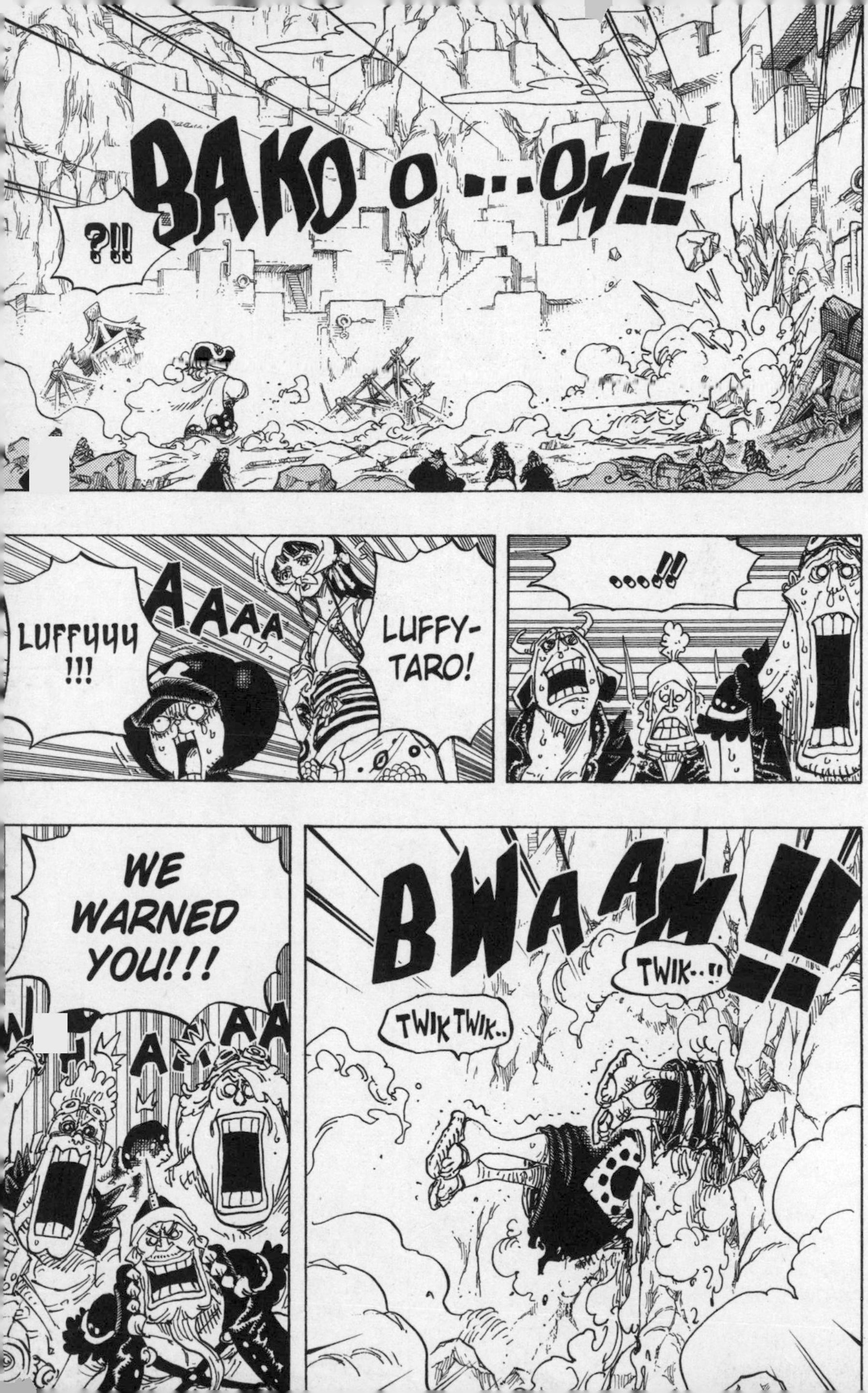
BAKO O...OM!!
?!!
....!!
LUFFY-TARO!
AAAA
LUFFYYY!!!
BWAAM!!
TWIK..!!
TWIK TWIK..
WE WARNED YOU!!!

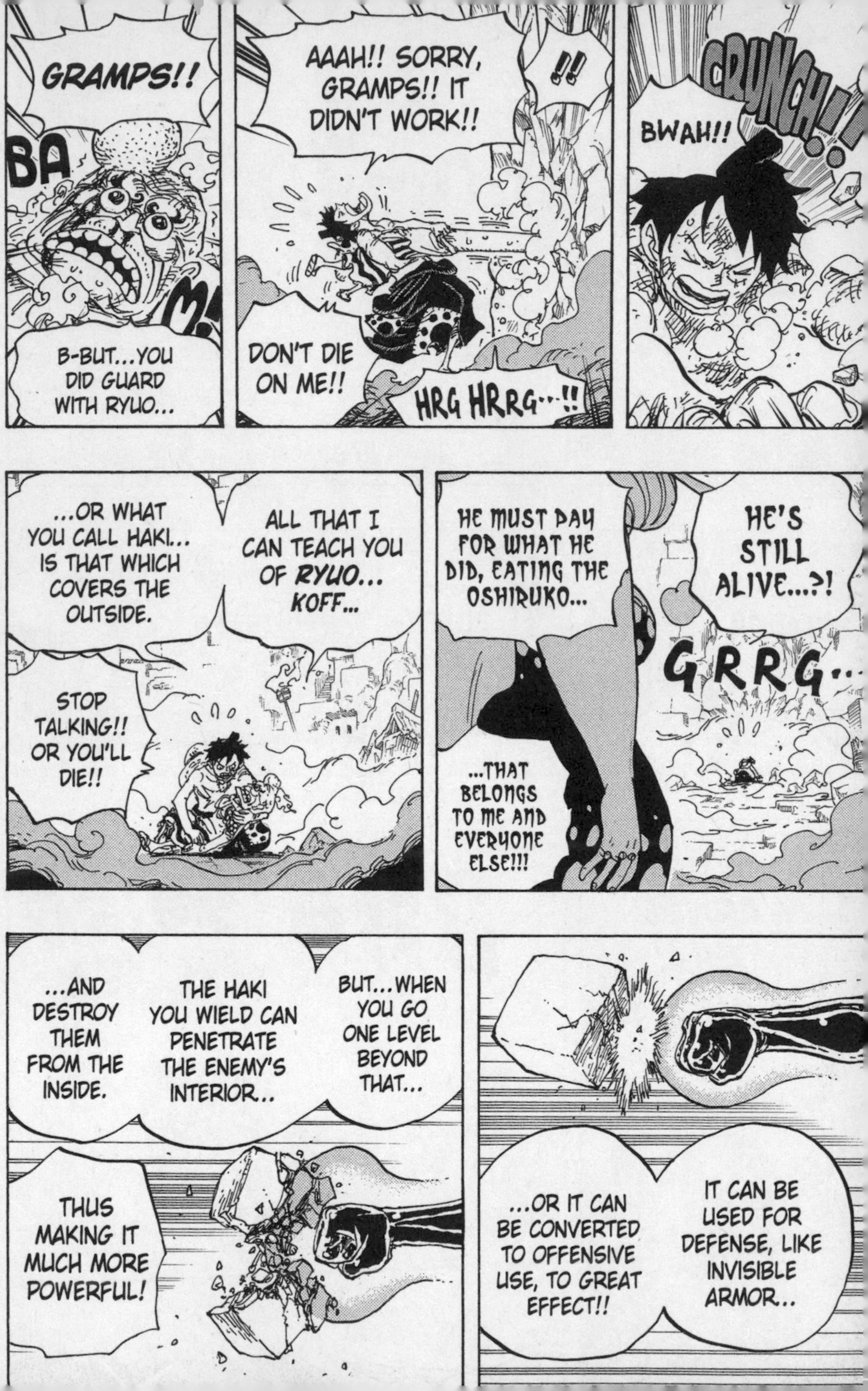
CRUNCH!!
BWAH!!
!!
AAAH!! SORRY, GRAMPS!! IT DIDN'T WORK!!
DON'T DIE ON ME!!
HRG HRRG...!!
GRAMPS!!
BA
M!
B-BUT...YOU DID GUARD WITH RYUO...
HE'S STILL ALIVE...?!
HE MUST PAY FOR WHAT HE DID, EATING THE OSHIRUKO...
GRRG...
...THAT BELONGS TO ME AND EVERYONE ELSE!!!
ALL THAT I CAN TEACH YOU OF *RYUO... KOFF...*
...OR WHAT YOU CALL HAKI... IS THAT WHICH COVERS THE OUTSIDE.
STOP TALKING!! OR YOU'LL DIE!!
IT CAN BE USED FOR DEFENSE, LIKE INVISIBLE ARMOR...
...OR IT CAN BE CONVERTED TO OFFENSIVE USE, TO GREAT EFFECT!!
BUT...WHEN YOU GO ONE LEVEL BEYOND THAT...
THE HAKI YOU WIELD CAN PENETRATE THE ENEMY'S INTERIOR...
...AND DESTROY THEM FROM THE INSIDE.
THUS MAKING IT MUCH MORE POWERFUL!

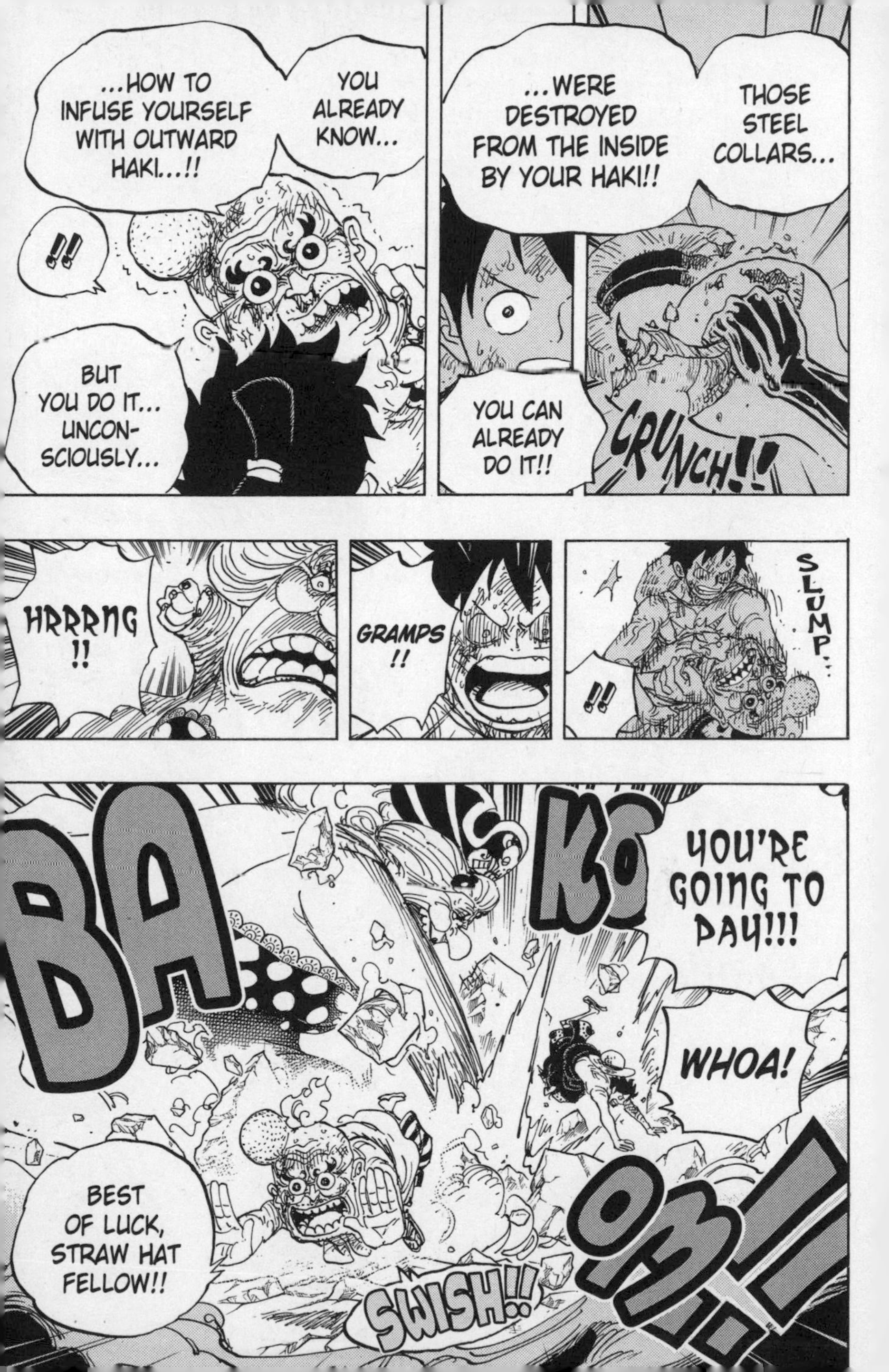
THOSE STEEL COLLARS...
...WERE DESTROYED FROM THE INSIDE BY YOUR HAKI!!
YOU CAN ALREADY DO IT!!
CRUNCH!!
YOU ALREADY KNOW...
...HOW TO INFUSE YOURSELF WITH OUTWARD HAKI...!!
!!
BUT YOU DO IT... UNCONSCIOUSLY...
SLUMP...
!!
GRAMPS !!
HRRRNG !!
YOU'RE GOING TO PAY!!!
BAKOOM!!
WHOA!
BEST OF LUCK, STRAW HAT FELLOW!!
SWISH!!

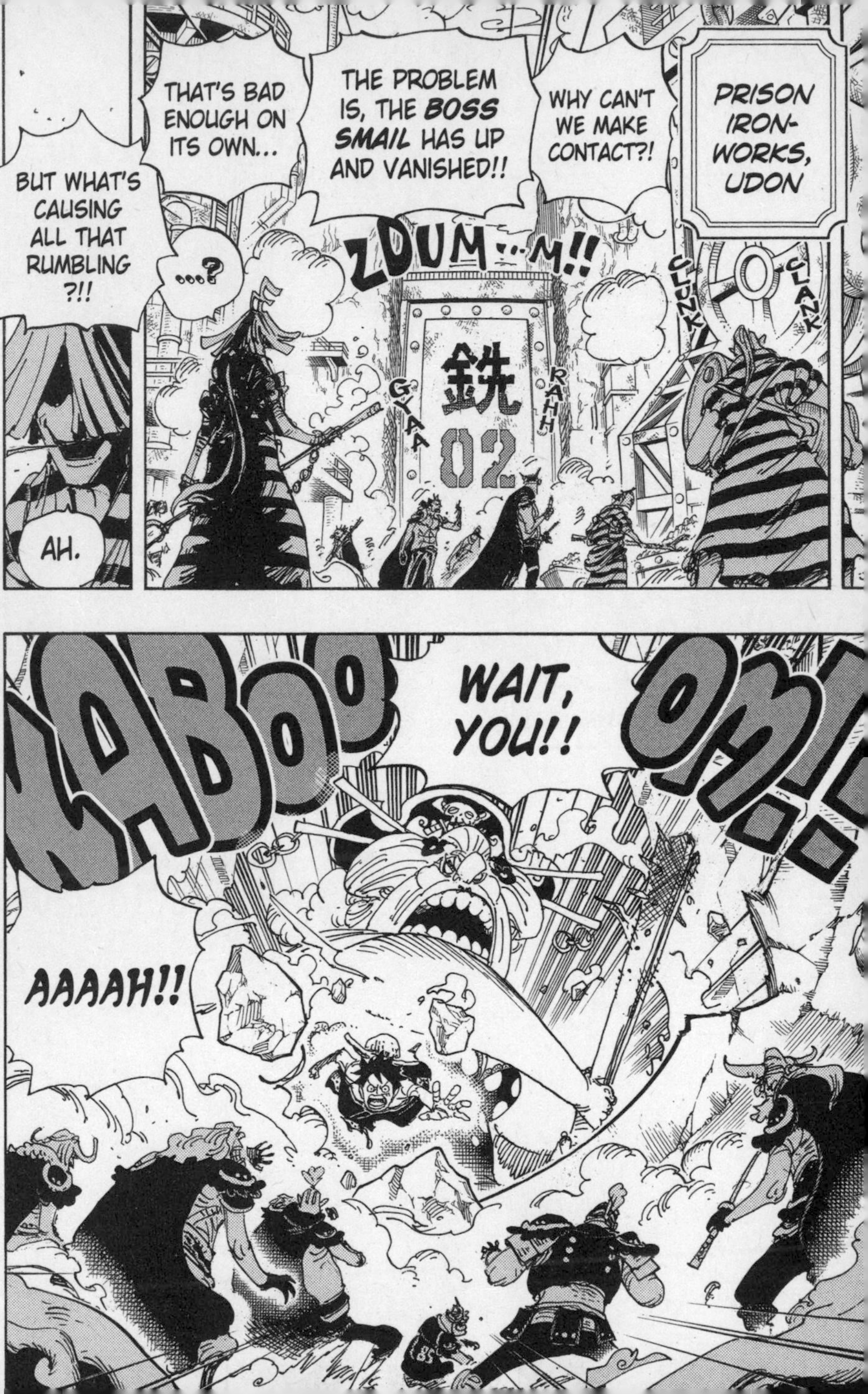
PRISON IRON-WORKS, UDON
CLUNK
CLANK
WHY CAN'T WE MAKE CONTACT?!
THE PROBLEM IS, THE **BOSS SMAIL** HAS UP AND VANISHED!!
THAT'S BAD ENOUGH ON ITS OWN...
BUT WHAT'S CAUSING ALL THAT RUMBLING ?!!
ZDUM...M!!
鉄
02
RAHH
GYAA
...?
AH.
KABOOOM!!
WAIT, YOU!!
AAAAH!!

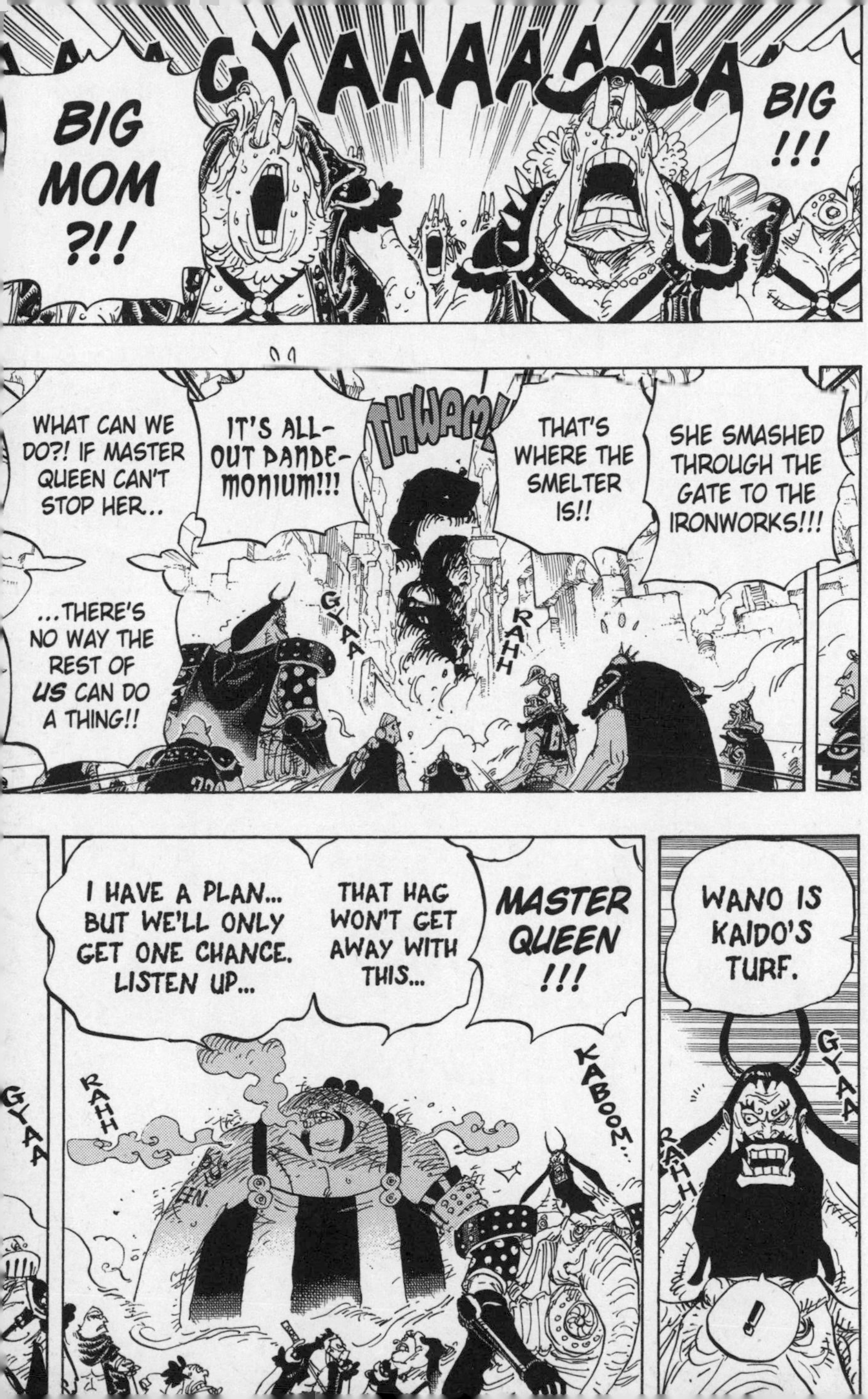
GYAAAAAAAA
BIG !!!
BIG MOM ?!!
SHE SMASHED THROUGH THE GATE TO THE IRONWORKS!!!
THAT'S WHERE THE SMELTER IS!!
THWAM!
IT'S ALL-OUT PANDEMONIUM!!!
RAHH
GYAA
WHAT CAN WE DO?! IF MASTER QUEEN CAN'T STOP HER...
...THERE'S NO WAY THE REST OF US CAN DO A THING!!
WANO IS KAIDO'S TURF.
GYAA
RAHH
!
MASTER QUEEN !!!
KABOOM
THAT HAG WON'T GET AWAY WITH THIS...
I HAVE A PLAN... BUT WE'LL ONLY GET ONE CHANCE. LISTEN UP...
RAHH
GYAA

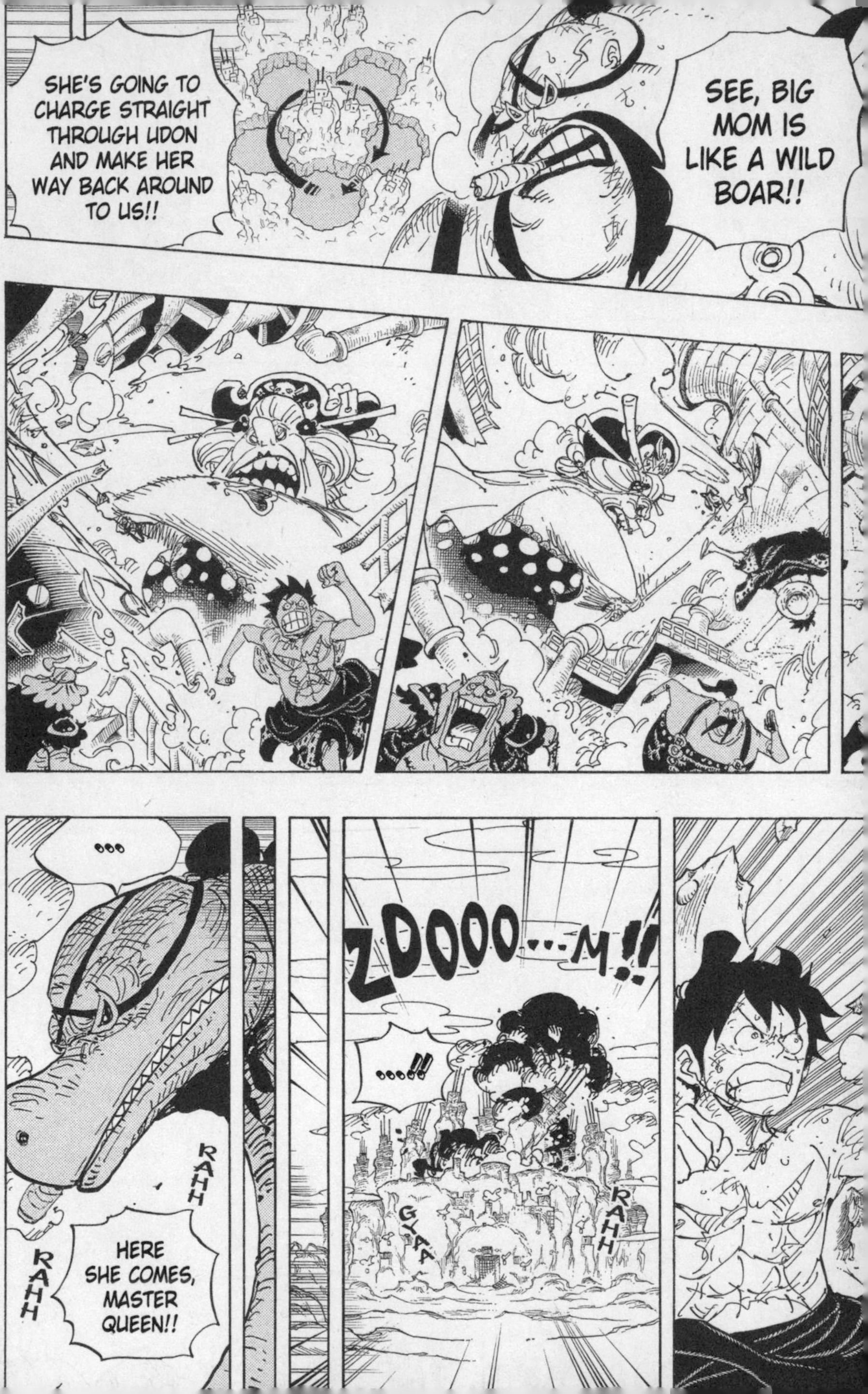
SEE, BIG MOM IS LIKE A WILD BOAR!!
SHE'S GOING TO CHARGE STRAIGHT THROUGH UDON AND MAKE HER WAY BACK AROUND TO US!!
ZDOOO...M!!
.....!!
RAHH
GYAA
RAHH
...
RAHH
HERE SHE COMES, MASTER QUEEN!!
RAHH

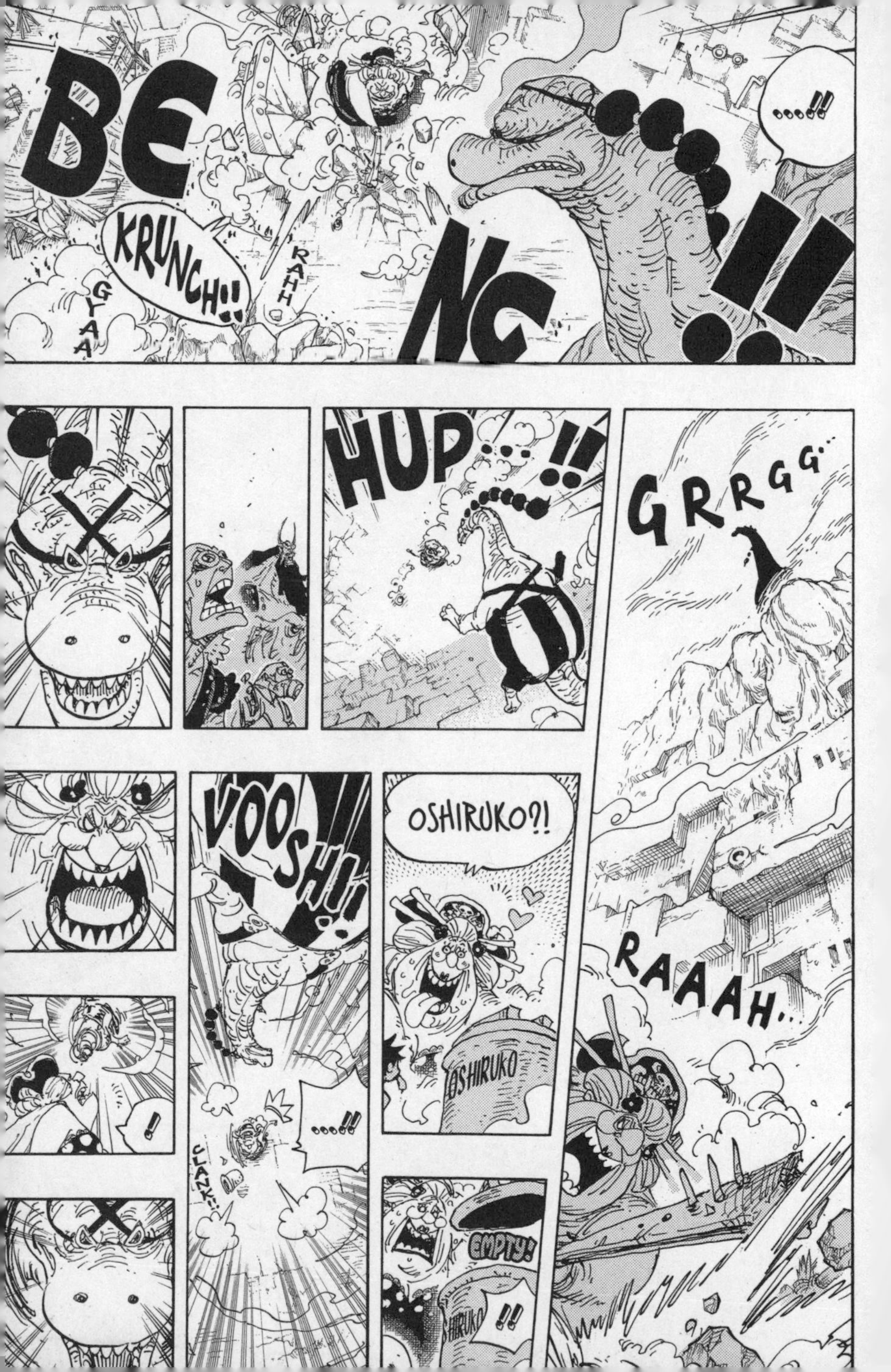

....!!
BENG!!
KRUNCH!!
RAHH
GYAA
GRRGG...
RAAAH...
HUP...!!
OSHIRUKO?!
OSHIRUKO
EMPTY!
SHIRUKO
!!
VOOSH!!
....!!
CLANK!!
!

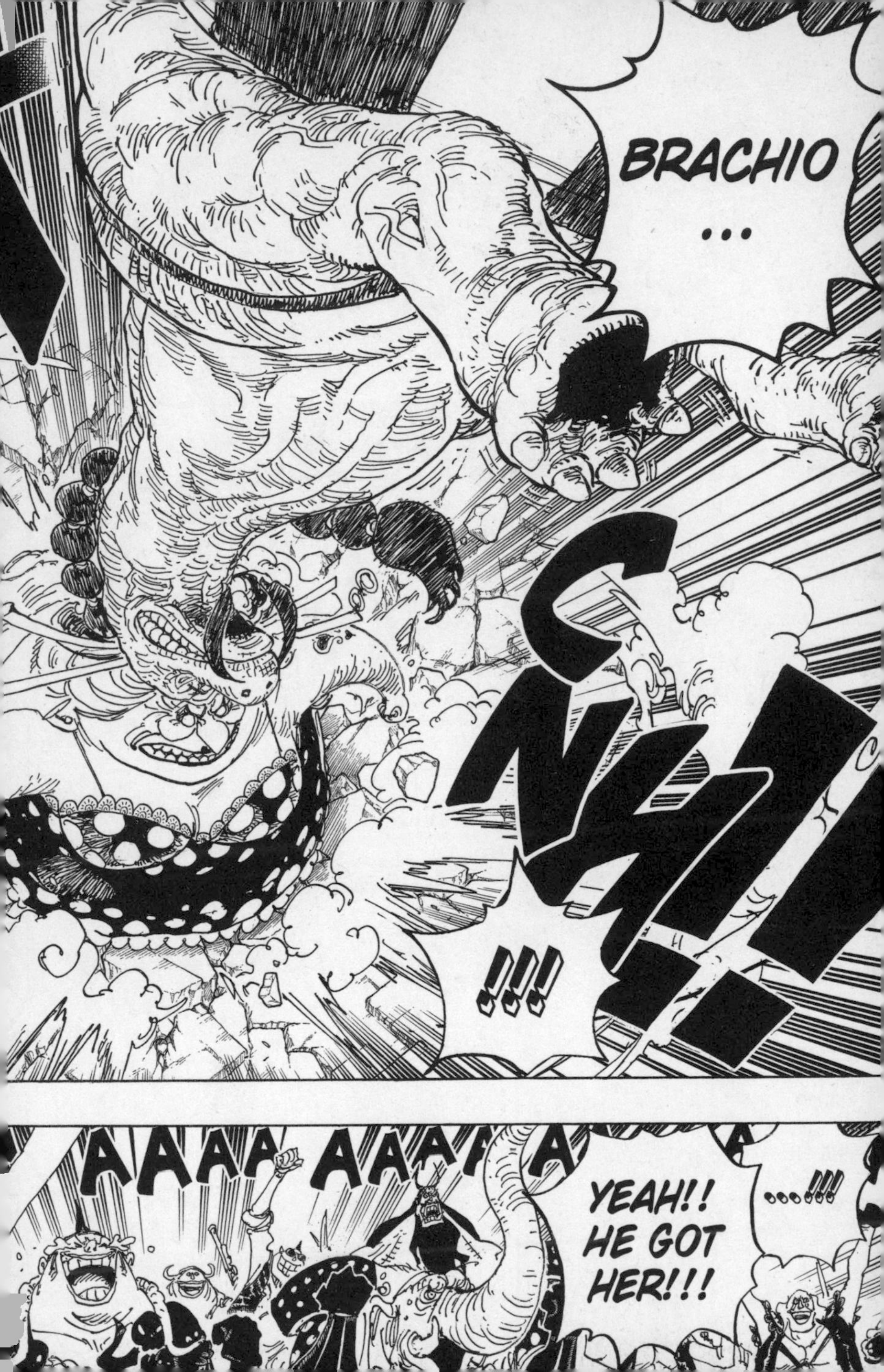
BRACHIO ...
!!!
...!!!
YEAH!! HE GOT HER!!!
AAAA AAAA A

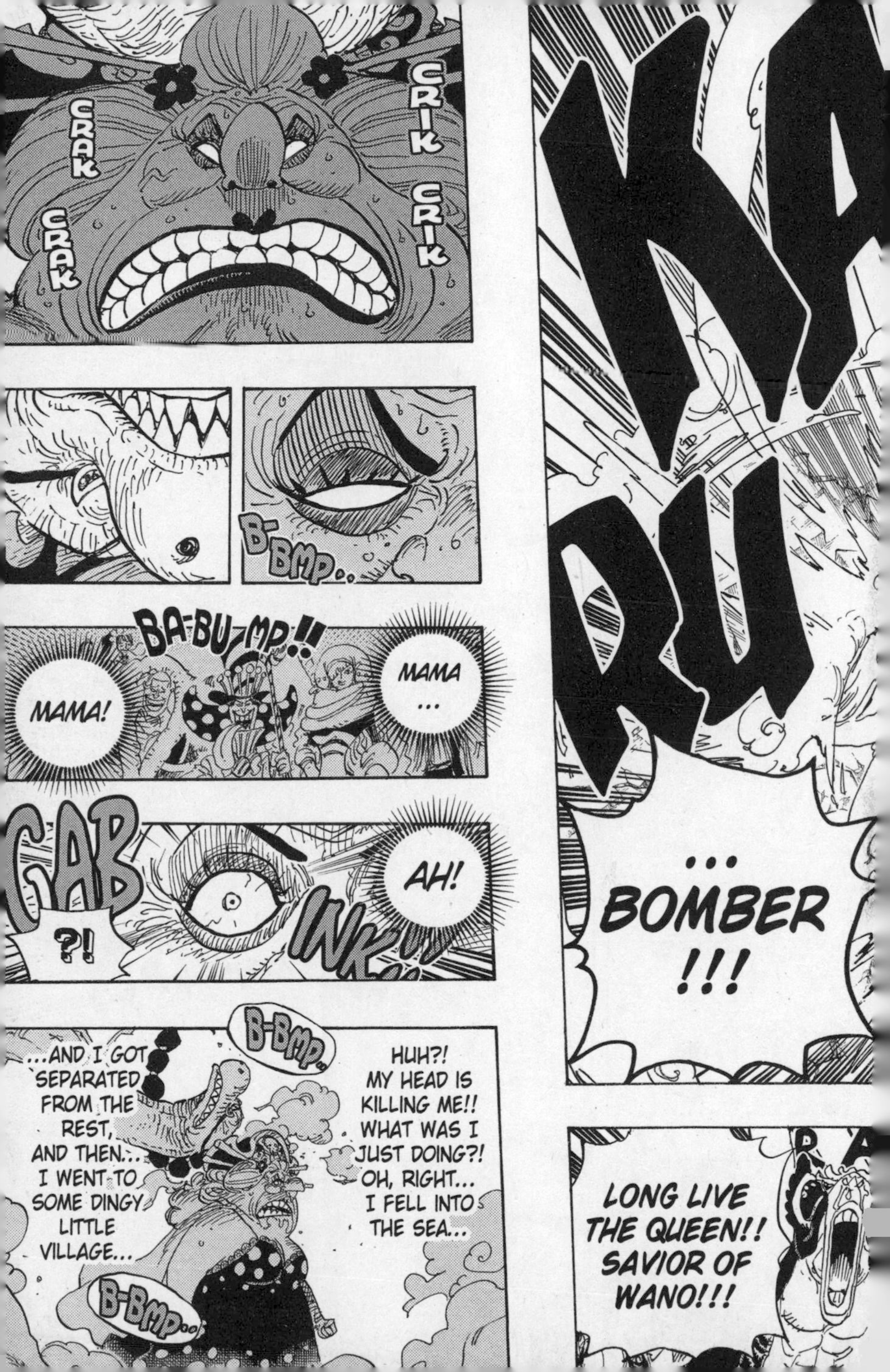
... BOMBER !!!
LONG LIVE THE QUEEN!! SAVIOR OF WANO!!!
CRIK CRIK
CRAK CRAK
B-BMP..
BA-BUMP!!
MAMA ...
MAMA!
AH!
GAB INK
?!
B-BMP..
HUH?! MY HEAD IS KILLING ME!! WHAT WAS I JUST DOING?! OH, RIGHT... I FELL INTO THE SEA...
...AND I GOT SEPARATED FROM THE REST, AND THEN... I WENT TO SOME DINGY LITTLE VILLAGE...
B-BMP..

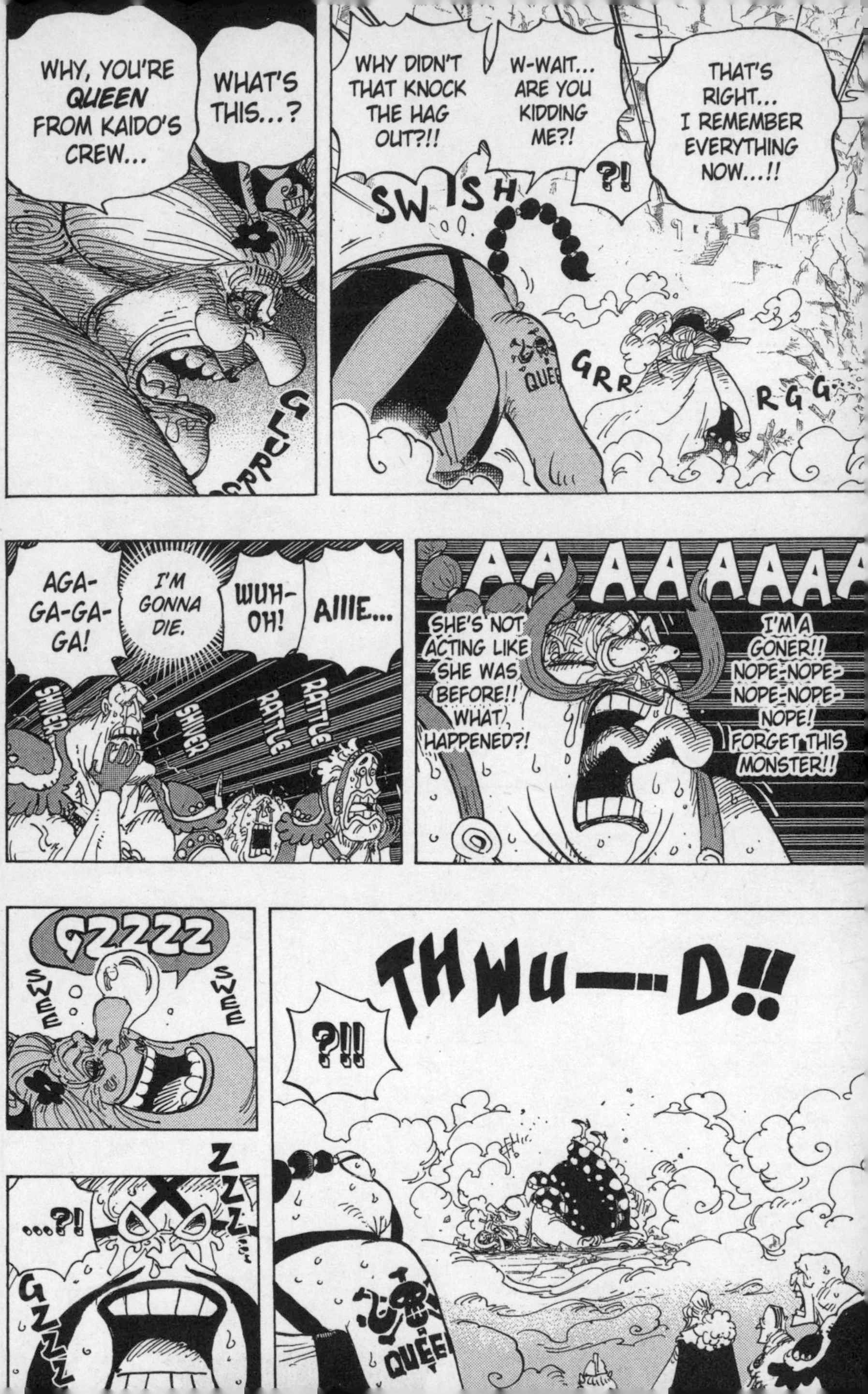
THAT'S RIGHT... I REMEMBER EVERYTHING NOW...!!
?!
W-WAIT... ARE YOU KIDDING ME?!
WHY DIDN'T THAT KNOCK THE HAG OUT?!!
SWISH
GRR
RGG
QUEE
WHAT'S THIS...?
WHY, YOU'RE QUEEN FROM KAIDO'S CREW...
AAAAAAA
I'M A GONER!! NOPE-NOPE-NOPE-NOPE-NOPE! FORGET THIS MONSTER!!
SHE'S NOT ACTING LIKE SHE WAS BEFORE!! WHAT HAPPENED?!
AIIIE...
WUH-OH!
I'M GONNA DIE.
AGA-GA-GA-GA!
RATTLE
RATTLE
SHIVER
SHIVER
THWU—D!!
?!!
QUEE
GZZZZ
SWEE
SWEE
ZZZZ...
...?!
GZZZ

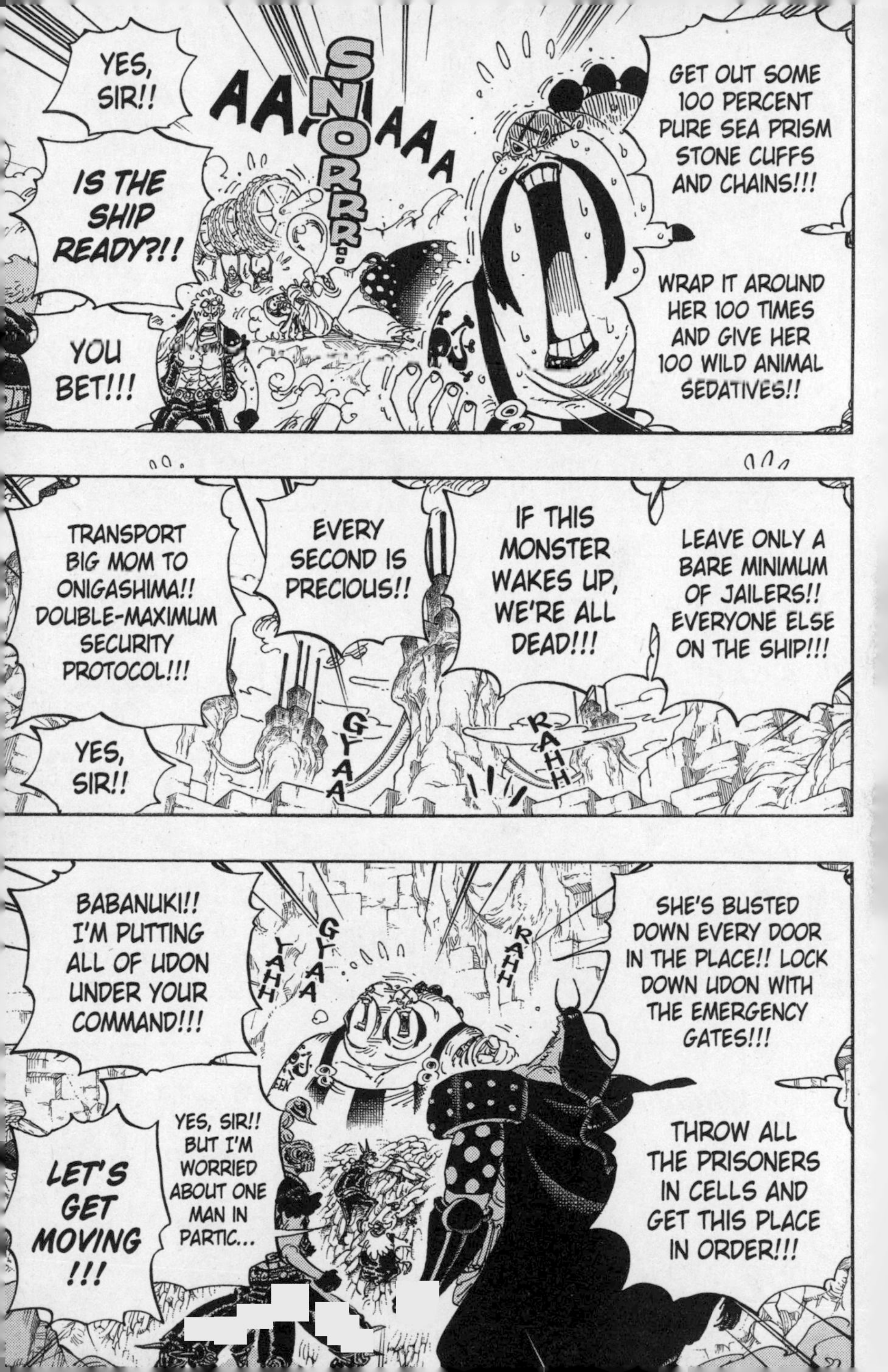
GET OUT SOME 100 PERCENT PURE SEA PRISM STONE CUFFS AND CHAINS!!!
WRAP IT AROUND HER 100 TIMES AND GIVE HER 100 WILD ANIMAL SEDATIVES!!
AAAAAAA
SNORRR..
YES, SIR!!
IS THE SHIP READY?!!
YOU BET!!!
LEAVE ONLY A BARE MINIMUM OF JAILERS!! EVERYONE ELSE ON THE SHIP!!!
IF THIS MONSTER WAKES UP, WE'RE ALL DEAD!!!
EVERY SECOND IS PRECIOUS!!
TRANSPORT BIG MOM TO ONIGASHIMA!! DOUBLE-MAXIMUM SECURITY PROTOCOL!!!
RAHH
GYAA
YES, SIR!!
SHE'S BUSTED DOWN EVERY DOOR IN THE PLACE!! LOCK DOWN UDON WITH THE EMERGENCY GATES!!!
RAHH
GYAA
YAHH
BABANUKI!! I'M PUTTING ALL OF UDON UNDER YOUR COMMAND!!!
THROW ALL THE PRISONERS IN CELLS AND GET THIS PLACE IN ORDER!!!
YES, SIR!! BUT I'M WORRIED ABOUT ONE MAN IN PARTIC...
LET'S GET MOVING!!!

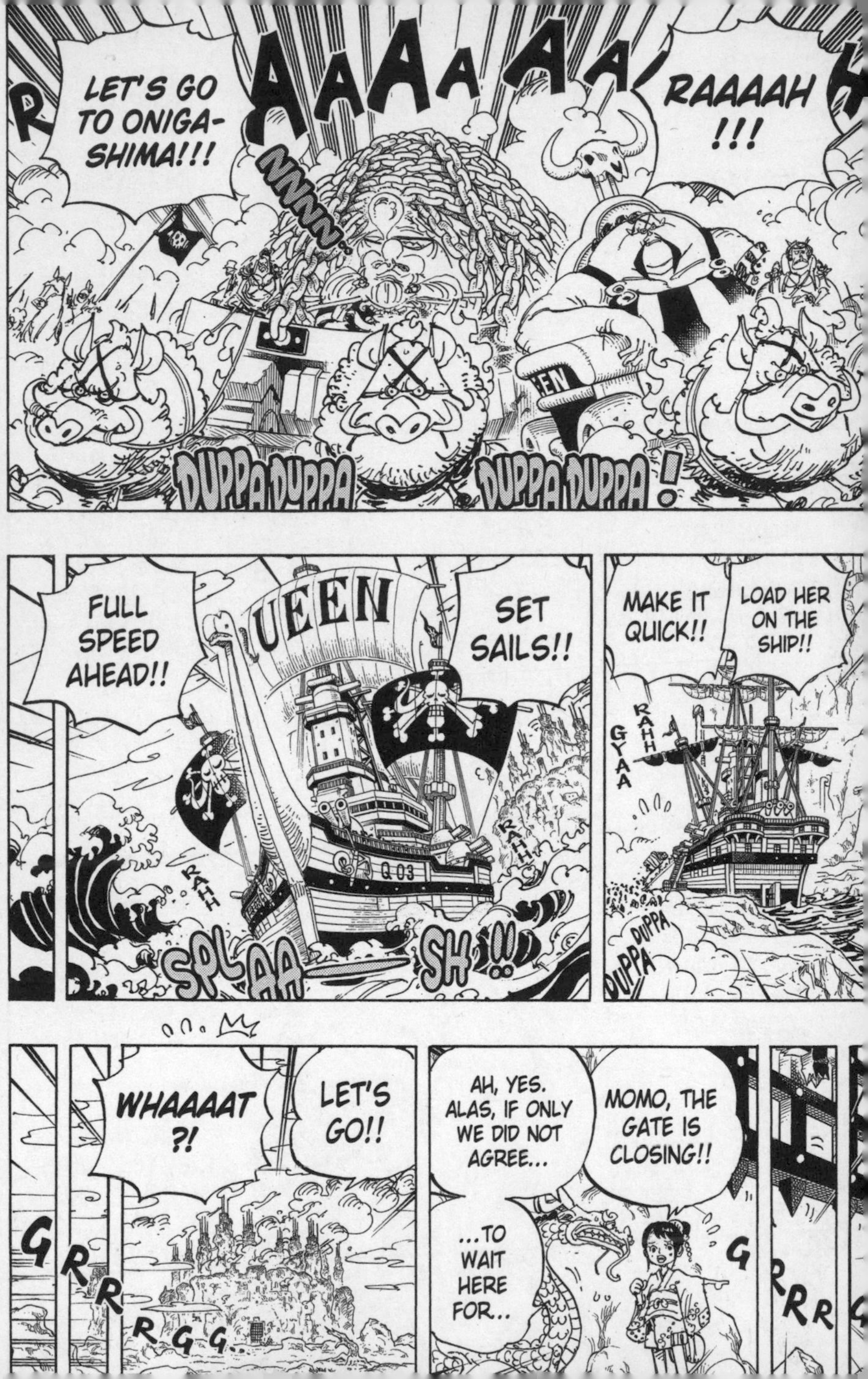
RAAAAH !!!
AAAAAA
NNNN
LET'S GO TO ONIGA-SHIMA!!!
R
DUPPA DUPPA DUPPA DUPPA!
LOAD HER ON THE SHIP!!
MAKE IT QUICK!!
GYAA
RAHH
DUPPA DUPPA
SET SAILS!!
FULL SPEED AHEAD!!
UEEN
Q03
RAHH
RAHH
SPLAASH!!
MOMO, THE GATE IS CLOSING!!
AH, YES. ALAS, IF ONLY WE DID NOT AGREE...
...TO WAIT HERE FOR...
GRRRR
LET'S GO!!
WHAAAAT ?!
GRRRRGG..

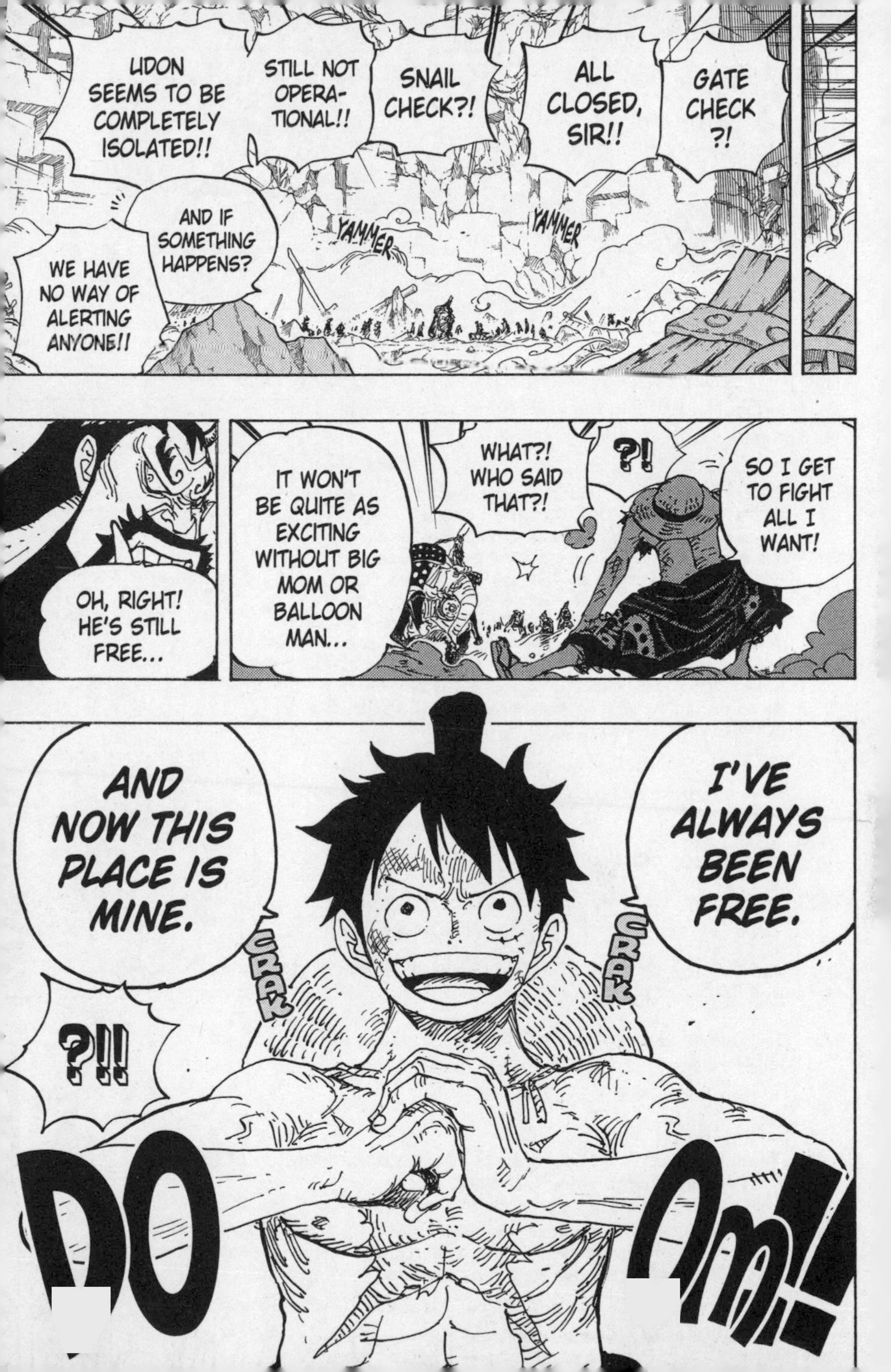

GATE CHECK?!
ALL CLOSED, SIR!!
SNAIL CHECK?!
STILL NOT OPERA-TIONAL!!
UDON SEEMS TO BE COMPLETELY ISOLATED!!
YAMMER
YAMMER
AND IF SOMETHING HAPPENS?
WE HAVE NO WAY OF ALERTING ANYONE!!
SO I GET TO FIGHT ALL I WANT!
?!
WHAT?! WHO SAID THAT?!
IT WON'T BE QUITE AS EXCITING WITHOUT BIG MOM OR BALLOON MAN...
OH, RIGHT! HE'S STILL FREE...
I'VE ALWAYS BEEN FREE.
CRAK
AND NOW THIS PLACE IS MINE.
CRAK
?!!
DO
OM!!

SBS Question Corner

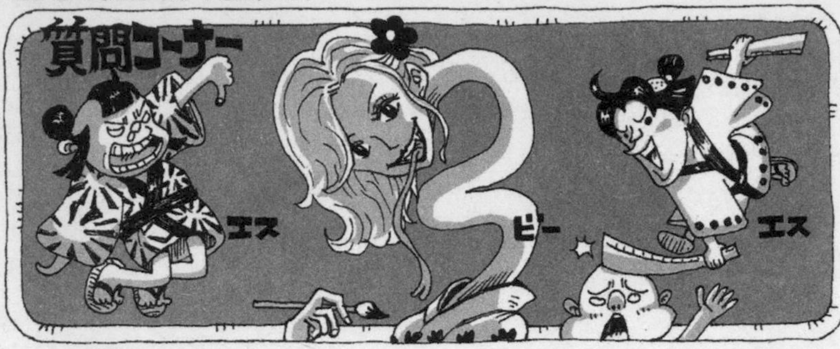
質問コーナー
エス
ビー
エス

(Buchonosuke, Tochigi)

Q: Oda Sensei, I want to be a person who helps others, so I'd like to work as a bathhouse assistant. But since I only have two arms, I can only help the women.

--Sanadacchi

A: There you are, Sanada the pervert!! You can't work here. The only future I can envision is you getting arrested!! Unfortunately, to explain the full history of bathhouse assistants, known as "Sansuke," would take too much time, so if you're curious, look them up yourself. The short story is that it's a fact that in the Edo period, there were male employees at mixed-use bathhouses who helped to wash the customers' bodies. But they would never hire a pervo like Sanada! So don't even think about it!!

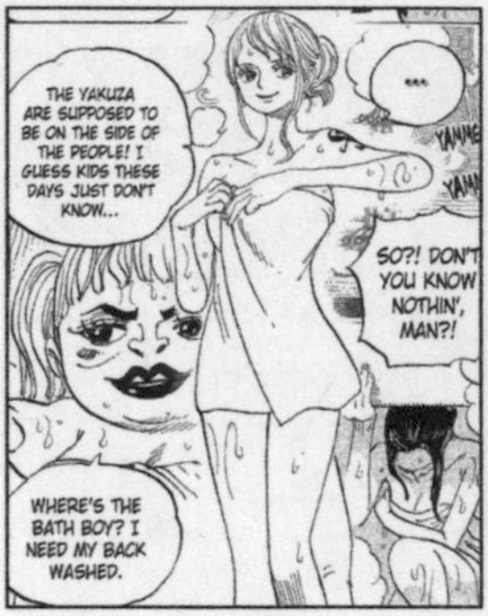
...
THE YAKUZA ARE SUPPOSED TO BE ON THE SIDE OF THE PEOPLE! I GUESS KIDS THESE DAYS JUST DON'T KNOW...
SO?! DON'T YOU KNOW NOTHIN', MAN?!
WHERE'S THE BATH BOY? I NEED MY BACK WASHED.

Q: I just saw Sanada, and he said he wanted to see more scenes at the mixed bath.

--Match and Takeshi

A: Sanada, you jerk!!

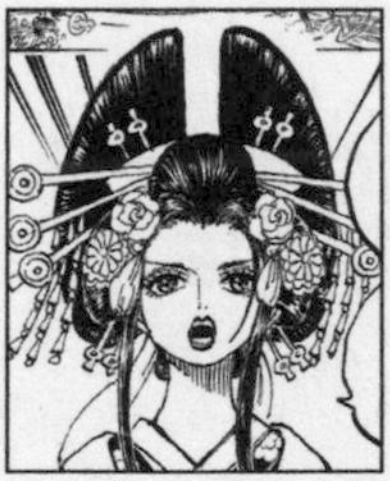

Q: Sanada just said he wants Komurasaki to step on him.

--Match and Takeshi

A: Sanada!! Stop ruining the sanctity of the SBS!!

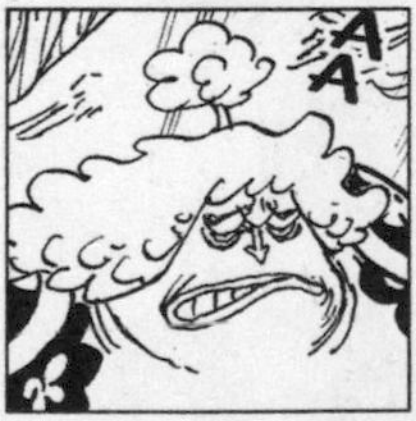

Q: The tree on Shutenmaru's head is from a rakugo routine called Atamayama, right? So where does the tree grow out of your body, Oda Sensei?

--Kinbo

A: That's right! There's a story in rakugo called Atamayama, meaning "head mountain." It's a strange and surreal story where a little cherry blossom tree grows out of a man's head, and then everyone goes up onto his head to watch the blossoms fall. Now, you asked where the tree grows out of my own body? Obviously, my crotch!! Come and watch the flowers bloom!! Huh? I hear police sirens...

Chapter 948:
INTRODUCING KAWAMATSU THE KAPPA

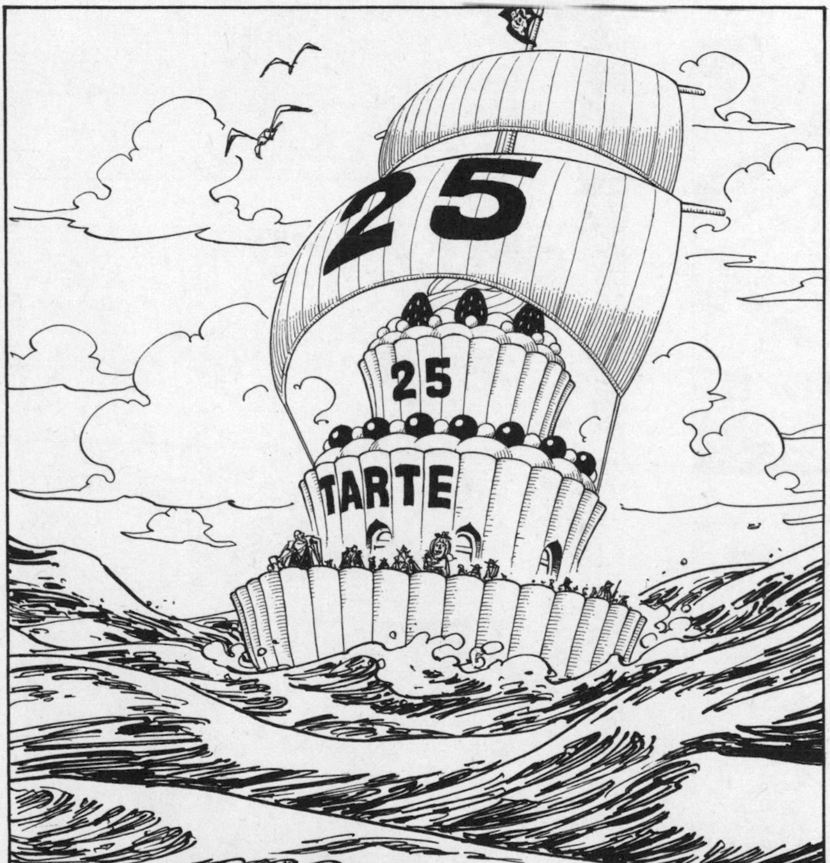
25
25
TARTE

LIMITED COVER SERIES, NO. 24
VOL. 1: "ESCAPE SUCCESSFUL"

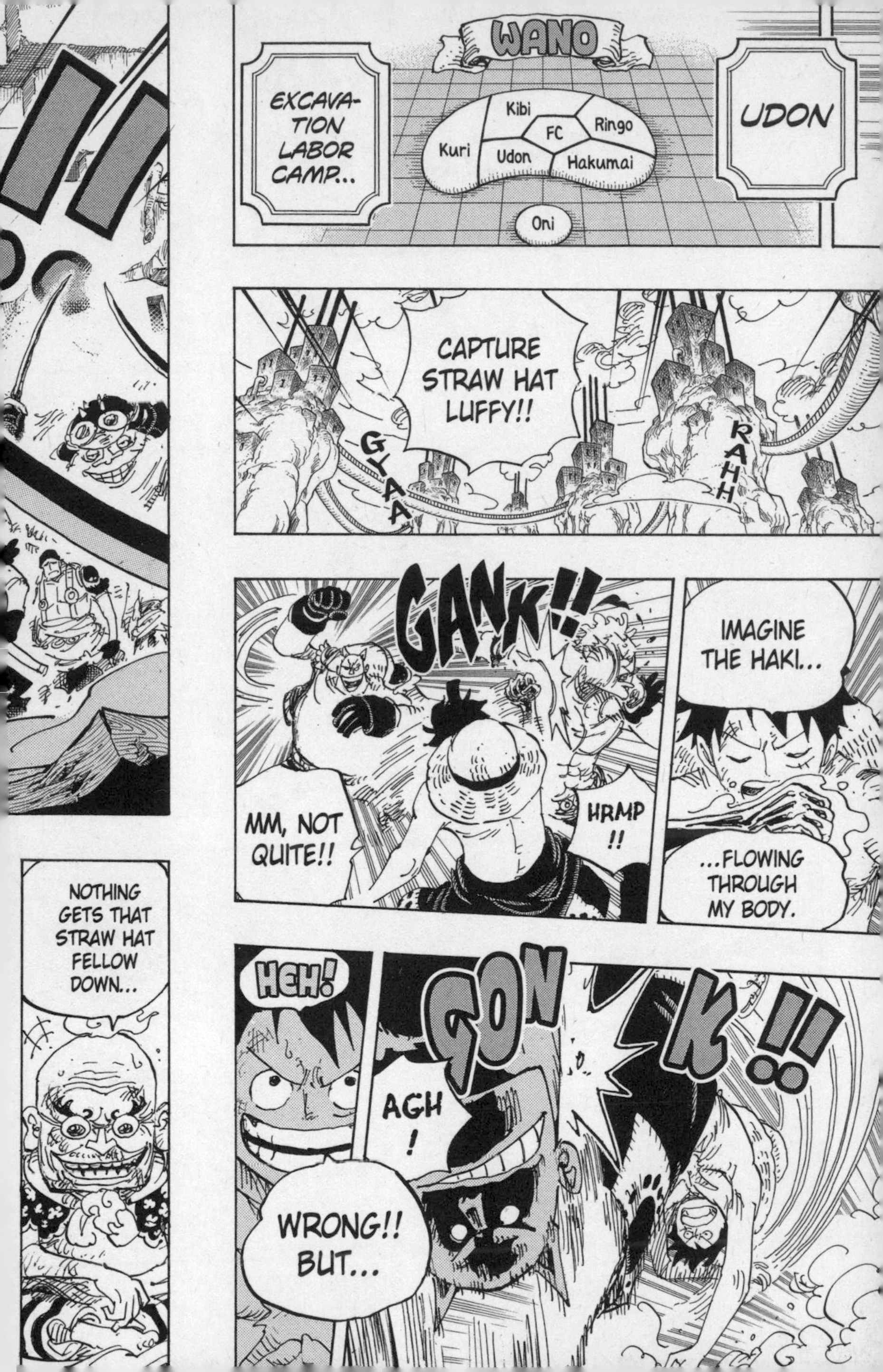
UDON
WANO
EXCAVATION LABOR CAMP...
Kibi
Ringo
FC
Kuri
Udon
Hakumai
Oni
RAHH
CAPTURE STRAW HAT LUFFY!!
GYAA
IMAGINE THE HAKI...
...FLOWING THROUGH MY BODY.
GANK!!
HRMP !!
MM, NOT QUITE!!
GONK!!
AGH !
HEH!
WRONG!! BUT...
NOTHING GETS THAT STRAW HAT FELLOW DOWN...

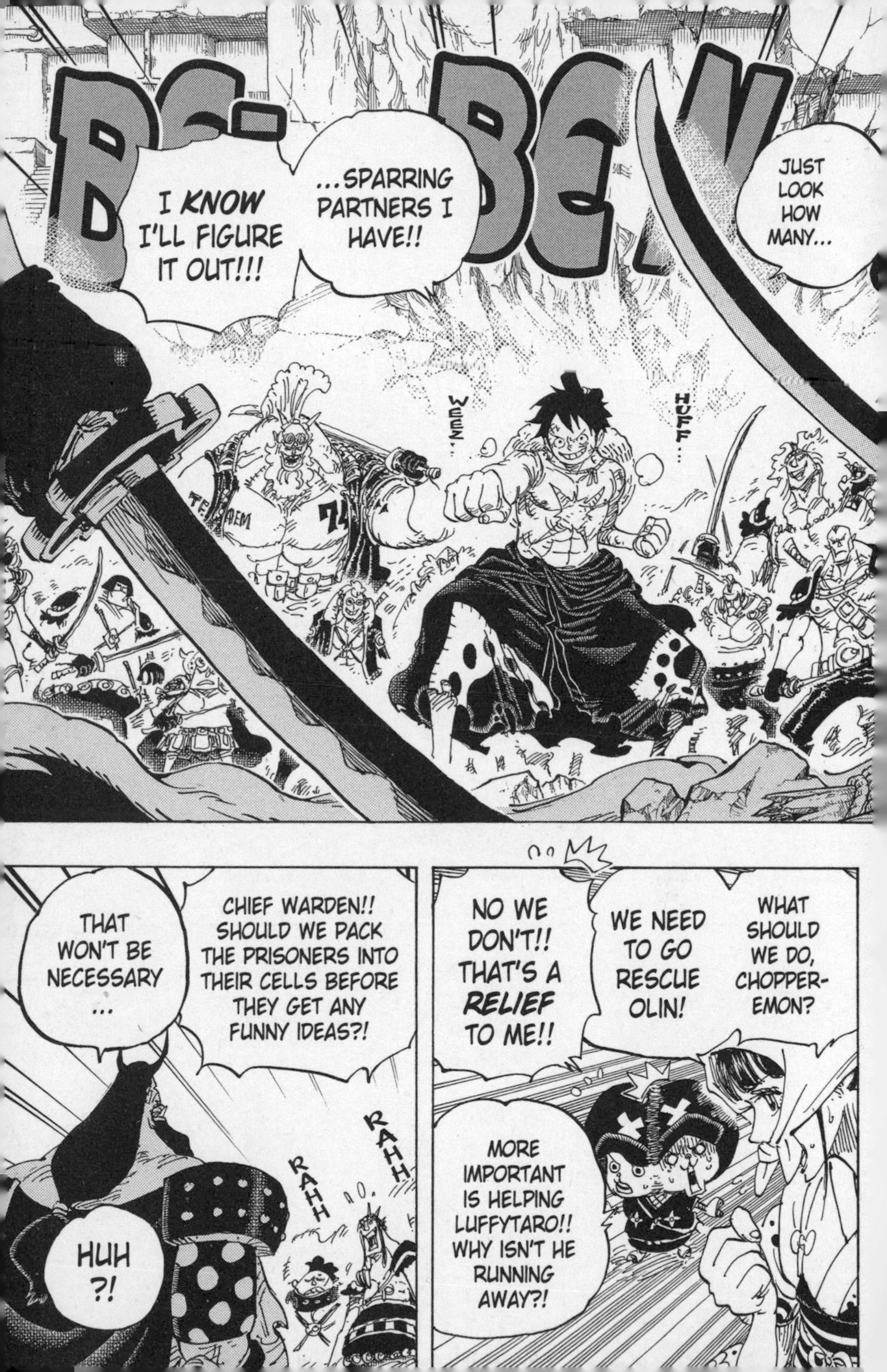
JUST LOOK HOW MANY...
...SPARRING PARTNERS I HAVE!!
I KNOW I'LL FIGURE IT OUT!!!
HUFF...
WEEZ...
WHAT SHOULD WE DO, CHOPPER-EMON?
WE NEED TO GO RESCUE OLIN!
NO WE DON'T!! THAT'S A RELIEF TO ME!!
MORE IMPORTANT IS HELPING LUFFYTARO!! WHY ISN'T HE RUNNING AWAY?!
CHIEF WARDEN!! SHOULD WE PACK THE PRISONERS INTO THEIR CELLS BEFORE THEY GET ANY FUNNY IDEAS?!
THAT WON'T BE NECESSARY ...
RAHH
RAHH
HUH ?!

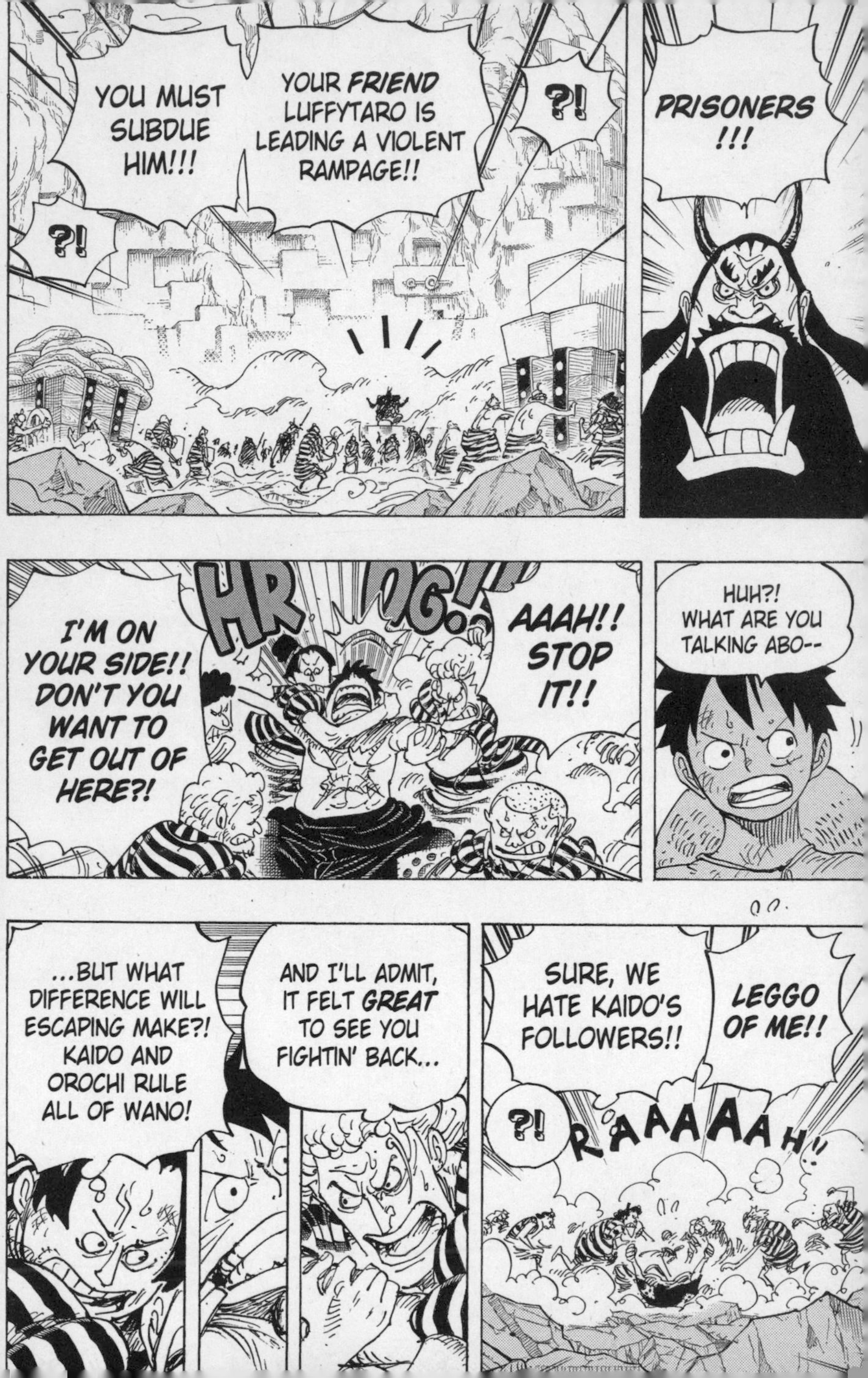
PRISONERS!!!
?!
YOUR FRIEND LUFFYTARO IS LEADING A VIOLENT RAMPAGE!!
YOU MUST SUBDUE HIM!!!
?!
HUH?! WHAT ARE YOU TALKING ABO--
AAAH!! STOP IT!!
I'M ON YOUR SIDE!! DON'T YOU WANT TO GET OUT OF HERE?!
LEGGO OF ME!!
SURE, WE HATE KAIDO'S FOLLOWERS!!
?!
RAAAAAH!!
AND I'LL ADMIT, IT FELT GREAT TO SEE YOU FIGHTIN' BACK...
...BUT WHAT DIFFERENCE WILL ESCAPING MAKE?! KAIDO AND OROCHI RULE ALL OF WANO!

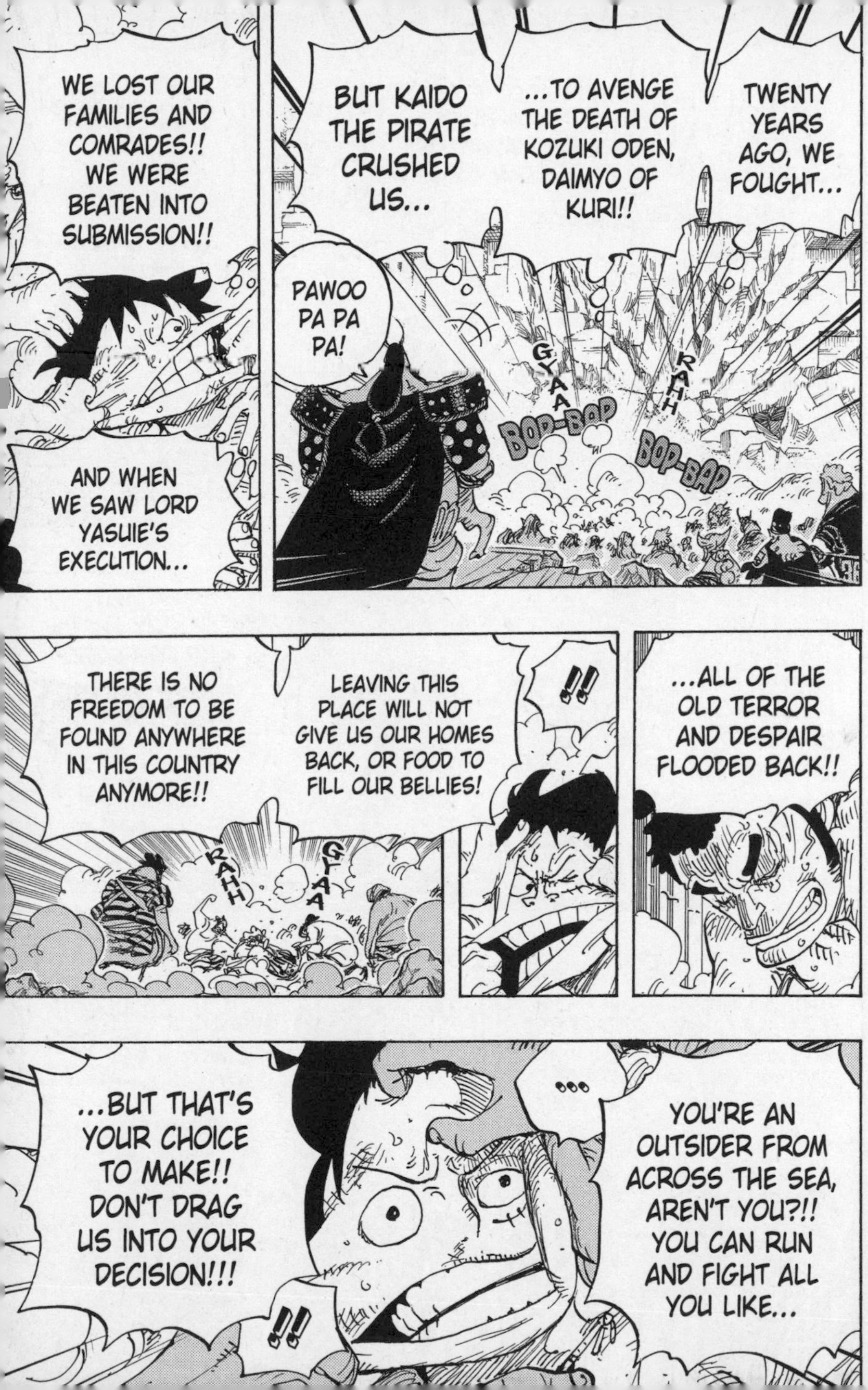
TWENTY YEARS AGO, WE FOUGHT...
...TO AVENGE THE DEATH OF KOZUKI ODEN, DAIMYO OF KURI!!
BUT KAIDO THE PIRATE CRUSHED US...
PAWOO PA PA PA!
RAHH
GYAAA
BOP-BOP
BOP-BAP
WE LOST OUR FAMILIES AND COMRADES!! WE WERE BEATEN INTO SUBMISSION!!
AND WHEN WE SAW LORD YASUIE'S EXECUTION...
...ALL OF THE OLD TERROR AND DESPAIR FLOODED BACK!!
!!
LEAVING THIS PLACE WILL NOT GIVE US OUR HOMES BACK, OR FOOD TO FILL OUR BELLIES!
THERE IS NO FREEDOM TO BE FOUND ANYWHERE IN THIS COUNTRY ANYMORE!!
GYAAA
RAHH
...
YOU'RE AN OUTSIDER FROM ACROSS THE SEA, AREN'T YOU?!! YOU CAN RUN AND FIGHT ALL YOU LIKE...
...BUT THAT'S YOUR CHOICE TO MAKE!! DON'T DRAG US INTO YOUR DECISION!!!
!!

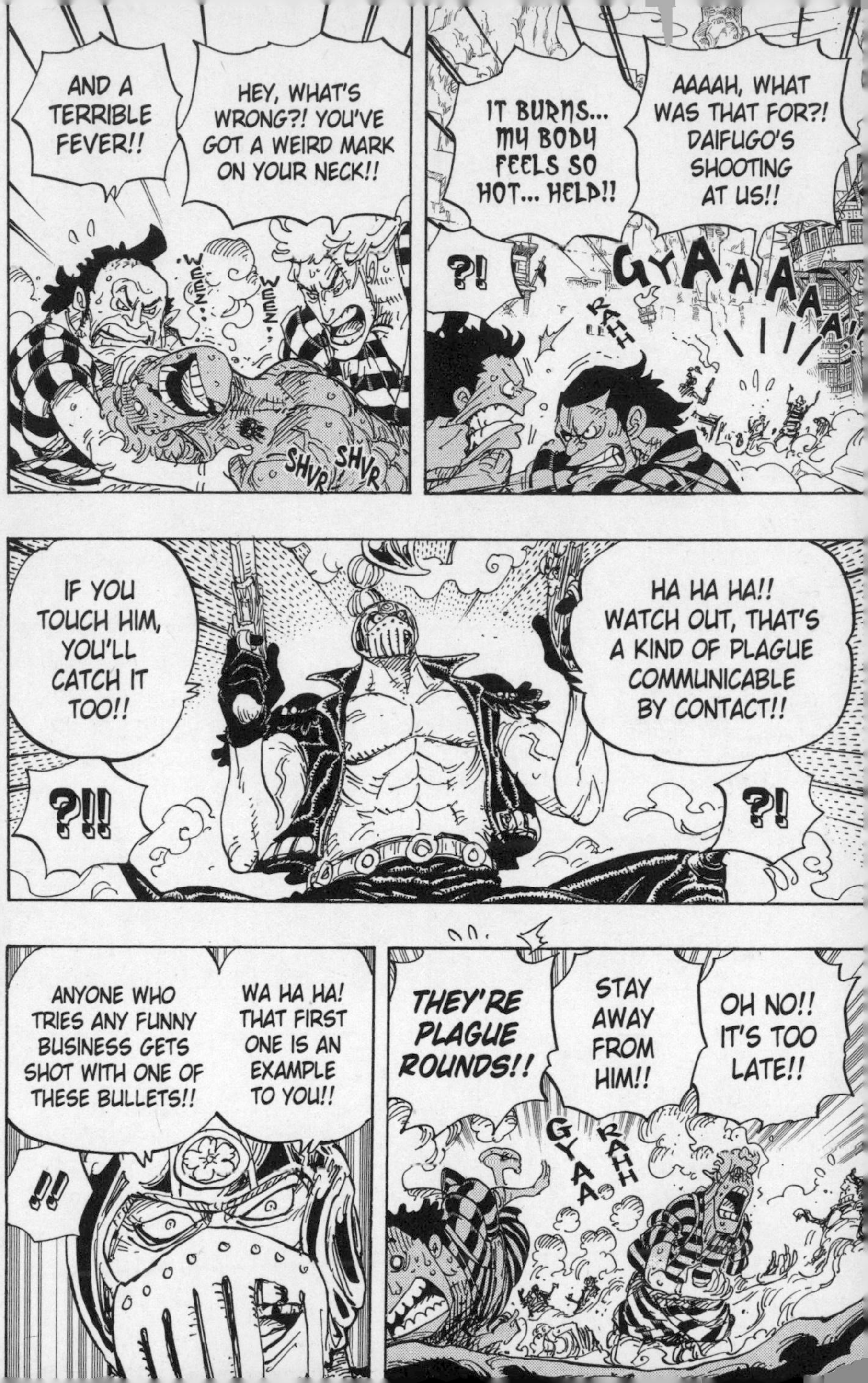
AAAAH, WHAT WAS THAT FOR?! DAIFUGO'S SHOOTING AT US!!
IT BURNS... MY BODY FEELS SO HOT... HELP!!
?!
GYAAAAAAA!
RAHH
HEY, WHAT'S WRONG?! YOU'VE GOT A WEIRD MARK ON YOUR NECK!!
AND A TERRIBLE FEVER!!
WEEZ
WEEZ
SHVR
SHVR
HA HA HA!! WATCH OUT, THAT'S A KIND OF PLAGUE COMMUNICABLE BY CONTACT!!
IF YOU TOUCH HIM, YOU'LL CATCH IT TOO!!
?!
?!!
OH NO!! IT'S TOO LATE!!
STAY AWAY FROM HIM!!
THEY'RE PLAGUE ROUNDS!!
RAHH
GYAA
WA HA HA! THAT FIRST ONE IS AN EXAMPLE TO YOU!!
ANYONE WHO TRIES ANY FUNNY BUSINESS GETS SHOT WITH ONE OF THESE BULLETS!!
!!

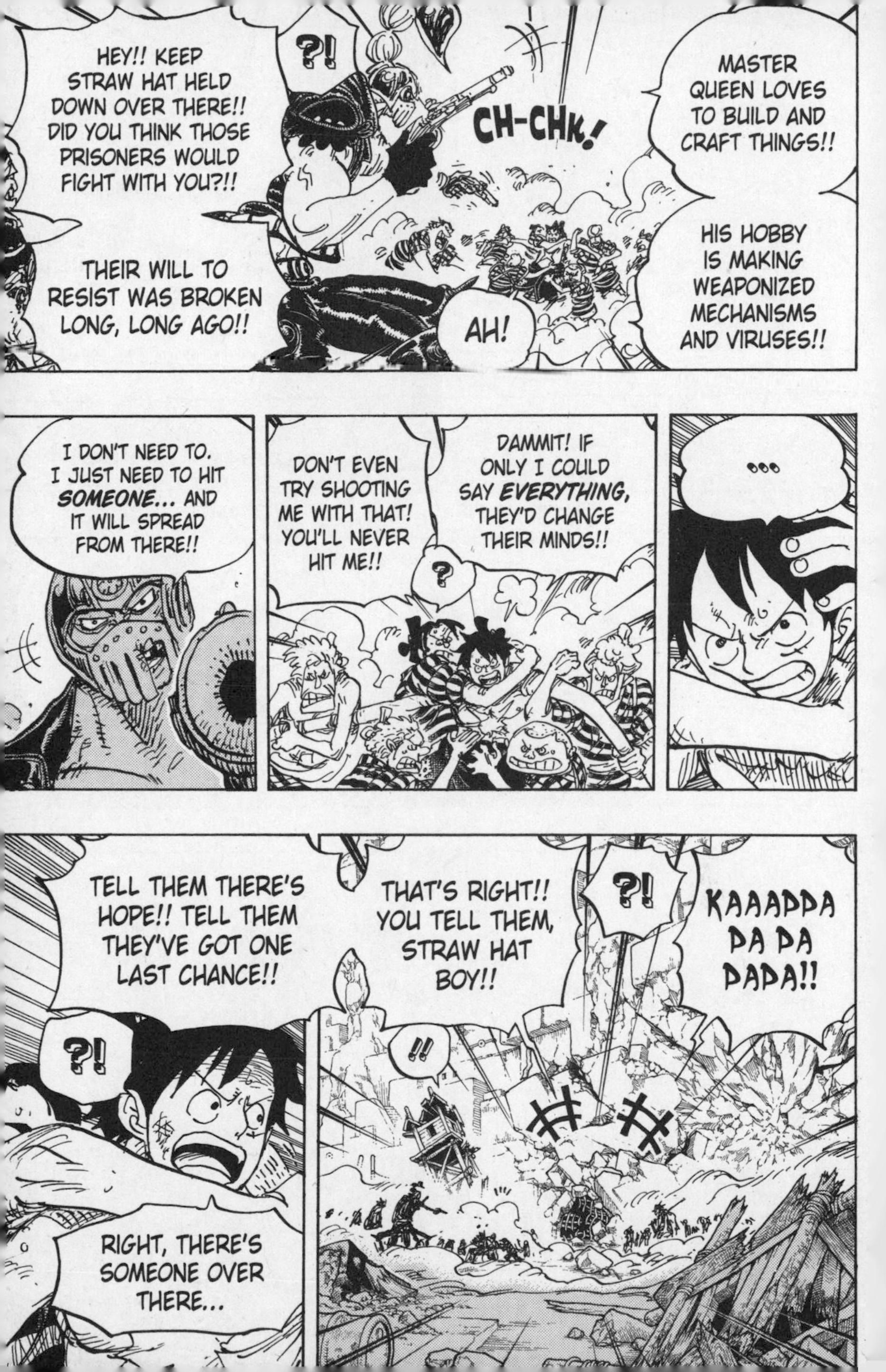
MASTER QUEEN LOVES TO BUILD AND CRAFT THINGS!!
CH-CHK!
?!
HIS HOBBY IS MAKING WEAPONIZED MECHANISMS AND VIRUSES!!
AH!
HEY!! KEEP STRAW HAT HELD DOWN OVER THERE!! DID YOU THINK THOSE PRISONERS WOULD FIGHT WITH YOU?!!
THEIR WILL TO RESIST WAS BROKEN LONG, LONG AGO!!
...
DAMMIT! IF ONLY I COULD SAY *EVERYTHING*, THEY'D CHANGE THEIR MINDS!!
DON'T EVEN TRY SHOOTING ME WITH THAT! YOU'LL NEVER HIT ME!!
?
I DON'T NEED TO. I JUST NEED TO HIT *SOMEONE...* AND IT WILL SPREAD FROM THERE!!
KAAAPPA PA PA PAPA!!
?!
THAT'S RIGHT!! YOU TELL THEM, STRAW HAT BOY!!
!!
TELL THEM THERE'S HOPE!! TELL THEM THEY'VE GOT ONE LAST CHANCE!!
?!
RIGHT, THERE'S SOMEONE OVER THERE...

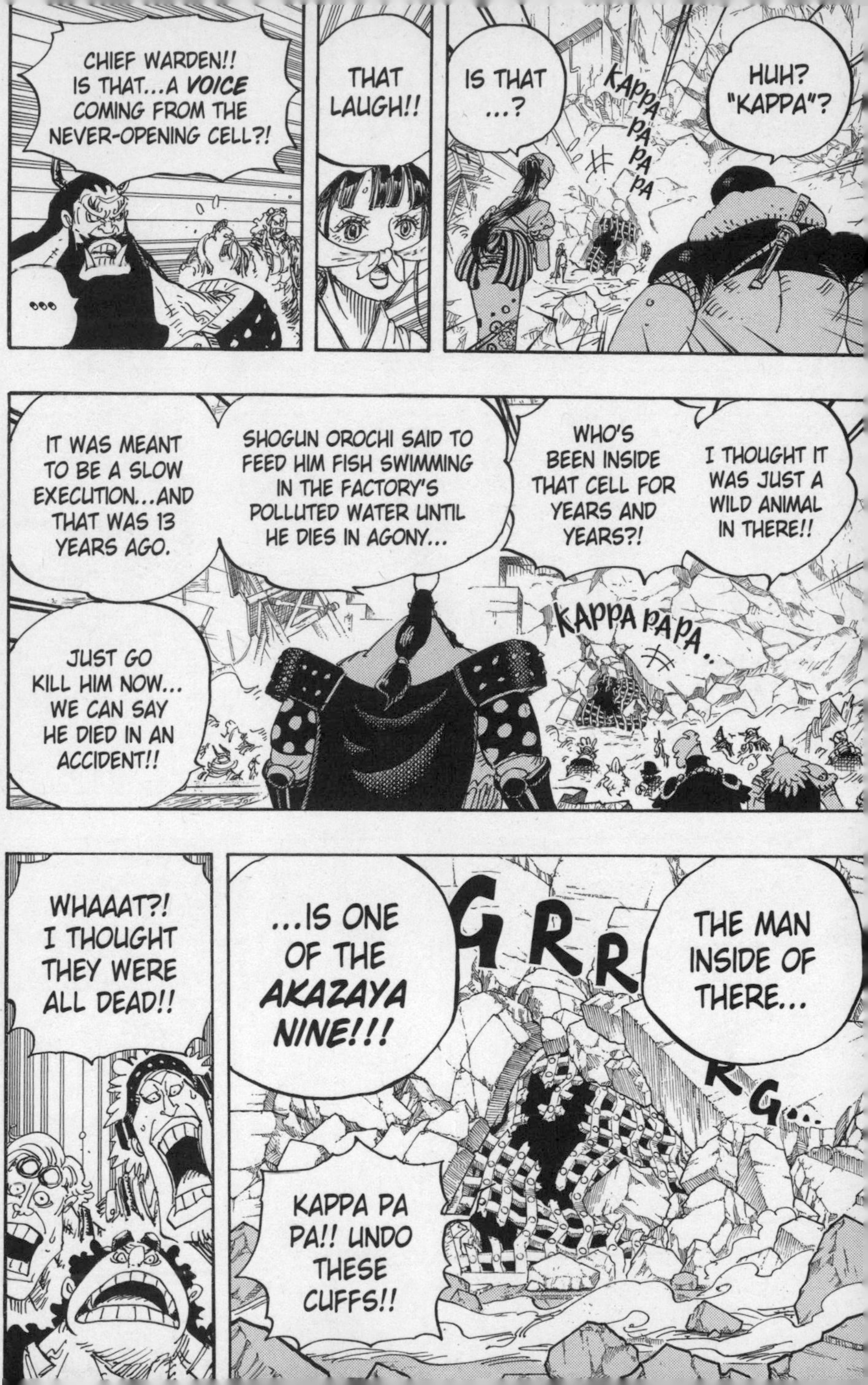
HUH? "KAPPA"?
IS THAT ...?
KAPPA PA PA PA PA
THAT LAUGH!!
CHIEF WARDEN!! IS THAT...A *VOICE* COMING FROM THE NEVER-OPENING CELL?!
...
I THOUGHT IT WAS JUST A WILD ANIMAL IN THERE!!
WHO'S BEEN INSIDE THAT CELL FOR YEARS AND YEARS?!
SHOGUN OROCHI SAID TO FEED HIM FISH SWIMMING IN THE FACTORY'S POLLUTED WATER UNTIL HE DIES IN AGONY...
IT WAS MEANT TO BE A SLOW EXECUTION...AND THAT WAS 13 YEARS AGO.
KAPPA PAPA..
JUST GO KILL HIM NOW... WE CAN SAY HE DIED IN AN ACCIDENT!!
THE MAN INSIDE OF THERE...
...IS ONE OF THE *AKAZAYA NINE!!!*
GRRRRG..
KAPPA PA PA!! UNDO THESE CUFFS!!
WHAAAT?! I THOUGHT THEY WERE ALL DEAD!!

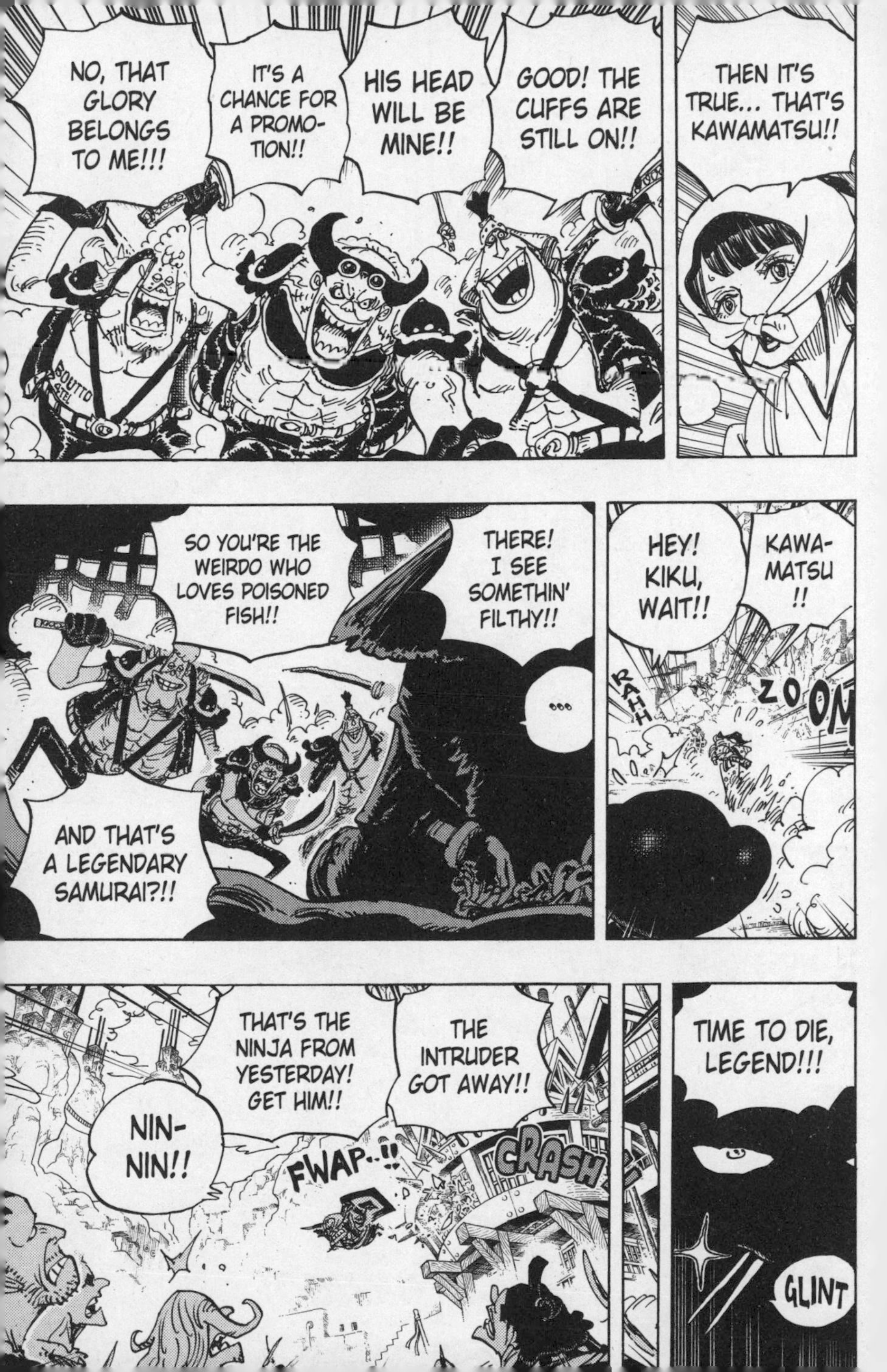
THEN IT'S TRUE... THAT'S KAWAMATSU!!
GOOD! THE CUFFS ARE STILL ON!!
HIS HEAD WILL BE MINE!!
IT'S A CHANCE FOR A PROMOTION!!
NO, THAT GLORY BELONGS TO ME!!!
KAWAMATSU!!
HEY! KIKU, WAIT!!
RAHH
ZOOM
THERE! I SEE SOMETHIN' FILTHY!!
SO YOU'RE THE WEIRDO WHO LOVES POISONED FISH!!
...
AND THAT'S A LEGENDARY SAMURAI?!!
TIME TO DIE, LEGEND!!!
GLINT
THE INTRUDER GOT AWAY!!
THAT'S THE NINJA FROM YESTERDAY! GET HIM!!
CRASH
FWAP..!!
NIN-NIN!!

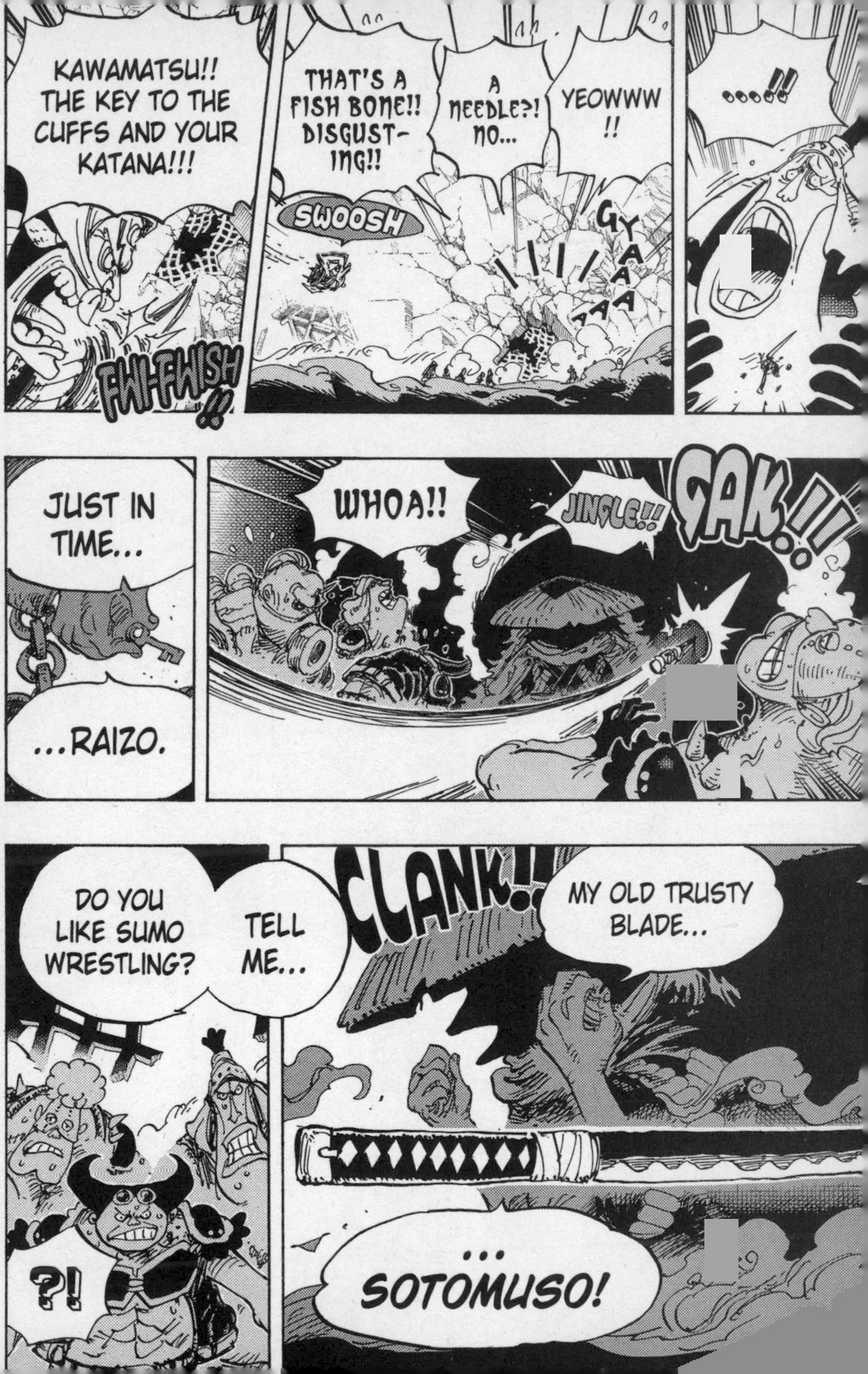

....!!
YEOWWW!!
A NEEDLE?! NO...
THAT'S A FISH BONE!! DISGUSTING!!
GYAAAAA
SWOOSH
KAWAMATSU!! THE KEY TO THE CUFFS AND YOUR KATANA!!!
FWI-FWISH!!
GAK...!!
JINGLE!!
WHOA!!
JUST IN TIME...
...RAIZO.
CLANK!!
MY OLD TRUSTY BLADE...
...SOTOMUSO!
TELL ME...
DO YOU LIKE SUMO WRESTLING?
?!

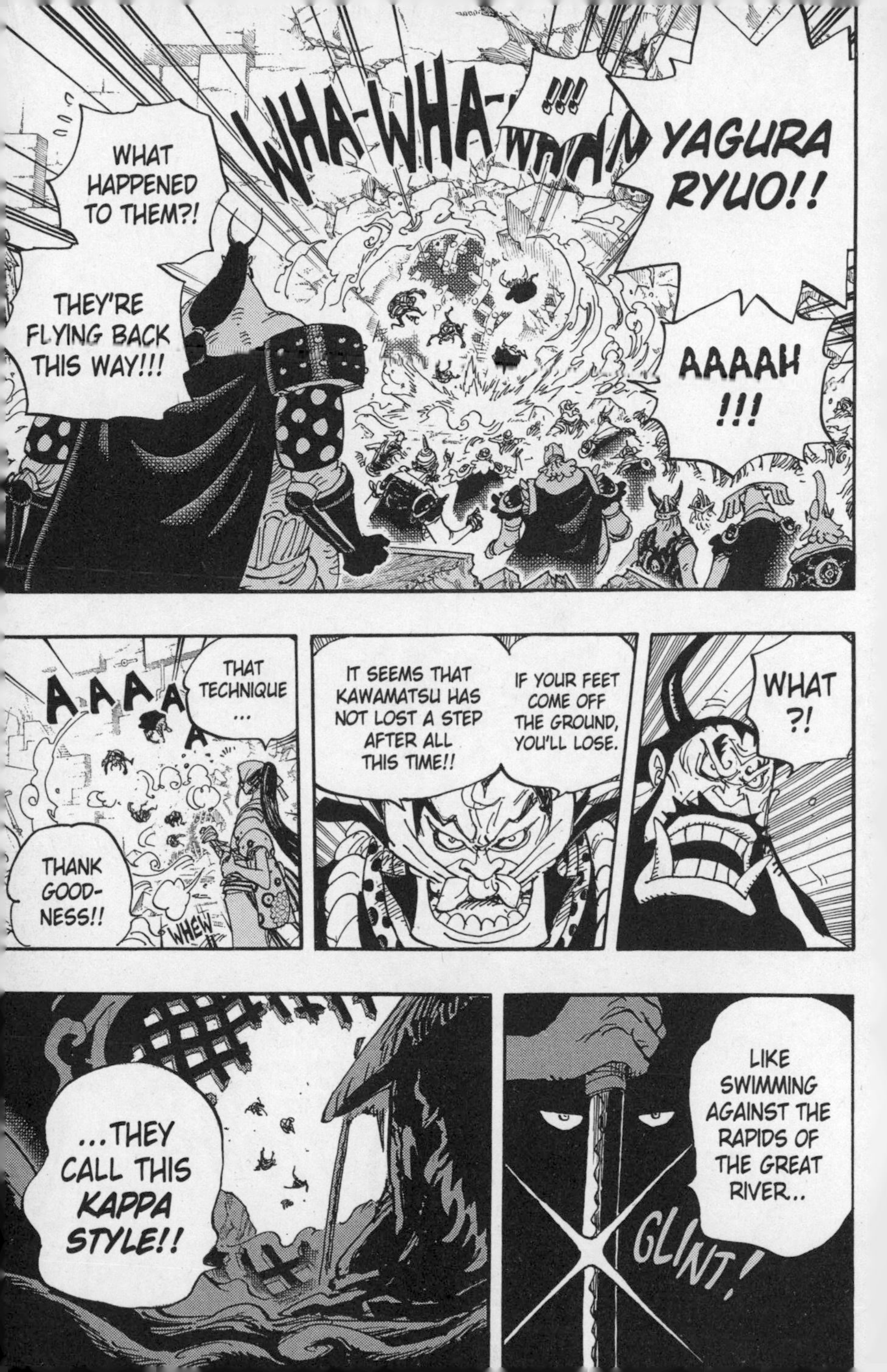
!!!
WHA-WHA-WHAN
YAGURA RYUO!!
AAAAH !!!
WHAT HAPPENED TO THEM?!
THEY'RE FLYING BACK THIS WAY!!!
WHAT ?!
IF YOUR FEET COME OFF THE GROUND, YOU'LL LOSE.
IT SEEMS THAT KAWAMATSU HAS NOT LOST A STEP AFTER ALL THIS TIME!!
THAT TECHNIQUE ...
AAAAA
THANK GOODNESS!!
WHEW
LIKE SWIMMING AGAINST THE RAPIDS OF THE GREAT RIVER..
GLINT!
...THEY CALL THIS KAPPA STYLE!!

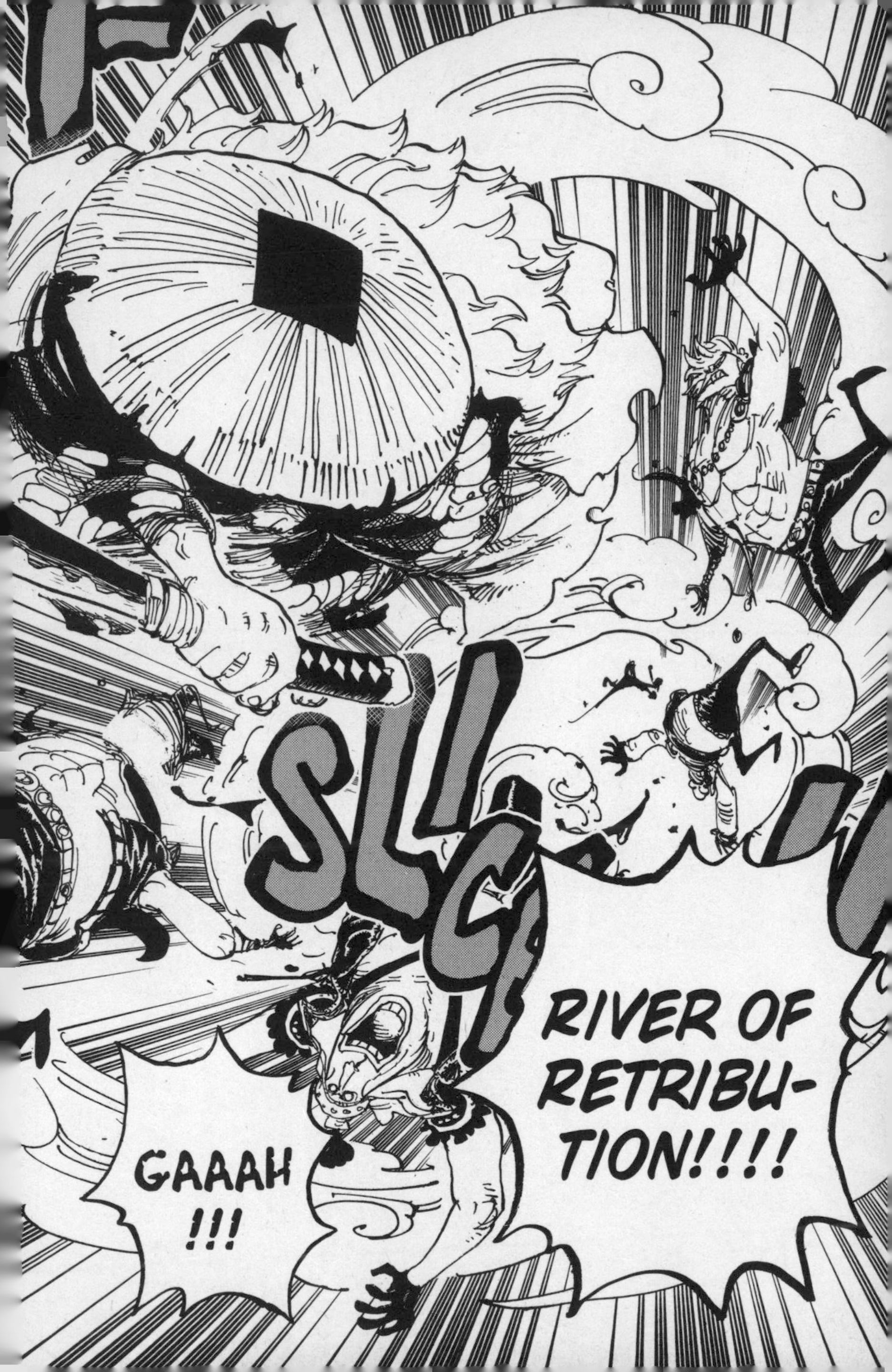
RIVER OF RETRIBU-TION!!!!
GAAAH !!!

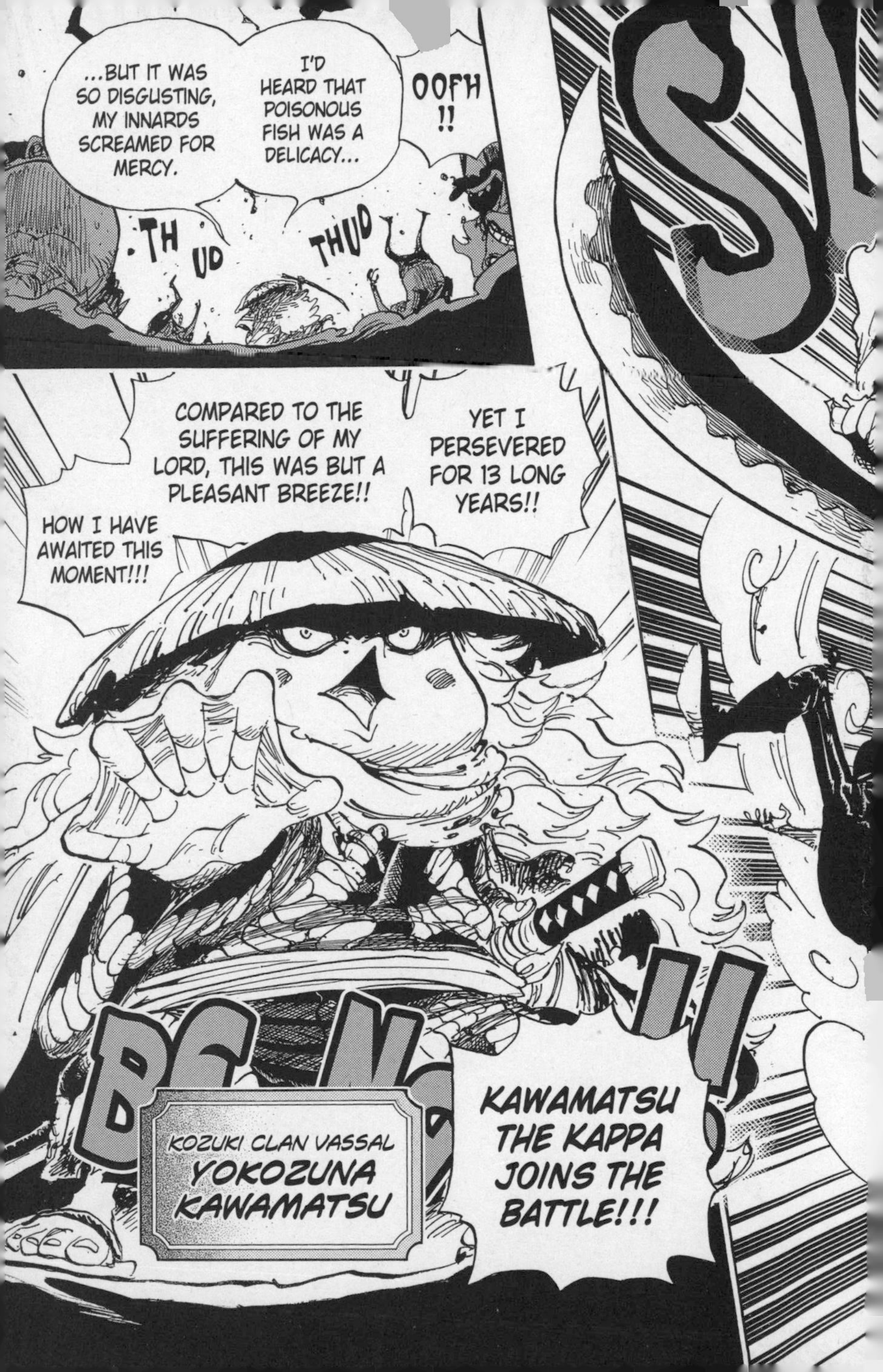
OOFH !!
I'D HEARD THAT POISONOUS FISH WAS A DELICACY...
...BUT IT WAS SO DISGUSTING, MY INNARDS SCREAMED FOR MERCY.
THUD
THUD
YET I PERSEVERED FOR 13 LONG YEARS!!
COMPARED TO THE SUFFERING OF MY LORD, THIS WAS BUT A PLEASANT BREEZE!!
HOW I HAVE AWAITED THIS MOMENT!!!
KOZUKI CLAN VASSAL
YOKOZUNA KAWAMATSU
KAWAMATSU THE KAPPA JOINS THE BATTLE!!!

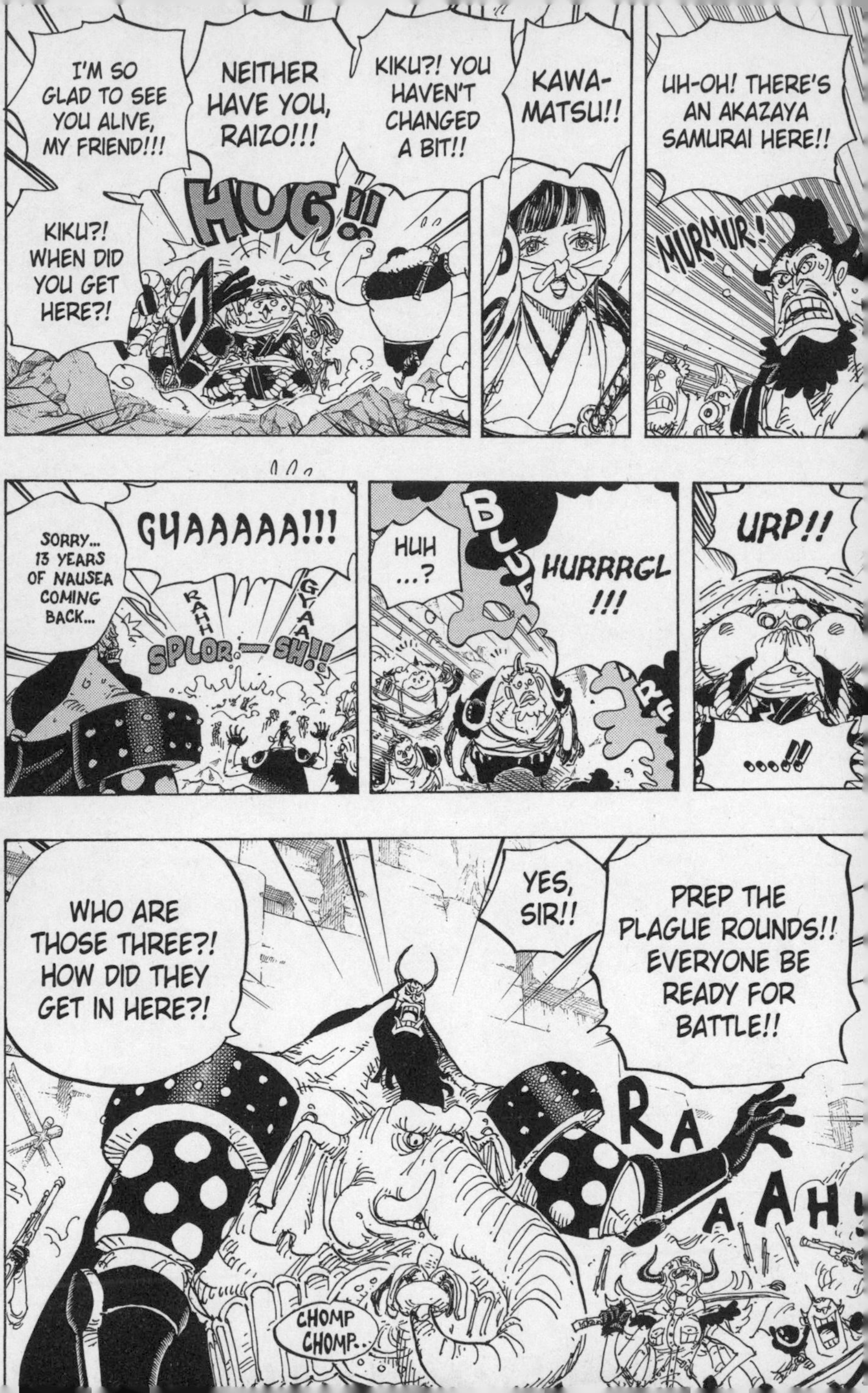
UH-OH! THERE'S AN AKAZAYA SAMURAI HERE!!
MURMUR!
KAWA-MATSU!!
KIKU?! YOU HAVEN'T CHANGED A BIT!!
NEITHER HAVE YOU, RAIZO!!!
I'M SO GLAD TO SEE YOU ALIVE, MY FRIEND!!!
HUG!!
KIKU?! WHEN DID YOU GET HERE?!
URP!!
...!!
HUH ...?
HURRRGL !!!
GYAAAAA!!!
SORRY... 13 YEARS OF NAUSEA COMING BACK...
RAHH
GYAAA
SPLOR—SH!!
PREP THE PLAGUE ROUNDS!! EVERYONE BE READY FOR BATTLE!!
YES, SIR!!
WHO ARE THOSE THREE?! HOW DID THEY GET IN HERE?!
RAAAH!
CHOMP CHOMP...

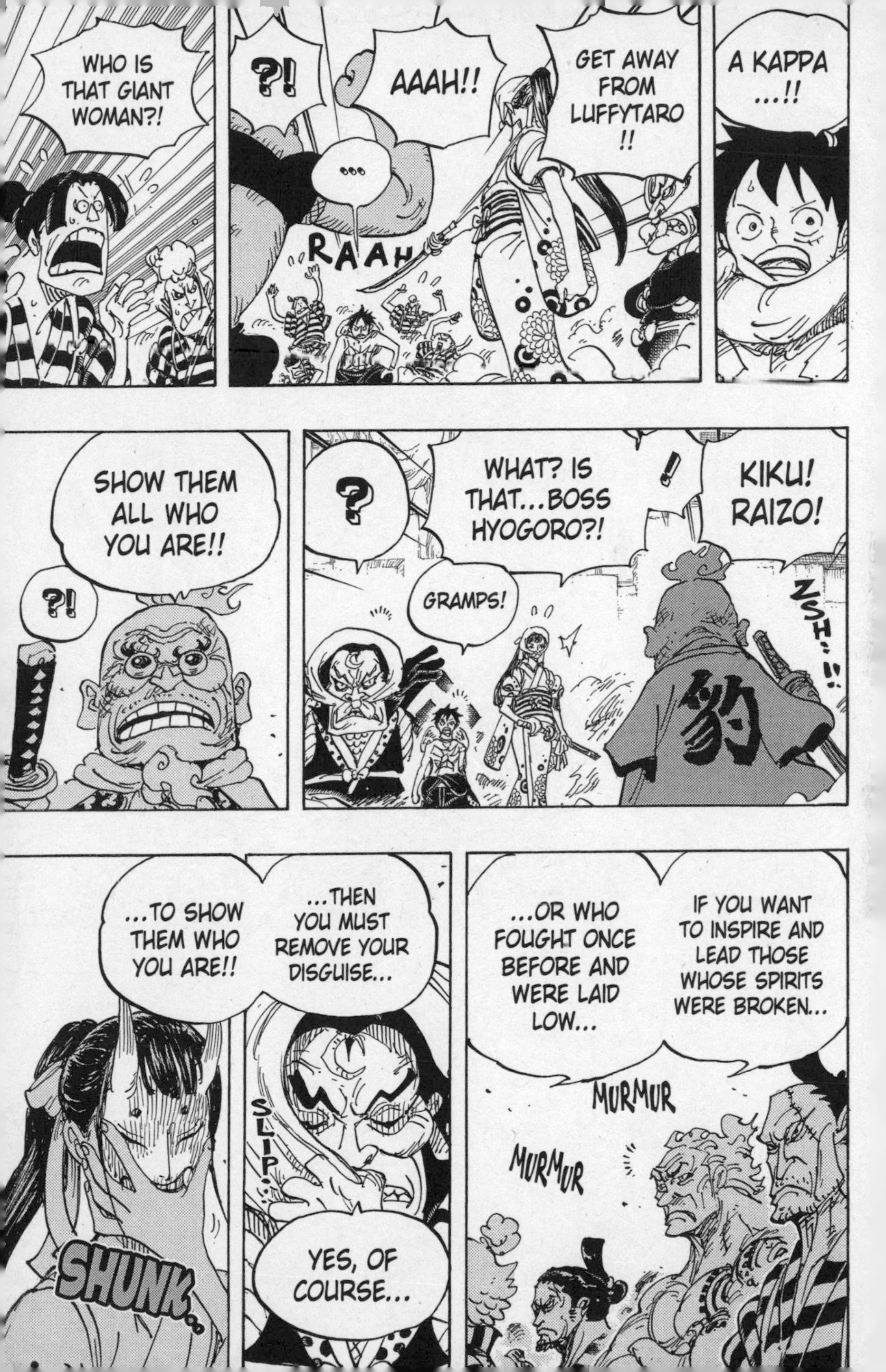
A KAPPA ...!!
GET AWAY FROM LUFFYTARO !!
AAAH!!
?!
...
RAAH
WHO IS THAT GIANT WOMAN?!
KIKU! RAIZO!
!
WHAT? IS THAT...BOSS HYOGORO?!
?
GRAMPS!
ZSH!!
SHOW THEM ALL WHO YOU ARE!!
?!
IF YOU WANT TO INSPIRE AND LEAD THOSE WHOSE SPIRITS WERE BROKEN...
...OR WHO FOUGHT ONCE BEFORE AND WERE LAID LOW...
MURMUR
MURMUR
...THEN YOU MUST REMOVE YOUR DISGUISE...
SLIP
YES, OF COURSE...
...TO SHOW THEM WHO YOU ARE!!
SHUNK

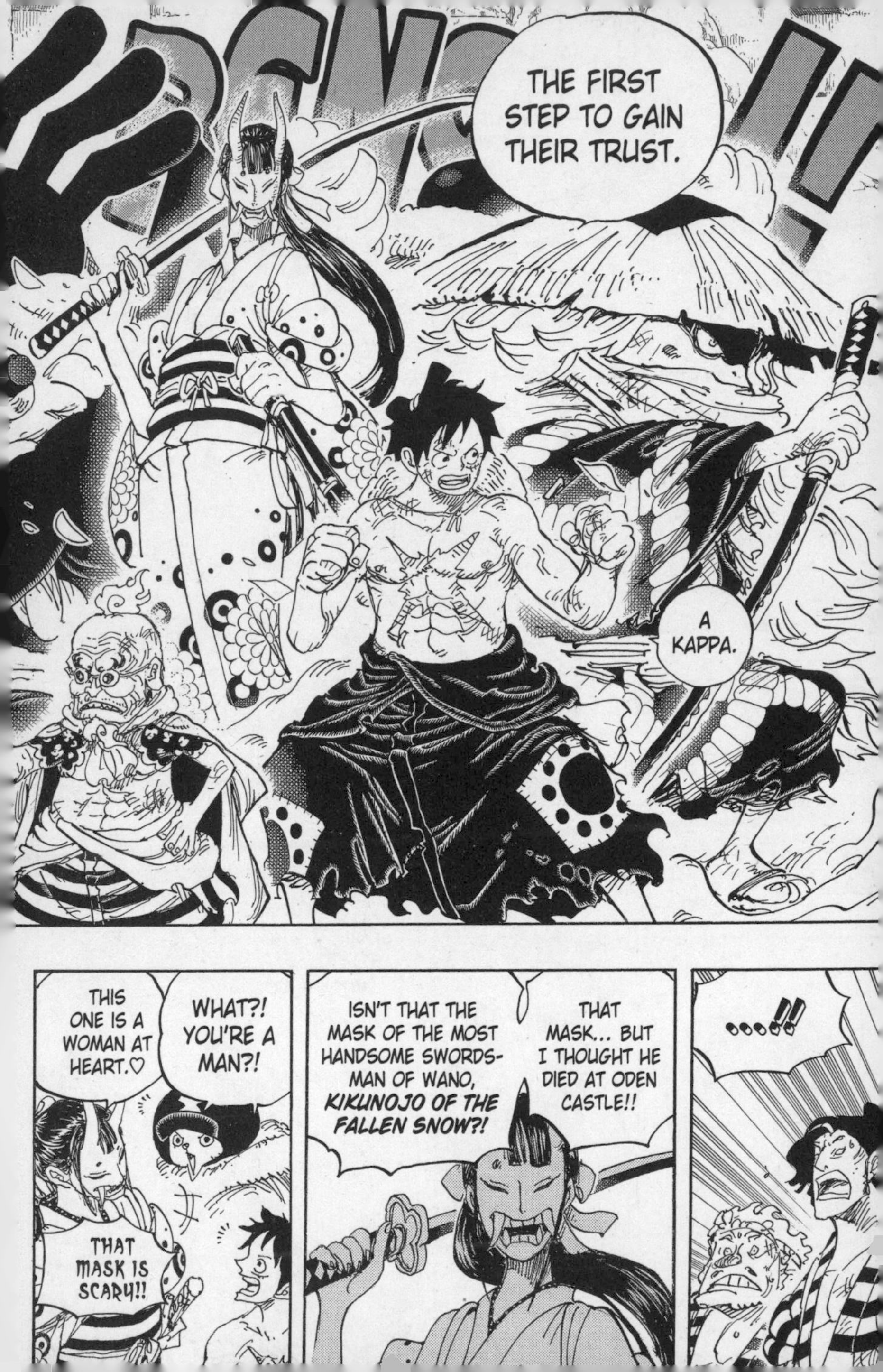
THE FIRST STEP TO GAIN THEIR TRUST.
A KAPPA.
...!!
THAT MASK... BUT I THOUGHT HE DIED AT ODEN CASTLE!!
ISN'T THAT THE MASK OF THE MOST HANDSOME SWORDS-MAN OF WANO, *KIKUNOJO OF THE FALLEN SNOW?!*
WHAT?! YOU'RE A MAN?!
THIS ONE IS A WOMAN AT HEART.♡
THAT MASK IS SCARY!!

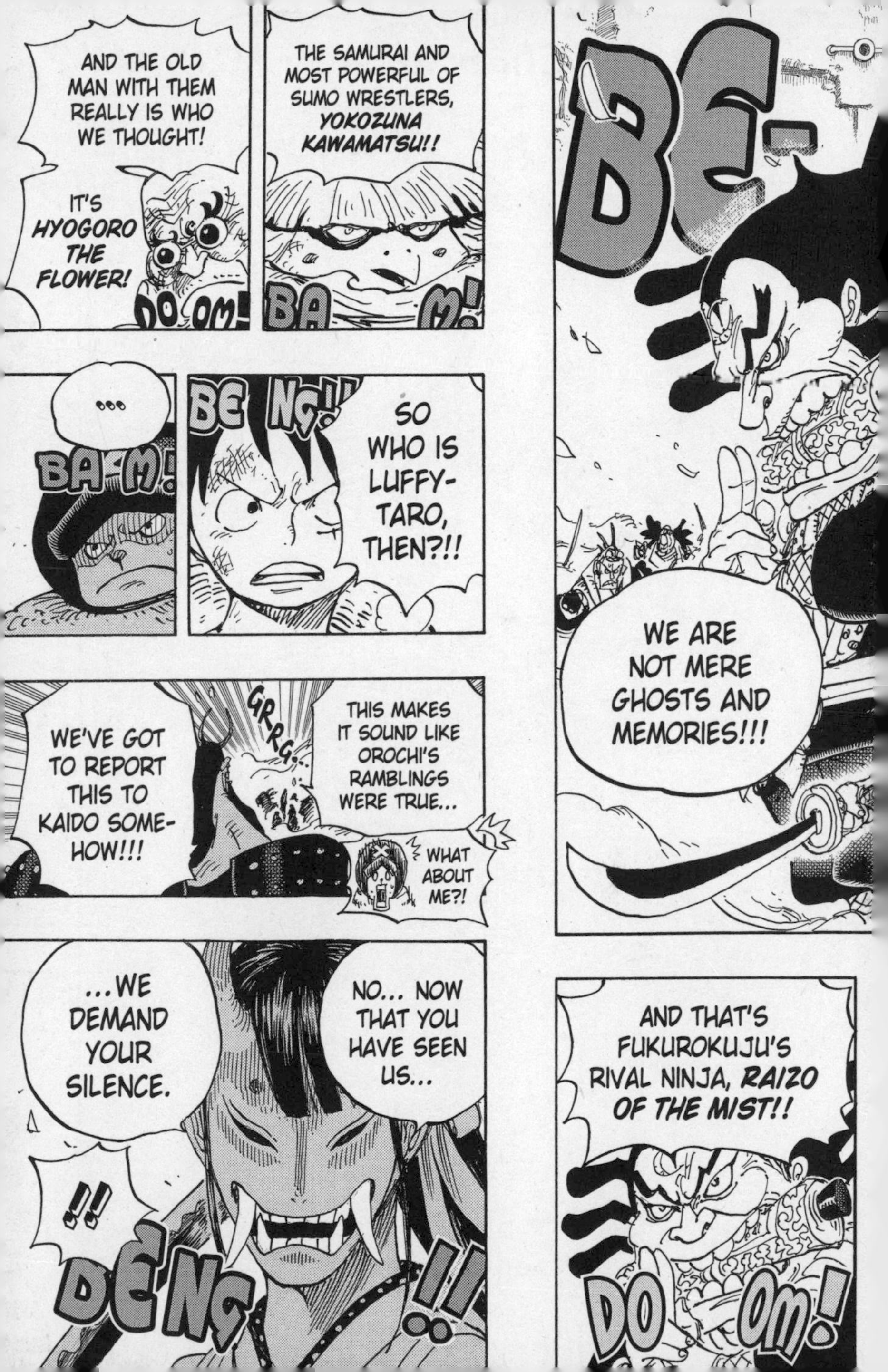
BE-
WE ARE NOT MERE GHOSTS AND MEMORIES!!!
THE SAMURAI AND MOST POWERFUL OF SUMO WRESTLERS, *YOKOZUNA KAWAMATSU!!*
BA M!
AND THE OLD MAN WITH THEM REALLY IS WHO WE THOUGHT!
IT'S *HYOGORO THE FLOWER!*
DO OM!
BE NG!!
SO WHO IS LUFFY-TARO, THEN?!!
...
BA M!
THIS MAKES IT SOUND LIKE OROCHI'S RAMBLINGS WERE TRUE...
GRRRG...
WHAT ABOUT ME?!
WE'VE GOT TO REPORT THIS TO KAIDO SOME-HOW!!!
AND THAT'S FUKUROKUJU'S RIVAL NINJA, *RAIZO OF THE MIST!!*
DO OM!
NO... NOW THAT YOU HAVE SEEN US...
...WE DEMAND YOUR SILENCE.
!!
DENG!!

Chapter 949: MUMMY

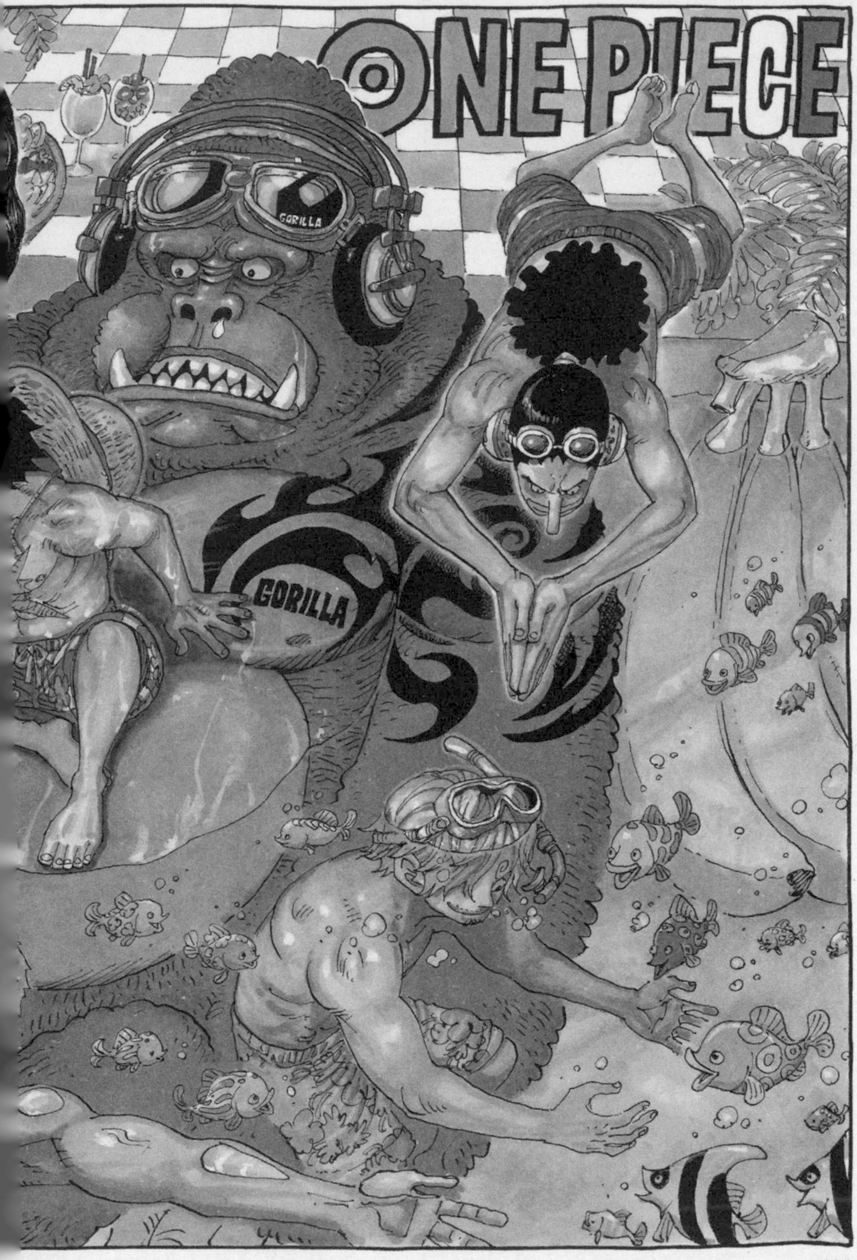
ONE PIECE
GORILLA
GORILLA

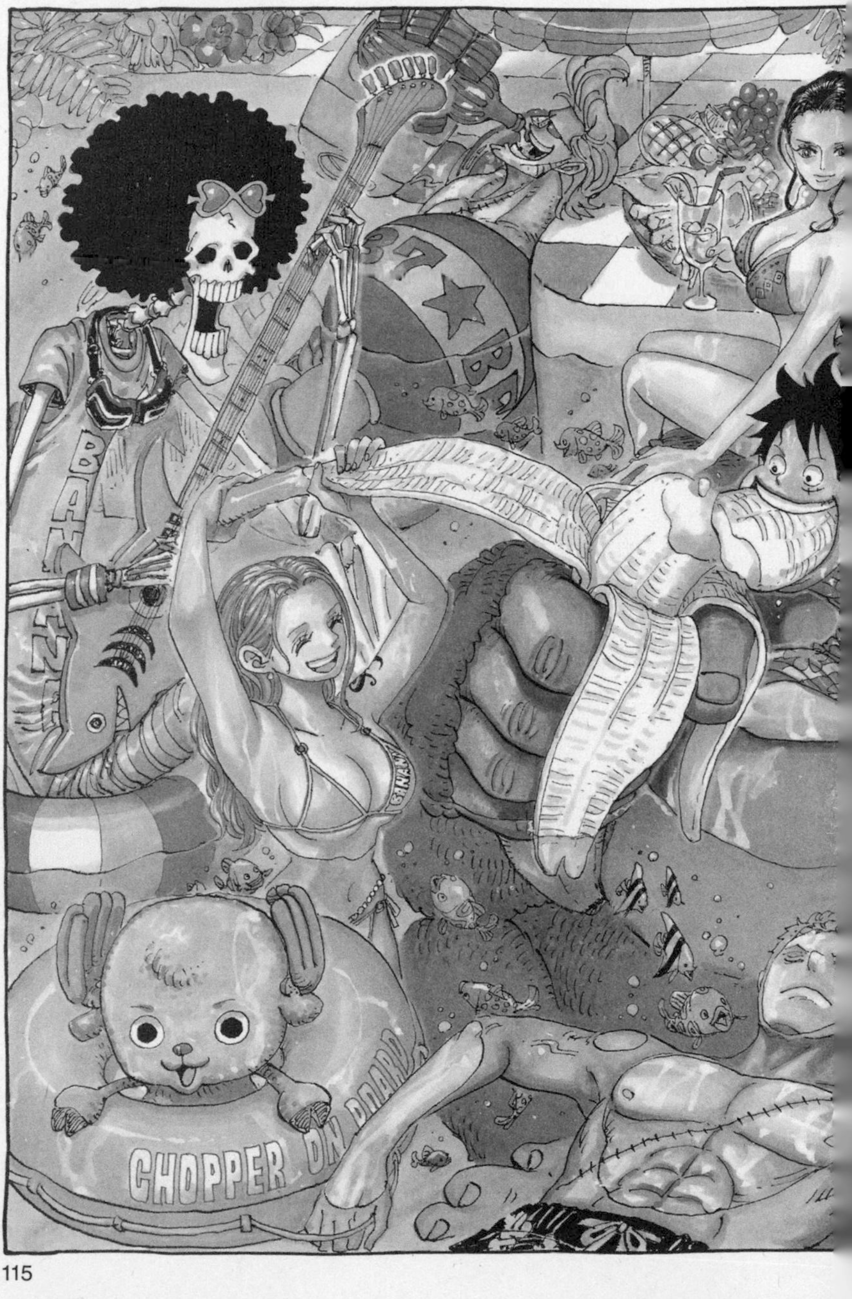
CHOPPER ON BOARD

ONE PIECE ^{vol.}94

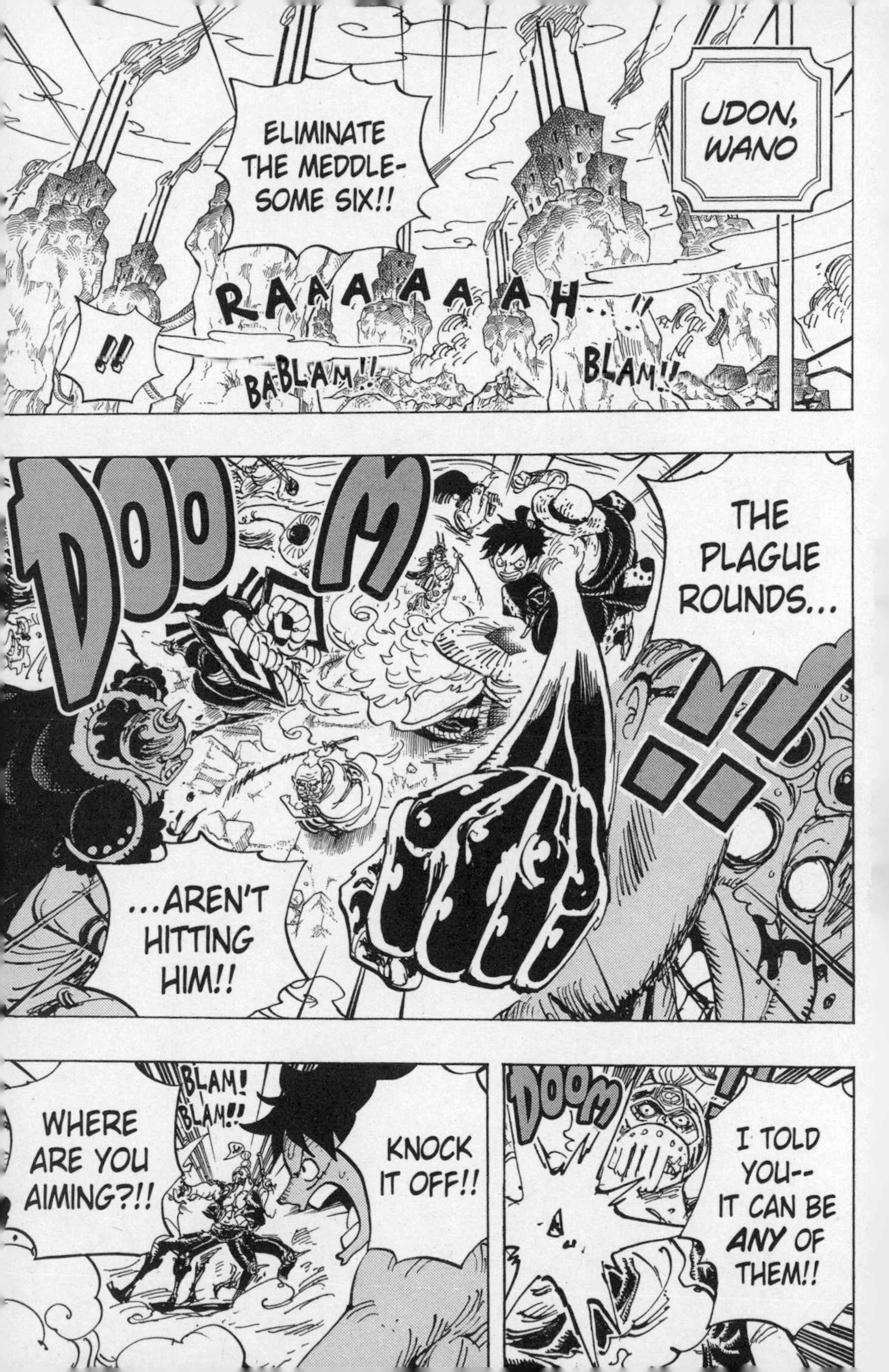
UDON, WANO
ELIMINATE THE MEDDLE-SOME SIX!!
RAAAAAAH
BLAM!!
BABLAM!!
!!
THE PLAGUE ROUNDS...
DOOM
...AREN'T HITTING HIM!!
DOOM
I TOLD YOU-- IT CAN BE ANY OF THEM!!
KNOCK IT OFF!!
BLAM! BLAM!!
WHERE ARE YOU AIMING?!!

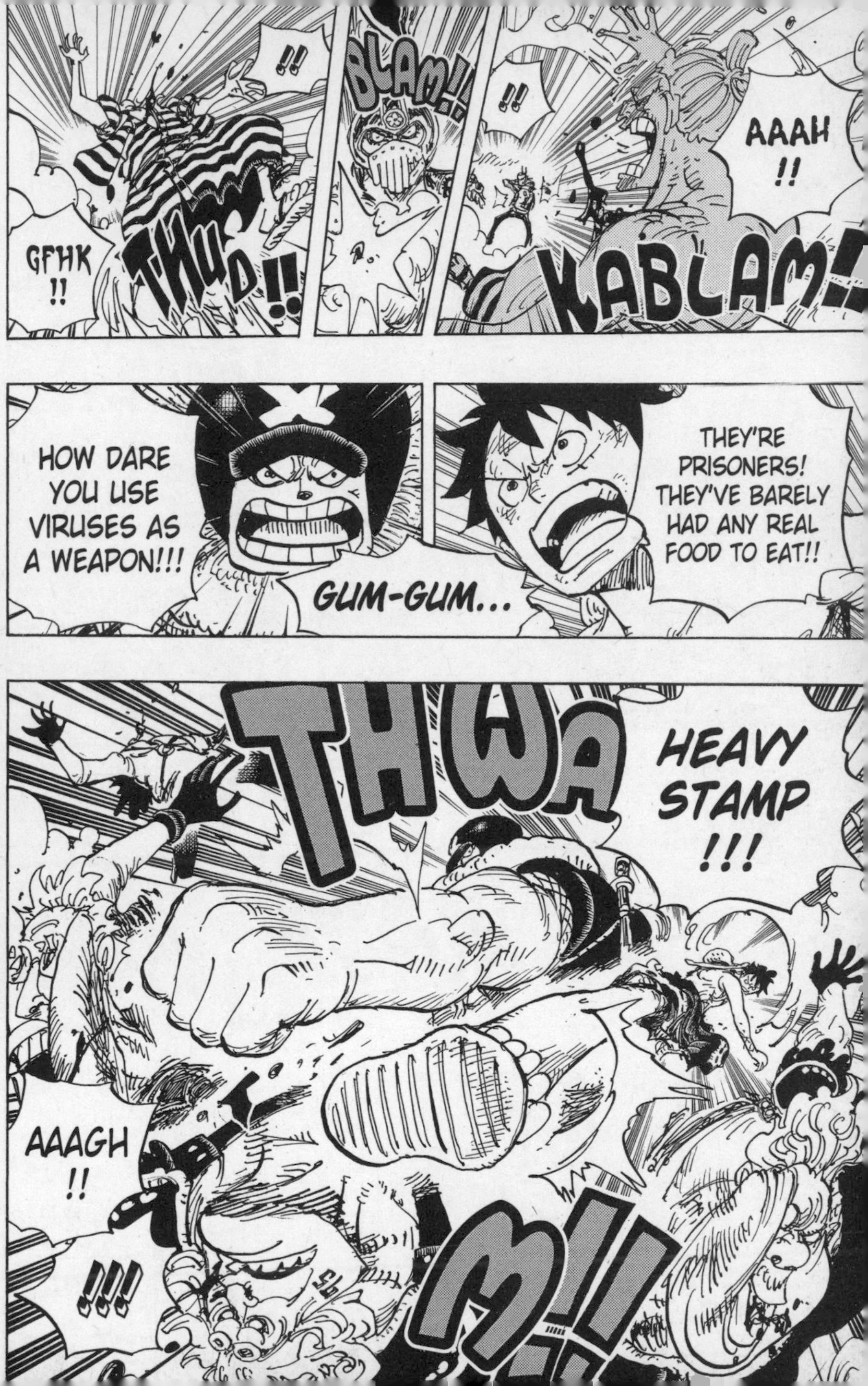
!!
AAAH !!
KABLAM!!
BLAM!!
!!
GFHK !!
THUD!!
THEY'RE PRISONERS! THEY'VE BARELY HAD ANY REAL FOOD TO EAT!!
HOW DARE YOU USE VIRUSES AS A WEAPON!!!
GUM-GUM...
HEAVY STAMP !!!
THWAM!!
AAAGH !!
!!!

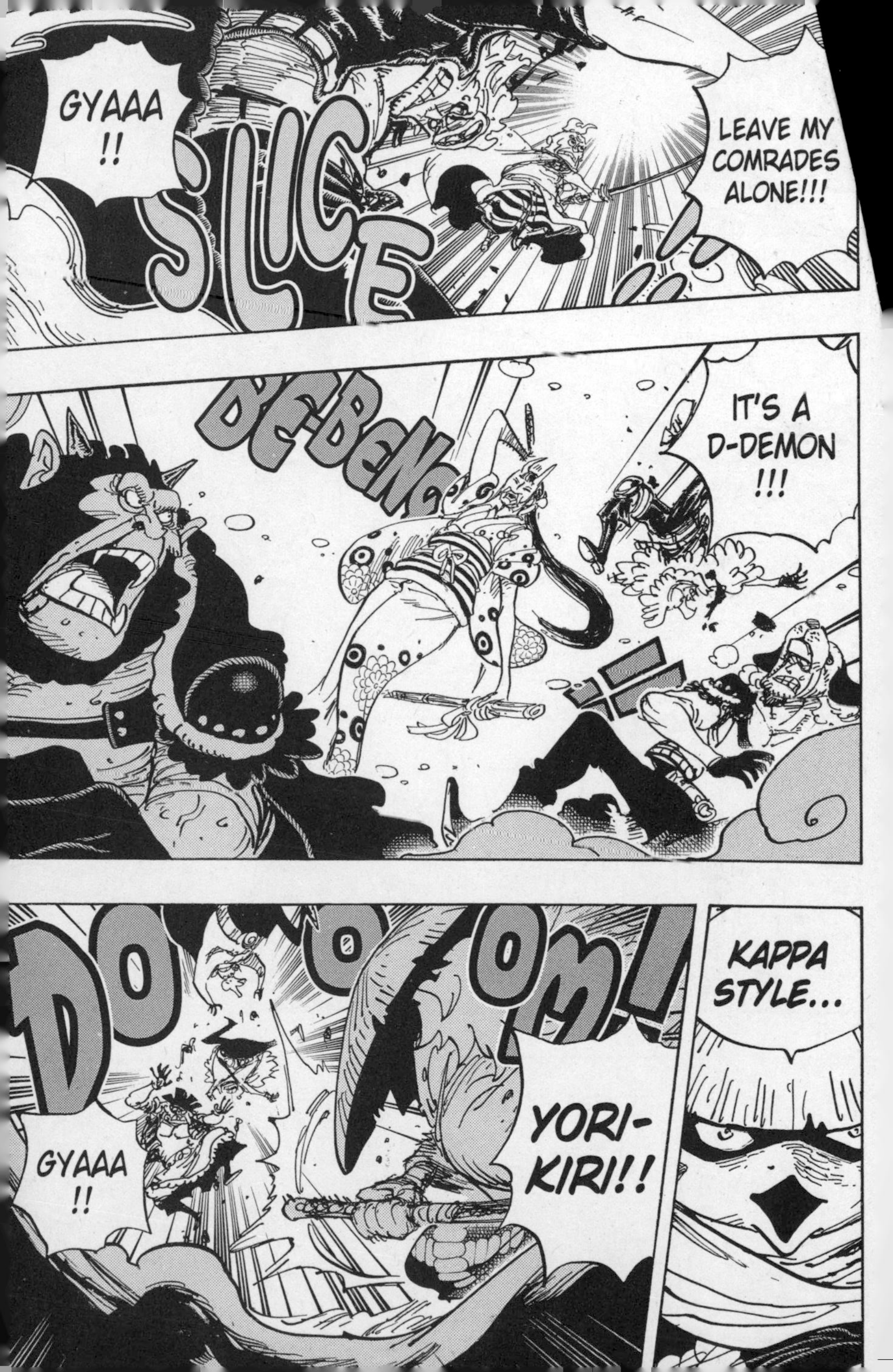

LEAVE MY COMRADES ALONE!!!
SLICE
GYAAA !!
IT'S A D-DEMON !!!
BE-BENG
KAPPA STYLE...
DOOOOM!
YORI-KIRI!!
GYAAA !!

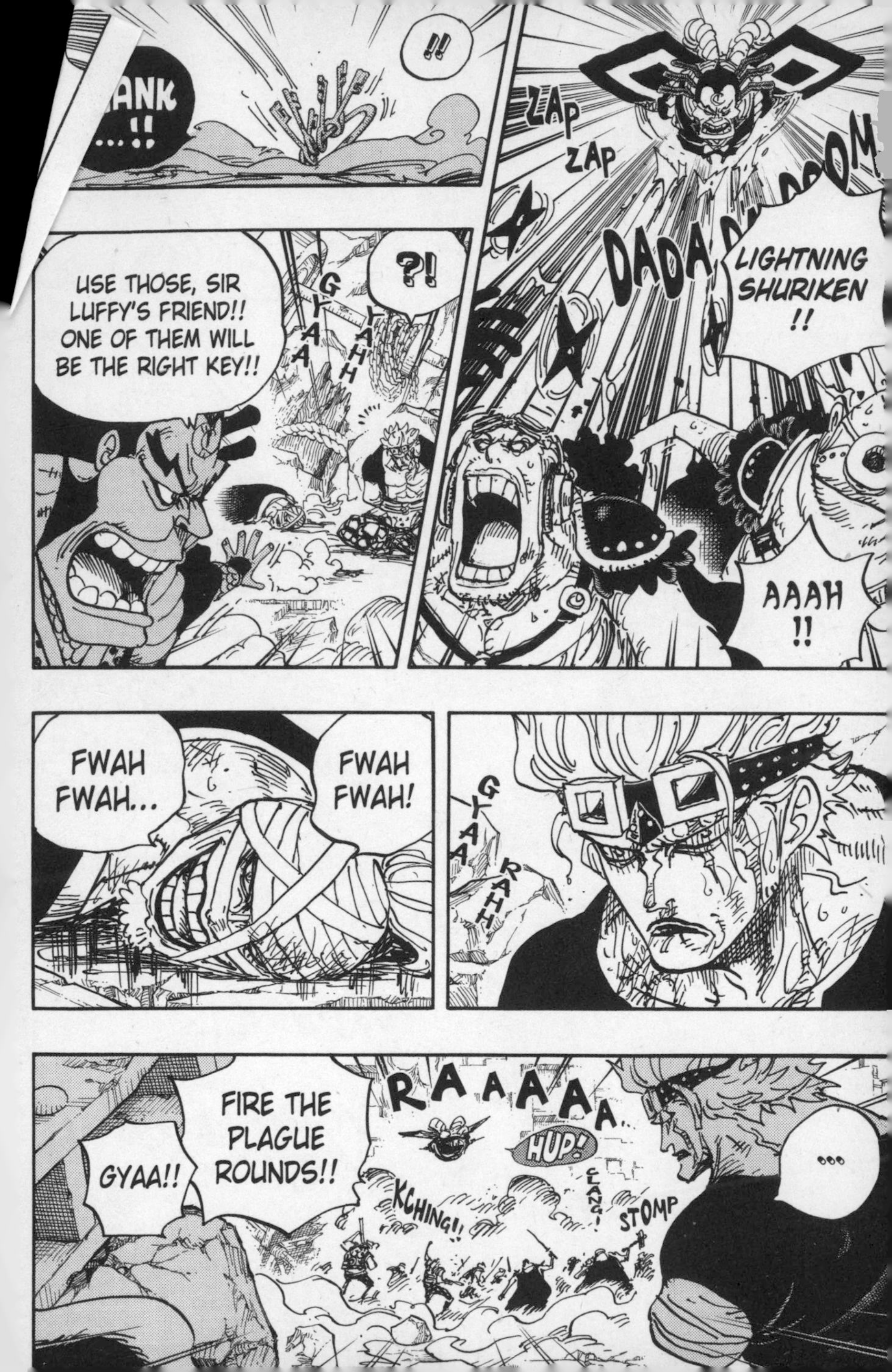
ZAP
ZAP
DOOM
DADA
LIGHTNING SHURIKEN !!
AAAH !!
ANK …!!
!!
?!
GYAA
YAHH
USE THOSE, SIR LUFFY'S FRIEND!! ONE OF THEM WILL BE THE RIGHT KEY!!
GYAAA
RAHH
FWAH FWAH!
FWAH FWAH…
…
STOMP
CLANG!
HUP!
RAAAAAA…
KCHING!!
FIRE THE PLAGUE ROUNDS!!
GYAA!!

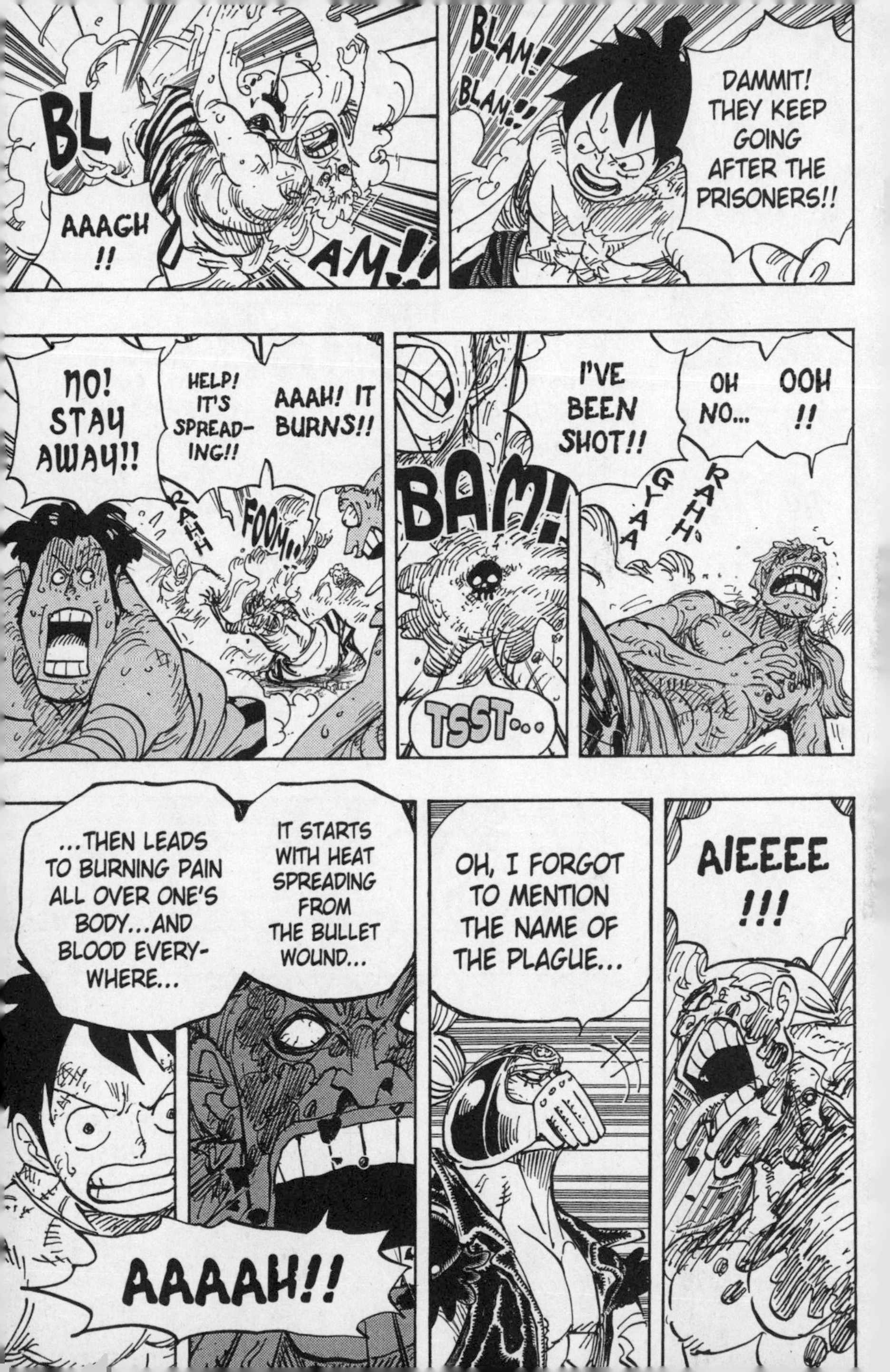
BLAM!!
BLAM!!
DAMMIT! THEY KEEP GOING AFTER THE PRISONERS!!
BLAM!!
AAAGH !!
OOH !!
OH NO...
I'VE BEEN SHOT!!
RAHH
GYAA
BAM!!
TSST...
AAAH! IT BURNS!!
HELP! IT'S SPREAD-ING!!
NO! STAY AWAY!!
RAHH
FOOM...
AIEEEE !!!
OH, I FORGOT TO MENTION THE NAME OF THE PLAGUE...
IT STARTS WITH HEAT SPREADING FROM THE BULLET WOUND...
...THEN LEADS TO BURNING PAIN ALL OVER ONE'S BODY...AND BLOOD EVERY-WHERE...
AAAAH!!

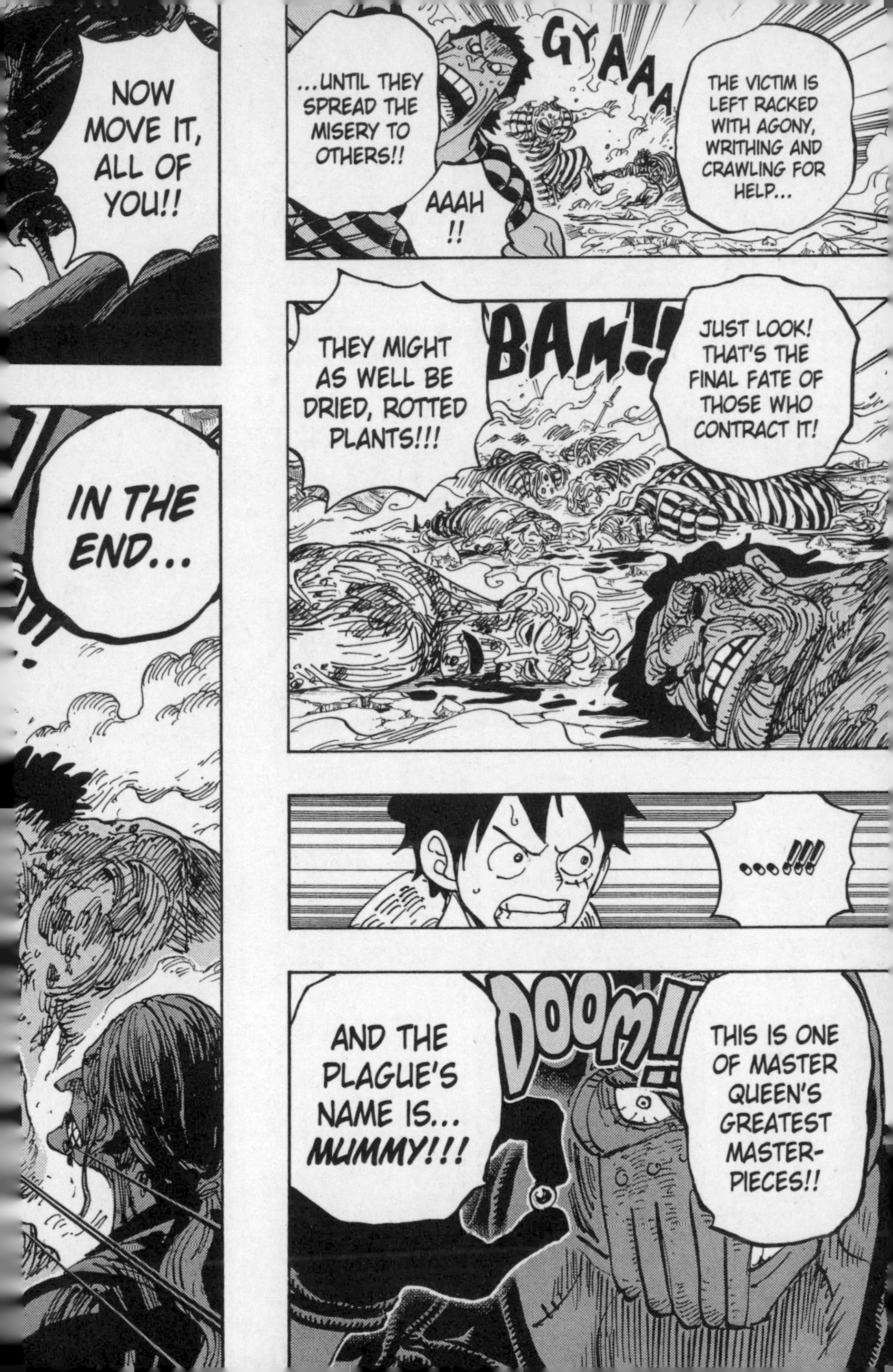
THE VICTIM IS LEFT RACKED WITH AGONY, WRITHING AND CRAWLING FOR HELP...
GYAAA
...UNTIL THEY SPREAD THE MISERY TO OTHERS!!
AAAH !!
JUST LOOK! THAT'S THE FINAL FATE OF THOSE WHO CONTRACT IT!
BAM!!
THEY MIGHT AS WELL BE DRIED, ROTTED PLANTS!!!
...!!!
THIS IS ONE OF MASTER QUEEN'S GREATEST MASTER-PIECES!!
DOOM!!
AND THE PLAGUE'S NAME IS... *MUMMY!!!*
NOW MOVE IT, ALL OF YOU!!
IN THE END...

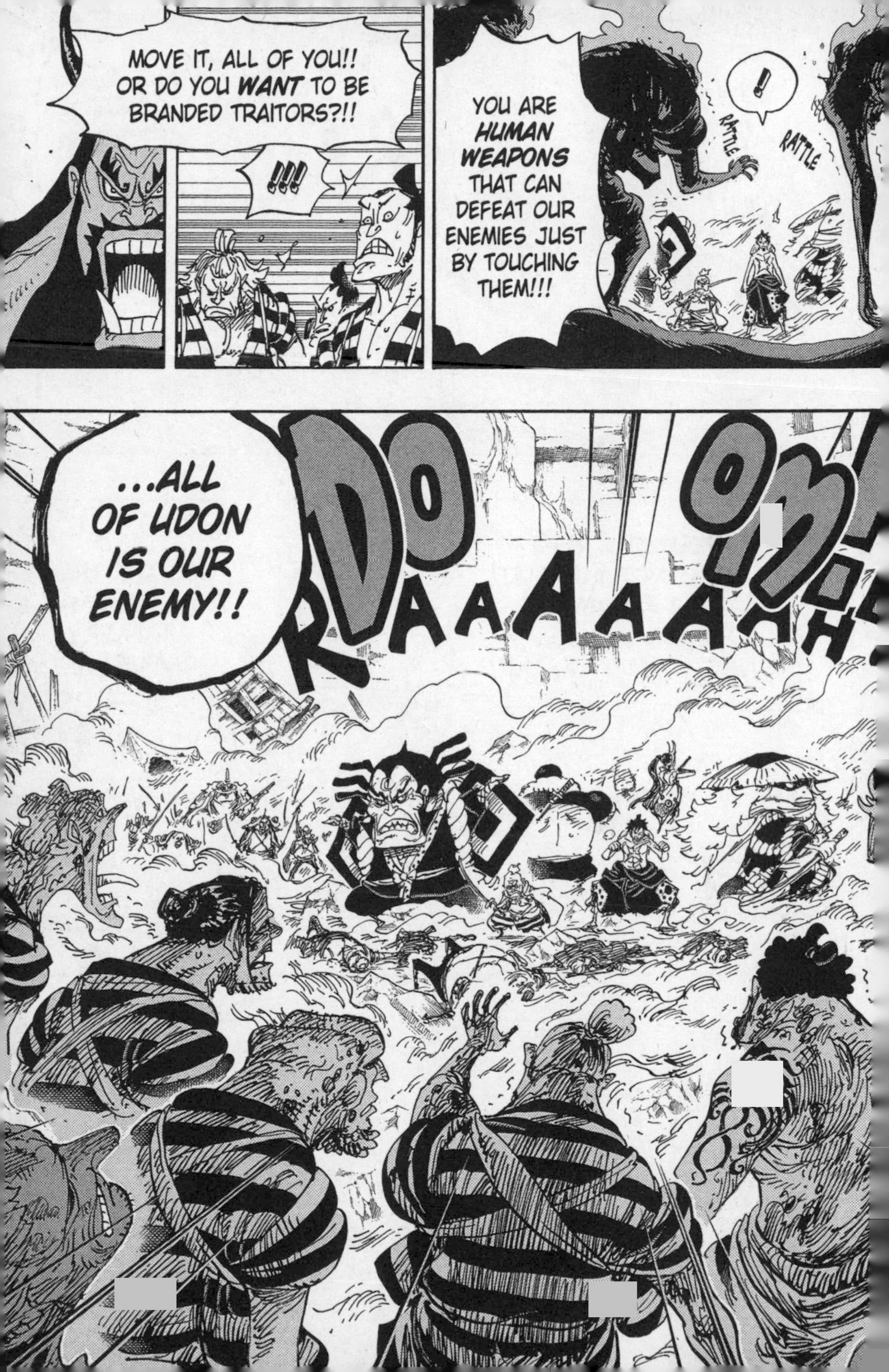
YOU ARE HUMAN WEAPONS THAT CAN DEFEAT OUR ENEMIES JUST BY TOUCHING THEM!!!
!
RATTLE
RATTLE
MOVE IT, ALL OF YOU!! OR DO YOU WANT TO BE BRANDED TRAITORS?!!
!!!
DOOM
RAAAAAAAH
...ALL OF UDON IS OUR ENEMY!!

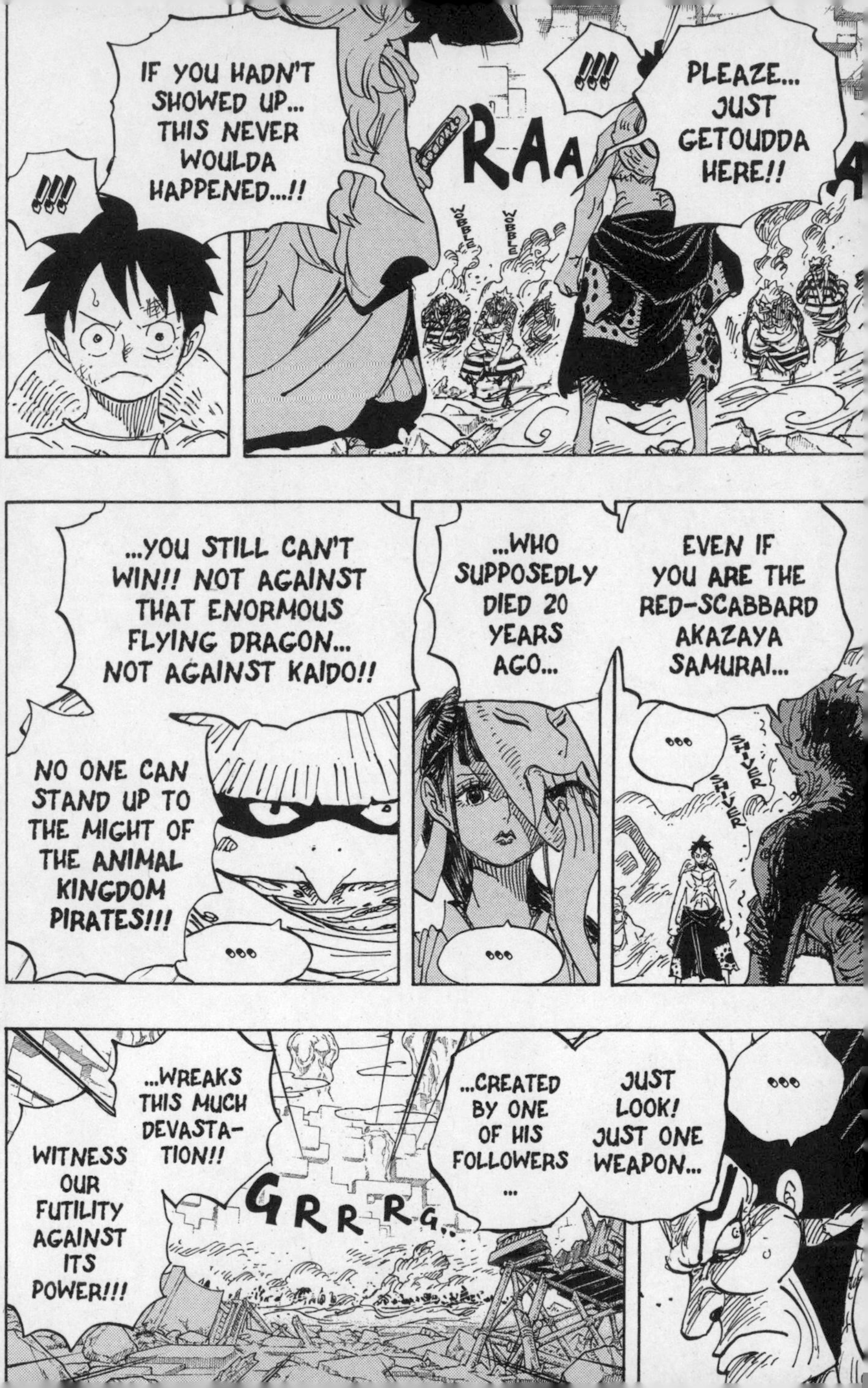
!!!
PLEAZE... JUST GETOUDDA HERE!!
RAA
WOBBLE
WOBBLE
IF YOU HADN'T SHOWED UP... THIS NEVER WOULDA HAPPENED...!!
!!!
EVEN IF YOU ARE THE RED-SCABBARD AKAZAYA SAMURAI...
...
SHIVER
SHIVER
...WHO SUPPOSEDLY DIED 20 YEARS AGO...
...
...YOU STILL CAN'T WIN!! NOT AGAINST THAT ENORMOUS FLYING DRAGON... NOT AGAINST KAIDO!!
NO ONE CAN STAND UP TO THE MIGHT OF THE ANIMAL KINGDOM PIRATES!!!
...
...
JUST LOOK! JUST ONE WEAPON...
...CREATED BY ONE OF HIS FOLLOWERS ...
...WREAKS THIS MUCH DEVASTATION!!
WITNESS OUR FUTILITY AGAINST ITS POWER!!!
GRRRRG..

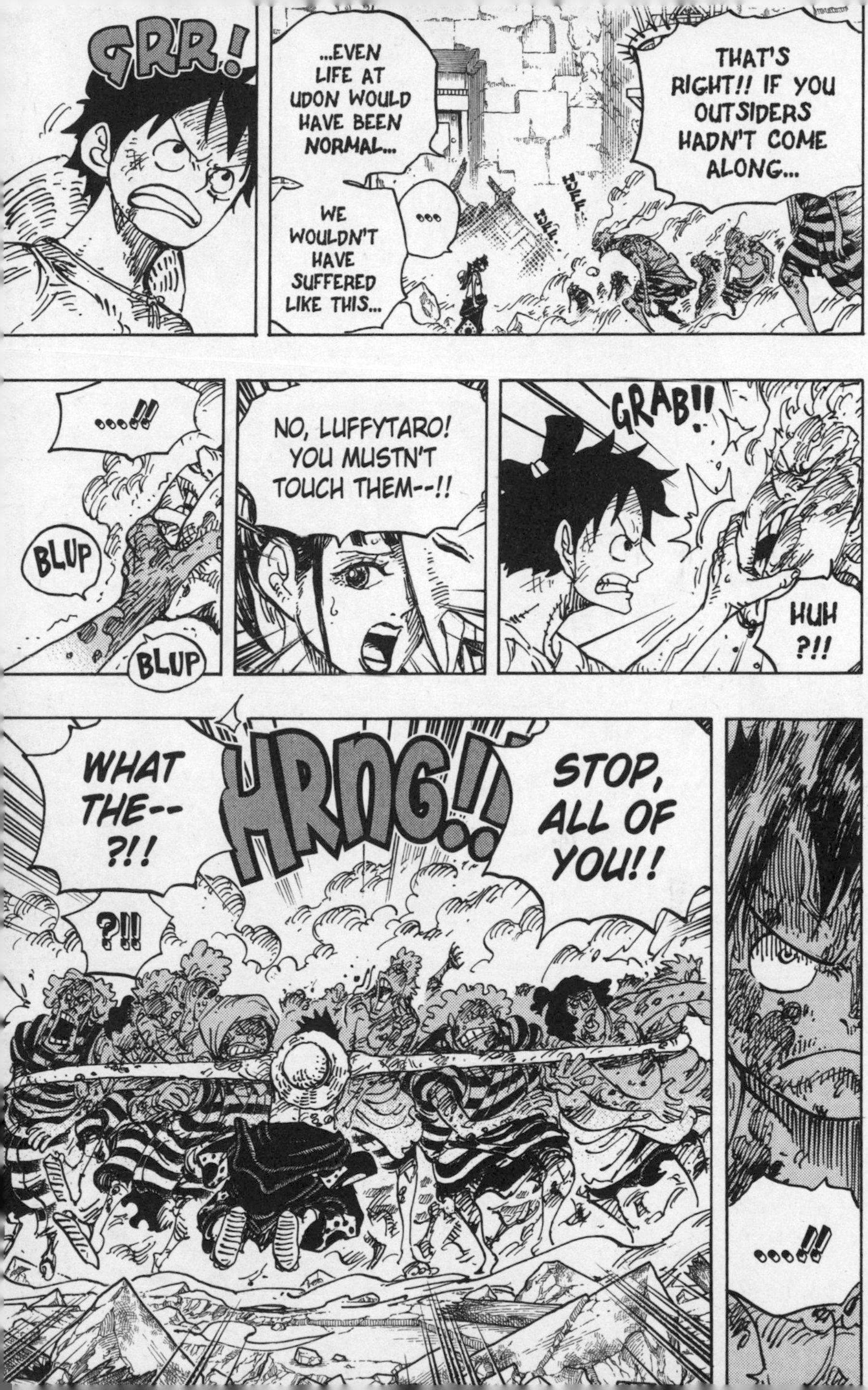
THAT'S RIGHT!! IF YOU OUTSIDERS HADN'T COME ALONG...
...EVEN LIFE AT UDON WOULD HAVE BEEN NORMAL...
WE WOULDN'T HAVE SUFFERED LIKE THIS...
...
HUFF
HUFF
GRR!
GRAB!!
HUH ?!!
NO, LUFFYTARO! YOU MUSTN'T TOUCH THEM--!!
...!!
BLUP
BLUP
...!!
STOP, ALL OF YOU!!
HRNG..!!
WHAT THE-- ?!!
?!!

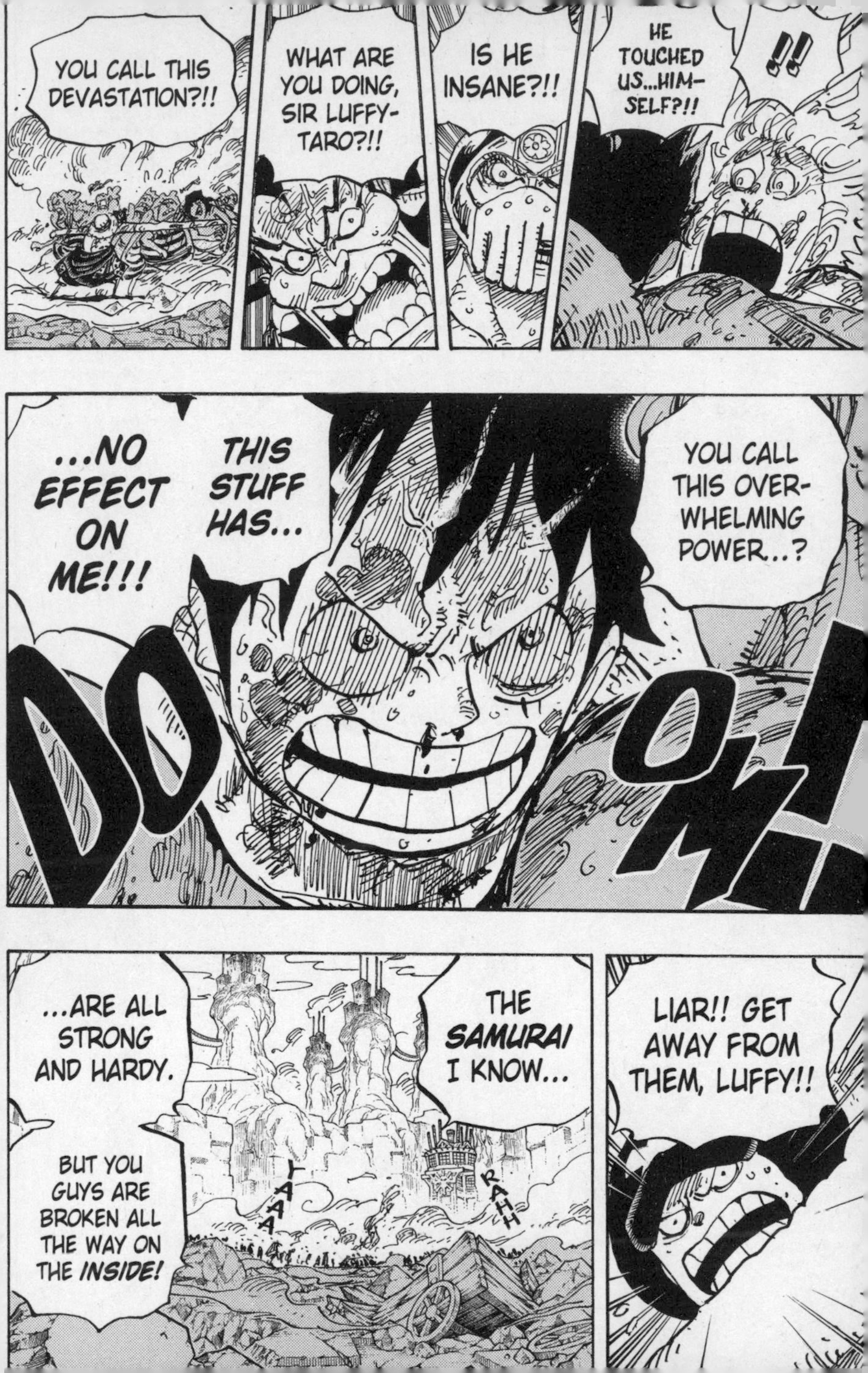
!!
HE TOUCHED US...HIM-SELF?!!
IS HE INSANE?!!
WHAT ARE YOU DOING, SIR LUFFY-TARO?!!
YOU CALL THIS DEVASTATION?!!
YOU CALL THIS OVER-WHELMING POWER...?
THIS STUFF HAS...
...NO EFFECT ON ME!!!
DOOM!!
LIAR!! GET AWAY FROM THEM, LUFFY!!
THE SAMURAI I KNOW...
...ARE ALL STRONG AND HARDY.
BUT YOU GUYS ARE BROKEN ALL THE WAY ON THE INSIDE!
RAHH
YAAAA

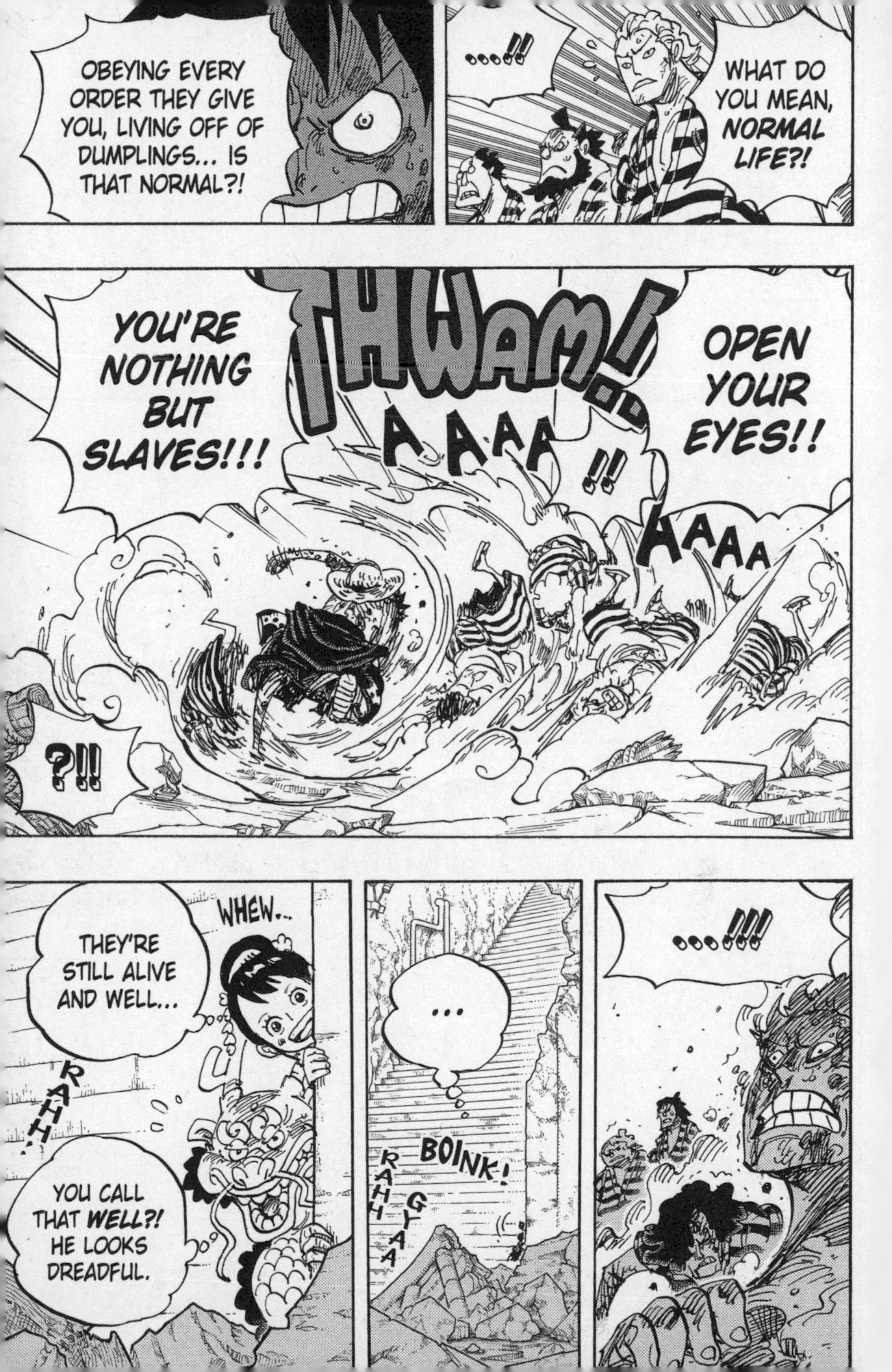
WHAT DO YOU MEAN, NORMAL LIFE?!
...!!
OBEYING EVERY ORDER THEY GIVE YOU, LIVING OFF OF DUMPLINGS... IS THAT NORMAL?!
OPEN YOUR EYES!!
THWAM!!
YOU'RE NOTHING BUT SLAVES!!!
AAAA!!
AAAA
?!!
...!!!
...
BOINK!
RAHH
GYAA
WHEW...
THEY'RE STILL ALIVE AND WELL...
RAHH!
YOU CALL THAT WELL?! HE LOOKS DREADFUL.

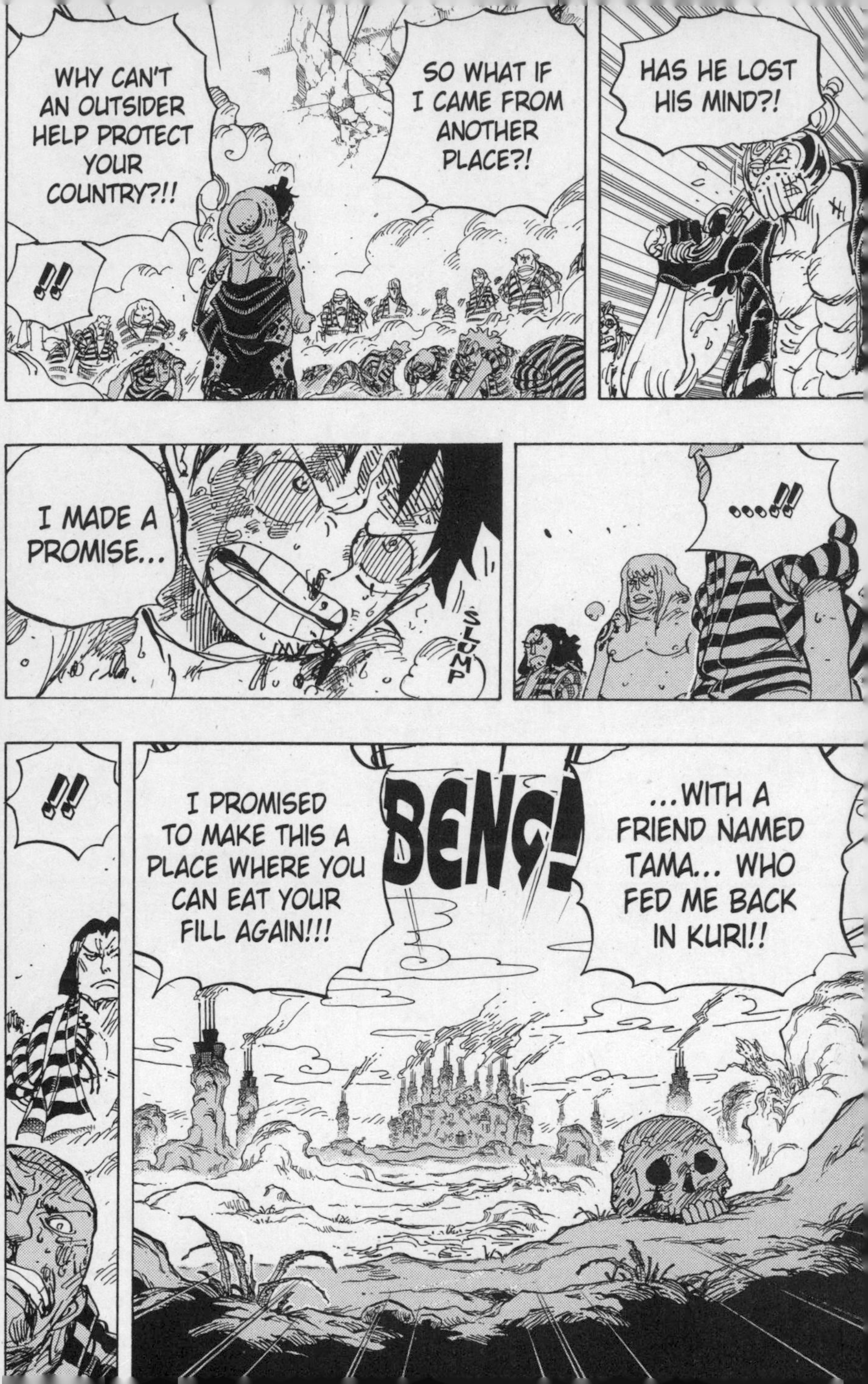
HAS HE LOST HIS MIND?!
SO WHAT IF I CAME FROM ANOTHER PLACE?!
WHY CAN'T AN OUTSIDER HELP PROTECT YOUR COUNTRY?!!
!!
...!!
I MADE A PROMISE...
SLUMP
...WITH A FRIEND NAMED TAMA... WHO FED ME BACK IN KURI!!
BENG!
I PROMISED TO MAKE THIS A PLACE WHERE YOU CAN EAT YOUR FILL AGAIN!!!
!!

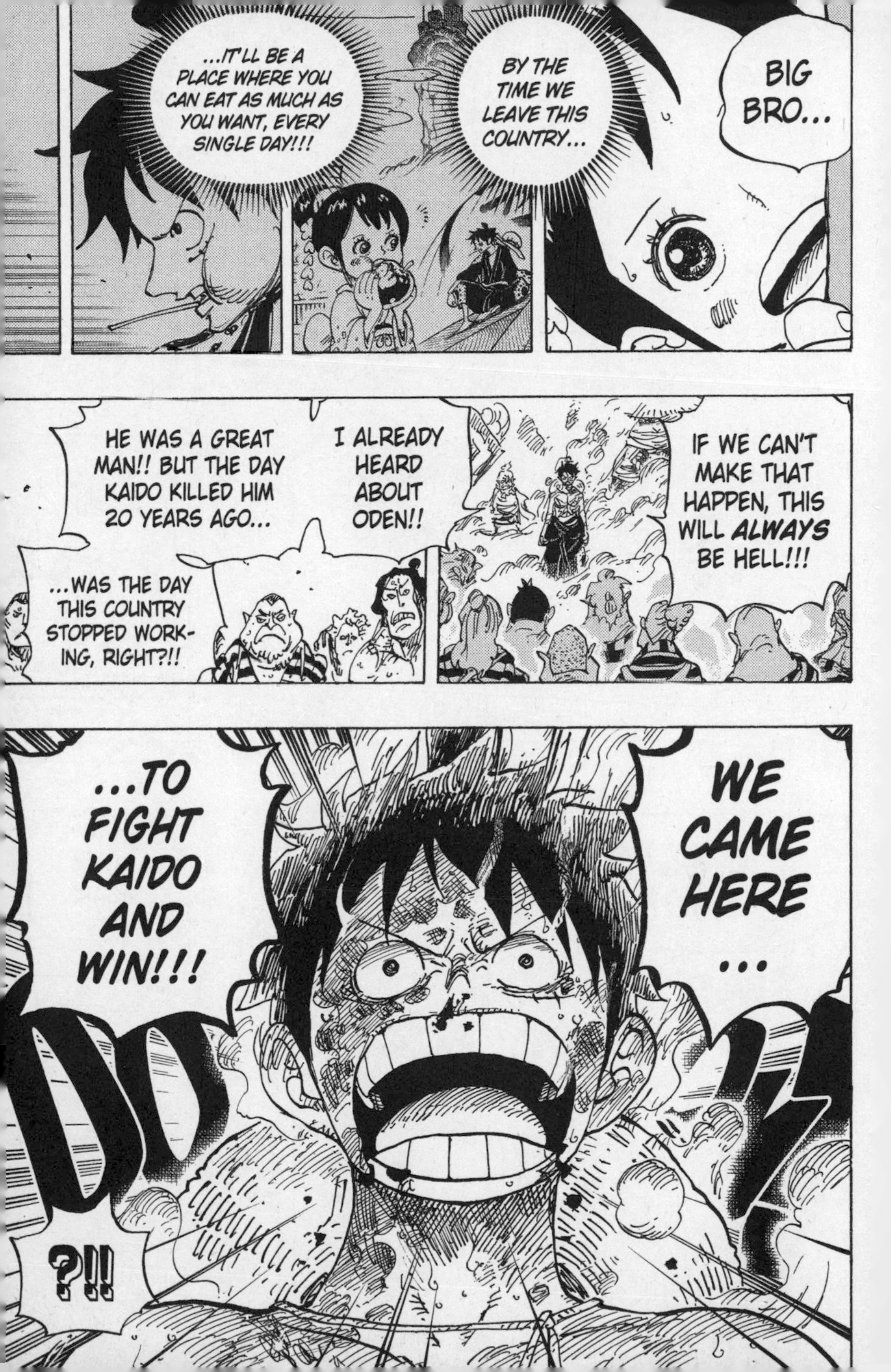
BIG BRO...
BY THE TIME WE LEAVE THIS COUNTRY...
...IT'LL BE A PLACE WHERE YOU CAN EAT AS MUCH AS YOU WANT, EVERY SINGLE DAY!!!
IF WE CAN'T MAKE THAT HAPPEN, THIS WILL ALWAYS BE HELL!!!
I ALREADY HEARD ABOUT ODEN!!
HE WAS A GREAT MAN!! BUT THE DAY KAIDO KILLED HIM 20 YEARS AGO...
...WAS THE DAY THIS COUNTRY STOPPED WORKING, RIGHT?!!
WE CAME HERE ...
...TO FIGHT KAIDO AND WIN!!!
?!!

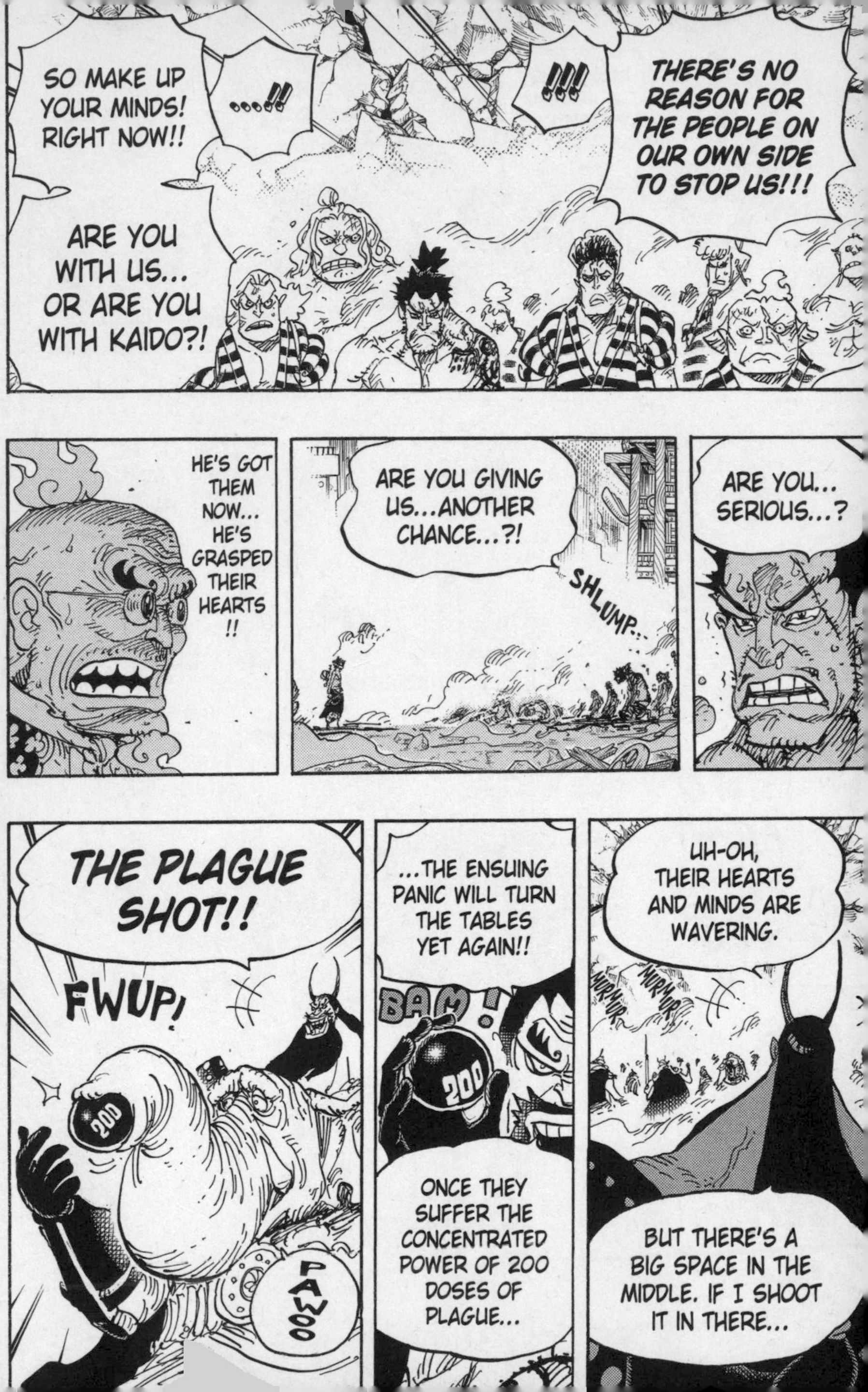
THERE'S NO REASON FOR THE PEOPLE ON OUR OWN SIDE TO STOP US!!!
!!!
...!!
SO MAKE UP YOUR MINDS! RIGHT NOW!!
ARE YOU WITH US... OR ARE YOU WITH KAIDO?!
ARE YOU... SERIOUS...?
ARE YOU GIVING US...ANOTHER CHANCE...?!
SHLUMP...
HE'S GOT THEM NOW... HE'S GRASPED THEIR HEARTS!!
UH-OH, THEIR HEARTS AND MINDS ARE WAVERING.
MURMUR
MURMUR
BUT THERE'S A BIG SPACE IN THE MIDDLE. IF I SHOOT IT IN THERE...
BAM!
200
...THE ENSUING PANIC WILL TURN THE TABLES YET AGAIN!!
ONCE THEY SUFFER THE CONCENTRATED POWER OF 200 DOSES OF PLAGUE...
THE PLAGUE SHOT!!
FWUP!
200
PAWOO

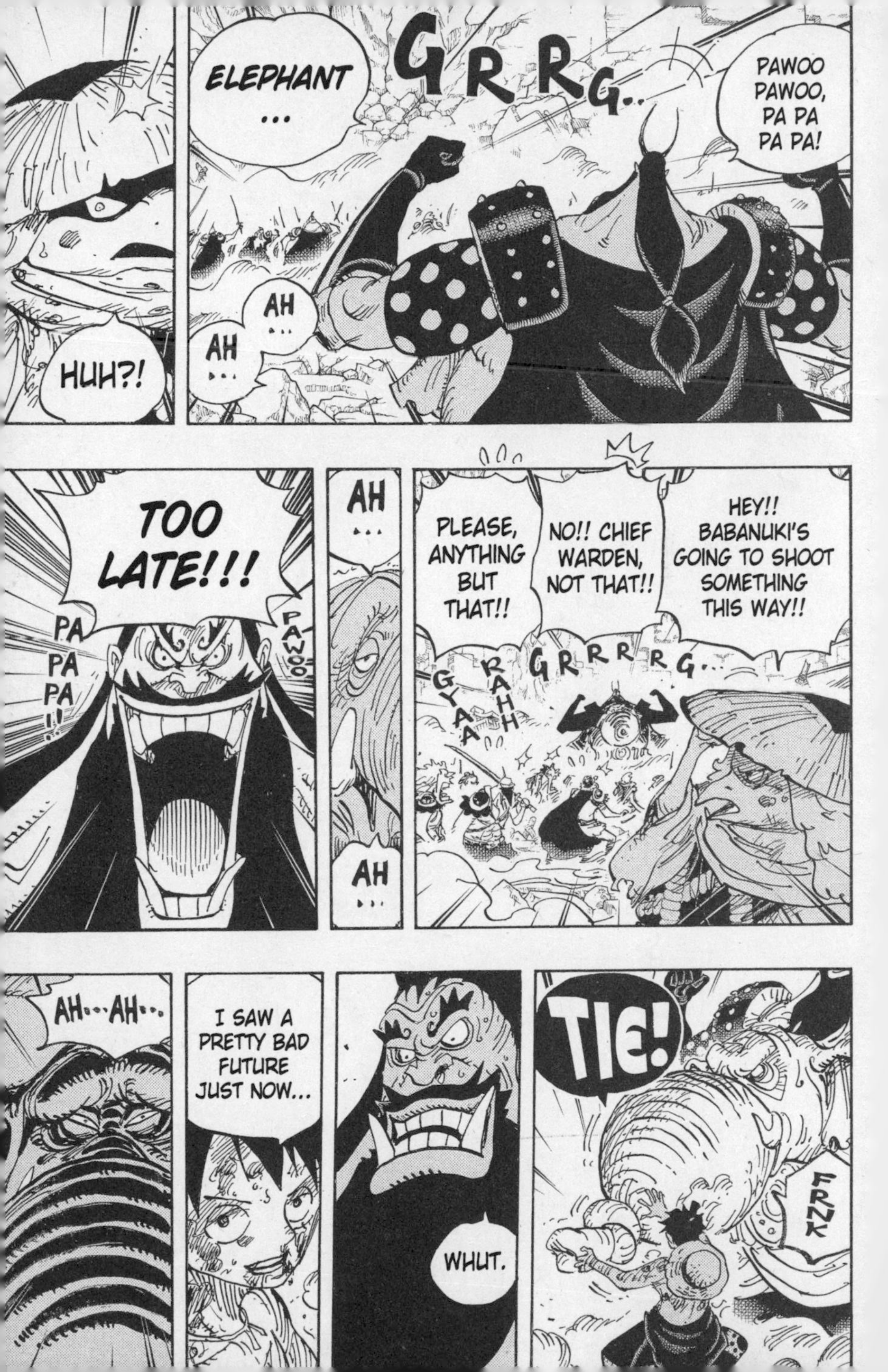
PAWOO PAWOO, PA PA PA PA!
GRRG...
ELEPHANT ...
AH ...
AH ...
HUH?!
HEY!! BABANUKI'S GOING TO SHOOT SOMETHING THIS WAY!!
NO!! CHIEF WARDEN, NOT THAT!!
PLEASE, ANYTHING BUT THAT!!
GRRRRRG...
RAHH
GYAA
AH ...
AH ...
TOO LATE!!!
PAWOO
PA PA PA PA!!
TIE!
FRNK
WHUT.
I SAW A PRETTY BAD FUTURE JUST NOW...
AH...AH...

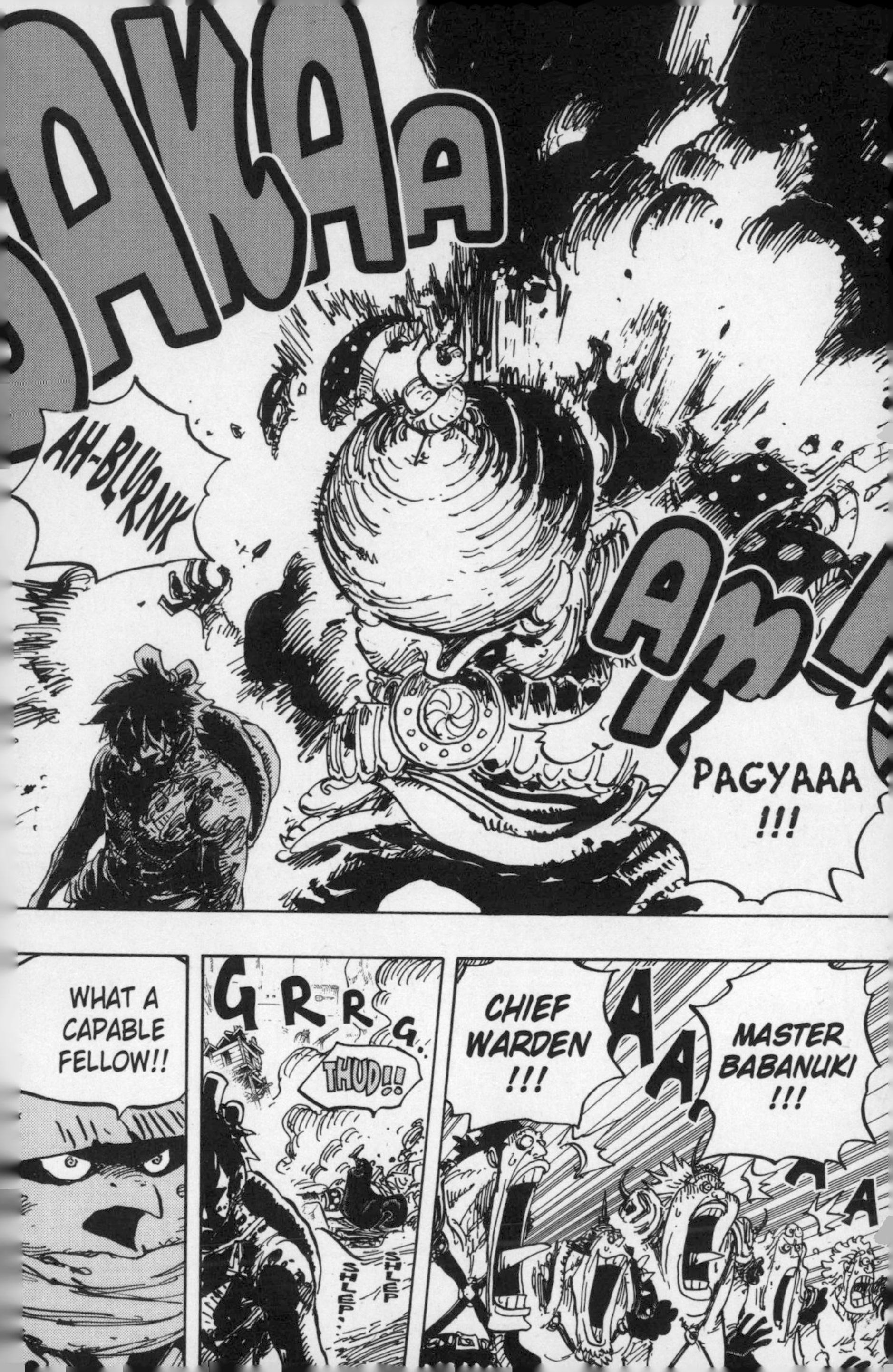
PAGYAAA !!!
AH-BLURNK
MASTER BABANUKI !!!
CHIEF WARDEN !!!
GRRG
THUD!!
SHLEP
SHLEP
WHAT A CAPABLE FELLOW!!

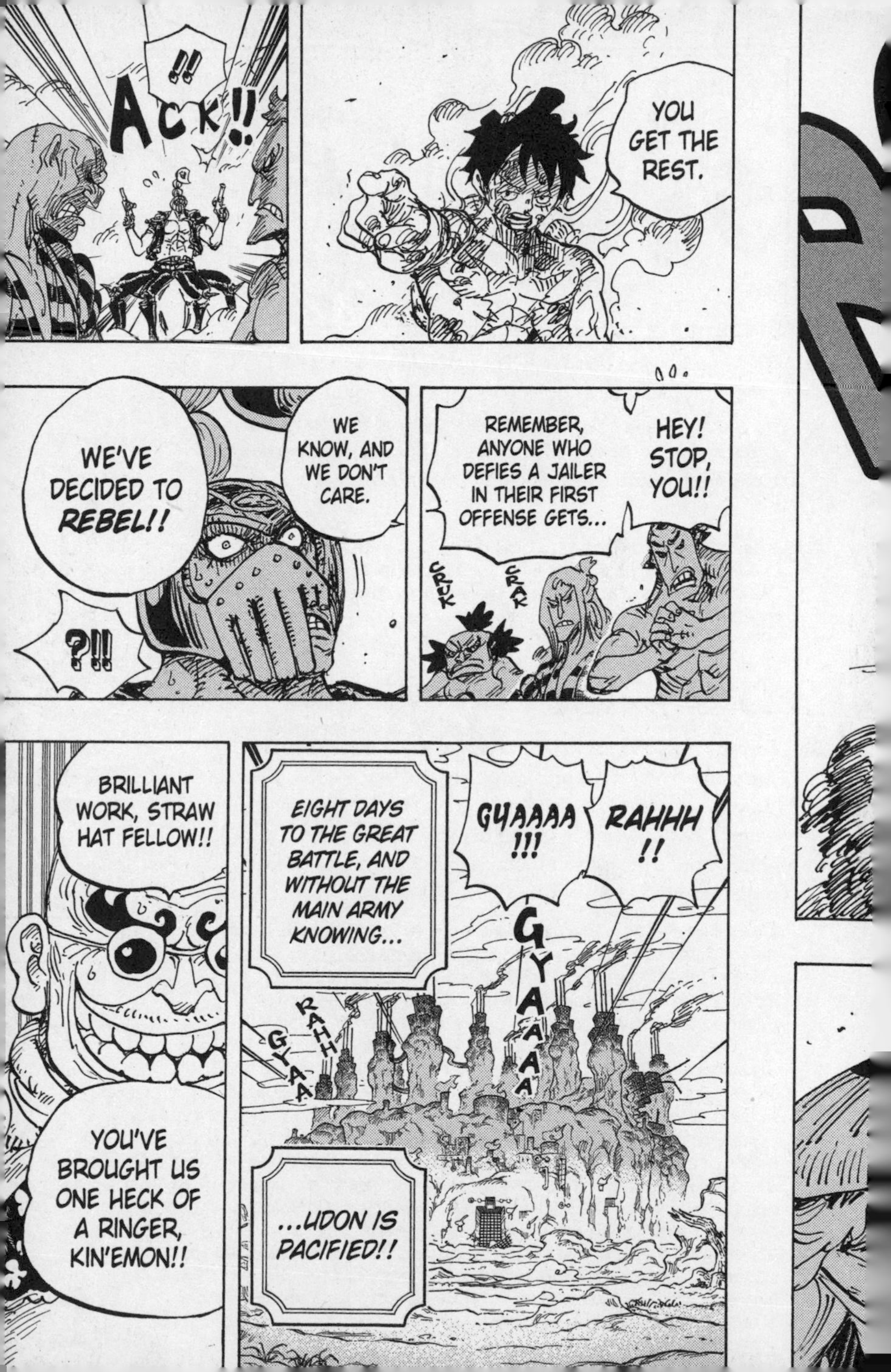

YOU GET THE REST.
!!
ACK!!
HEY! STOP, YOU!!
REMEMBER, ANYONE WHO DEFIES A JAILER IN THEIR FIRST OFFENSE GETS...
CRAK
CRUK
WE KNOW, AND WE DON'T CARE.
WE'VE DECIDED TO REBEL!!
?!!
RAHHH!!
GYAAAA!!!
EIGHT DAYS TO THE GREAT BATTLE, AND WITHOUT THE MAIN ARMY KNOWING...
GYAAAAA
RAHH
GYAA
...UDON IS PACIFIED!!
BRILLIANT WORK, STRAW HAT FELLOW!!
YOU'VE BROUGHT US ONE HECK OF A RINGER, KIN'EMON!!

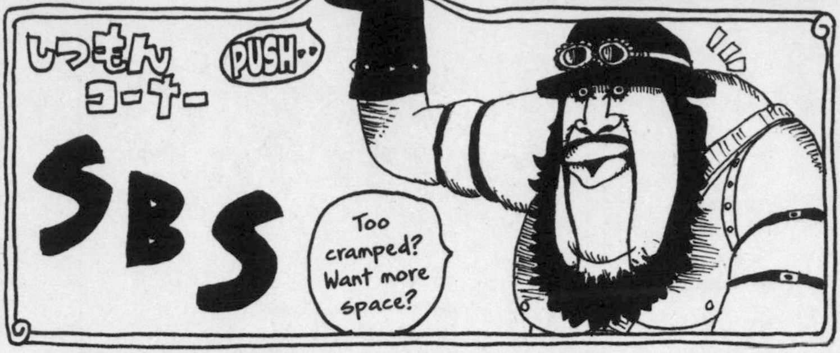
しつもんコーナー
PUSH..
SBS
Too cramped? Want more space?

(Art Club Member, Hokkaido)

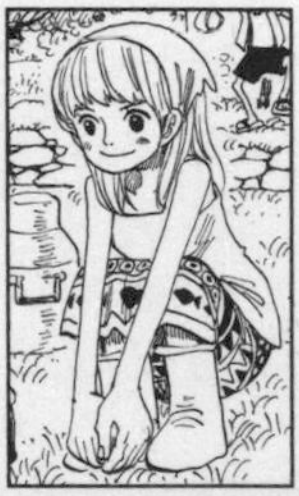

Q: Mr. Oda! I have a question!! The skirt on the girl who collapsed against Belo Betty on page 67 of volume 90 sure looks a lot like the skirt of the milk maid Moda's skirt from when she appears in the "Ace's Great Search for Blackbeard" cover story, starting in chapter 278! Is that Moda?!

--Kyarin

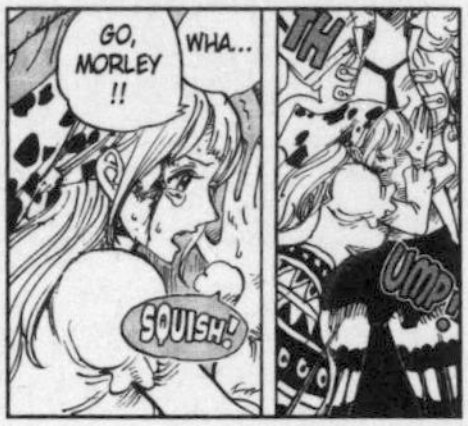
GO, MORLEY !!
WHA...
SQUISH!

A: Yes, that's correct. Good catch. At the time, Lulucia was still a peaceful kingdom, but King Seki has been a terrible ruler, and the people are miserable now. Hopefully the courage the Revolutionaries brought to them will help Moda keep going.

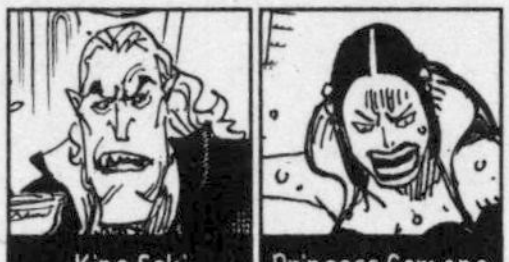
King Seki | Princess Comane

Q: I have a question about the reader request chapter covers. In volume 56, it said, "covers with an animal and one Straw Hat member at a time," but now you're taking requests that don't have animals or Straw Hats in them, right? What are the actual requirements to get your idea picked?

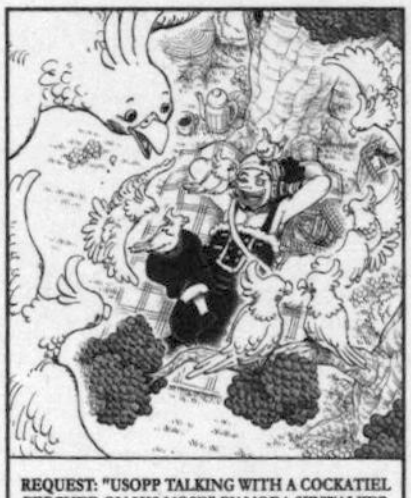
REQUEST: "USOPP TALKING WITH A COCKATIEL PERCHED ON HIS NOSE" BY NODA SKYWALKER

A: Well, I've never actually put out an official set of rules for them or anything, if I'm remembering correctly. Thank you all for your many reader requests. The basic format is just "Animal plus Character doing ____," and I like having a lot of them involve the Straw Hats. At first I thought, I want to get as many people's requests in as possible, so I only drew one for each individual. But some people are so good at making requests that tickle my fancy, and I got tired of worrying, "I can't draw this person's request for a second time, even though I really like this prompt," so I decided that I'll just draw the ones I like, no matter what. If you can capture my interest through the animal choice and character choice, I will happily draw your request. Drawing is my hobby, after all. If I want to draw it, I'll even use it for a two-page color spread. So put animals in those too. After 22 years of this, I've drawn just about everything, so the newer and fresher the request, the more fun it is for me.

Chapter 950:
A SOLDIER'S DREAM

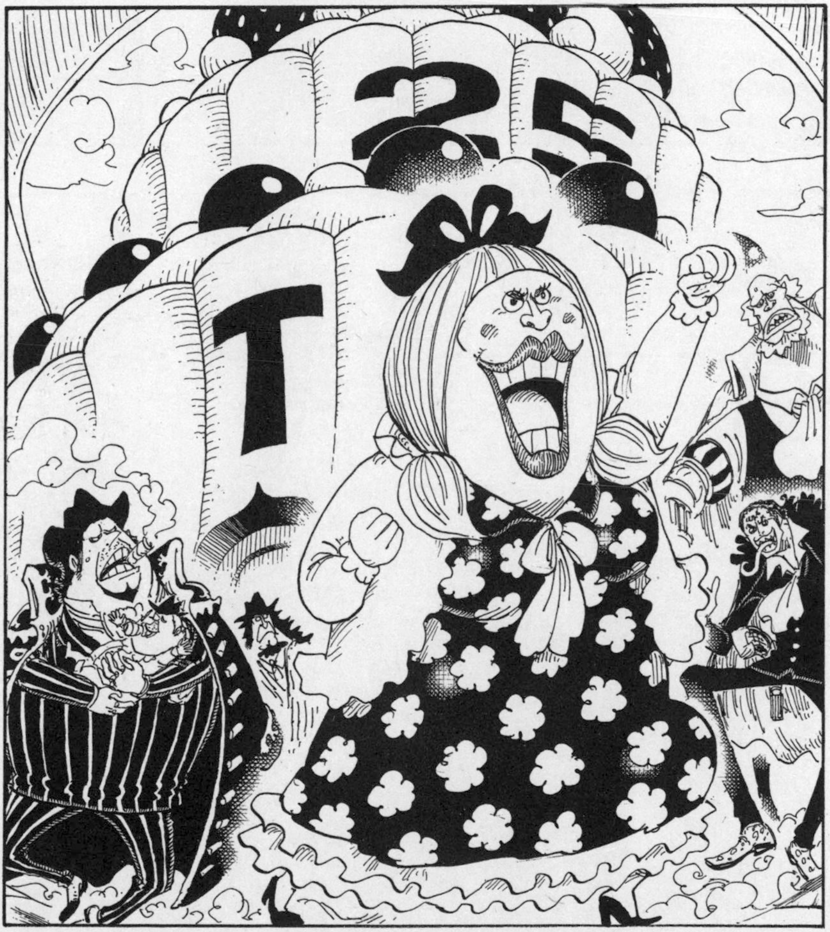
T
25

GANG BEGE'S OH MY FAMILY
VOL. 2: "I WANT TO SEE MY TWIN SISTER LOLA!!"

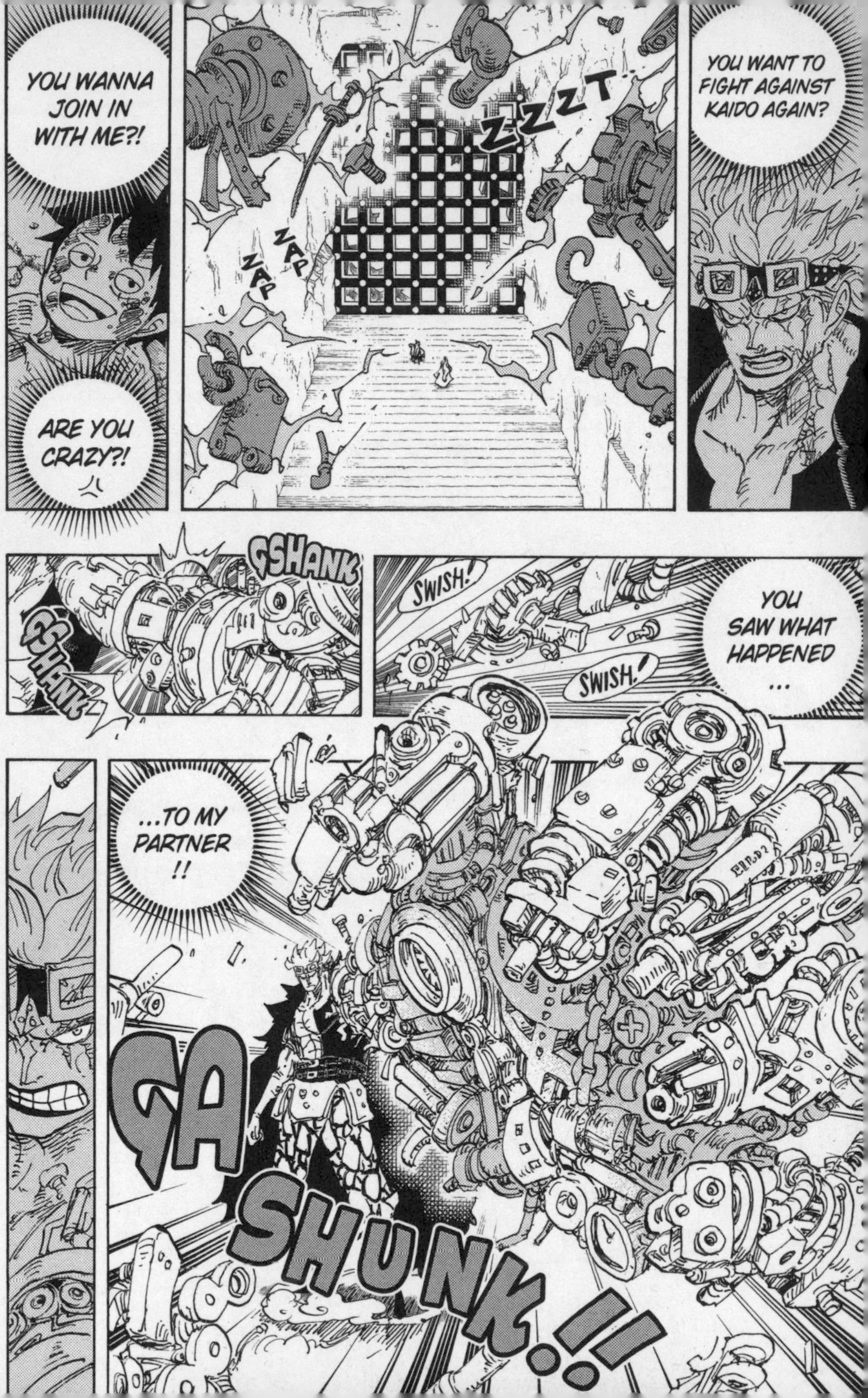

YOU WANT TO FIGHT AGAINST KAIDO AGAIN?
ZZZZT
ZAP
ZAP
YOU WANNA JOIN IN WITH ME?!
ARE YOU CRAZY?!
SWISH!
SWISH!
YOU SAW WHAT HAPPENED ...
GSHANK
GSHANK
...TO MY PARTNER !!
GASHUNK..!!

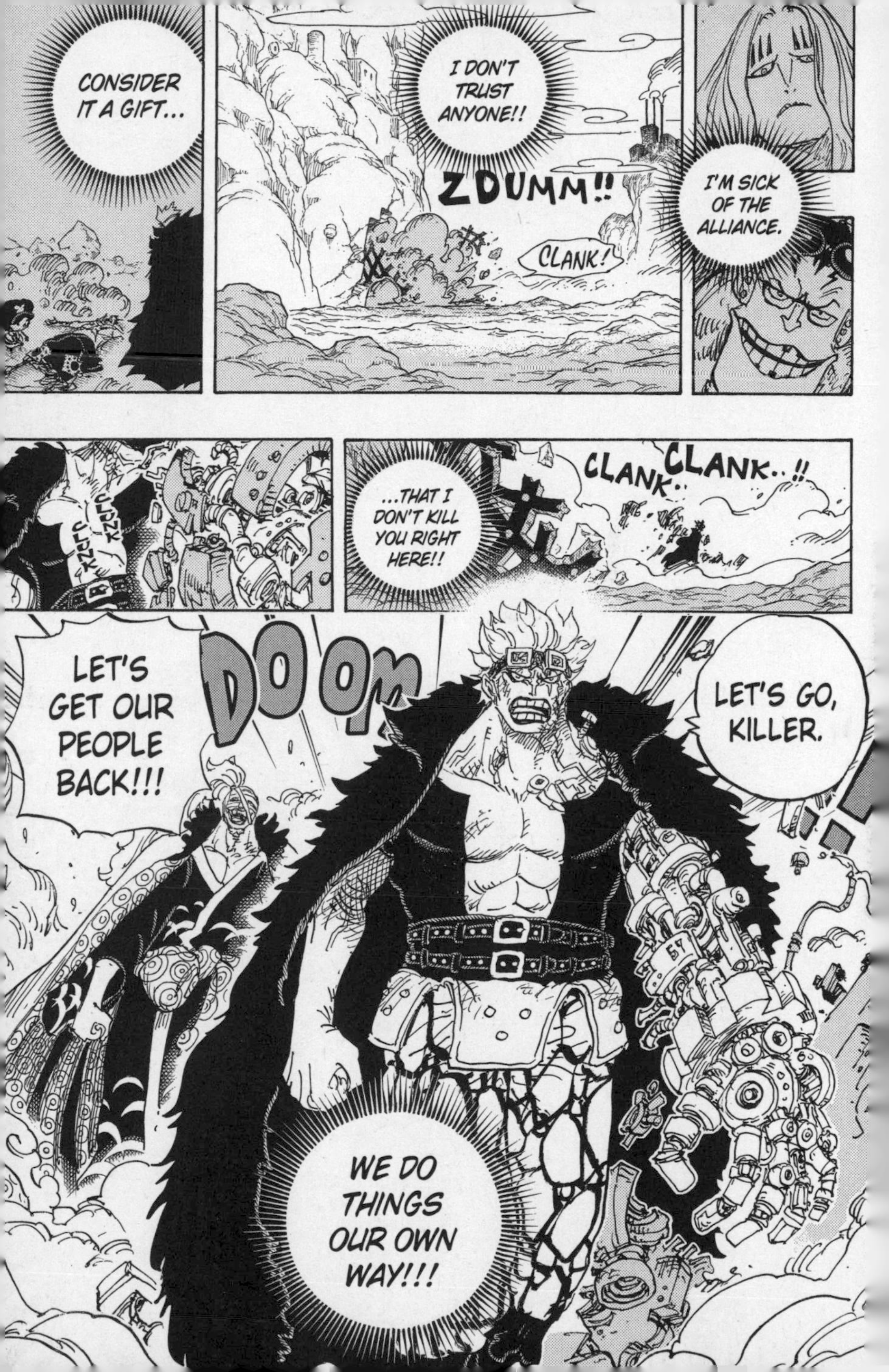
I'M SICK OF THE ALLIANCE.
I DON'T TRUST ANYONE!!
ZDUMM!!
CLANK!
CONSIDER IT A GIFT...
CLANK..!!
CLANK..
...THAT I DON'T KILL YOU RIGHT HERE!!
CLANK
CLANK
LET'S GO, KILLER.
DOOM
LET'S GET OUR PEOPLE BACK!!!
WE DO THINGS OUR OWN WAY!!!

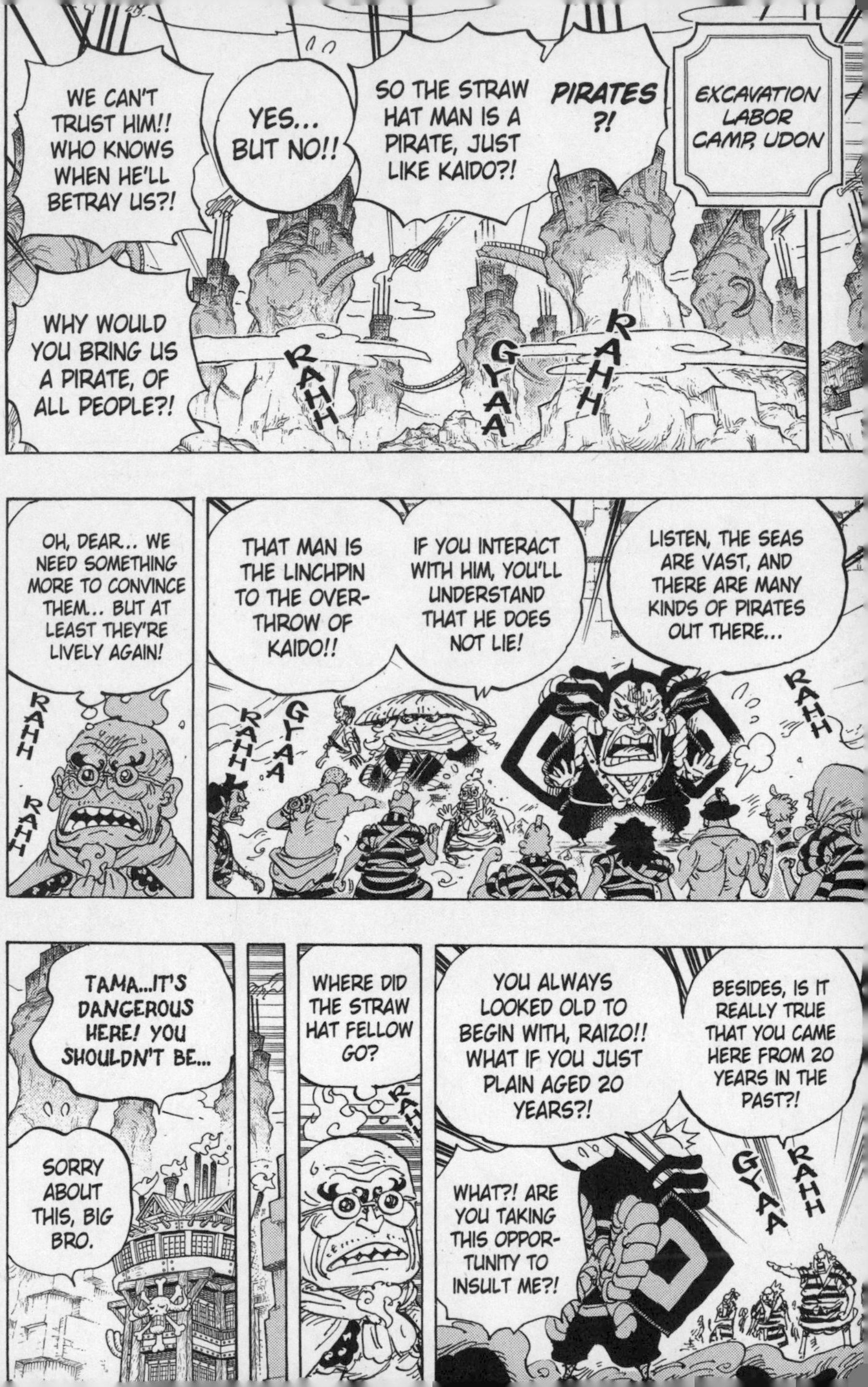
EXCAVATION LABOR CAMP, UDON
PIRATES ?!
SO THE STRAW HAT MAN IS A PIRATE, JUST LIKE KAIDO?!
YES... BUT NO!!
WE CAN'T TRUST HIM!! WHO KNOWS WHEN HE'LL BETRAY US?!
RAHH
GYAA
RAHH
WHY WOULD YOU BRING US A PIRATE, OF ALL PEOPLE?!
LISTEN, THE SEAS ARE VAST, AND THERE ARE MANY KINDS OF PIRATES OUT THERE...
IF YOU INTERACT WITH HIM, YOU'LL UNDERSTAND THAT HE DOES NOT LIE!
THAT MAN IS THE LINCHPIN TO THE OVER-THROW OF KAIDO!!
RAHH
GYAA
RAHH
OH, DEAR... WE NEED SOMETHING MORE TO CONVINCE THEM... BUT AT LEAST THEY'RE LIVELY AGAIN!
RAHH
RAHH
BESIDES, IS IT REALLY TRUE THAT YOU CAME HERE FROM 20 YEARS IN THE PAST?!
YOU ALWAYS LOOKED OLD TO BEGIN WITH, RAIZO!! WHAT IF YOU JUST PLAIN AGED 20 YEARS?!
RAHH
GYAA
WHAT?! ARE YOU TAKING THIS OPPOR-TUNITY TO INSULT ME?!
WHERE DID THE STRAW HAT FELLOW GO?
RAHH
TAMA...IT'S DANGEROUS HERE! YOU SHOULDN'T BE...
SORRY ABOUT THIS, BIG BRO.

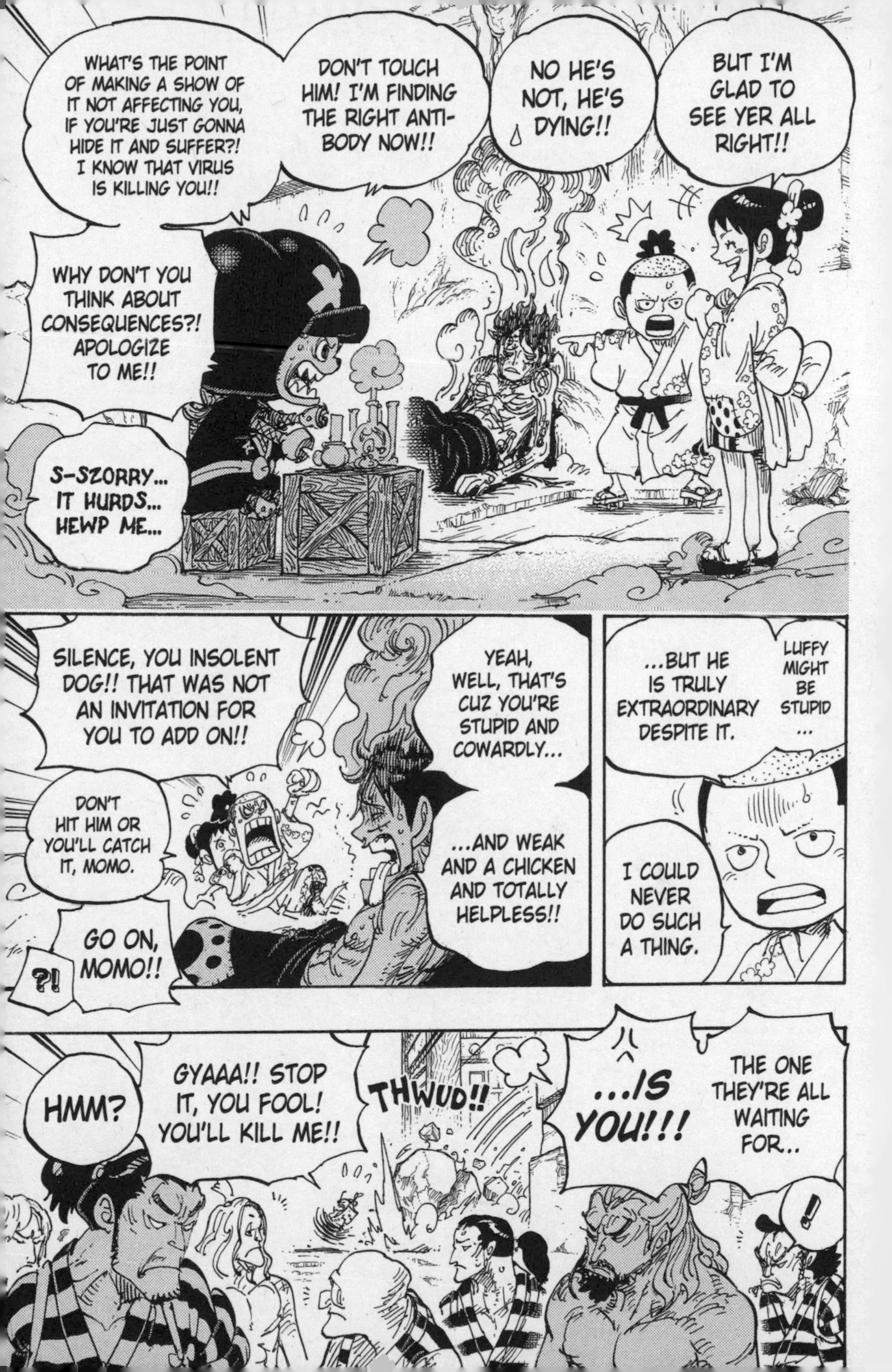
BUT I'M GLAD TO SEE YER ALL RIGHT!!
NO HE'S NOT, HE'S DYING!!
DON'T TOUCH HIM! I'M FINDING THE RIGHT ANTI-BODY NOW!!
WHAT'S THE POINT OF MAKING A SHOW OF IT NOT AFFECTING YOU, IF YOU'RE JUST GONNA HIDE IT AND SUFFER?! I KNOW THAT VIRUS IS KILLING YOU!!
WHY DON'T YOU THINK ABOUT CONSEQUENCES?! APOLOGIZE TO ME!!
S-SZORRY... IT HURDS... HEWP ME...
LUFFY MIGHT BE STUPID ...
...BUT HE IS TRULY EXTRAORDINARY DESPITE IT.
I COULD NEVER DO SUCH A THING.
YEAH, WELL, THAT'S CUZ YOU'RE STUPID AND COWARDLY...
SILENCE, YOU INSOLENT DOG!! THAT WAS NOT AN INVITATION FOR YOU TO ADD ON!!
...AND WEAK AND A CHICKEN AND TOTALLY HELPLESS!!
DON'T HIT HIM OR YOU'LL CATCH IT, MOMO.
GO ON, MOMO!!
?!
THE ONE THEY'RE ALL WAITING FOR..
...IS YOU!!!
!
THWUD!!
GYAAA!! STOP IT, YOU FOOL! YOU'LL KILL ME!!
HMM?

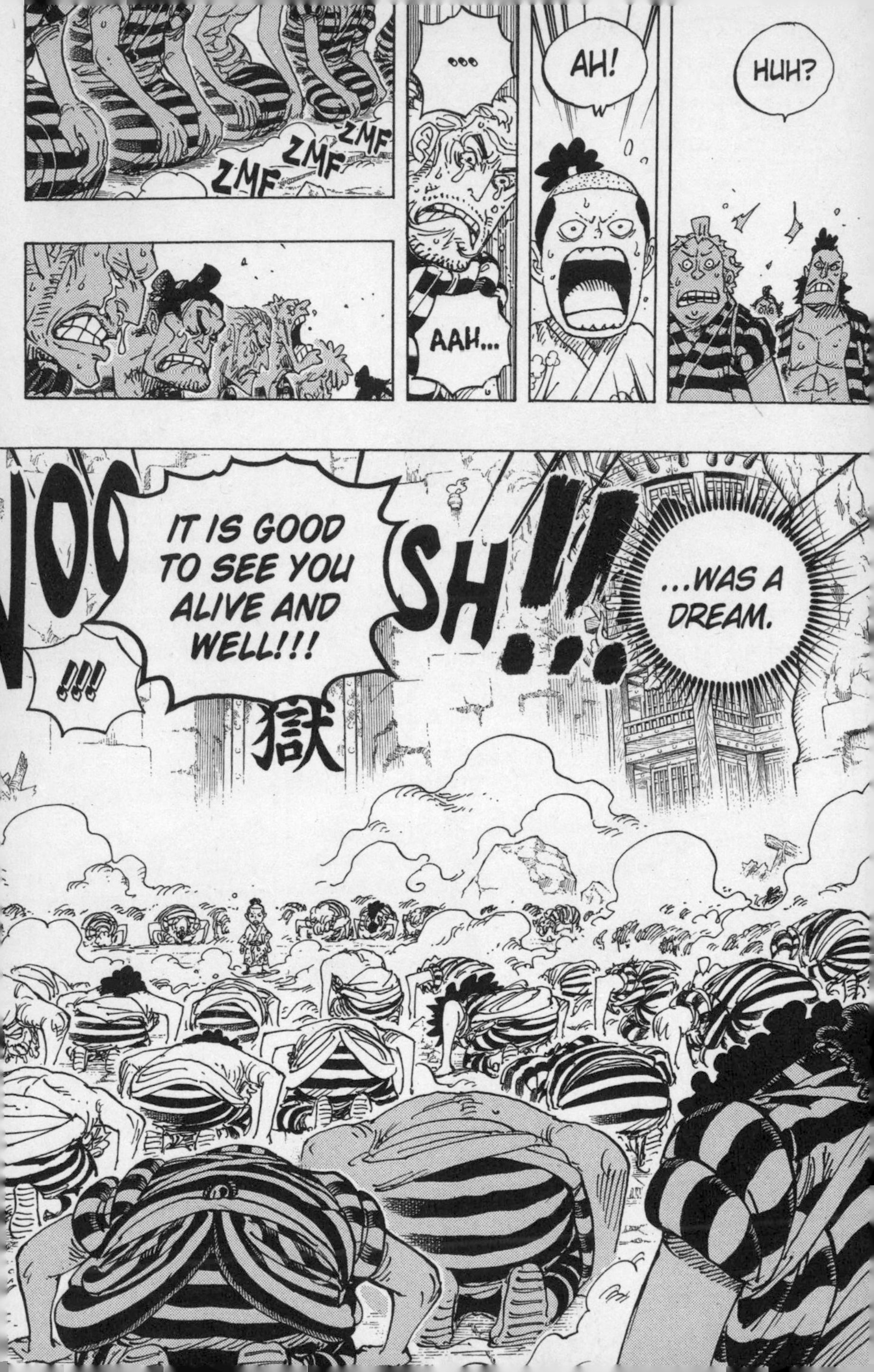
HUH?
AH!
...
AAH...
ZMF
ZMF
ZMF
...WAS A DREAM.
IT IS GOOD TO SEE YOU ALIVE AND WELL!!!
!!!
獄

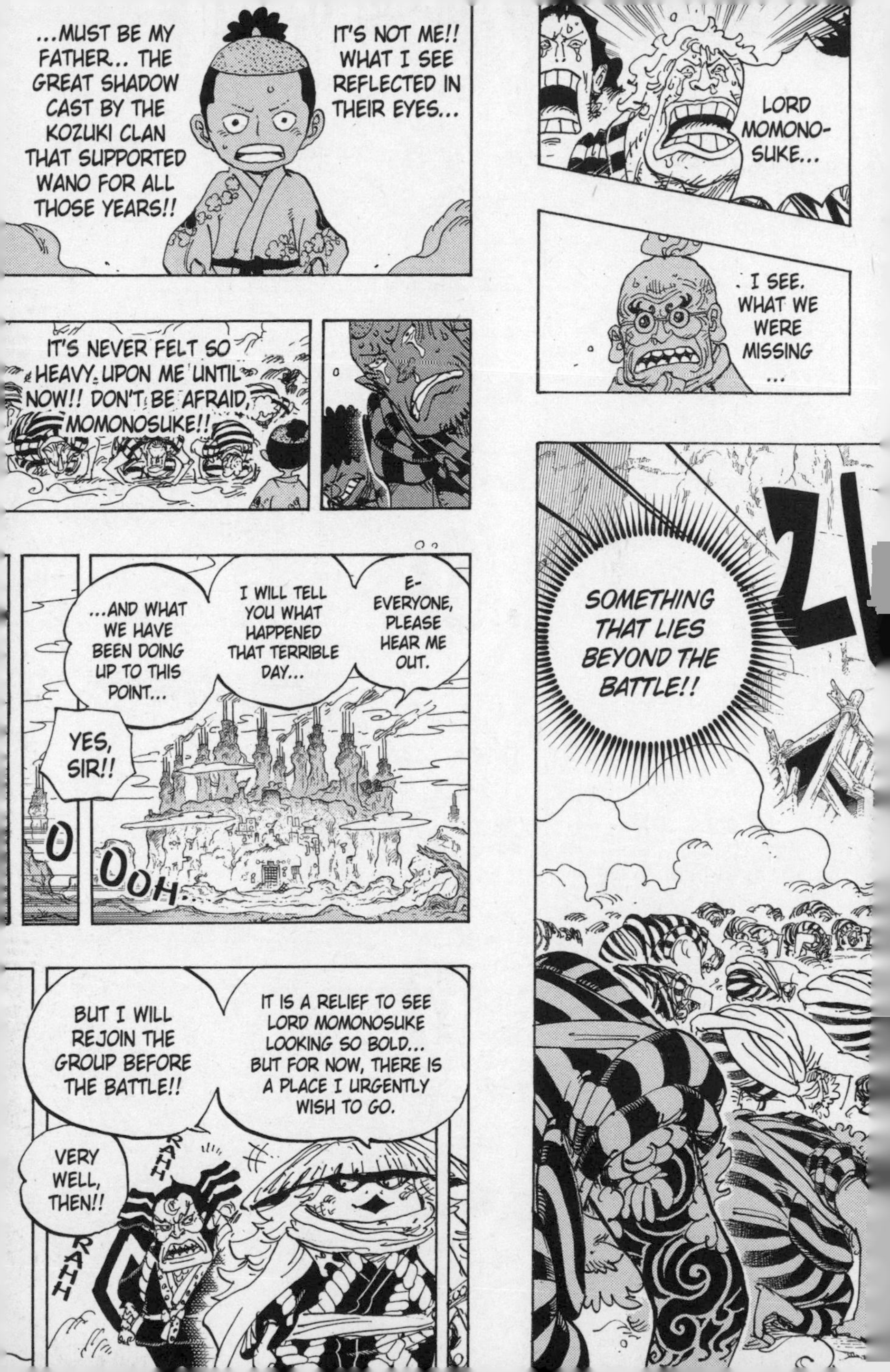
LORD MOMONOSUKE...
I SEE. WHAT WE WERE MISSING...
SOMETHING THAT LIES BEYOND THE BATTLE!!
IT'S NOT ME!! WHAT I SEE REFLECTED IN THEIR EYES...
...MUST BE MY FATHER... THE GREAT SHADOW CAST BY THE KOZUKI CLAN THAT SUPPORTED WANO FOR ALL THOSE YEARS!!
IT'S NEVER FELT SO HEAVY UPON ME UNTIL NOW!! DON'T BE AFRAID, MOMONOSUKE!!
E-EVERYONE, PLEASE HEAR ME OUT.
I WILL TELL YOU WHAT HAPPENED THAT TERRIBLE DAY...
...AND WHAT WE HAVE BEEN DOING UP TO THIS POINT...
YES, SIR!!
OOOH
IT IS A RELIEF TO SEE LORD MOMONOSUKE LOOKING SO BOLD... BUT FOR NOW, THERE IS A PLACE I URGENTLY WISH TO GO.
BUT I WILL REJOIN THE GROUP BEFORE THE BATTLE!!
VERY WELL, THEN!!
RAHH
RAHH

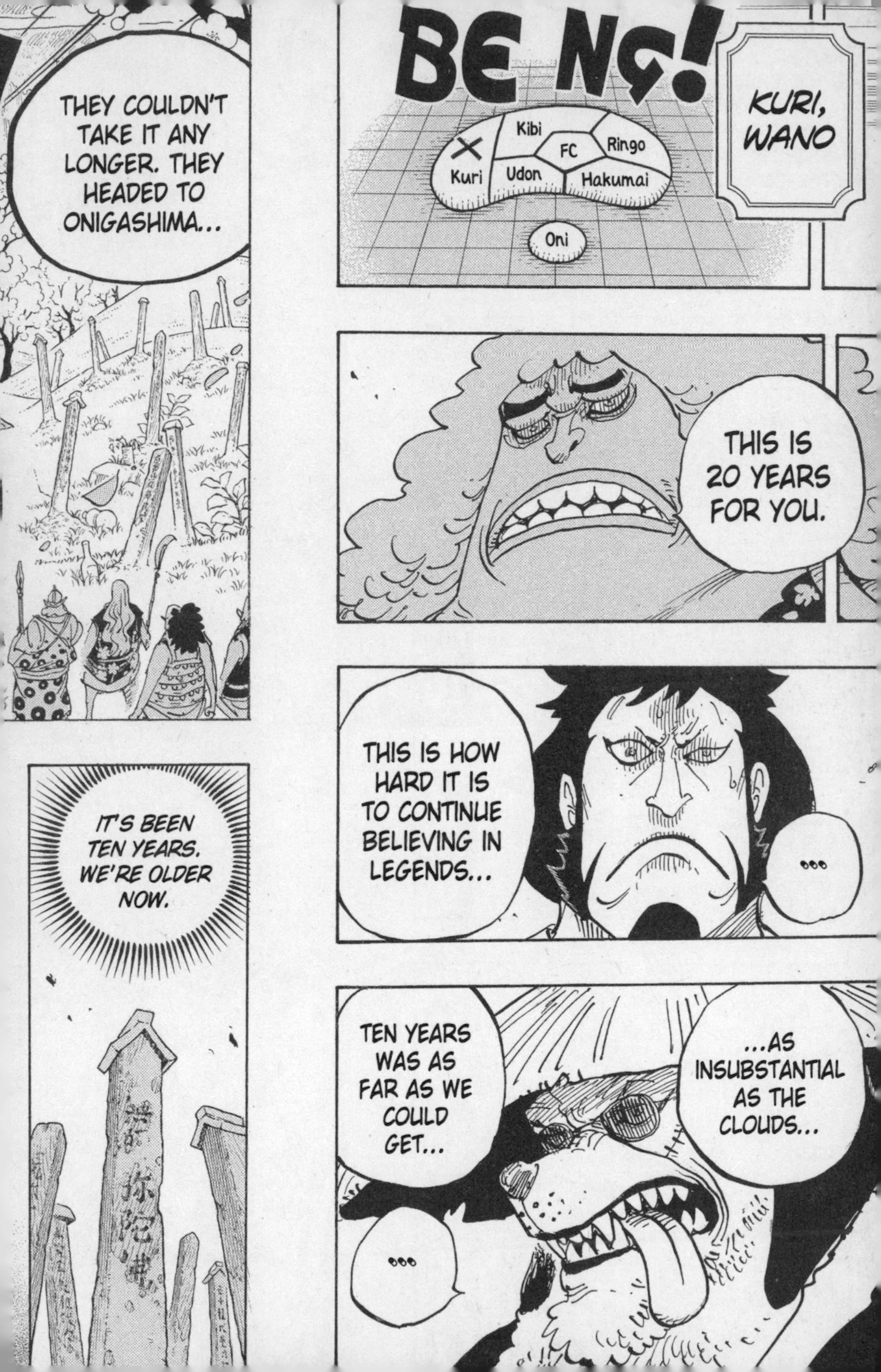
KURI, WANO
BENG!
Kibi
FC
Ringo
Kuri
Udon
Hakumai
Oni
THIS IS 20 YEARS FOR YOU.
...
THIS IS HOW HARD IT IS TO CONTINUE BELIEVING IN LEGENDS...
...AS INSUBSTANTIAL AS THE CLOUDS...
TEN YEARS WAS AS FAR AS WE COULD GET...
...
THEY COULDN'T TAKE IT ANY LONGER. THEY HEADED TO ONIGASHIMA...
IT'S BEEN TEN YEARS. WE'RE OLDER NOW.

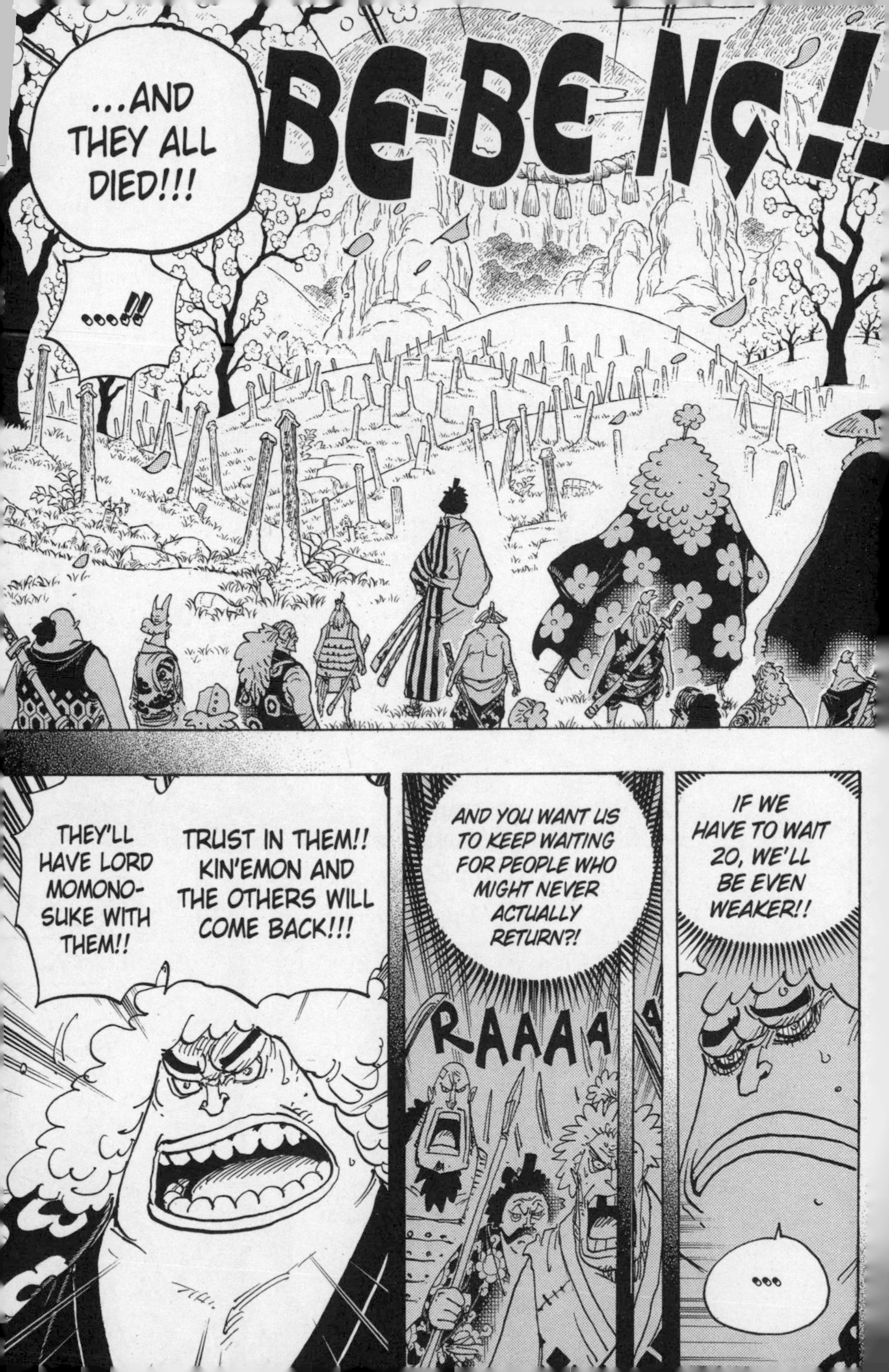
BE-BENG!!
...AND THEY ALL DIED!!!
...!!
IF WE HAVE TO WAIT 20, WE'LL BE EVEN WEAKER!!
...
AND YOU WANT US TO KEEP WAITING FOR PEOPLE WHO MIGHT NEVER ACTUALLY RETURN?!
RAAAAA
TRUST IN THEM!! KIN'EMON AND THE OTHERS WILL COME BACK!!!
THEY'LL HAVE LORD MOMONO-SUKE WITH THEM!!

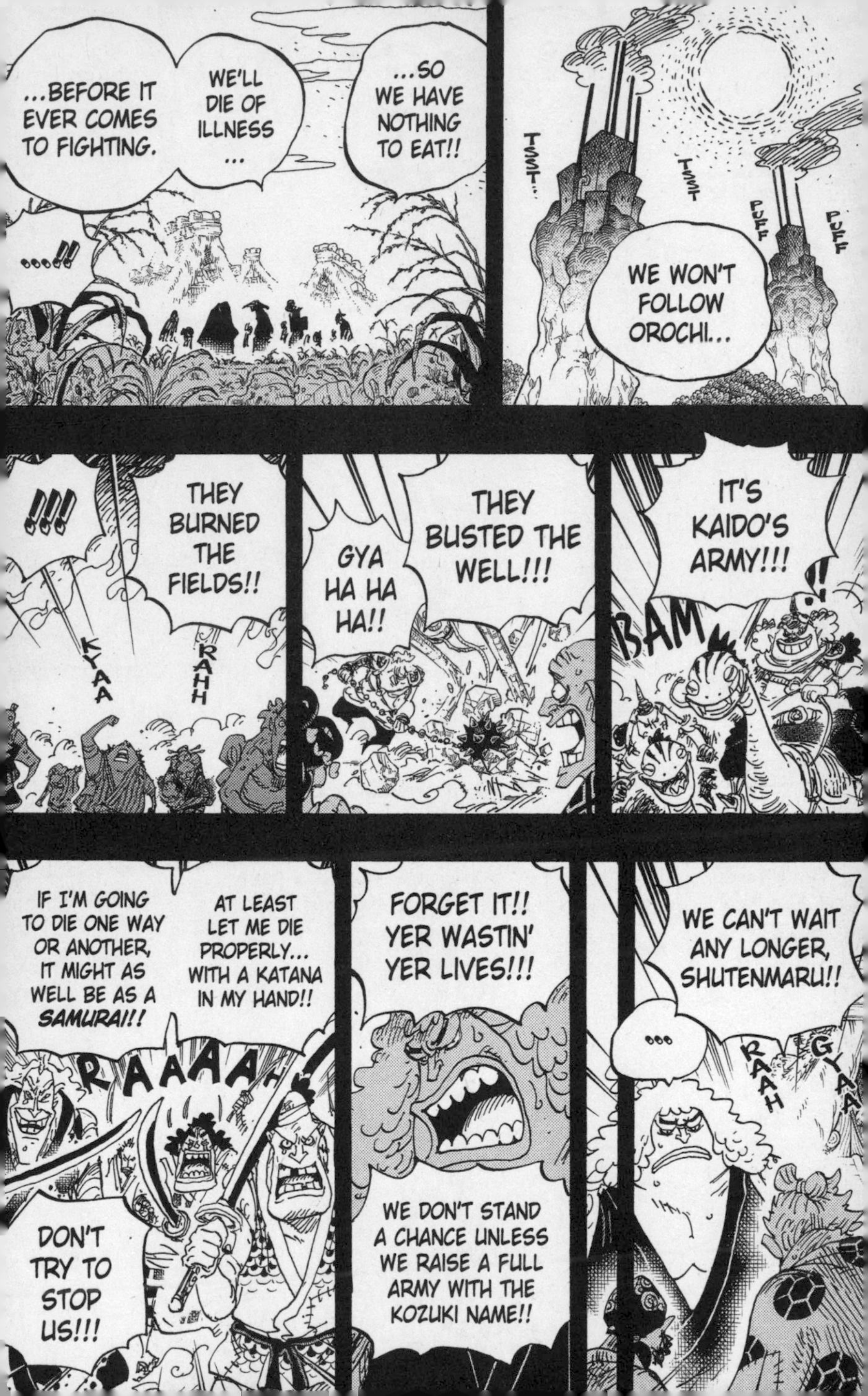
TSST...
TSST
PUFF
PUFF
WE WON'T FOLLOW OROCHI...
...SO WE HAVE NOTHING TO EAT!!
WE'LL DIE OF ILLNESS ...
...BEFORE IT EVER COMES TO FIGHTING.
...!!
IT'S KAIDO'S ARMY!!!
!
BAM
THEY BUSTED THE WELL!!!
GYA HA HA HA!!
THEY BURNED THE FIELDS!!
!!!
RAHH
KYAA
WE CAN'T WAIT ANY LONGER, SHUTENMARU!!
GYAA
RAAH
...
FORGET IT!! YER WASTIN' YER LIVES!!!
WE DON'T STAND A CHANCE UNLESS WE RAISE A FULL ARMY WITH THE KOZUKI NAME!!
AT LEAST LET ME DIE PROPERLY... WITH A KATANA IN MY HAND!!
IF I'M GOING TO DIE ONE WAY OR ANOTHER, IT MIGHT AS WELL BE AS A *SAMURAI*!!
RAAAAH
DON'T TRY TO STOP US!!!

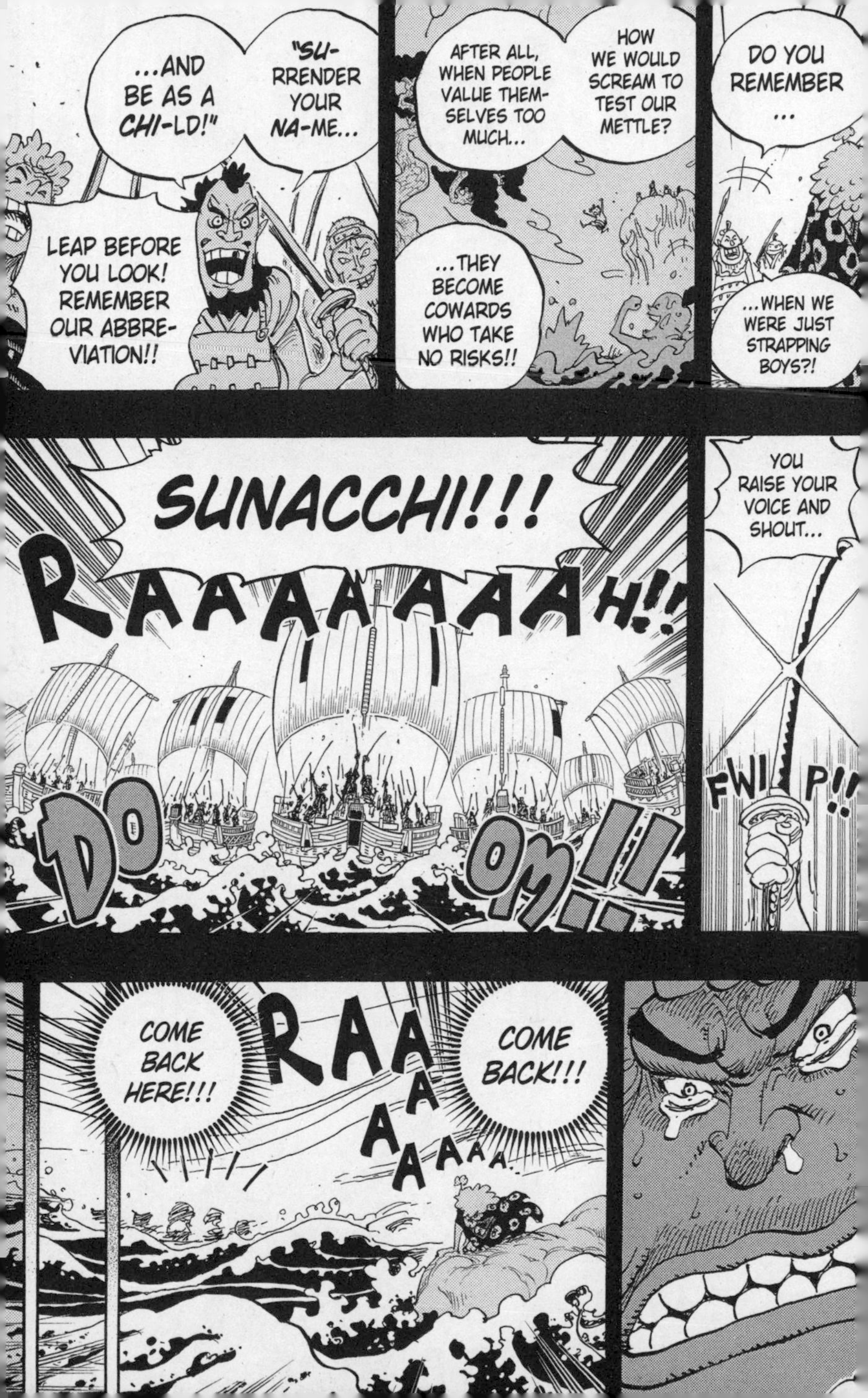
DO YOU REMEMBER ...
...WHEN WE WERE JUST STRAPPING BOYS?!
HOW WE WOULD SCREAM TO TEST OUR METTLE?
AFTER ALL, WHEN PEOPLE VALUE THEM-SELVES TOO MUCH...
...THEY BECOME COWARDS WHO TAKE NO RISKS!!
"SU-RRENDER YOUR NA-ME...
...AND BE AS A CHI-LD!"
LEAP BEFORE YOU LOOK! REMEMBER OUR ABBRE-VIATION!!
YOU RAISE YOUR VOICE AND SHOUT...
FWIP!!
SUNACCHI!!!
RAAAAAAAH!!
DOOM!!
COME BACK!!!
RAAAAAAAAA
COME BACK HERE!!!

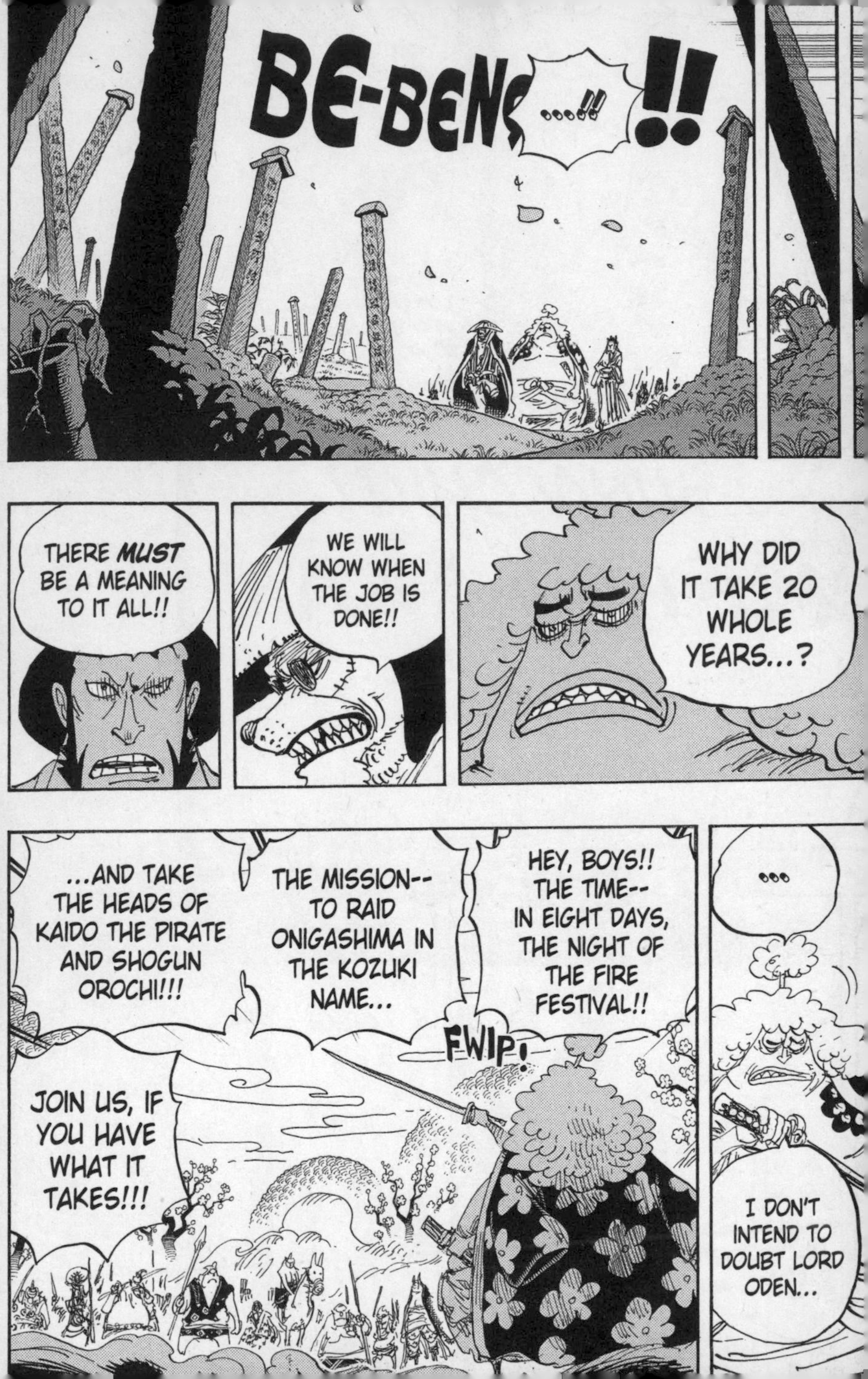
BE-BENG
...!!
!!
WHY DID IT TAKE 20 WHOLE YEARS...?
WE WILL KNOW WHEN THE JOB IS DONE!!
THERE MUST BE A MEANING TO IT ALL!!
...
I DON'T INTEND TO DOUBT LORD ODEN...
HEY, BOYS!! THE TIME-- IN EIGHT DAYS, THE NIGHT OF THE FIRE FESTIVAL!!
THE MISSION-- TO RAID ONIGASHIMA IN THE KOZUKI NAME...
...AND TAKE THE HEADS OF KAIDO THE PIRATE AND SHOGUN OROCHI!!!
FWIP
JOIN US, IF YOU HAVE WHAT IT TAKES!!!

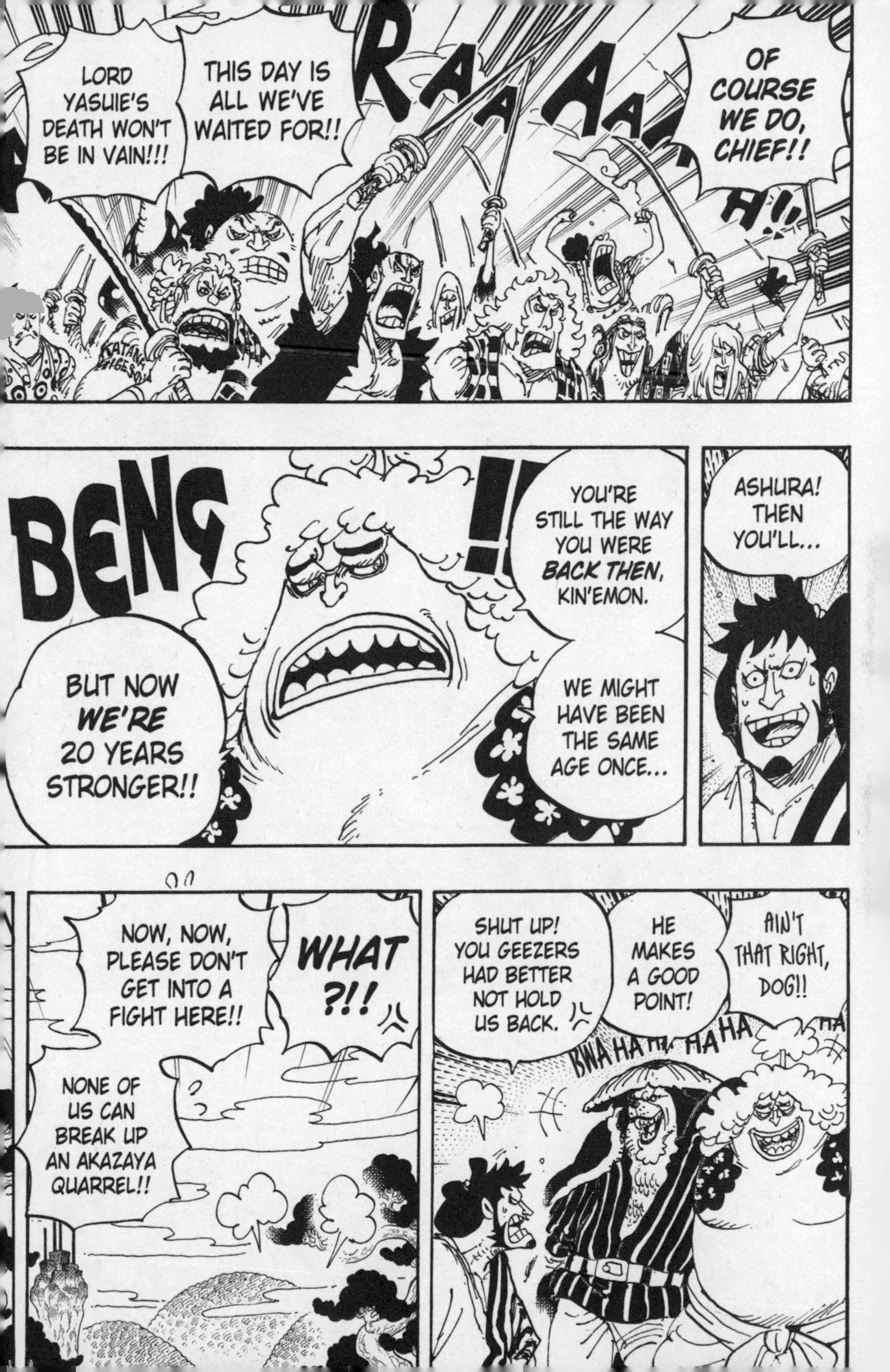
OF COURSE WE DO, CHIEF!!
RAAAAAH!!
THIS DAY IS ALL WE'VE WAITED FOR!!
LORD YASUIE'S DEATH WON'T BE IN VAIN!!!
ASHURA! THEN YOU'LL...
YOU'RE STILL THE WAY YOU WERE *BACK THEN*, KIN'EMON.
!!
BENG
WE MIGHT HAVE BEEN THE SAME AGE ONCE...
BUT NOW *WE'RE* 20 YEARS STRONGER!!
AIN'T THAT RIGHT, DOG!!
HE MAKES A GOOD POINT!
SHUT UP! YOU GEEZERS HAD BETTER NOT HOLD US BACK.
BWA HA HA HA HA HA
WHAT?!!
NOW, NOW, PLEASE DON'T GET INTO A FIGHT HERE!!
NONE OF US CAN BREAK UP AN AKAZAYA QUARREL!!

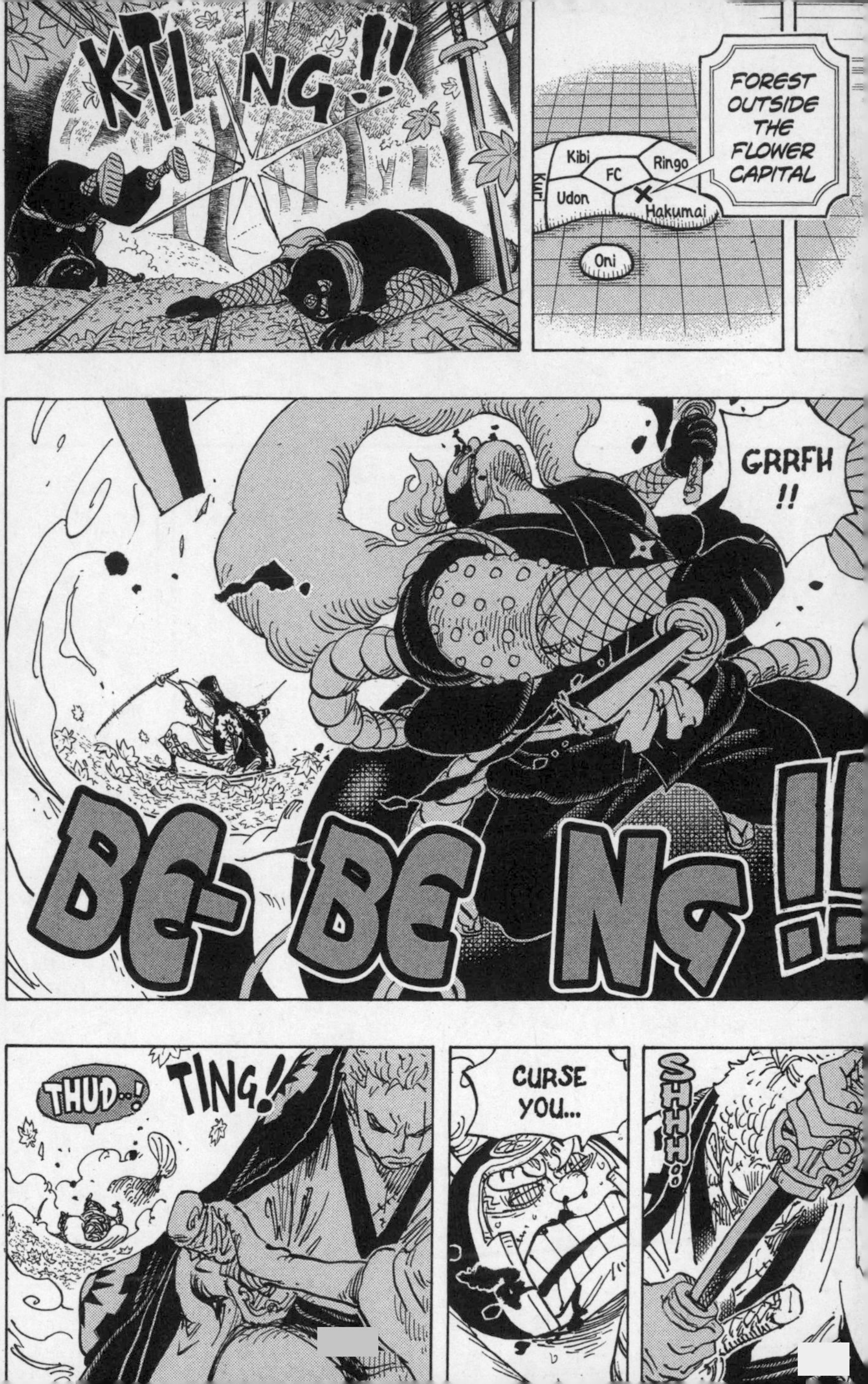
FOREST OUTSIDE THE FLOWER CAPITAL
Kibi
Ringo
FC
Kuri
Udon
Hakumai
Oni
KTING!!
GRRFH!!
BE-BENG!!
SHHHH..
CURSE YOU...
THUD..!
TING!!

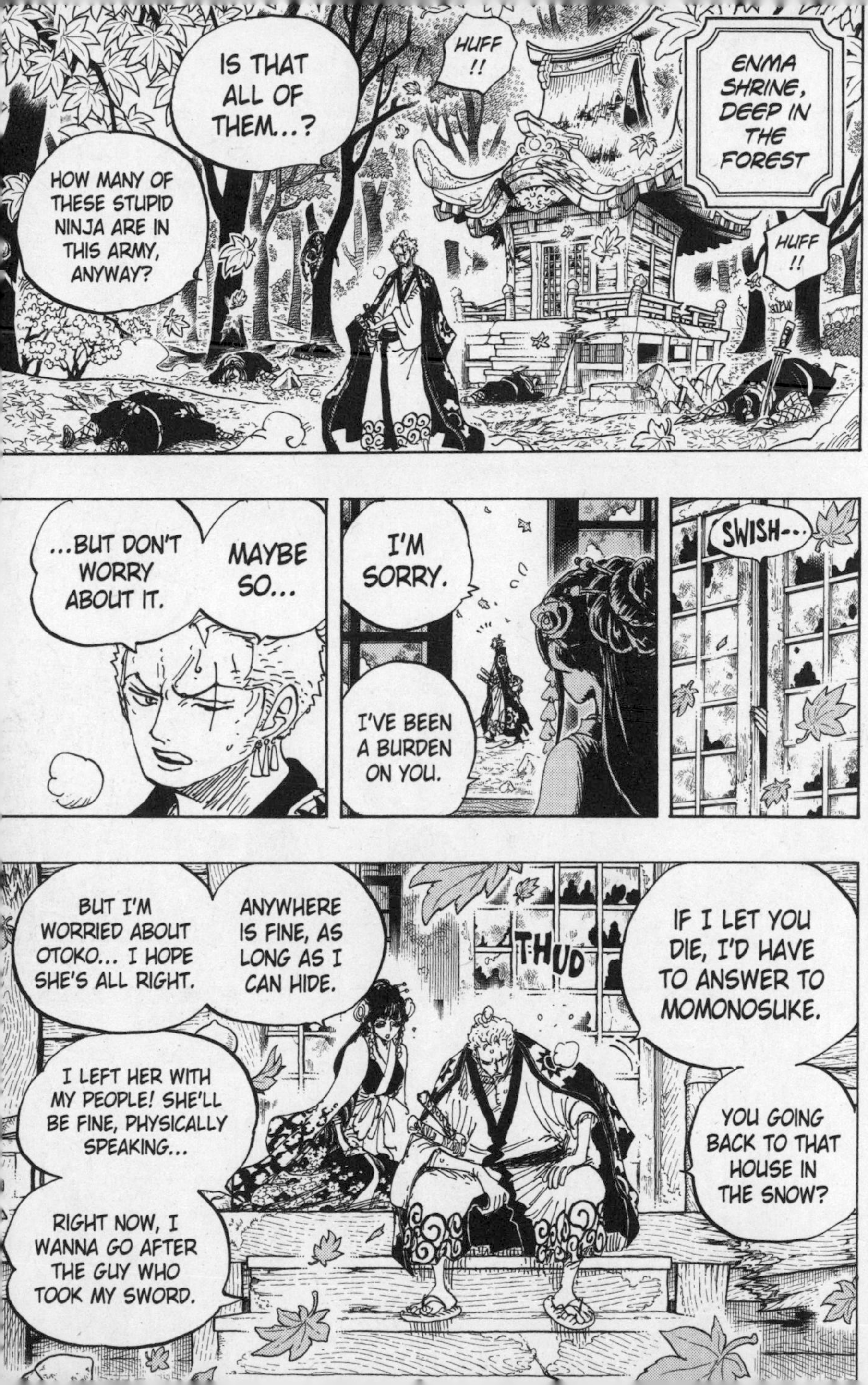
ENMA SHRINE, DEEP IN THE FOREST
HUFF !!
IS THAT ALL OF THEM...?
HUFF !!
HOW MANY OF THESE STUPID NINJA ARE IN THIS ARMY, ANYWAY?
SWISH-..
I'M SORRY.
I'VE BEEN A BURDEN ON YOU.
MAYBE SO...
...BUT DON'T WORRY ABOUT IT.
IF I LET YOU DIE, I'D HAVE TO ANSWER TO MOMONOSUKE.
THUD
YOU GOING BACK TO THAT HOUSE IN THE SNOW?
ANYWHERE IS FINE, AS LONG AS I CAN HIDE.
BUT I'M WORRIED ABOUT OTOKO... I HOPE SHE'S ALL RIGHT.
I LEFT HER WITH MY PEOPLE! SHE'LL BE FINE, PHYSICALLY SPEAKING...
RIGHT NOW, I WANNA GO AFTER THE GUY WHO TOOK MY SWORD.

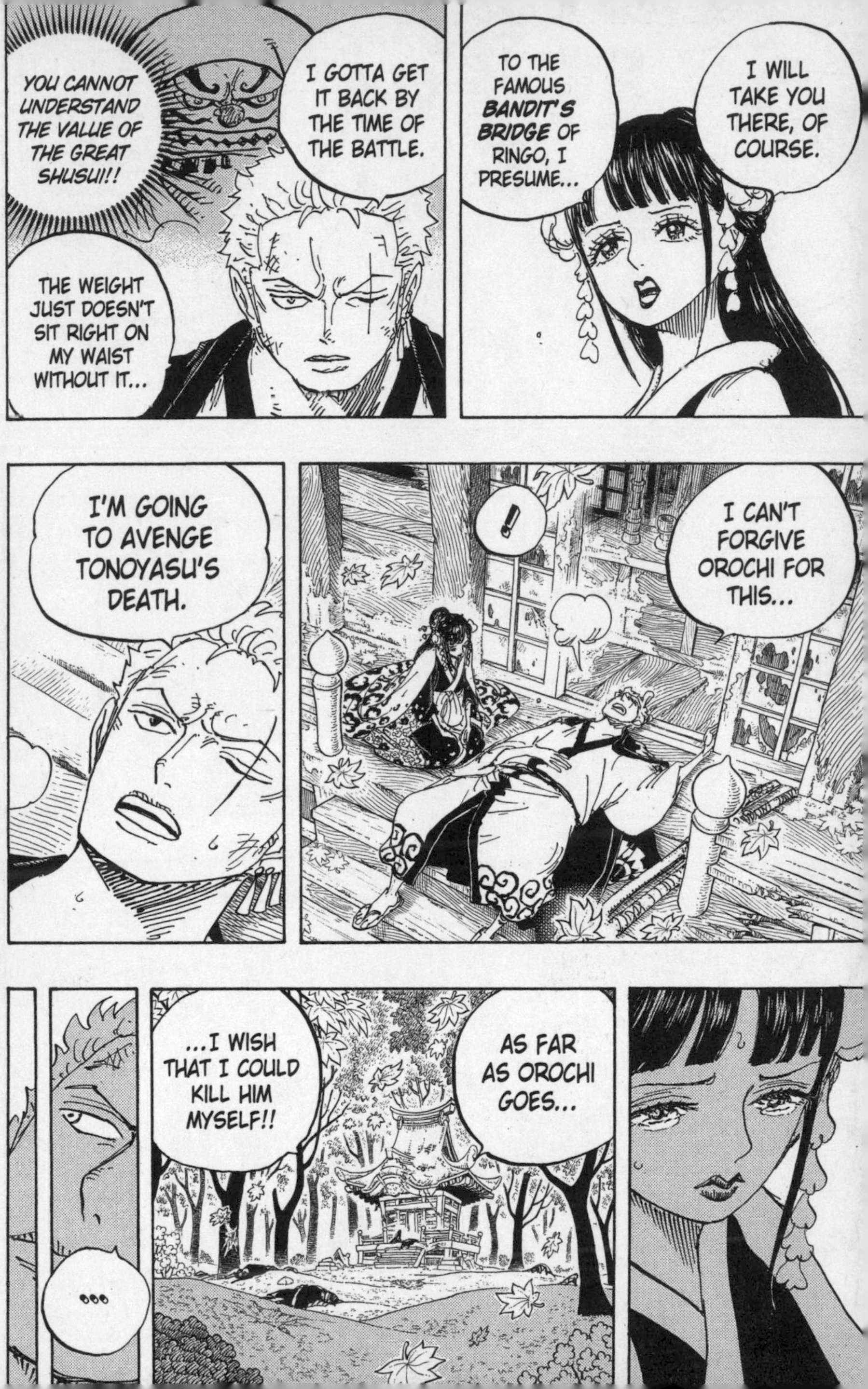

I WILL TAKE YOU THERE, OF COURSE.
TO THE FAMOUS BANDIT'S BRIDGE OF RINGO, I PRESUME...
I GOTTA GET IT BACK BY THE TIME OF THE BATTLE.
YOU CANNOT UNDERSTAND THE VALUE OF THE GREAT SHUSUI!!
THE WEIGHT JUST DOESN'T SIT RIGHT ON MY WAIST WITHOUT IT...
I CAN'T FORGIVE OROCHI FOR THIS...
!
I'M GOING TO AVENGE TONOYASU'S DEATH.
AS FAR AS OROCHI GOES...
...I WISH THAT I COULD KILL HIM MYSELF!!
...

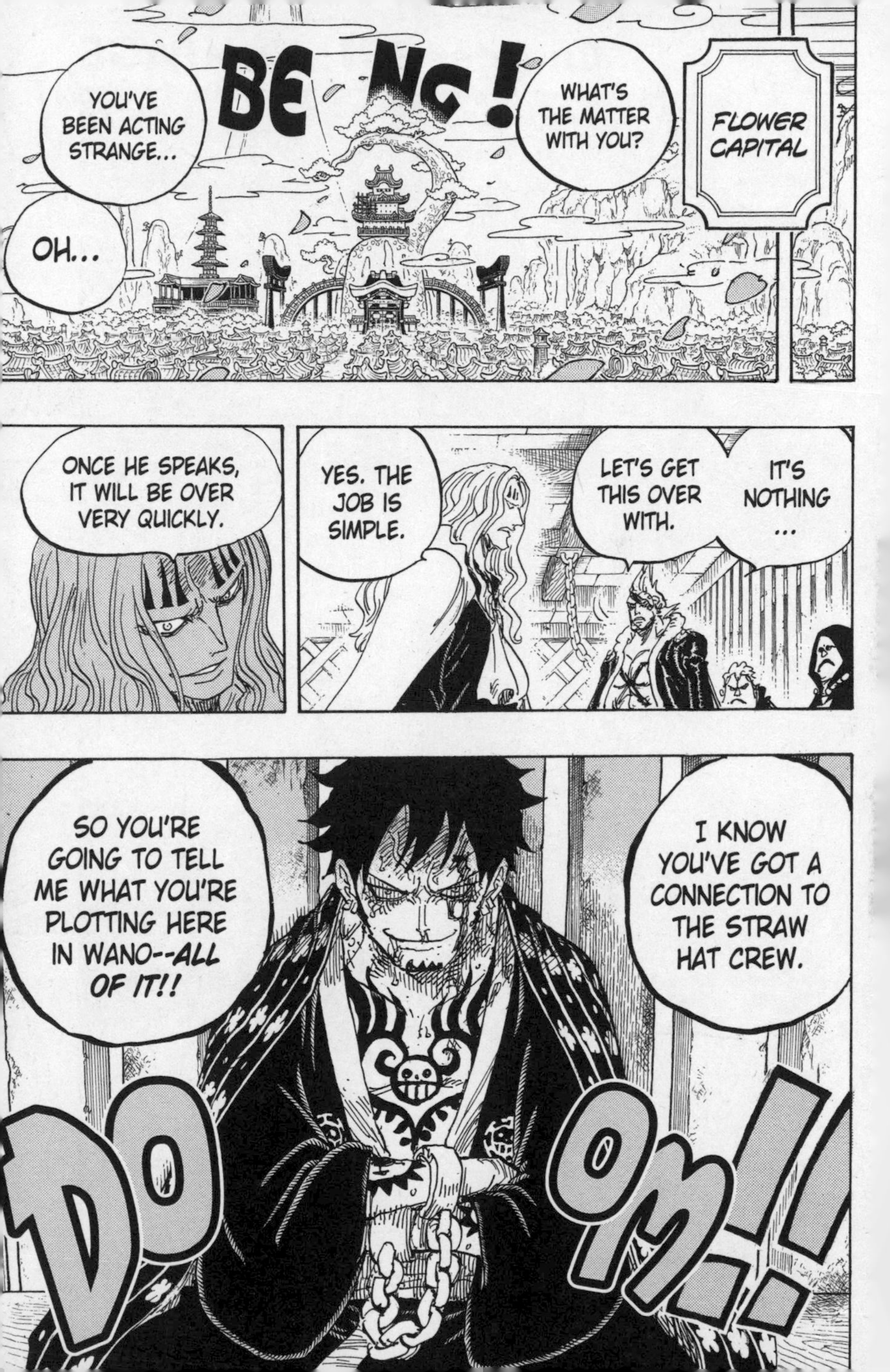
FLOWER CAPITAL
WHAT'S THE MATTER WITH YOU?
BE NG!
YOU'VE BEEN ACTING STRANGE...
OH...
IT'S NOTHING ...
LET'S GET THIS OVER WITH.
YES. THE JOB IS SIMPLE.
ONCE HE SPEAKS, IT WILL BE OVER VERY QUICKLY.
I KNOW YOU'VE GOT A CONNECTION TO THE STRAW HAT CREW.
SO YOU'RE GOING TO TELL ME WHAT YOU'RE PLOTTING HERE IN WANO--*ALL OF IT!!*
DOOM!!

Chapter 951: RAMPAGE

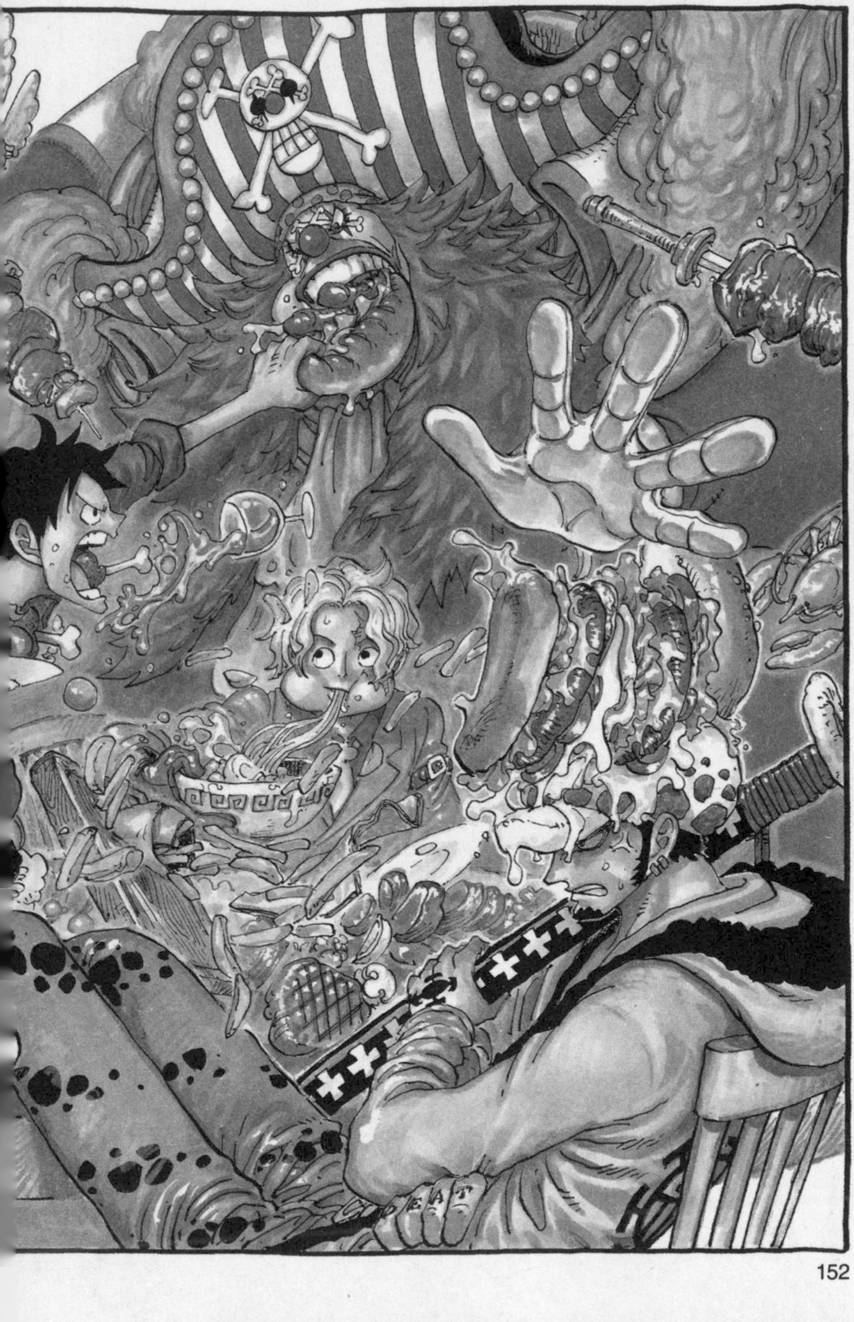

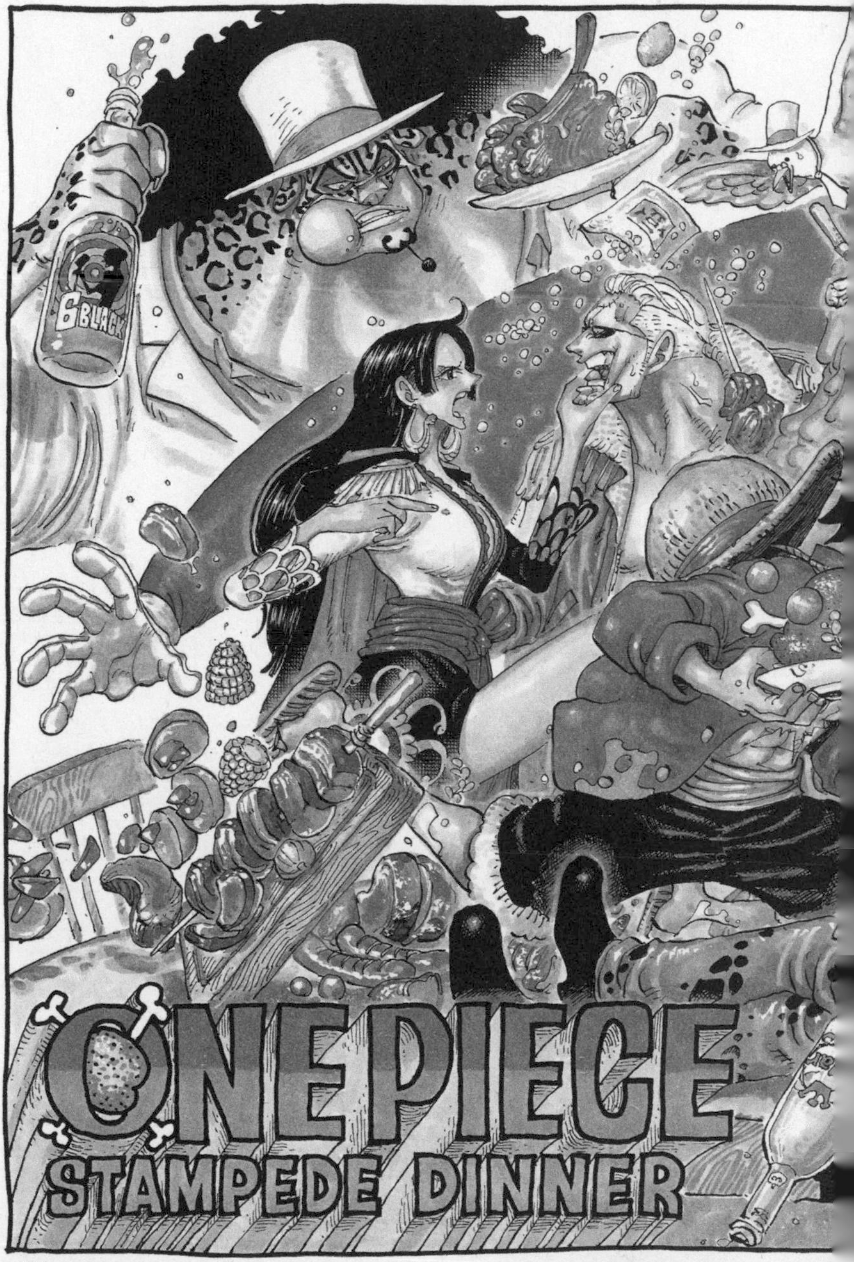
6 BLACK
ONE PIECE
STAMPEDE DINNER

vol.94
ONE PIECE

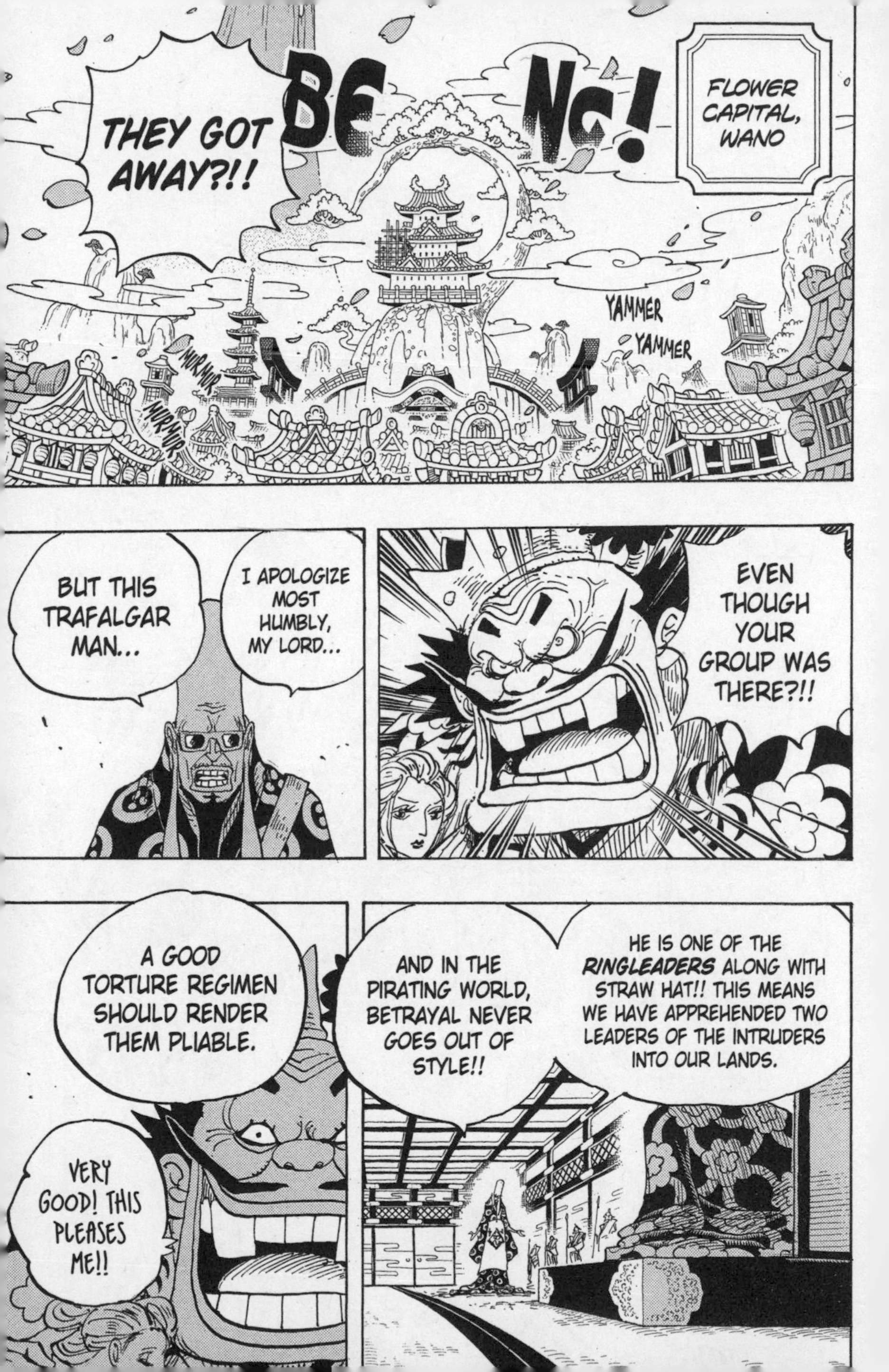
FLOWER CAPITAL, WANO
BE NG!
THEY GOT AWAY?!!
YAMMER YAMMER
MURMUR MURMUR
EVEN THOUGH YOUR GROUP WAS THERE?!!
I APOLOGIZE MOST HUMBLY, MY LORD...
BUT THIS TRAFALGAR MAN...
HE IS ONE OF THE *RINGLEADERS* ALONG WITH STRAW HAT!! THIS MEANS WE HAVE APPREHENDED TWO LEADERS OF THE INTRUDERS INTO OUR LANDS.
AND IN THE PIRATING WORLD, BETRAYAL NEVER GOES OUT OF STYLE!!
A GOOD TORTURE REGIMEN SHOULD RENDER THEM PLIABLE.
VERY GOOD! THIS PLEASES ME!!

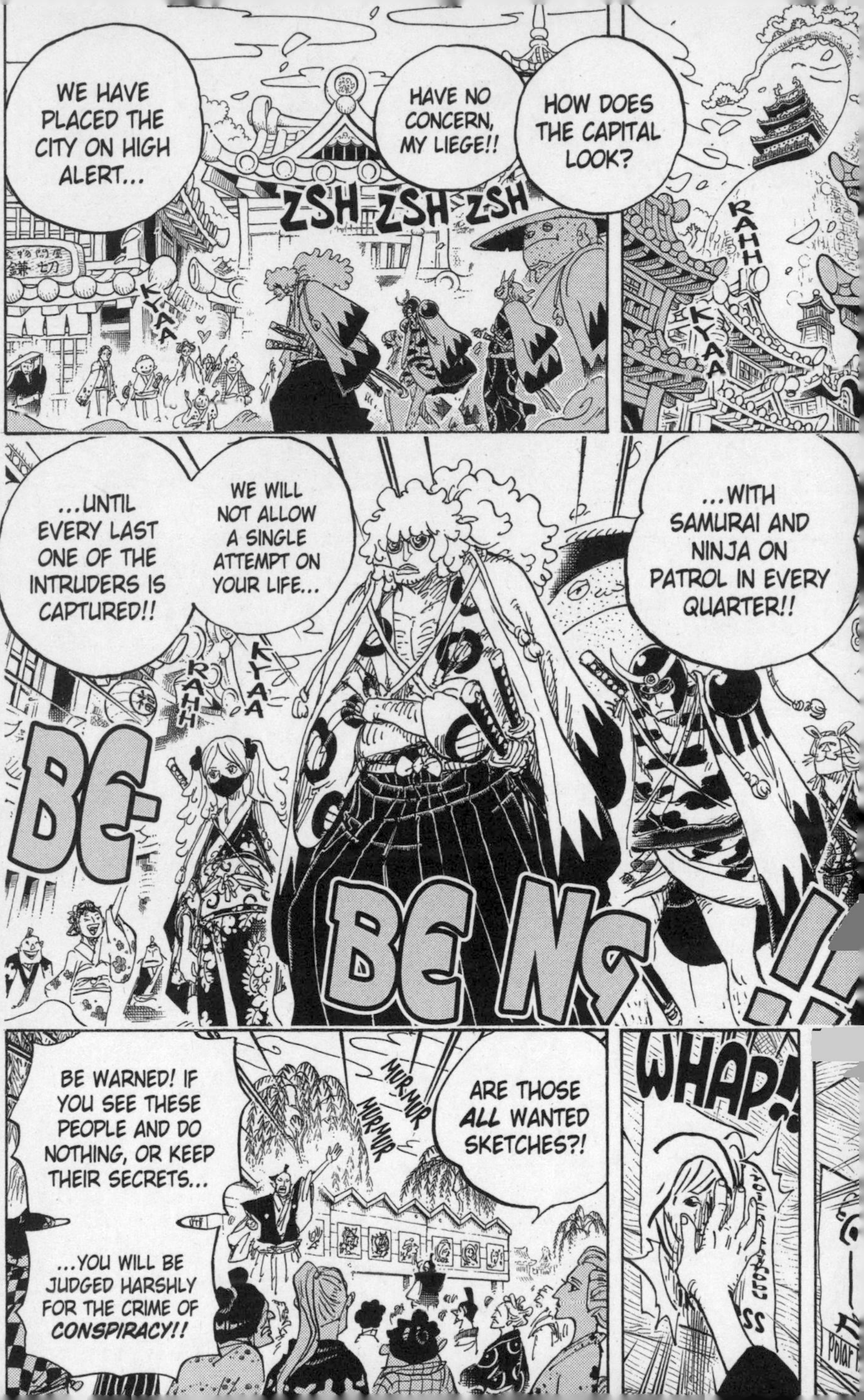
RAHHH
KYAA
HOW DOES THE CAPITAL LOOK?
HAVE NO CONCERN, MY LIEGE!!
WE HAVE PLACED THE CITY ON HIGH ALERT...
ZSH ZSH ZSH
KYAA
...WITH SAMURAI AND NINJA ON PATROL IN EVERY QUARTER!!
WE WILL NOT ALLOW A SINGLE ATTEMPT ON YOUR LIFE...
...UNTIL EVERY LAST ONE OF THE INTRUDERS IS CAPTURED!!
KYAA
RAHHH
BE-
BENG!!
WHAP!!
ARE THOSE *ALL* WANTED SKETCHES?!
MURMUR
MURMUR
BE WARNED! IF YOU SEE THESE PEOPLE AND DO NOTHING, OR KEEP THEIR SECRETS...
...YOU WILL BE JUDGED HARSHLY FOR THE CRIME OF *CONSPIRACY!!*

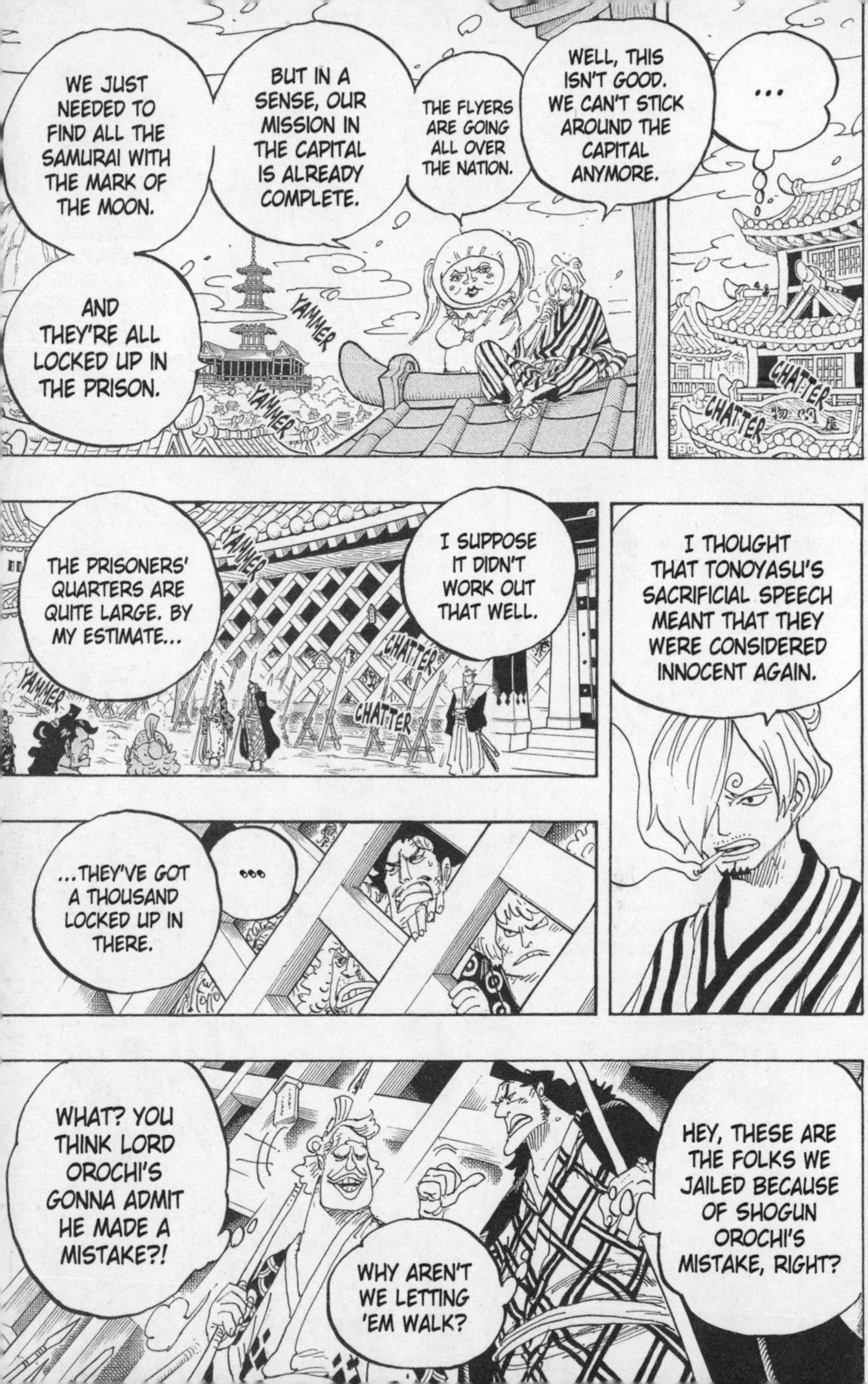
...
CHATTER
CHATTER
WELL, THIS ISN'T GOOD. WE CAN'T STICK AROUND THE CAPITAL ANYMORE.
THE FLYERS ARE GOING ALL OVER THE NATION.
BUT IN A SENSE, OUR MISSION IN THE CAPITAL IS ALREADY COMPLETE.
WE JUST NEEDED TO FIND ALL THE SAMURAI WITH THE MARK OF THE MOON.
YAMMER
YAMMER
AND THEY'RE ALL LOCKED UP IN THE PRISON.
I THOUGHT THAT TONOYASU'S SACRIFICIAL SPEECH MEANT THAT THEY WERE CONSIDERED INNOCENT AGAIN.
I SUPPOSE IT DIDN'T WORK OUT THAT WELL.
YAMMER
CHATTER
CHATTER
THE PRISONERS' QUARTERS ARE QUITE LARGE. BY MY ESTIMATE...
YAMMER
...
...THEY'VE GOT A THOUSAND LOCKED UP IN THERE.
HEY, THESE ARE THE FOLKS WE JAILED BECAUSE OF SHOGUN OROCHI'S MISTAKE, RIGHT?
WHY AREN'T WE LETTING 'EM WALK?
WHAT? YOU THINK LORD OROCHI'S GONNA ADMIT HE MADE A MISTAKE?!

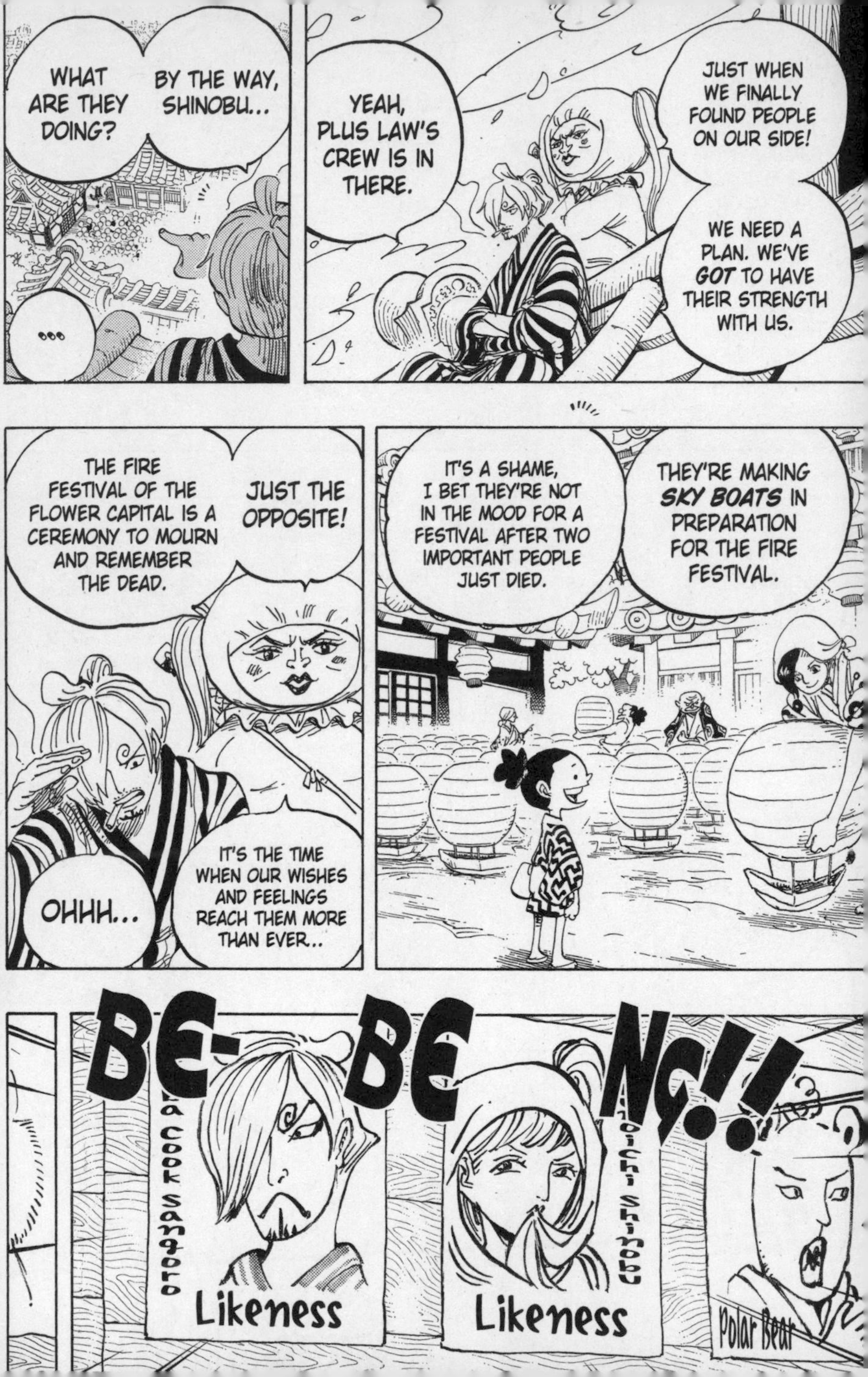
JUST WHEN WE FINALLY FOUND PEOPLE ON OUR SIDE!
WE NEED A PLAN. WE'VE *GOT* TO HAVE THEIR STRENGTH WITH US.
YEAH, PLUS LAW'S CREW IS IN THERE.
BY THE WAY, SHINOBU...
WHAT ARE THEY DOING?
...
THEY'RE MAKING *SKY BOATS* IN PREPARATION FOR THE FIRE FESTIVAL.
IT'S A SHAME, I BET THEY'RE NOT IN THE MOOD FOR A FESTIVAL AFTER TWO IMPORTANT PEOPLE JUST DIED.
JUST THE OPPOSITE!
THE FIRE FESTIVAL OF THE FLOWER CAPITAL IS A CEREMONY TO MOURN AND REMEMBER THE DEAD.
IT'S THE TIME WHEN OUR WISHES AND FEELINGS REACH THEM MORE THAN EVER...
OHHH...
BE-BE NG!!
Polar Bear
Likeness
Likeness

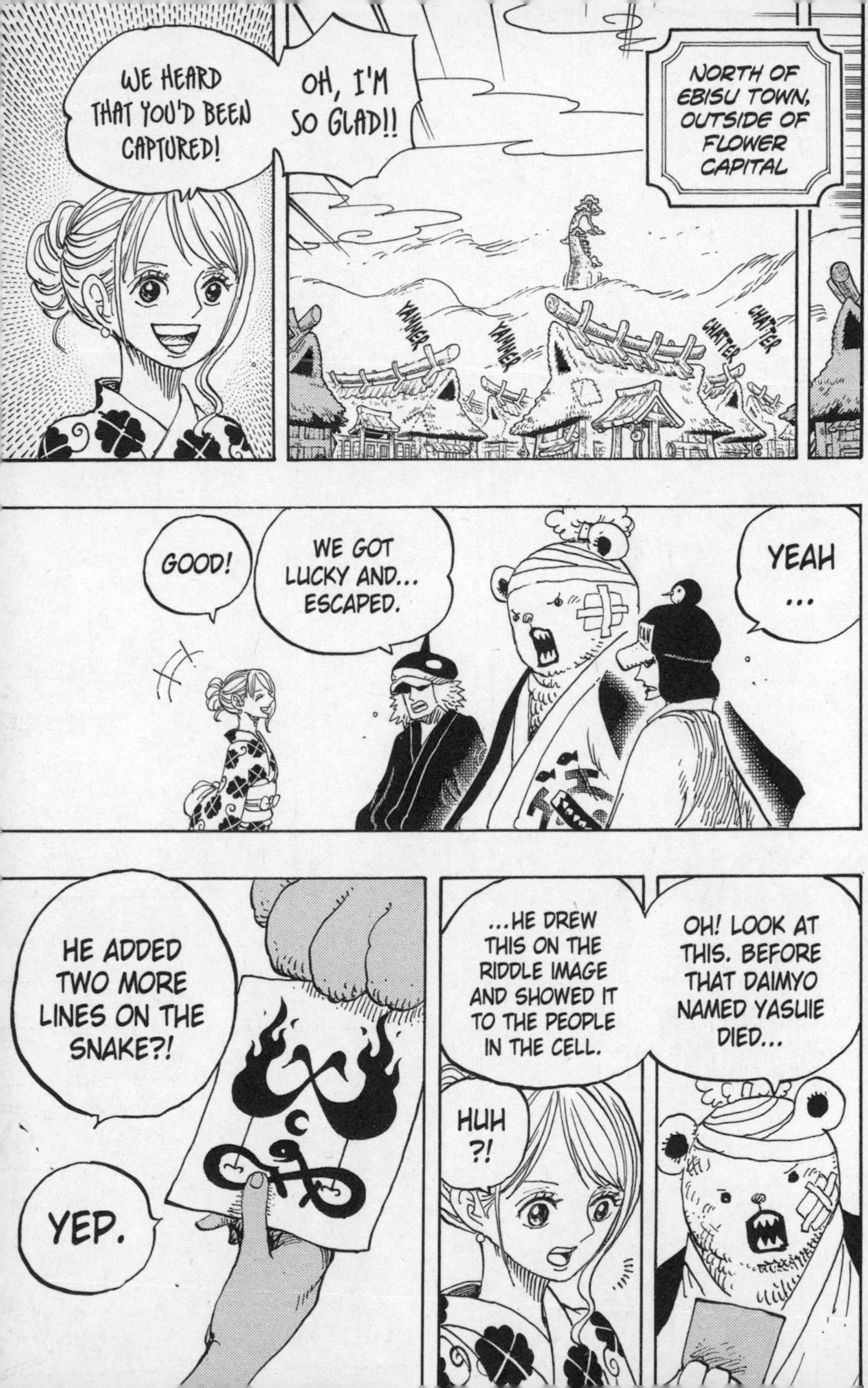
NORTH OF EBISU TOWN, OUTSIDE OF FLOWER CAPITAL
CHATTER
CHATTER
YAMMER
YAMMER
OH, I'M SO GLAD!!
WE HEARD THAT YOU'D BEEN CAPTURED!
YEAH ...
WE GOT LUCKY AND... ESCAPED.
GOOD!
OH! LOOK AT THIS. BEFORE THAT DAIMYO NAMED YASUIE DIED...
...HE DREW THIS ON THE RIDDLE IMAGE AND SHOWED IT TO THE PEOPLE IN THE CELL.
HUH ?!
HE ADDED TWO MORE LINES ON THE SNAKE?!
YEP.

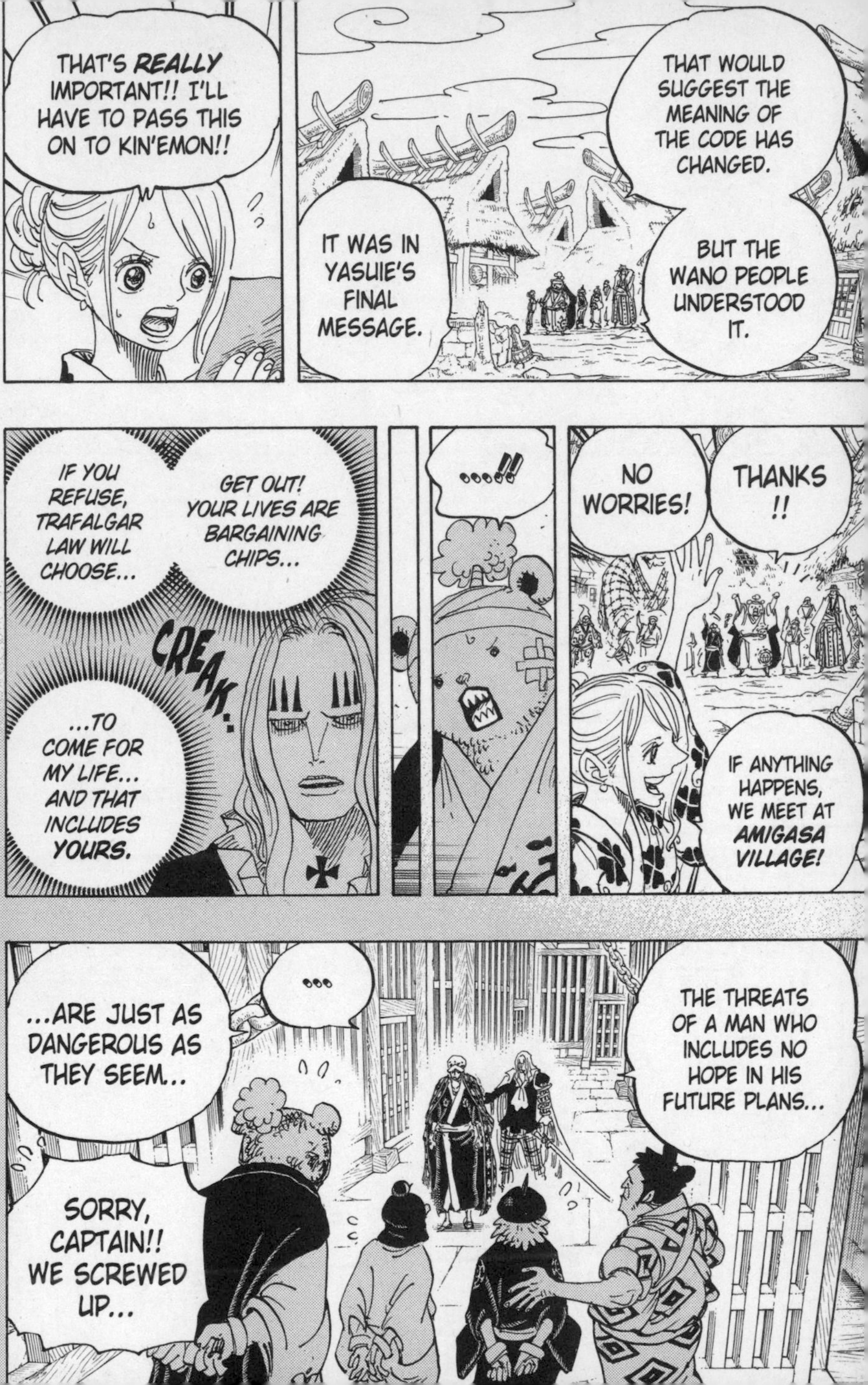
THAT WOULD SUGGEST THE MEANING OF THE CODE HAS CHANGED.
IT WAS IN YASUIE'S FINAL MESSAGE.
BUT THE WANO PEOPLE UNDERSTOOD IT.
THAT'S REALLY IMPORTANT!! I'LL HAVE TO PASS THIS ON TO KIN'EMON!!
THANKS!!
NO WORRIES!
IF ANYTHING HAPPENS, WE MEET AT AMIGASA VILLAGE!
...!!
GET OUT! YOUR LIVES ARE BARGAINING CHIPS...
IF YOU REFUSE, TRAFALGAR LAW WILL CHOOSE...
CREAK..
...TO COME FOR MY LIFE... AND THAT INCLUDES YOURS.
THE THREATS OF A MAN WHO INCLUDES NO HOPE IN HIS FUTURE PLANS...
...
...ARE JUST AS DANGEROUS AS THEY SEEM...
SORRY, CAPTAIN!! WE SCREWED UP...

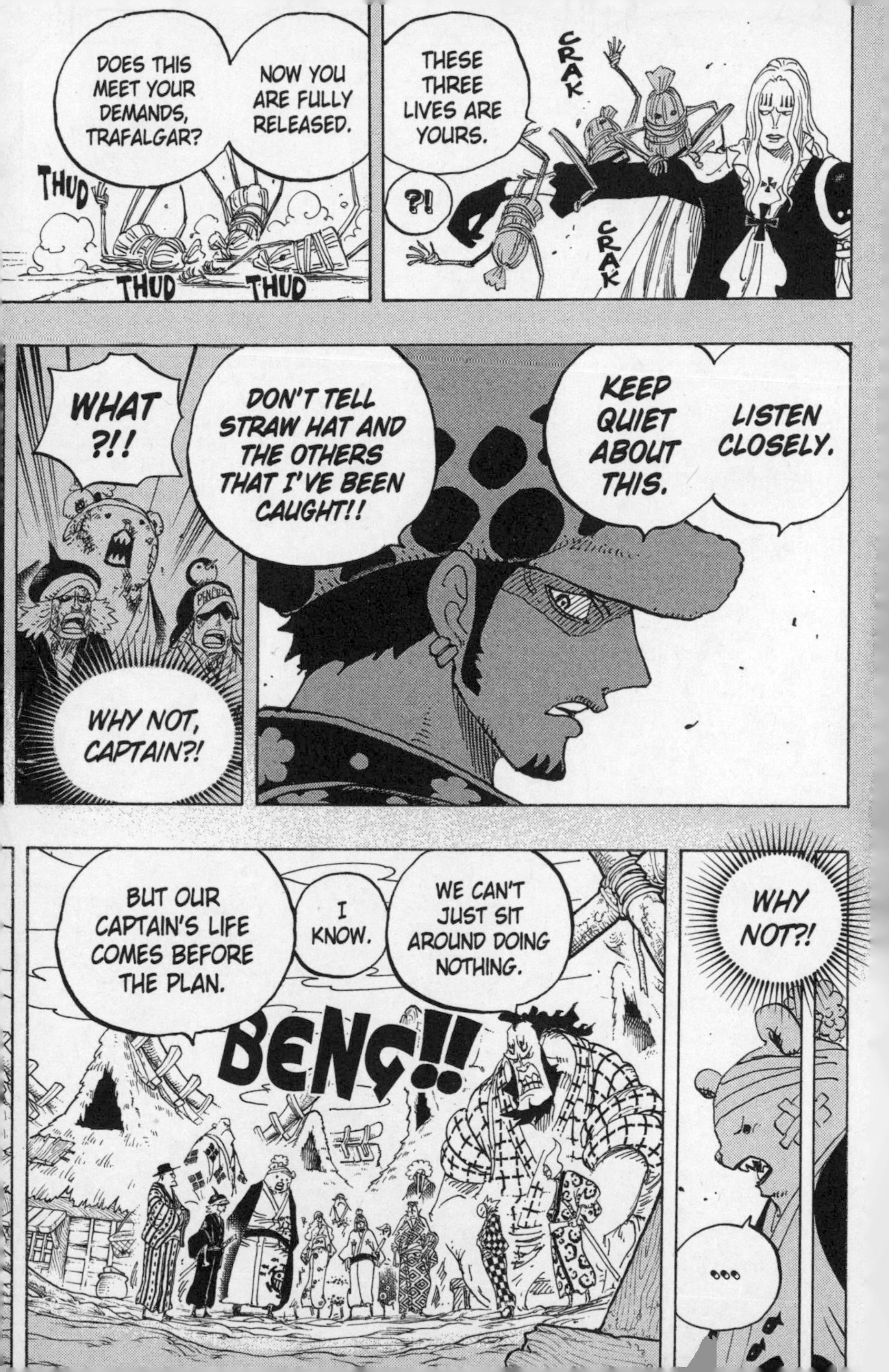
CRAK
THESE THREE LIVES ARE YOURS.
?!
CRAK
NOW YOU ARE FULLY RELEASED.
DOES THIS MEET YOUR DEMANDS, TRAFALGAR?
THUD
THUD
THUD
LISTEN CLOSELY.
KEEP QUIET ABOUT THIS.
DON'T TELL STRAW HAT AND THE OTHERS THAT I'VE BEEN CAUGHT!!
WHAT ?!!
WHY NOT, CAPTAIN?!
WHY NOT?!
...
WE CAN'T JUST SIT AROUND DOING NOTHING.
I KNOW.
BUT OUR CAPTAIN'S LIFE COMES BEFORE THE PLAN.
BENG!!

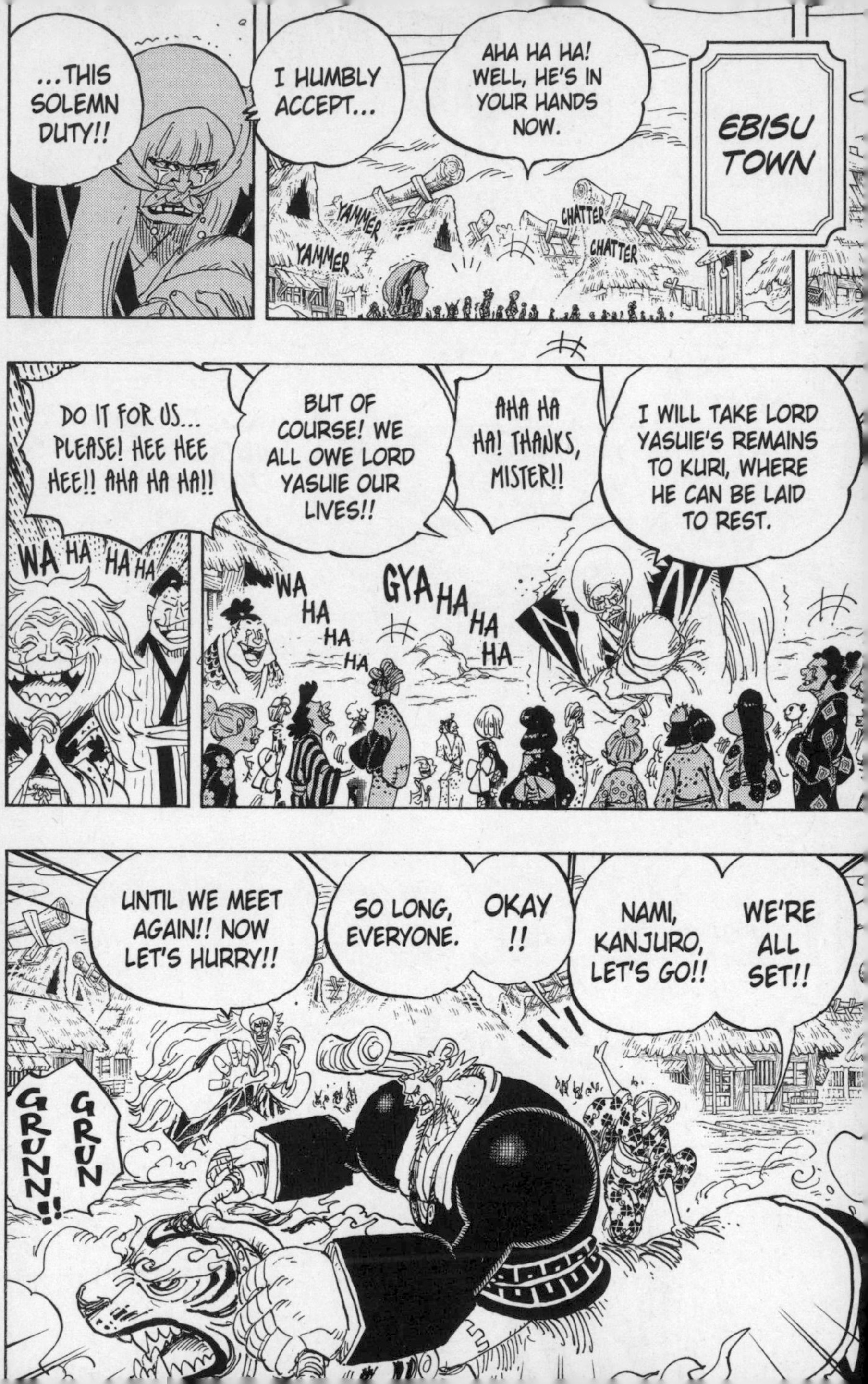
EBISU TOWN
AHA HA HA! WELL, HE'S IN YOUR HANDS NOW.
I HUMBLY ACCEPT...
CHATTER CHATTER
YAMMER YAMMER
...THIS SOLEMN DUTY!!
I WILL TAKE LORD YASUIE'S REMAINS TO KURI, WHERE HE CAN BE LAID TO REST.
AHA HA HA! THANKS, MISTER!!
BUT OF COURSE! WE ALL OWE LORD YASUIE OUR LIVES!!
GYA HA HA HA
WA HA HA HA
DO IT FOR US... PLEASE! HEE HEE HEE!! AHA HA HA!!
WA HA HA HA
WE'RE ALL SET!!
NAMI, KANJURO, LET'S GO!!
OKAY!!
SO LONG, EVERYONE.
UNTIL WE MEET AGAIN!! NOW LET'S HURRY!!
GRUN
GRUNN!!

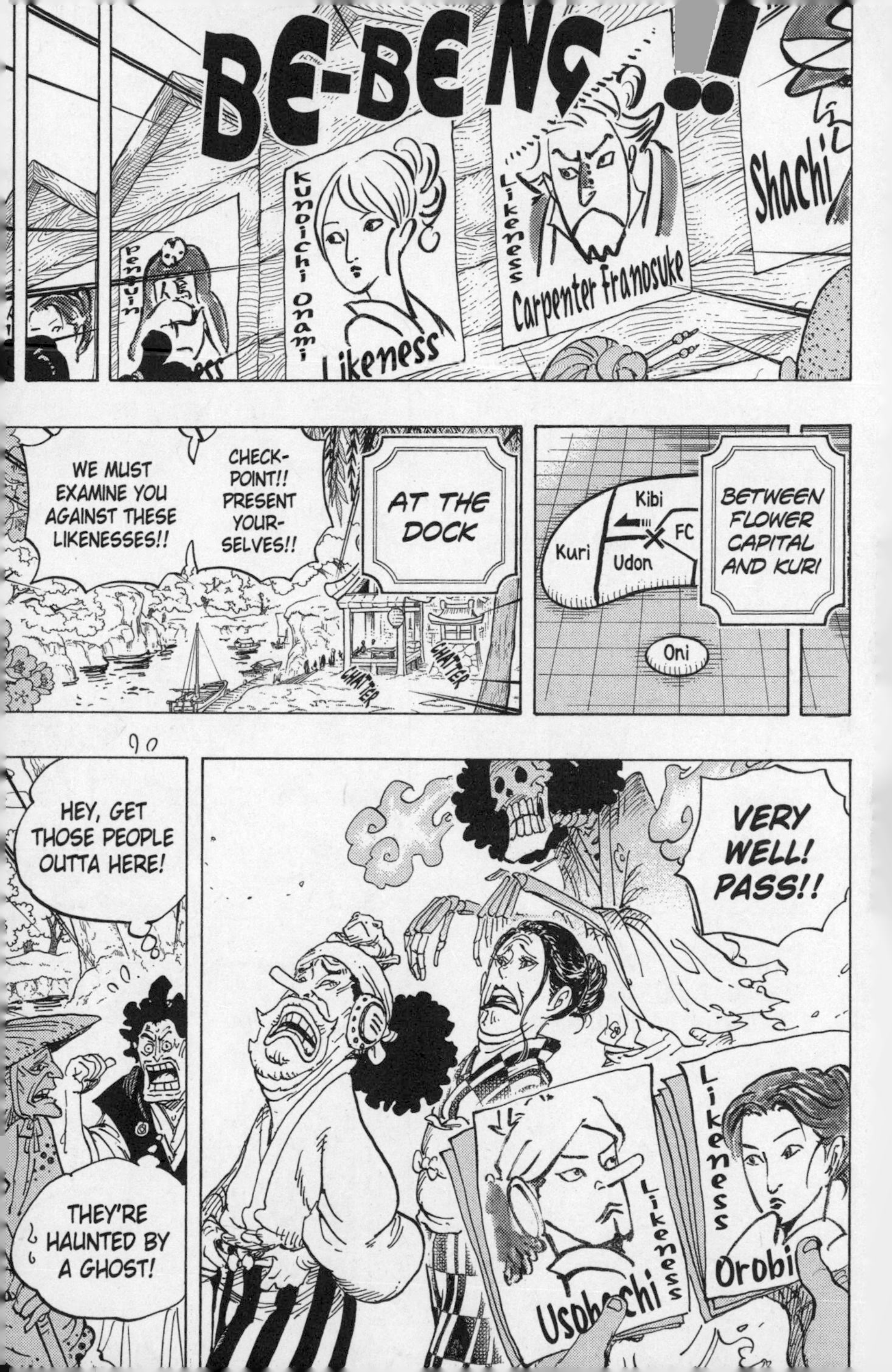
Shachi
Likeness
Carpenter Franosuke
BE-BENG!!
Kunoichi Onami
Likeness
Penguin
BETWEEN FLOWER CAPITAL AND KURI
Kibi
FC
Kuri
Udon
Oni
AT THE DOCK
CHECK-POINT!! PRESENT YOUR-SELVES!!
WE MUST EXAMINE YOU AGAINST THESE LIKENESSES!!
CHATTER
CHATTER
VERY WELL! PASS!!
Likeness
Orobi
Likeness
Usohachi
HEY, GET THOSE PEOPLE OUTTA HERE!
THEY'RE HAUNTED BY A GHOST!

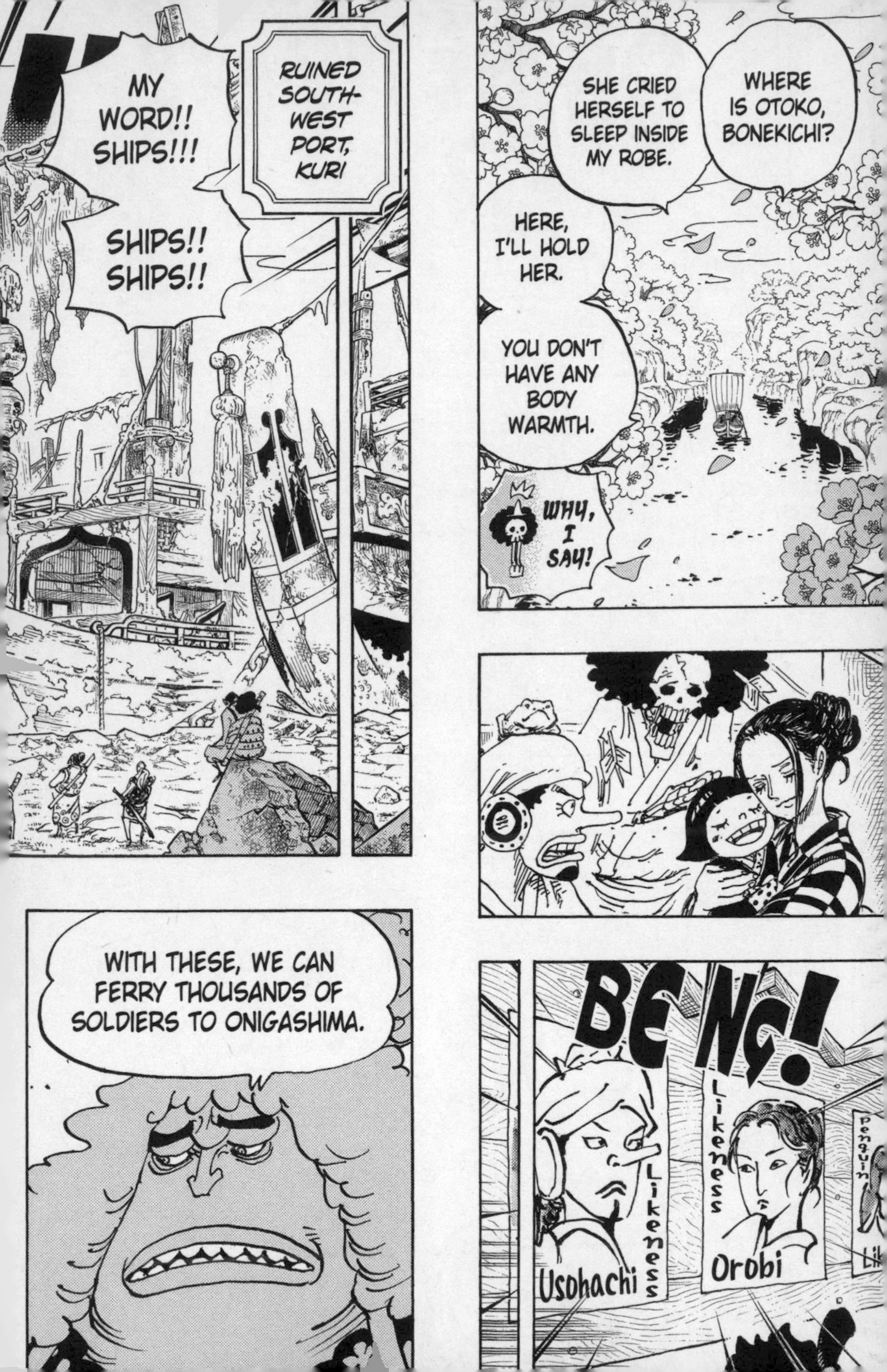
WHERE IS OTOKO, BONEKICHI?
SHE CRIED HERSELF TO SLEEP INSIDE MY ROBE.
HERE, I'LL HOLD HER.
YOU DON'T HAVE ANY BODY WARMTH.
WHY, I SAY!
RUINED SOUTH-WEST PORT, KURI
MY WORD!! SHIPS!!!
SHIPS!! SHIPS!!
BENG!
Penguin
Likeness
Orobi
Likeness
Usohachi
Likeness
WITH THESE, WE CAN FERRY THOUSANDS OF SOLDIERS TO ONIGASHIMA.

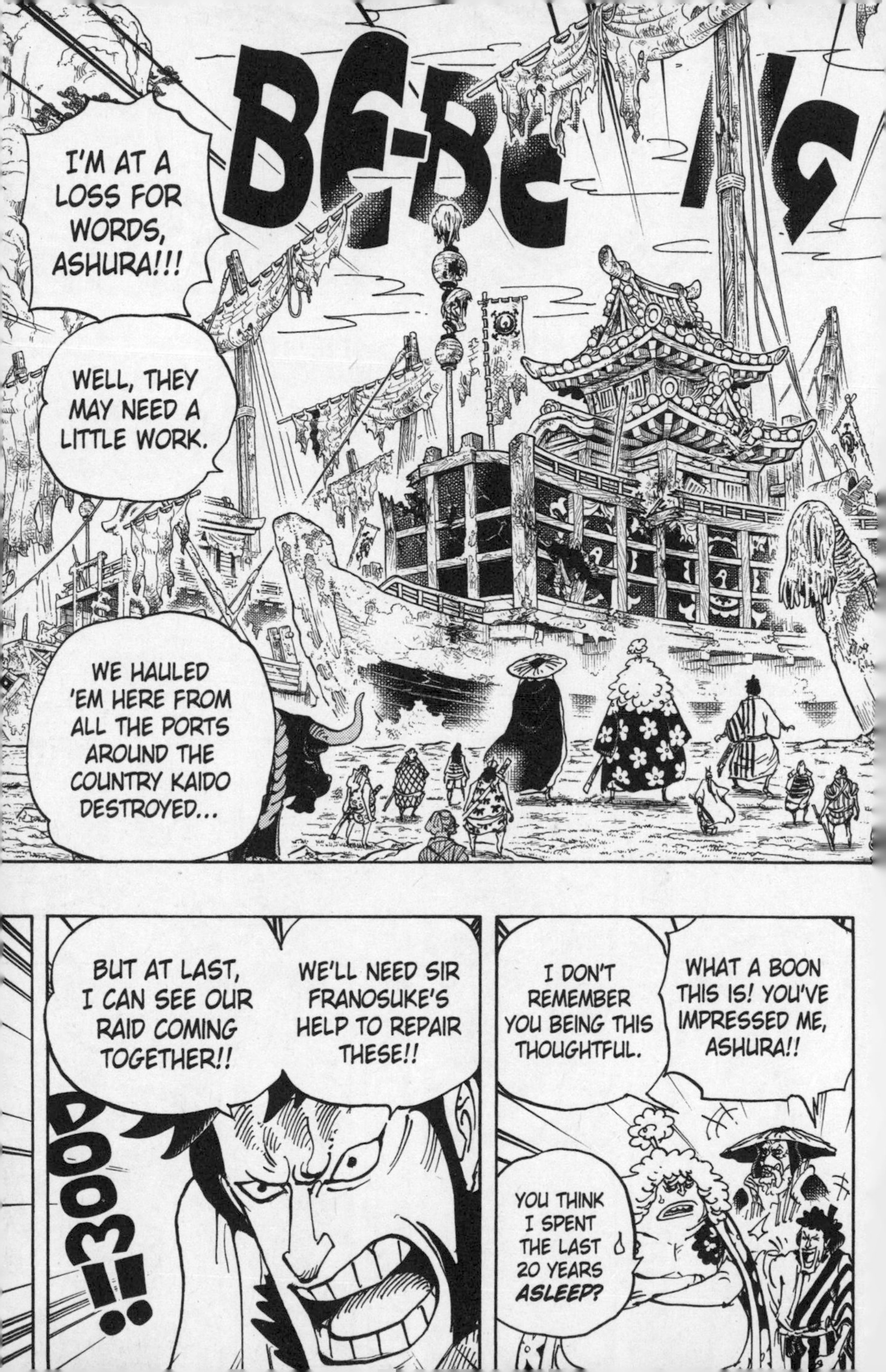
BE-BE NG
I'M AT A LOSS FOR WORDS, ASHURA!!!
WELL, THEY MAY NEED A LITTLE WORK.
WE HAULED 'EM HERE FROM ALL THE PORTS AROUND THE COUNTRY KAIDO DESTROYED...
WHAT A BOON THIS IS! YOU'VE IMPRESSED ME, ASHURA!!
I DON'T REMEMBER YOU BEING THIS THOUGHTFUL.
YOU THINK I SPENT THE LAST 20 YEARS ASLEEP?
WE'LL NEED SIR FRANOSUKE'S HELP TO REPAIR THESE!!
BUT AT LAST, I CAN SEE OUR RAID COMING TOGETHER!!
DOOO!!

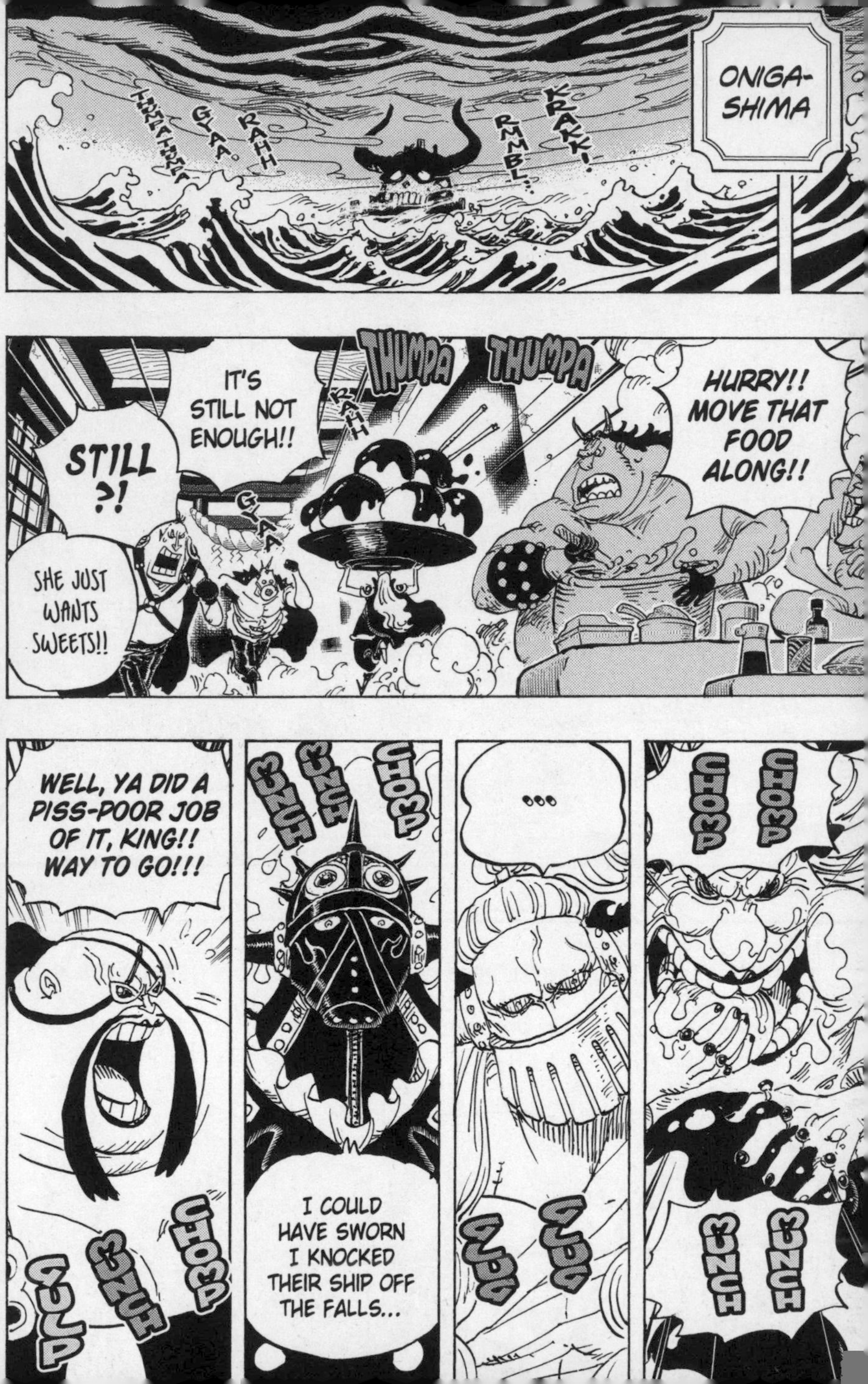
ONIGA-SHIMA
KRAKKI
RMMBL...
RAHH
GYAA
THUMPATHUMPA
HURRY!! MOVE THAT FOOD ALONG!!
THUMPA
THUMPA
RAHH
IT'S STILL NOT ENOUGH!!
STILL ?!
GYAA
SHE JUST WANTS SWEETS!!
CHOMP
CHOMP
MUNCH
MUNCH
...
GULP
GULP
CHOMP
MUNCH
MUNCH
I COULD HAVE SWORN I KNOCKED THEIR SHIP OFF THE FALLS...
WELL, YA DID A PISS-POOR JOB OF IT, KING!! WAY TO GO!!!
CHOMP
MUNCH
GULP

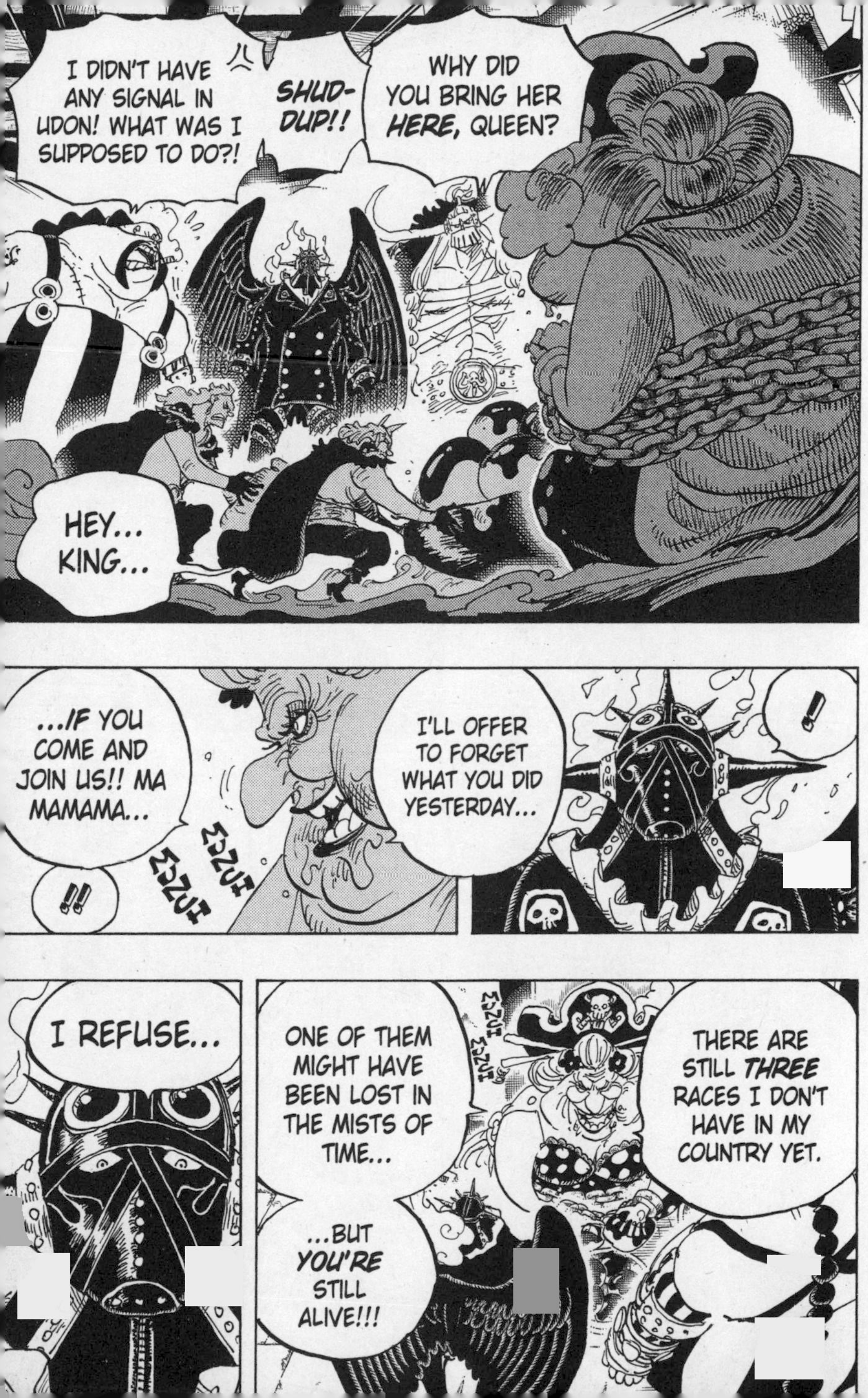

WHY DID YOU BRING HER *HERE,* QUEEN?
SHUD-DUP!!
I DIDN'T HAVE ANY SIGNAL IN UDON! WHAT WAS I SUPPOSED TO DO?!
HEY... KING...
!
I'LL OFFER TO FORGET WHAT YOU DID YESTERDAY...
...*IF* YOU COME AND JOIN US!! MA MAMAMA...
!!
THERE ARE STILL *THREE* RACES I DON'T HAVE IN MY COUNTRY YET.
ONE OF THEM MIGHT HAVE BEEN LOST IN THE MISTS OF TIME...
...BUT *YOU'RE* STILL ALIVE!!!
I REFUSE...

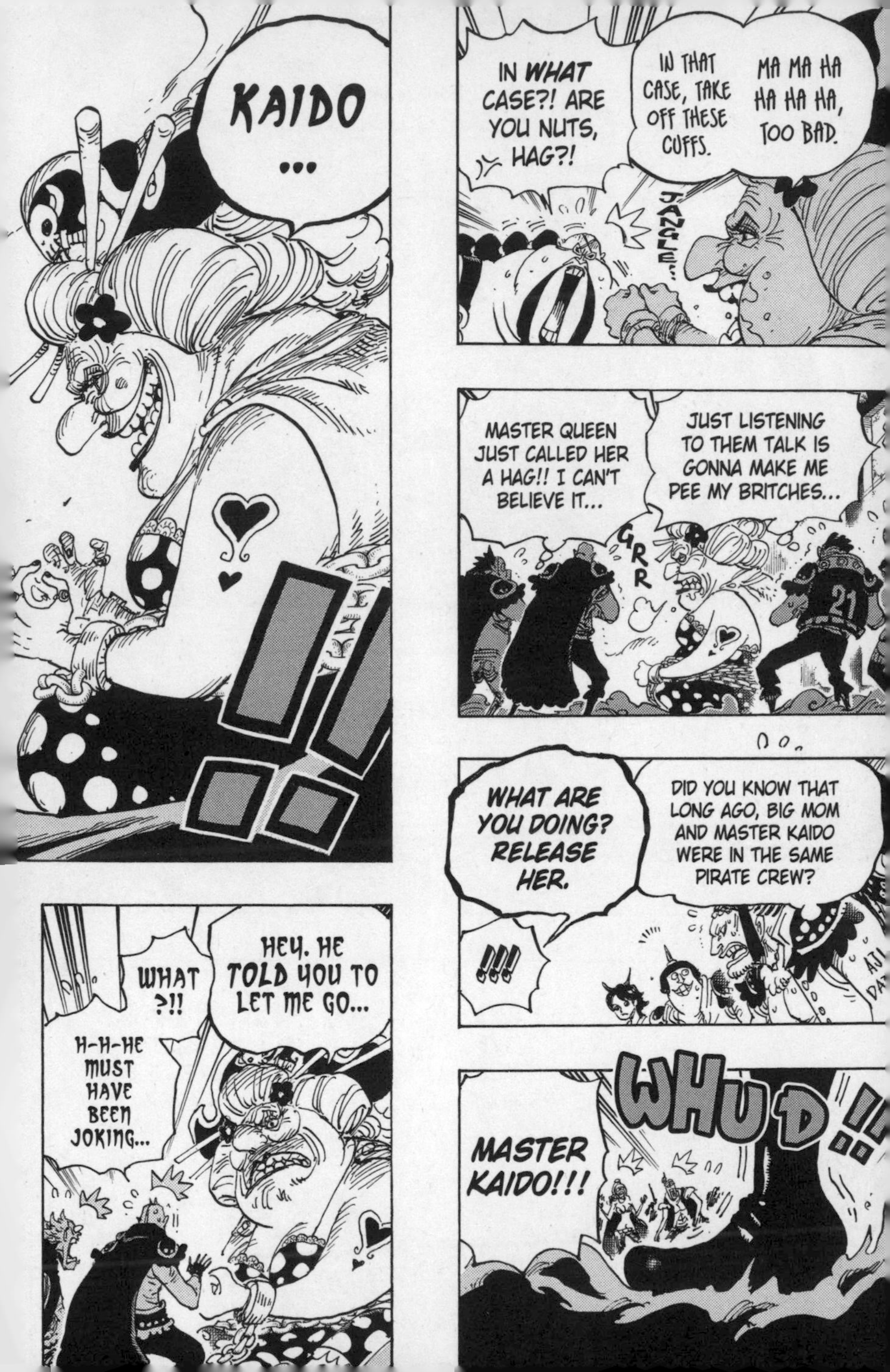
MA MA HA HA HA HA, TOO BAD.
IN THAT CASE, TAKE OFF THESE CUFFS.
IN WHAT CASE?! ARE YOU NUTS, HAG?!
JANGLE
JUST LISTENING TO THEM TALK IS GONNA MAKE ME PEE MY BRITCHES...
MASTER QUEEN JUST CALLED HER A HAG!! I CAN'T BELIEVE IT...
GRR
DID YOU KNOW THAT LONG AGO, BIG MOM AND MASTER KAIDO WERE IN THE SAME PIRATE CREW?
WHAT ARE YOU DOING? RELEASE HER.
!!!
WHUD!!
MASTER KAIDO!!!
KAIDO...
HEY. HE TOLD YOU TO LET ME GO...
WHAT ?!!
H-H-HE MUST HAVE BEEN JOKING...

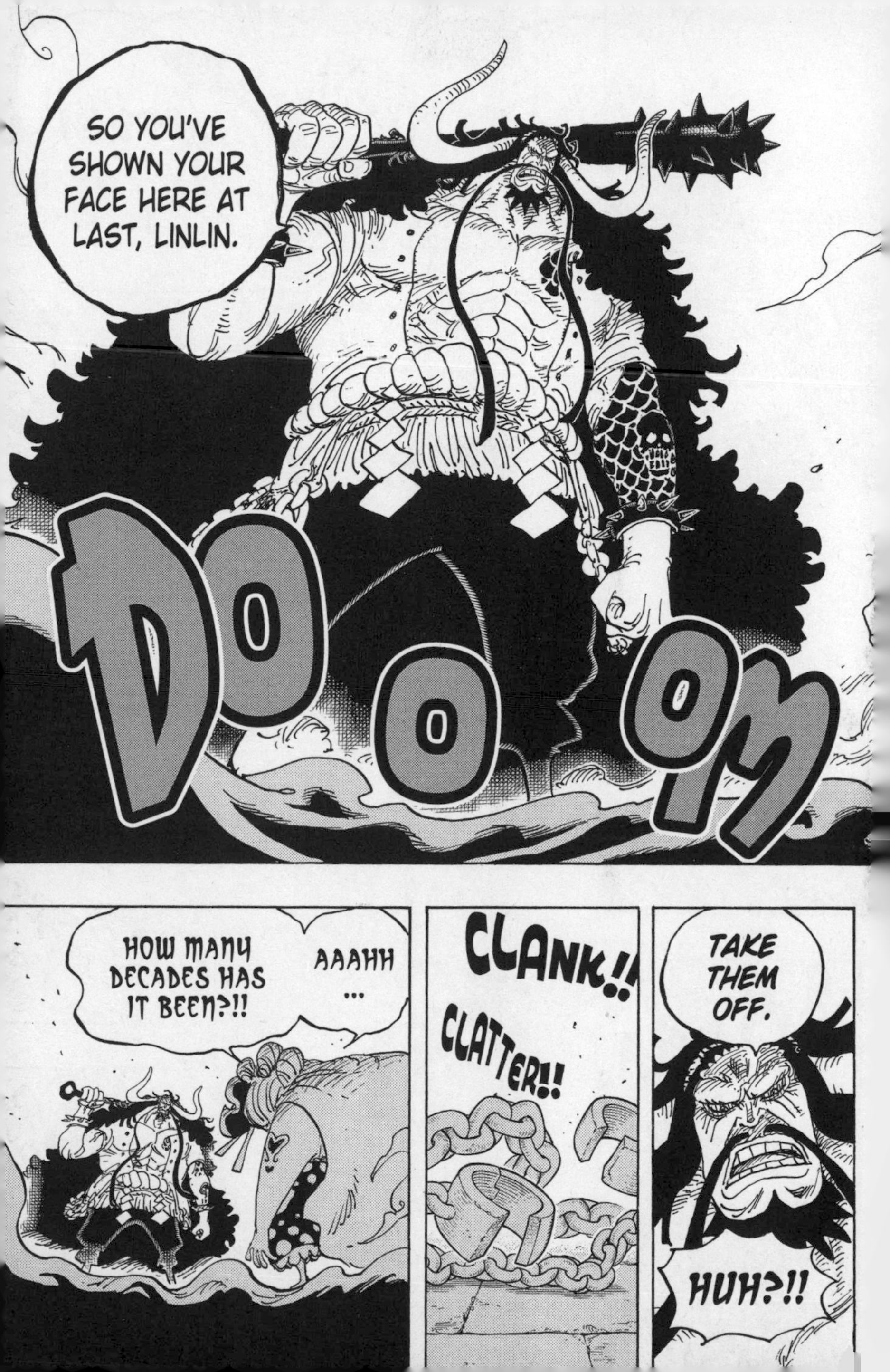
SO YOU'VE SHOWN YOUR FACE HERE AT LAST, LINLIN.
DOOOM
TAKE THEM OFF.
HUH?!!
CLANK!!
CLATTER!!
AAAHH ...
HOW MANY DECADES HAS IT BEEN?!!

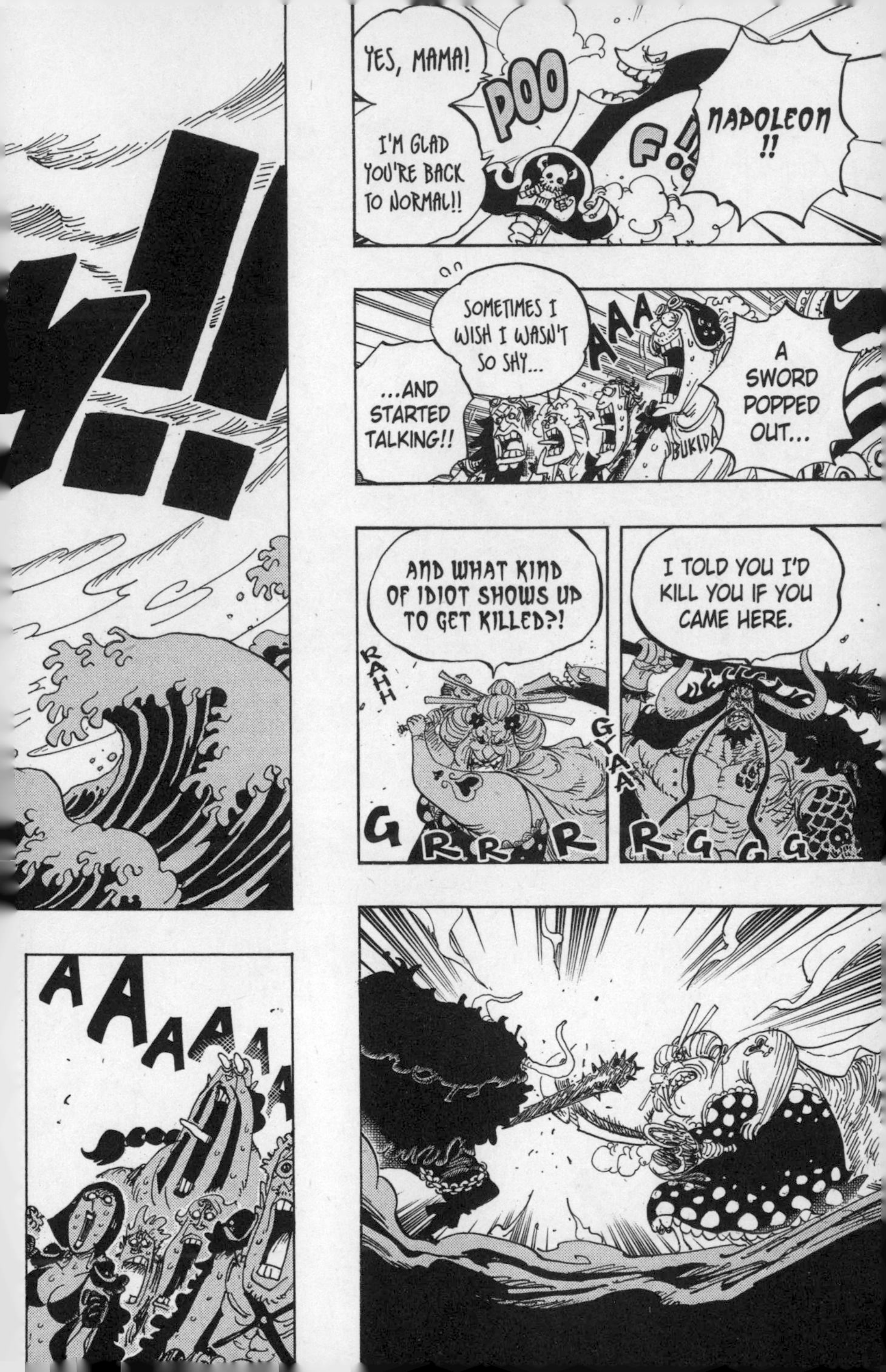
NAPOLEON!!
FOO
POO
YES, MAMA!
I'M GLAD YOU'RE BACK TO NORMAL!!
A SWORD POPPED OUT...
AAA
BUKIDA
SOMETIMES I WISH I WASN'T SO SHY...
...AND STARTED TALKING!!
I TOLD YOU I'D KILL YOU IF YOU CAME HERE.
GYAA
RGGG
AND WHAT KIND OF IDIOT SHOWS UP TO GET KILLED?!
RAHH
GRRRR
!!
AAAAAA

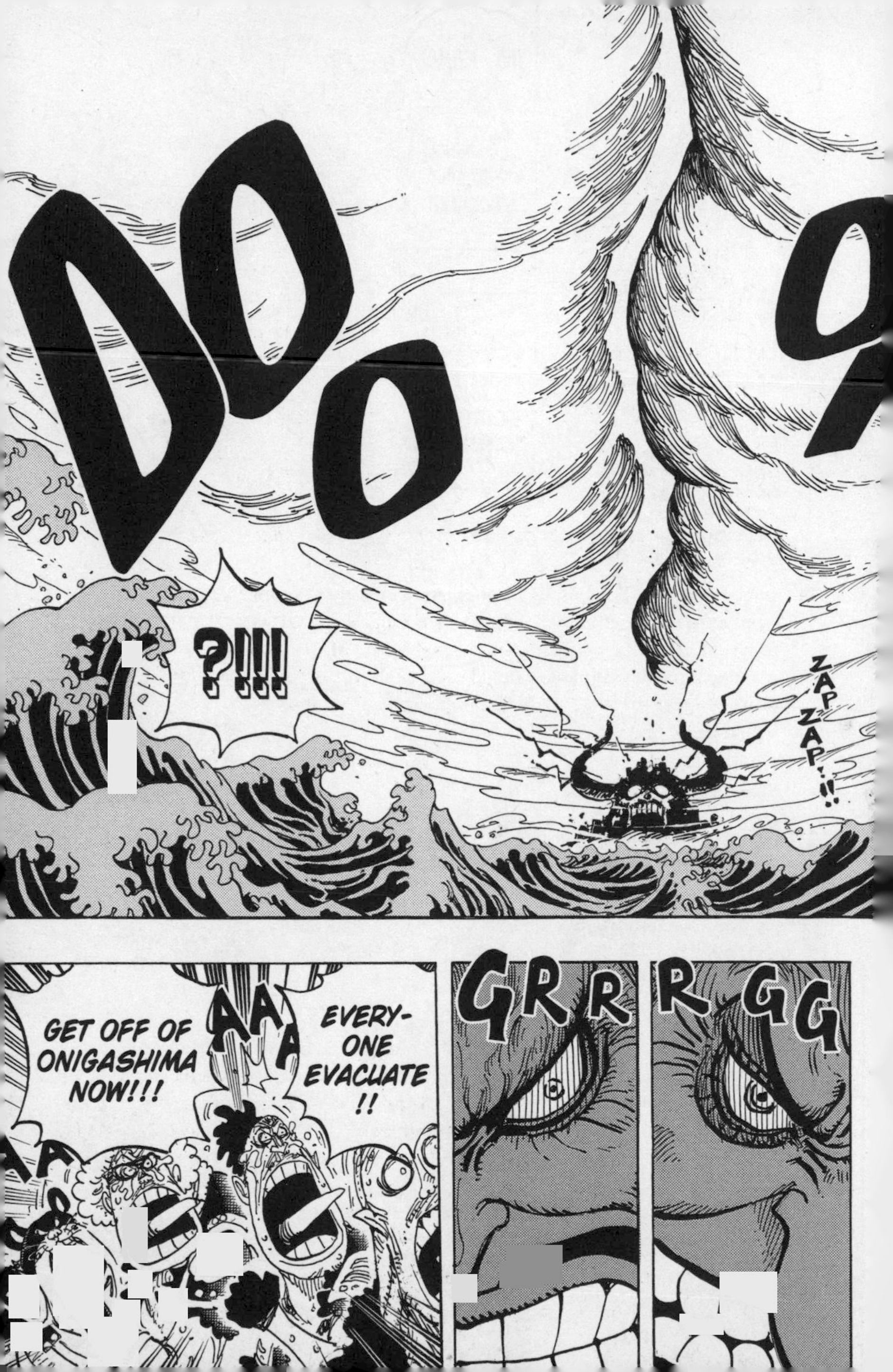
DOOO
?!!!
ZAP ZAP..!!
GRR
RGG
EVERY-ONE EVACUATE !!
AAA
GET OFF OF ONIGASHIMA NOW!!!

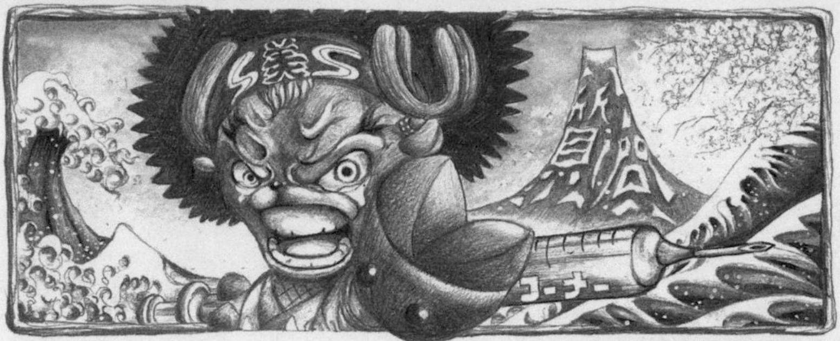
コーナー

(Takahisa Fujiwara, Nara)

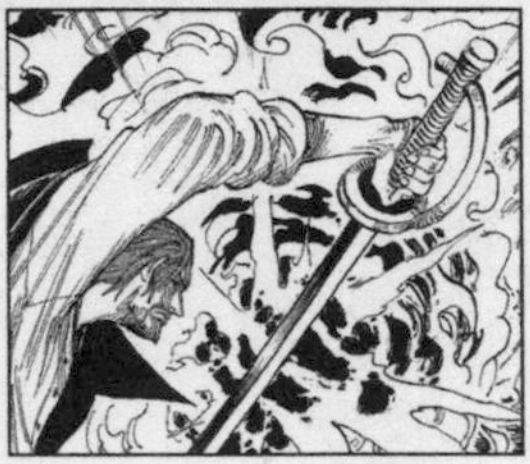

Q: I really want to see an anthropomorphized version of Griffon, the sword Shanks uses. I bet it looks really awesome as a person.

--Red-Haired Straw Hat

A: You wanna see Shanks's Griffon? I'm really good at drawing human versions of them! Don't worry, pal, I got you!!

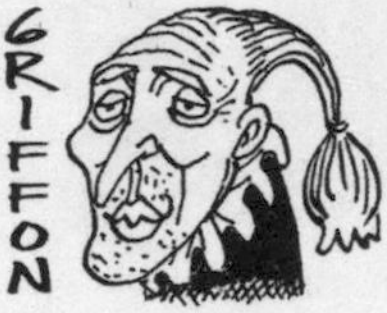
GRIFFON

Q: In chapter 931, "Soba Mask," Usopp and Franky are complaining about Sanji's wonderful character name, clamoring for a chance to give him a name of their own making. Now I'm wondering what that name would be. In fact, why don't you just tell us what all of the Straw Hats would name him?

--S. Masae

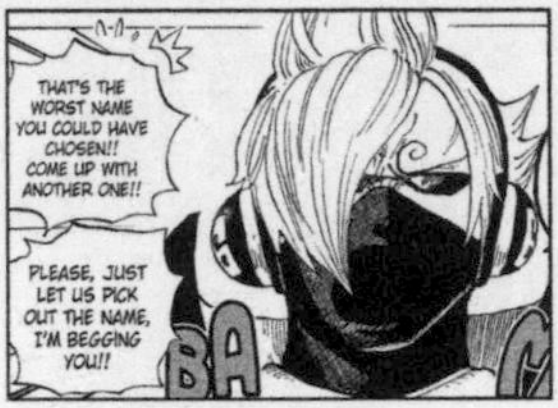
THAT'S THE WORST NAME YOU COULD HAVE CHOSEN!! COME UP WITH ANOTHER ONE!!
PLEASE, JUST LET US PICK OUT THE NAME, I'M BEGGING YOU!!

A: Okay. Let's ask them!

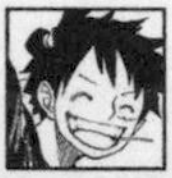 "Black! Mask! Crest!"

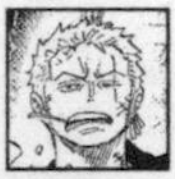 "Idiot"

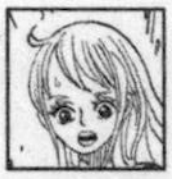 "Cape"

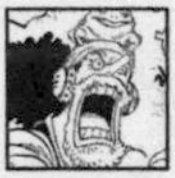 "Lightning Skyzer"

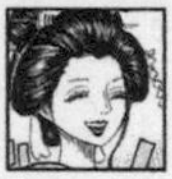 "Unfortunate Mask"

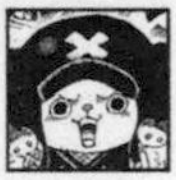 "Go Go Sanji!"

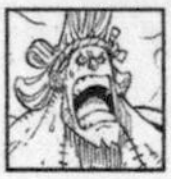 "Black Rolling Destroyer"

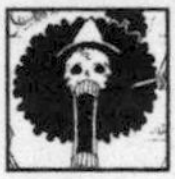 "Jealou-C Women's Bath-man"

Which one would you go by?

Q: When Reiju sucks the poison out of Luffy, she says "Thanks for the treat♡" and licks her lips at the same time. I thought that was cute, so I've been trying to mimic it, but the best I can do sounds more like "Hanks ho peep" or "Fank bo beep." How do you say that?

--Karinto

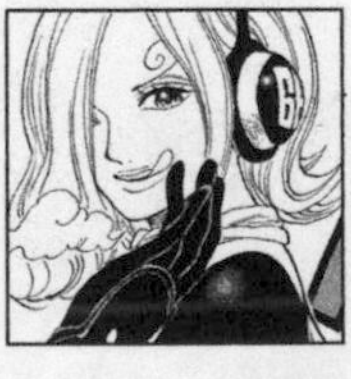

A: Well, the truth is, you're supposed to interpret that as "Thanks for the treat♡" and then she licks her lips. But if your hard work has already gotten you to the point of "Fank bo beep," then you're almost there! You can nearly do it already! "Thanks for the treat♡"!!

Chapter 952:
HIYORI AND KAWAMATSU

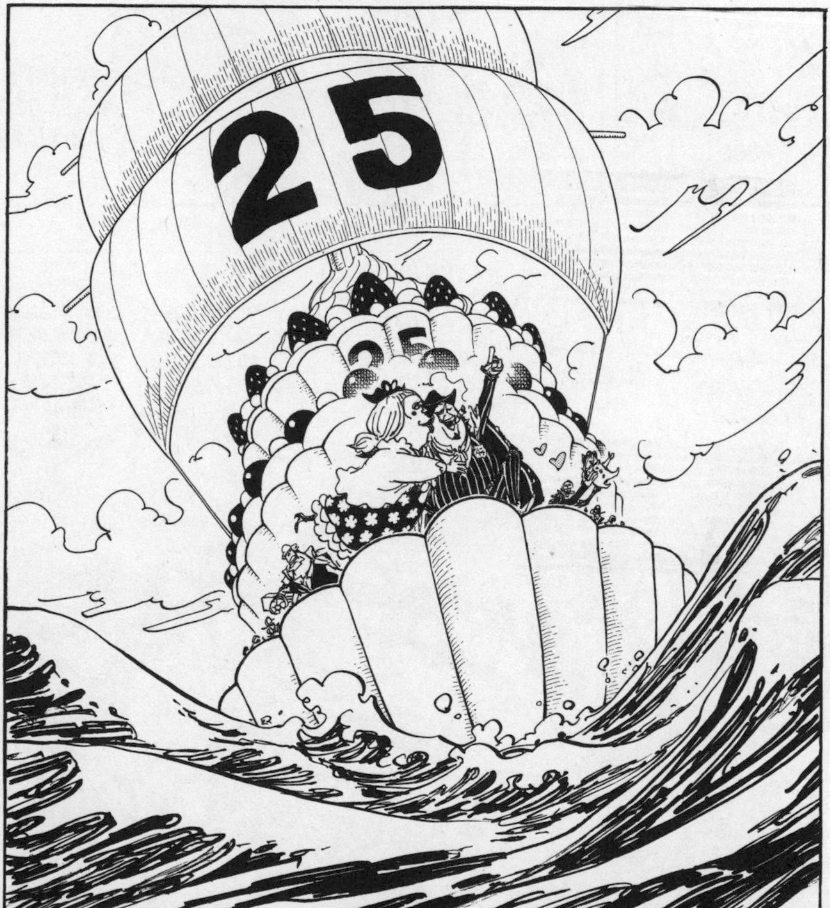
25

GANG BEGE'S OH MY FAMILY
VOL. 3: "WHAT MY WIFE WANTS, I WANT"

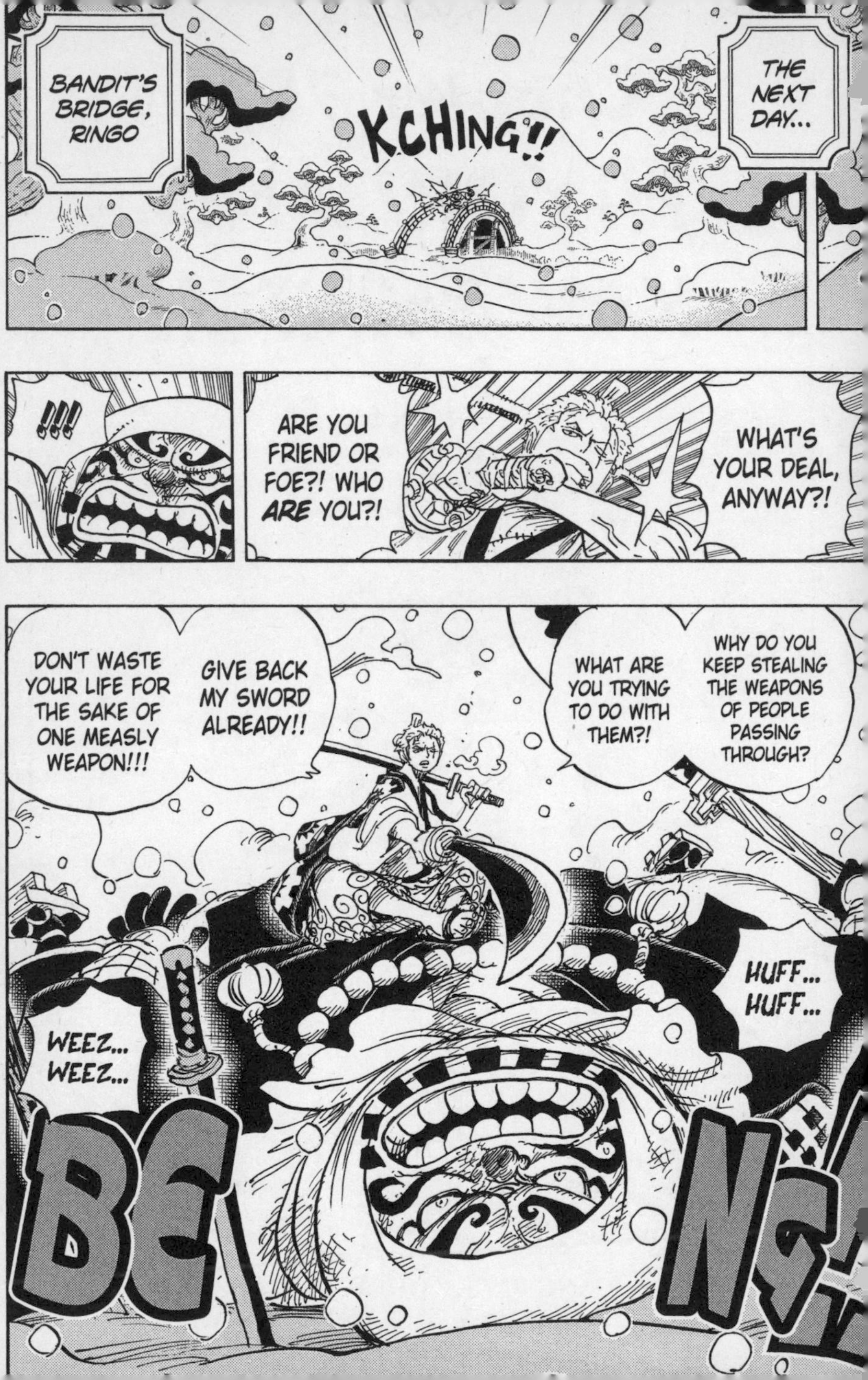
THE NEXT DAY...
KCHING!!
BANDIT'S BRIDGE, RINGO
WHAT'S YOUR DEAL, ANYWAY?!
ARE YOU FRIEND OR FOE?! WHO ARE YOU?!
!!!
WHY DO YOU KEEP STEALING THE WEAPONS OF PEOPLE PASSING THROUGH?
WHAT ARE YOU TRYING TO DO WITH THEM?!
GIVE BACK MY SWORD ALREADY!!
DON'T WASTE YOUR LIFE FOR THE SAKE OF ONE MEASLY WEAPON!!!
HUFF... HUFF...
WEEZ... WEEZ...
BE NG

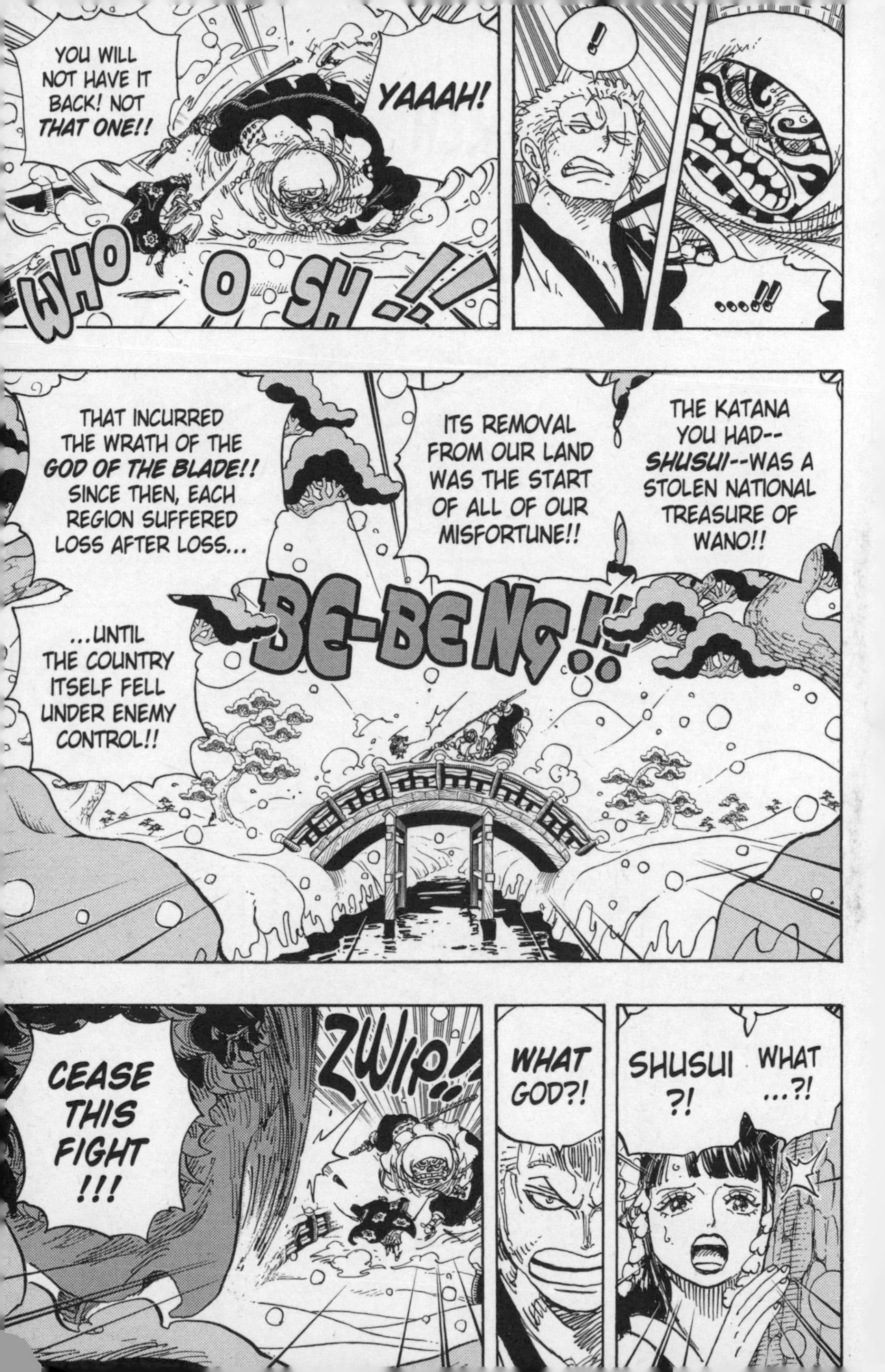

!
...!!
YAAAH!
YOU WILL NOT HAVE IT BACK! NOT THAT ONE!!
WHOOOSH!!
THE KATANA YOU HAD-- SHUSUI--WAS A STOLEN NATIONAL TREASURE OF WANO!!
ITS REMOVAL FROM OUR LAND WAS THE START OF ALL OF OUR MISFORTUNE!!
THAT INCURRED THE WRATH OF THE GOD OF THE BLADE!! SINCE THEN, EACH REGION SUFFERED LOSS AFTER LOSS...
...UNTIL THE COUNTRY ITSELF FELL UNDER ENEMY CONTROL!!
BE-BENG!!
WHAT ...?!
SHUSUI ?!
WHAT GOD?!
ZWIP!!
CEASE THIS FIGHT !!!

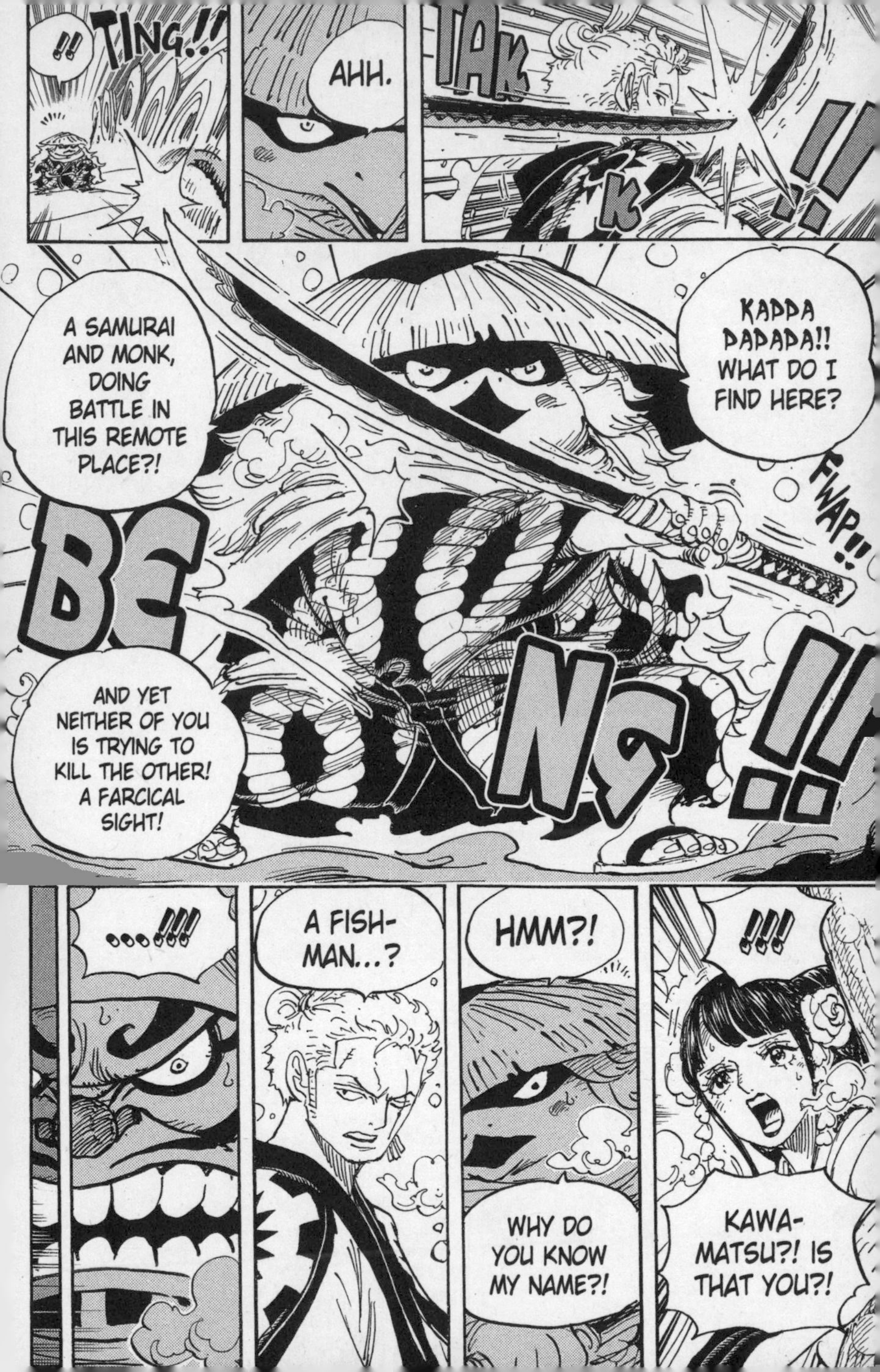
TAK
K
!!
AHH.
!!
TING!!
KAPPA PAPAPA!! WHAT DO I FIND HERE?
FWAP!!
A SAMURAI AND MONK, DOING BATTLE IN THIS REMOTE PLACE?!
BEDONG!!
AND YET NEITHER OF YOU IS TRYING TO KILL THE OTHER! A FARCICAL SIGHT!
!!!
KAWA-MATSU?! IS THAT YOU?!
HMM?!
WHY DO YOU KNOW MY NAME?!
A FISH-MAN...?
....!!!

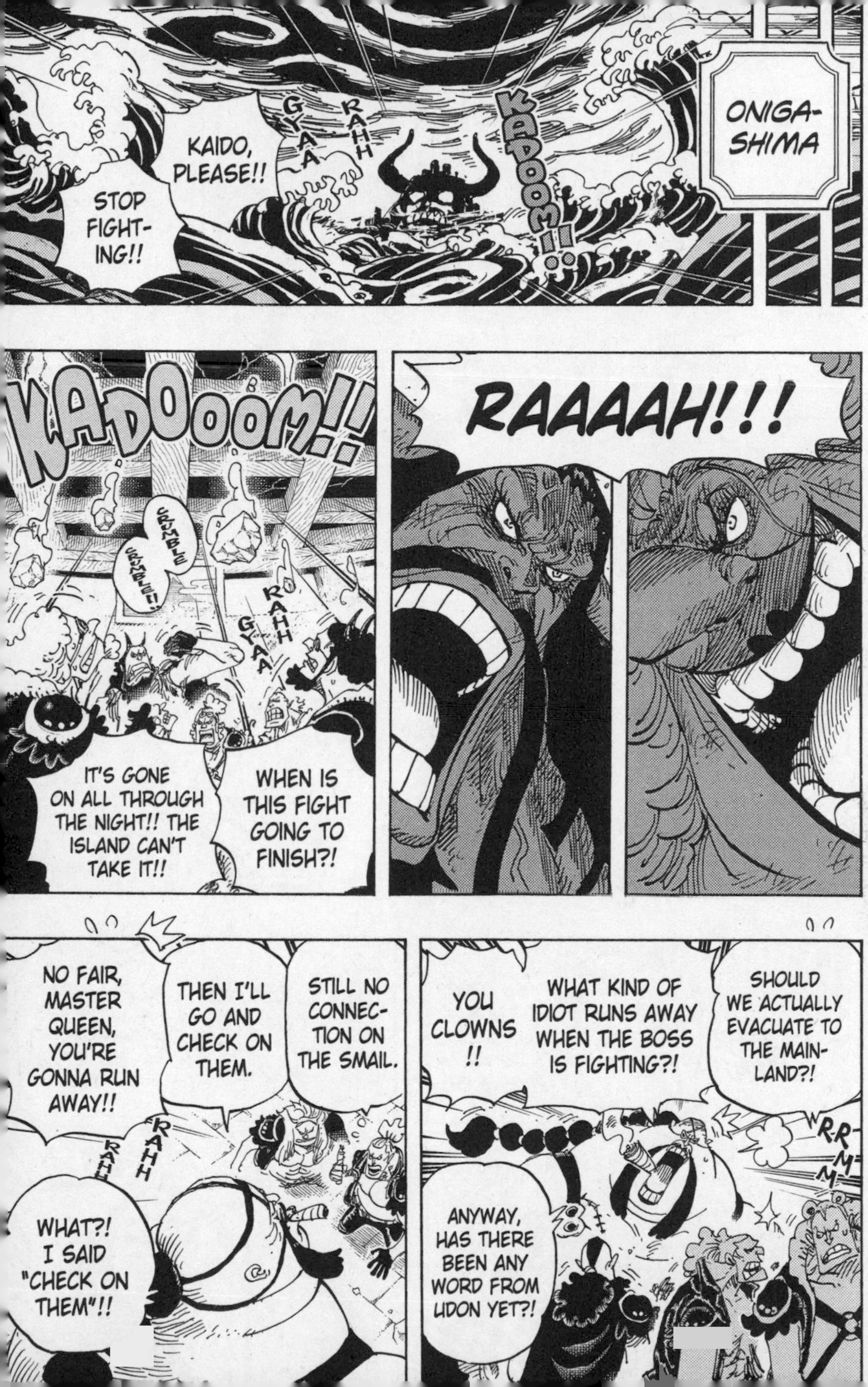
ONIGA-SHIMA
KADOOM!!
RAHH
GYAA
KAIDO, PLEASE!!
STOP FIGHT-ING!!
RAAAAH!!!
KADOOOM!!
CRUMBLE
CRUMBLE!!
RAHH
GYAA
WHEN IS THIS FIGHT GOING TO FINISH?!
IT'S GONE ON ALL THROUGH THE NIGHT!! THE ISLAND CAN'T TAKE IT!!
SHOULD WE ACTUALLY EVACUATE TO THE MAIN-LAND?!
WHAT KIND OF IDIOT RUNS AWAY WHEN THE BOSS IS FIGHTING?!
YOU CLOWNS!!
R-R-M-M
ANYWAY, HAS THERE BEEN ANY WORD FROM UDON YET?!
STILL NO CONNEC-TION ON THE SMAIL.
THEN I'LL GO AND CHECK ON THEM.
NO FAIR, MASTER QUEEN, YOU'RE GONNA RUN AWAY!!
RAHH
RAHH
WHAT?! I SAID "CHECK ON THEM"!!

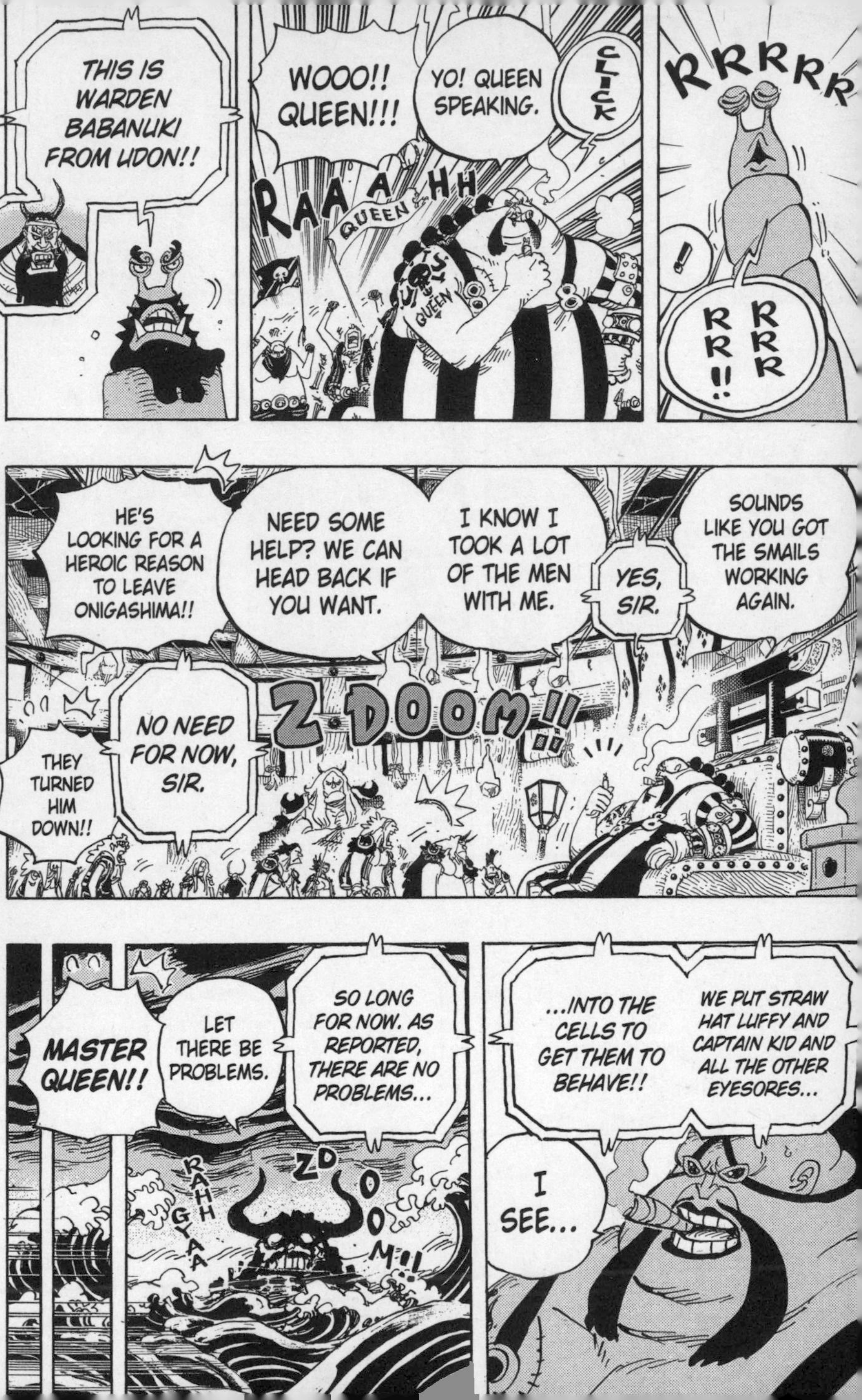
RRRRRR
!
RRR RRR
RR RR!!
CLICK
YO! QUEEN SPEAKING.
WOOO!! QUEEN!!!
RAAAHH
QUEEN
THIS IS WARDEN BABANUKI FROM UDON!!
SOUNDS LIKE YOU GOT THE SMAILS WORKING AGAIN.
YES, SIR.
I KNOW I TOOK A LOT OF THE MEN WITH ME.
NEED SOME HELP? WE CAN HEAD BACK IF YOU WANT.
HE'S LOOKING FOR A HEROIC REASON TO LEAVE ONIGASHIMA!!
ZDOOM!!
NO NEED FOR NOW, SIR.
THEY TURNED HIM DOWN!!
WE PUT STRAW HAT LUFFY AND CAPTAIN KID AND ALL THE OTHER EYESORES...
...INTO THE CELLS TO GET THEM TO BEHAVE!!
I SEE...
SO LONG FOR NOW. AS REPORTED, THERE ARE NO PROBLEMS...
LET THERE BE PROBLEMS.
MASTER QUEEN!!
ZDOOM!!
RAHH
GYAA

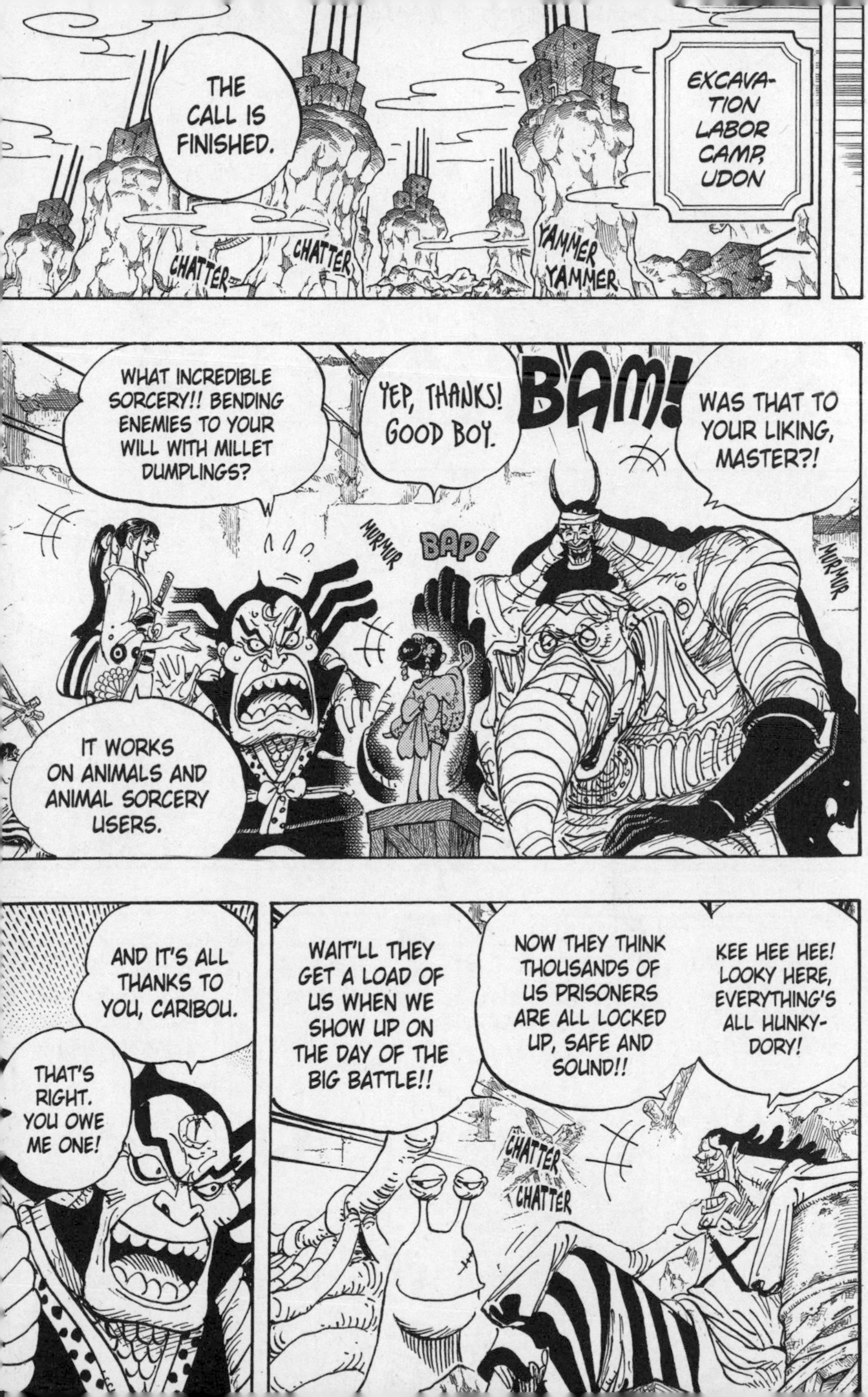
EXCAVATION LABOR CAMP, UDON
THE CALL IS FINISHED.
YAMMER YAMMER
CHATTER
CHATTER
WAS THAT TO YOUR LIKING, MASTER?!
BAM!
YEP, THANKS! GOOD BOY.
WHAT INCREDIBLE SORCERY!! BENDING ENEMIES TO YOUR WILL WITH MILLET DUMPLINGS?
MURMUR
BAP!
MURMUR
IT WORKS ON ANIMALS AND ANIMAL SORCERY USERS.
KEE HEE HEE! LOOKY HERE, EVERYTHING'S ALL HUNKY-DORY!
NOW THEY THINK THOUSANDS OF US PRISONERS ARE ALL LOCKED UP, SAFE AND SOUND!!
WAIT'LL THEY GET A LOAD OF US WHEN WE SHOW UP ON THE DAY OF THE BIG BATTLE!!
CHATTER CHATTER
AND IT'S ALL THANKS TO YOU, CARIBOU.
THAT'S RIGHT. YOU OWE ME ONE!

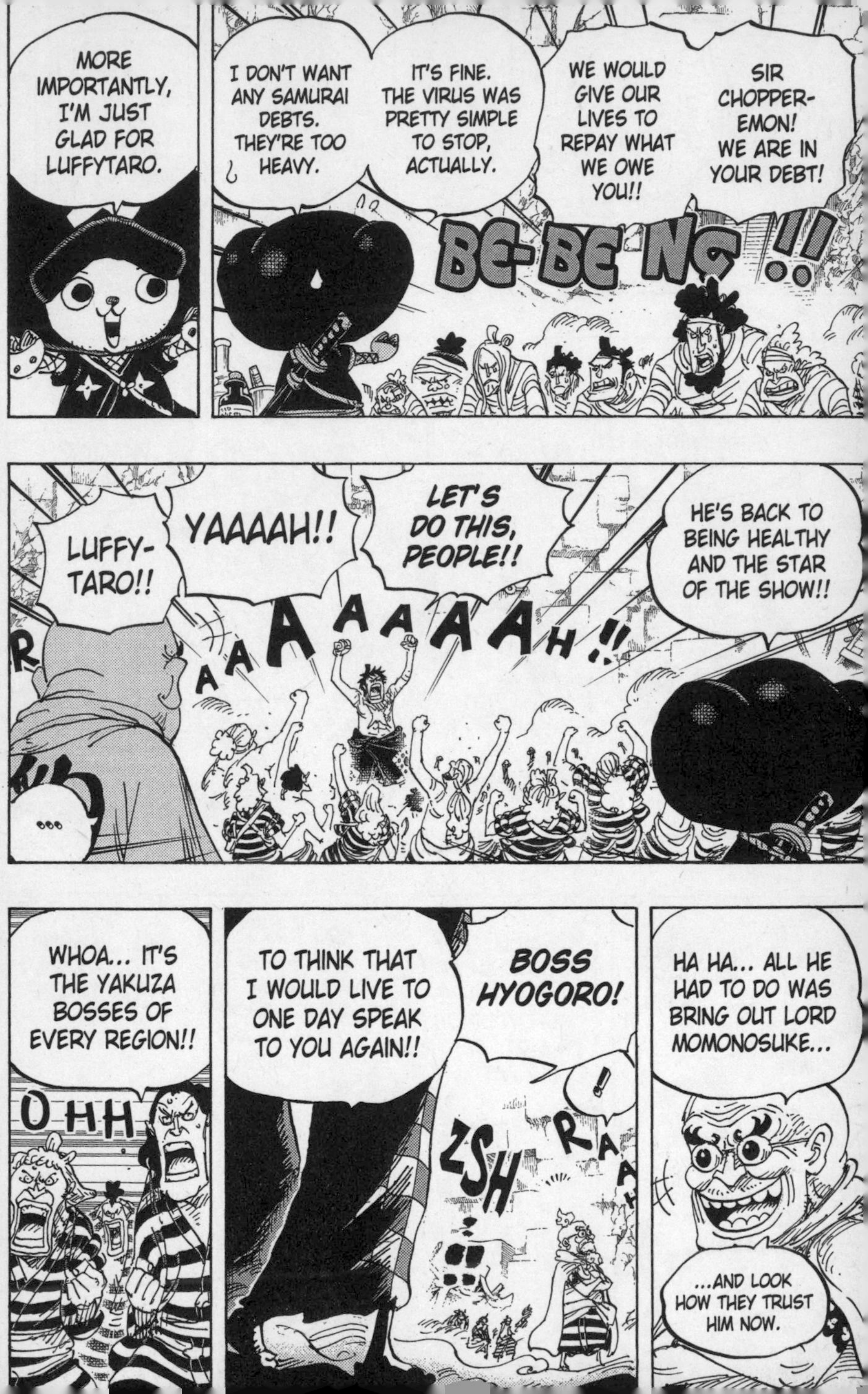

SIR CHOPPER-EMON! WE ARE IN YOUR DEBT!
WE WOULD GIVE OUR LIVES TO REPAY WHAT WE OWE YOU!!
BE-BE NG!!
IT'S FINE. THE VIRUS WAS PRETTY SIMPLE TO STOP, ACTUALLY.
I DON'T WANT ANY SAMURAI DEBTS. THEY'RE TOO HEAVY.
MORE IMPORTANTLY, I'M JUST GLAD FOR LUFFYTARO.
HE'S BACK TO BEING HEALTHY AND THE STAR OF THE SHOW!!
LET'S DO THIS, PEOPLE!!
YAAAAH!!
AAAAAAAH!!
LUFFY-TARO!!
R
...
HA HA... ALL HE HAD TO DO WAS BRING OUT LORD MOMONOSUKE...
...AND LOOK HOW THEY TRUST HIM NOW.
BOSS HYOGORO!
!
RAAH
ZSH
TO THINK THAT I WOULD LIVE TO ONE DAY SPEAK TO YOU AGAIN!!
WHOA... IT'S THE YAKUZA BOSSES OF EVERY REGION!!
OHH

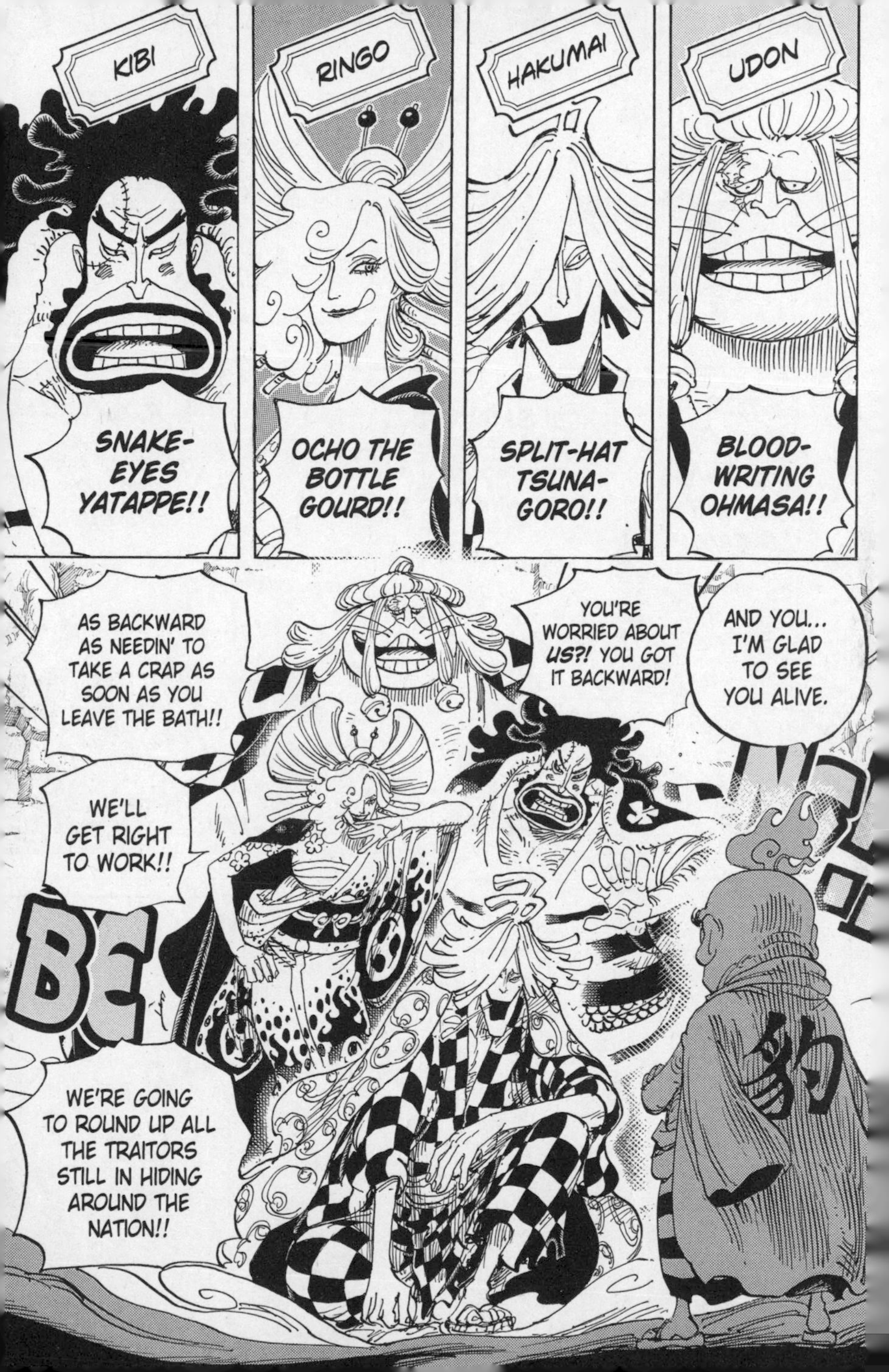
UDON
BLOOD-WRITING OHMASA!!
HAKUMAI
SPLIT-HAT TSUNA-GORO!!
RINGO
OCHO THE BOTTLE GOURD!!
KIBI
SNAKE-EYES YATAPPE!!
AND YOU... I'M GLAD TO SEE YOU ALIVE.
YOU'RE WORRIED ABOUT US?! YOU GOT IT BACKWARD!
AS BACKWARD AS NEEDIN' TO TAKE A CRAP AS SOON AS YOU LEAVE THE BATH!!
WE'LL GET RIGHT TO WORK!!
BE
WE'RE GOING TO ROUND UP ALL THE TRAITORS STILL IN HIDING AROUND THE NATION!!

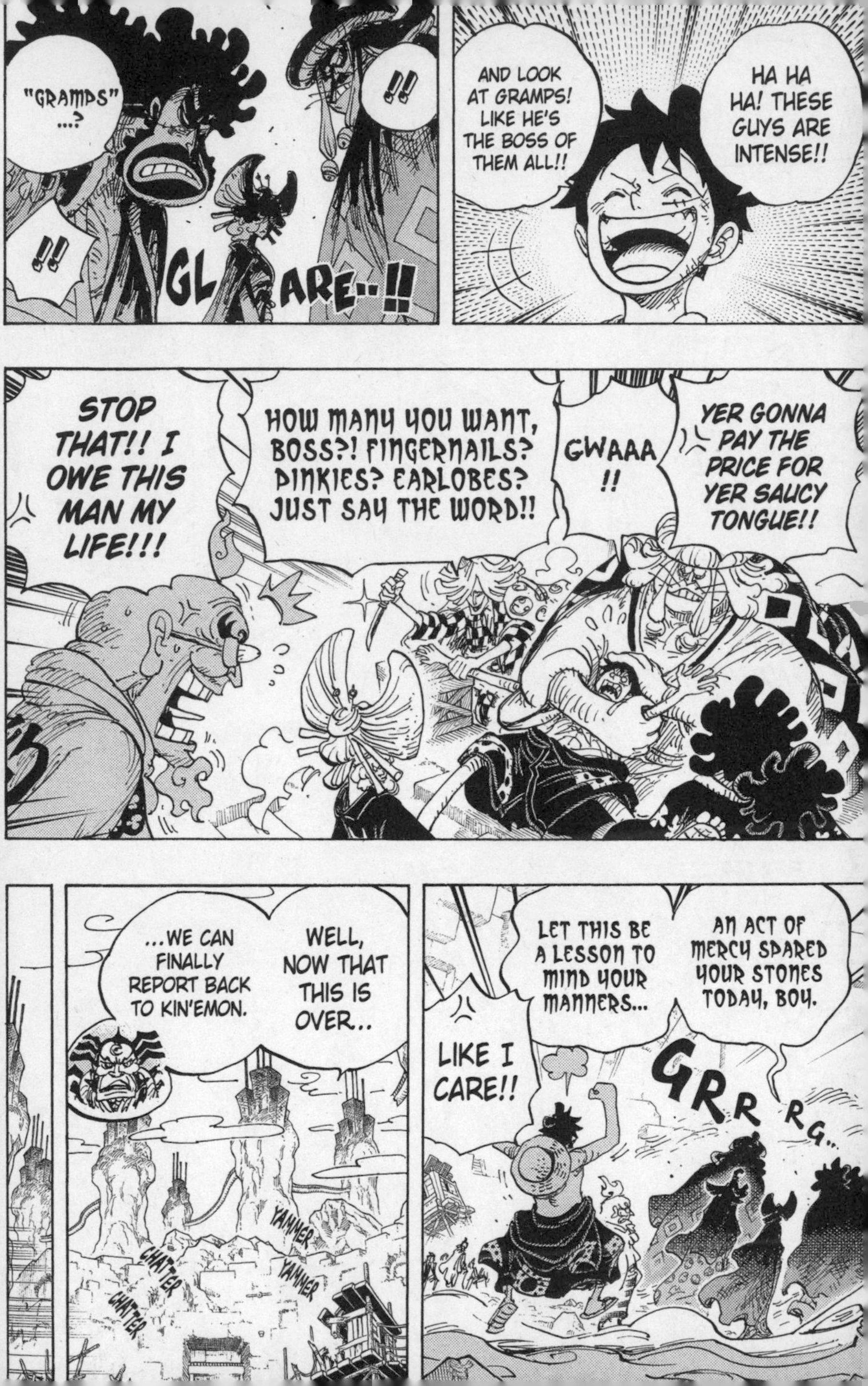
HA HA HA! THESE GUYS ARE INTENSE!!
AND LOOK AT GRAMPS! LIKE HE'S THE BOSS OF THEM ALL!!
!!
"GRAMPS" ...?
!!
GLARE..!!
YER GONNA PAY THE PRICE FOR YER SAUCY TONGUE!!
GWAAA !!
HOW MANY YOU WANT, BOSS?! FINGERNAILS? PINKIES? EARLOBES? JUST SAY THE WORD!!
STOP THAT!! I OWE THIS MAN MY LIFE!!!
AN ACT OF MERCY SPARED YOUR STONES TODAY, BOY.
LET THIS BE A LESSON TO MIND YOUR MANNERS...
LIKE I CARE!!
GRRRRG..
WELL, NOW THAT THIS IS OVER...
...WE CAN FINALLY REPORT BACK TO KIN'EMON.
YAMMER YAMMER
CHATTER CHATTER

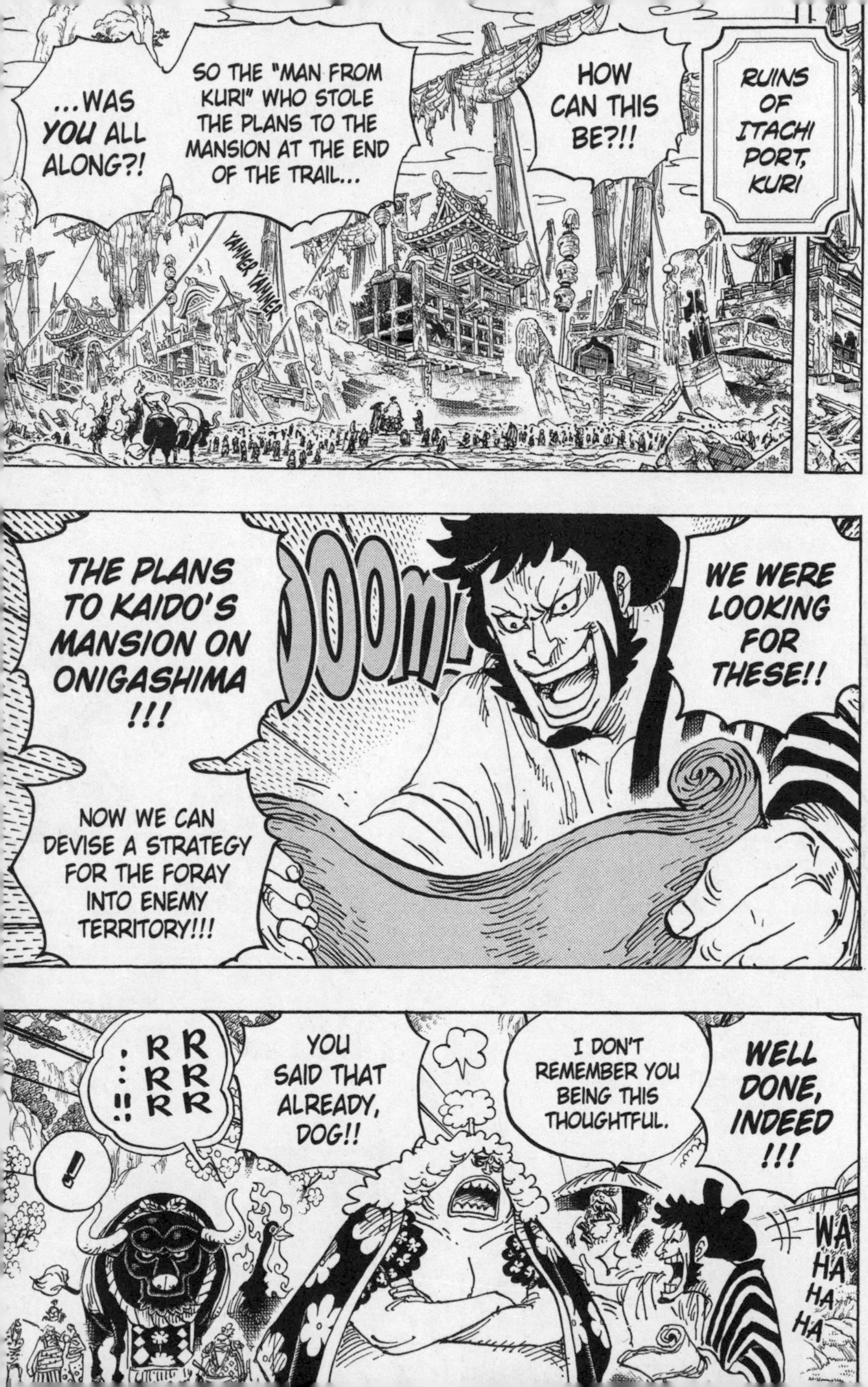
RUINS OF ITACHI PORT, KURI
HOW CAN THIS BE?!!
SO THE "MAN FROM KURI" WHO STOLE THE PLANS TO THE MANSION AT THE END OF THE TRAIL...
...WAS YOU ALL ALONG?!
YAMMER YAMMER
WE WERE LOOKING FOR THESE!!
THE PLANS TO KAIDO'S MANSION ON ONIGASHIMA !!!
NOW WE CAN DEVISE A STRATEGY FOR THE FORAY INTO ENEMY TERRITORY!!!
WELL DONE, INDEED !!!
WA HA HA HA HA
I DON'T REMEMBER YOU BEING THIS THOUGHTFUL.
YOU SAID THAT ALREADY, DOG!!
RRR RRR ...!!
!

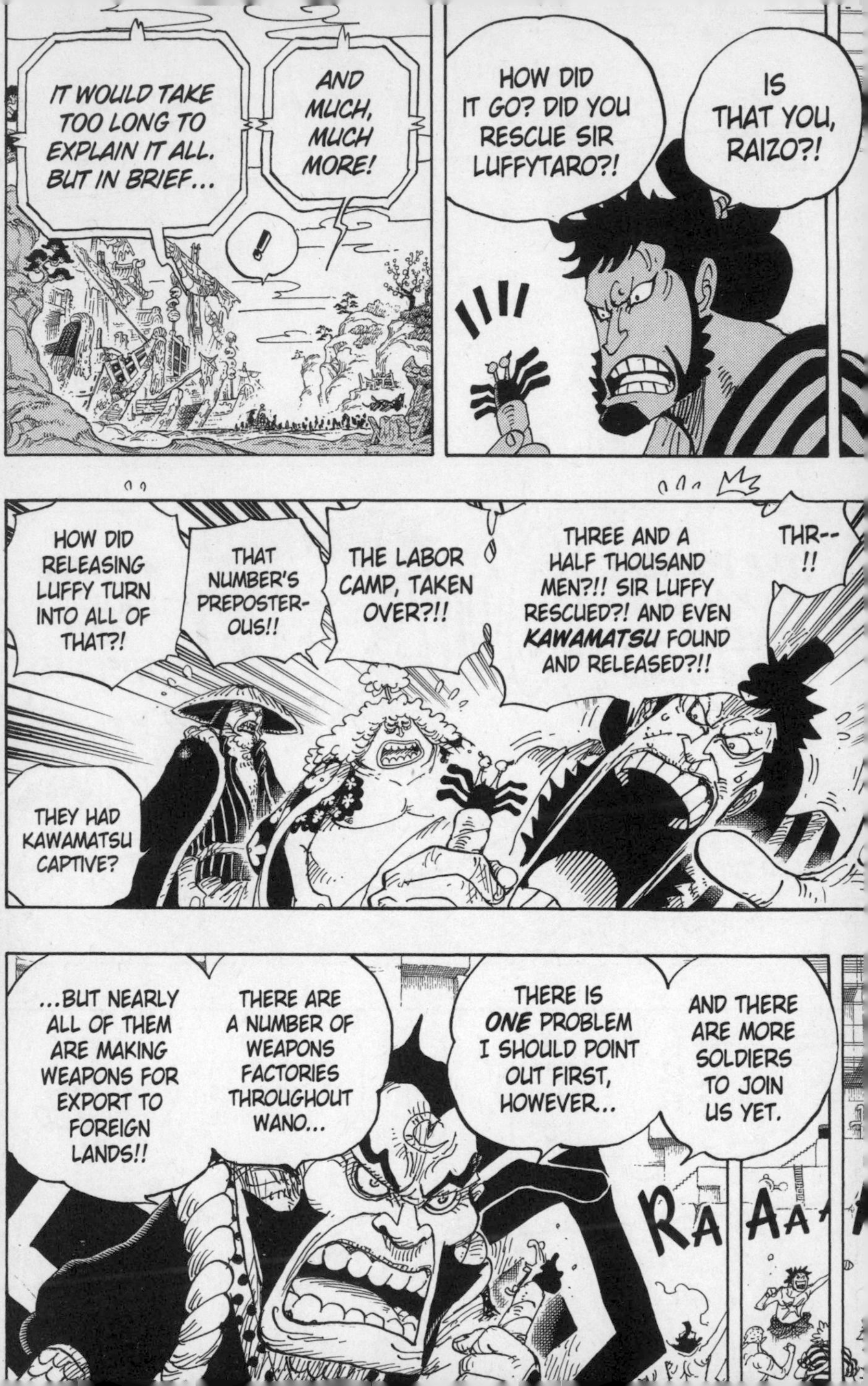
IS THAT YOU, RAIZO?!
HOW DID IT GO? DID YOU RESCUE SIR LUFFYTARO?!
IT WOULD TAKE TOO LONG TO EXPLAIN IT ALL. BUT IN BRIEF...
AND MUCH, MUCH MORE!
!
THR-- !!
THREE AND A HALF THOUSAND MEN?!! SIR LUFFY RESCUED?! AND EVEN KAWAMATSU FOUND AND RELEASED?!!
THE LABOR CAMP, TAKEN OVER?!!
THAT NUMBER'S PREPOSTEROUS!!
HOW DID RELEASING LUFFY TURN INTO ALL OF THAT?!
THEY HAD KAWAMATSU CAPTIVE?
AND THERE ARE MORE SOLDIERS TO JOIN US YET.
THERE IS ONE PROBLEM I SHOULD POINT OUT FIRST, HOWEVER...
THERE ARE A NUMBER OF WEAPONS FACTORIES THROUGHOUT WANO...
...BUT NEARLY ALL OF THEM ARE MAKING WEAPONS FOR EXPORT TO FOREIGN LANDS!!
RA AAA

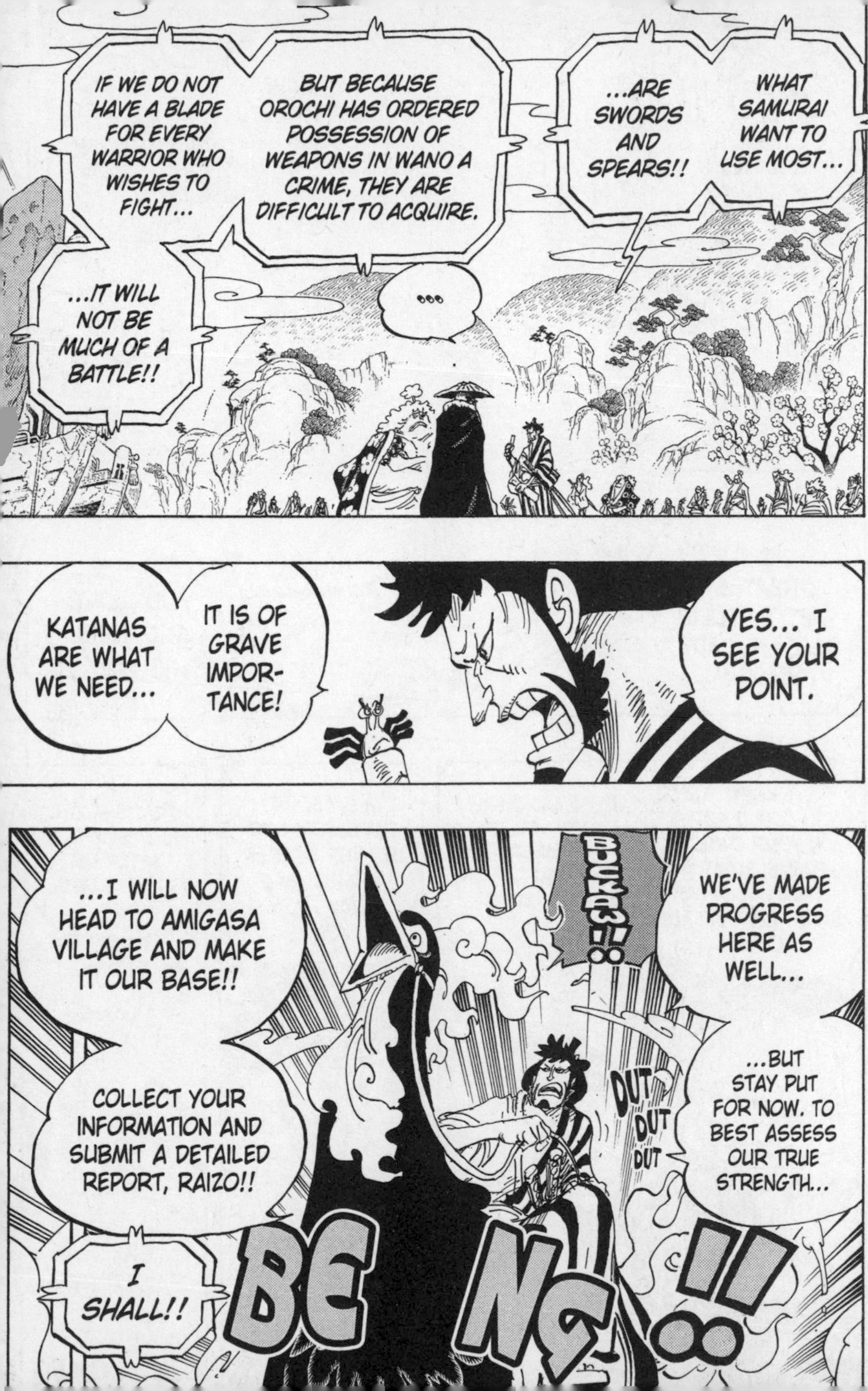
WHAT SAMURAI WANT TO USE MOST...
...ARE SWORDS AND SPEARS!!
...
BUT BECAUSE OROCHI HAS ORDERED POSSESSION OF WEAPONS IN WANO A CRIME, THEY ARE DIFFICULT TO ACQUIRE.
IF WE DO NOT HAVE A BLADE FOR EVERY WARRIOR WHO WISHES TO FIGHT...
...IT WILL NOT BE MUCH OF A BATTLE!!
YES... I SEE YOUR POINT.
IT IS OF GRAVE IMPORTANCE!
KATANAS ARE WHAT WE NEED...
WE'VE MADE PROGRESS HERE AS WELL...
BUCKAW!!
...BUT STAY PUT FOR NOW. TO BEST ASSESS OUR TRUE STRENGTH...
DUT DUT DUT
...I WILL NOW HEAD TO AMIGASA VILLAGE AND MAKE IT OUR BASE!!
COLLECT YOUR INFORMATION AND SUBMIT A DETAILED REPORT, RAIZO!!
BENG!!
I SHALL!!

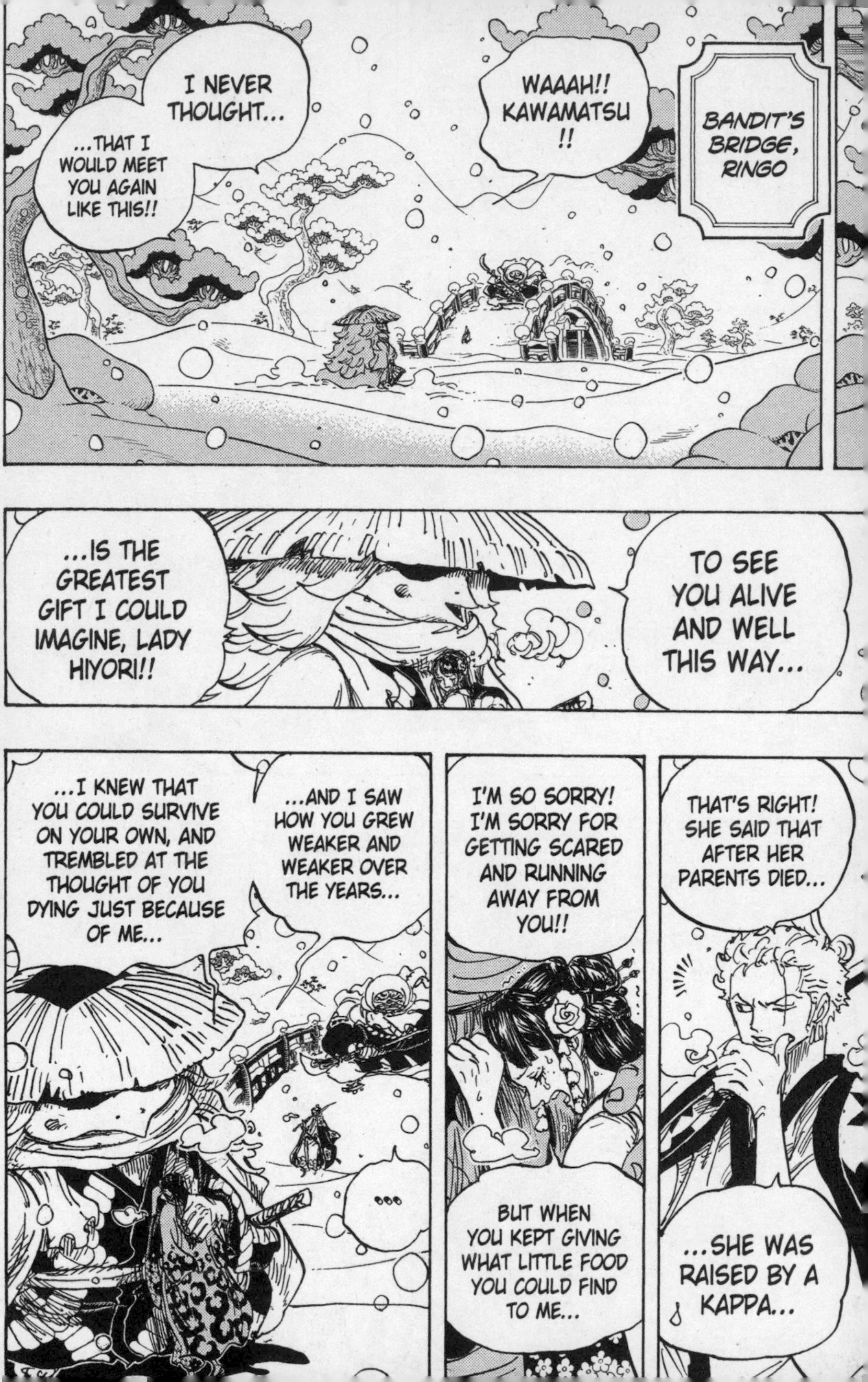
BANDIT'S BRIDGE, RINGO
WAAAH!! KAWAMATSU !!
I NEVER THOUGHT...
...THAT I WOULD MEET YOU AGAIN LIKE THIS!!
TO SEE YOU ALIVE AND WELL THIS WAY...
...IS THE GREATEST GIFT I COULD IMAGINE, LADY HIYORI!!
THAT'S RIGHT! SHE SAID THAT AFTER HER PARENTS DIED...
...SHE WAS RAISED BY A KAPPA...
I'M SO SORRY! I'M SORRY FOR GETTING SCARED AND RUNNING AWAY FROM YOU!!
BUT WHEN YOU KEPT GIVING WHAT LITTLE FOOD YOU COULD FIND TO ME...
...AND I SAW HOW YOU GREW WEAKER AND WEAKER OVER THE YEARS...
...I KNEW THAT YOU COULD SURVIVE ON YOUR OWN, AND TREMBLED AT THE THOUGHT OF YOU DYING JUST BECAUSE OF ME...
...

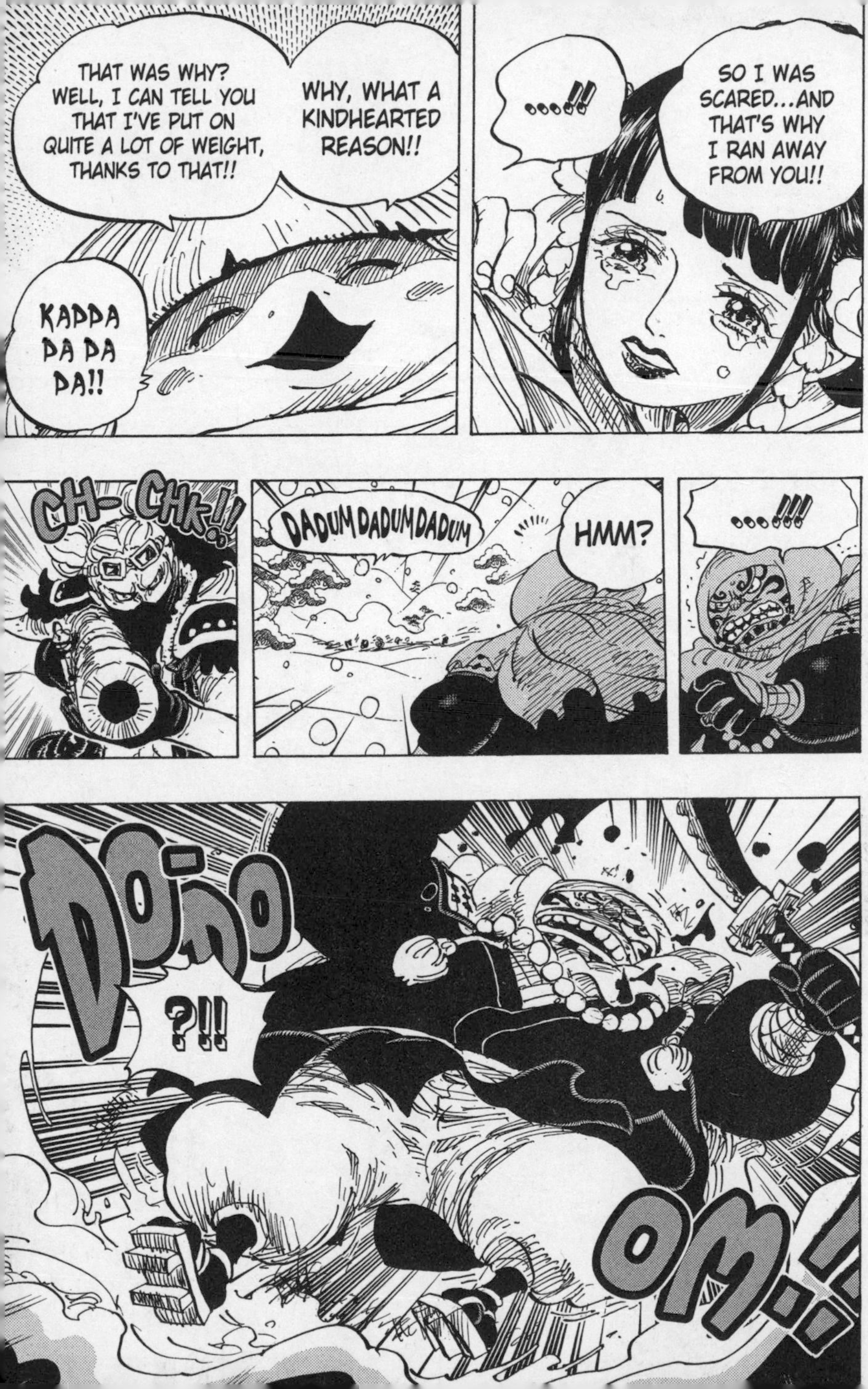
SO I WAS SCARED...AND THAT'S WHY I RAN AWAY FROM YOU!!
...!!
WHY, WHAT A KINDHEARTED REASON!!
THAT WAS WHY? WELL, I CAN TELL YOU THAT I'VE PUT ON QUITE A LOT OF WEIGHT, THANKS TO THAT!!
KAPPA PA PA PA!!
...!!!
HMM?
DADUM DADUM DADUM
CH-CHK!!
DO-OO
?!!
OM..!!

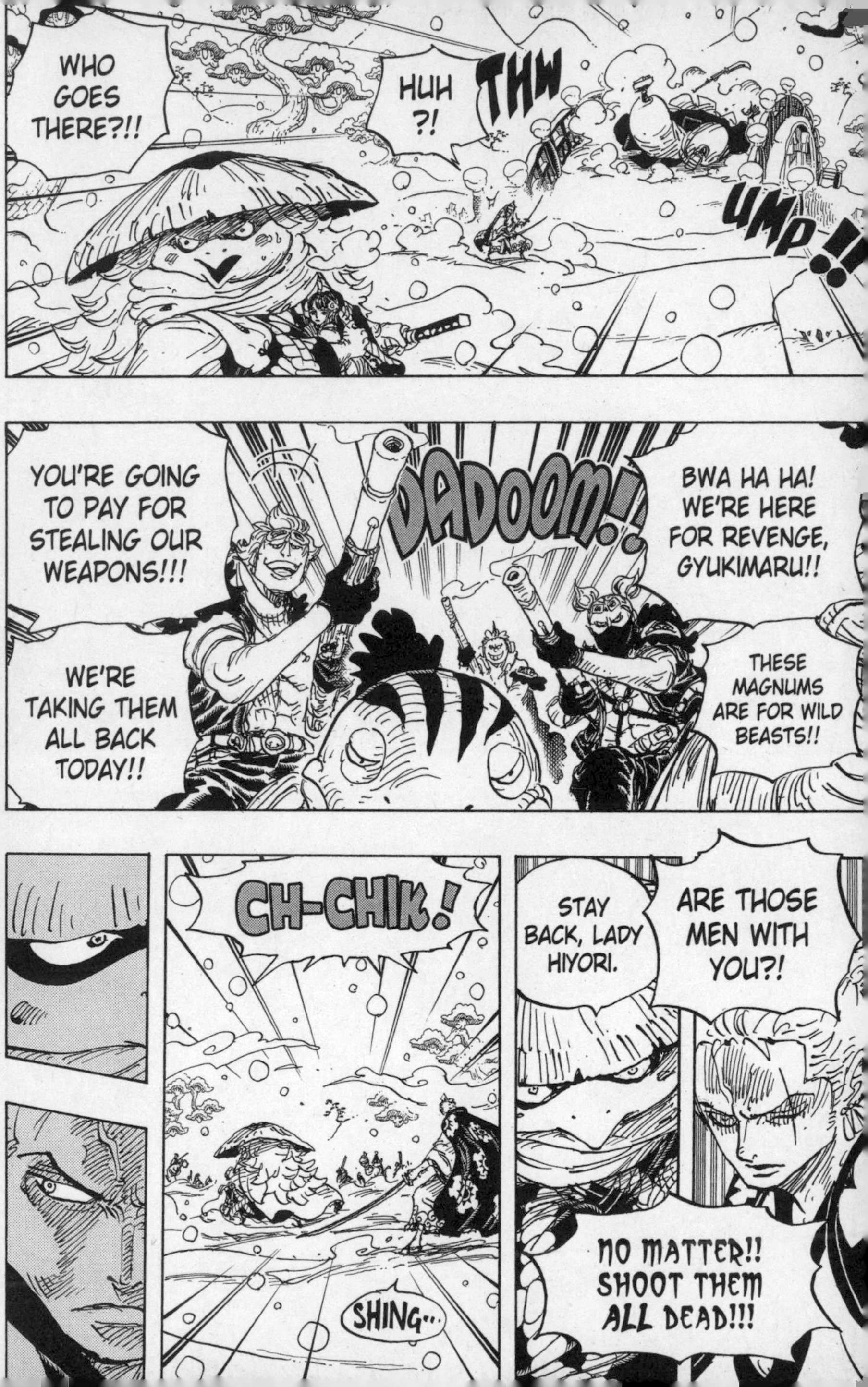
THWUMP!!
HUH ?!
WHO GOES THERE?!!
BWA HA HA! WE'RE HERE FOR REVENGE, GYUKIMARU!!
DADOOM!!
THESE MAGNUMS ARE FOR WILD BEASTS!!
YOU'RE GOING TO PAY FOR STEALING OUR WEAPONS!!!
WE'RE TAKING THEM ALL BACK TODAY!!
ARE THOSE MEN WITH YOU?!
STAY BACK, LADY HIYORI.
NO MATTER!! SHOOT THEM ALL DEAD!!!
CH-CHIK!
SHING...

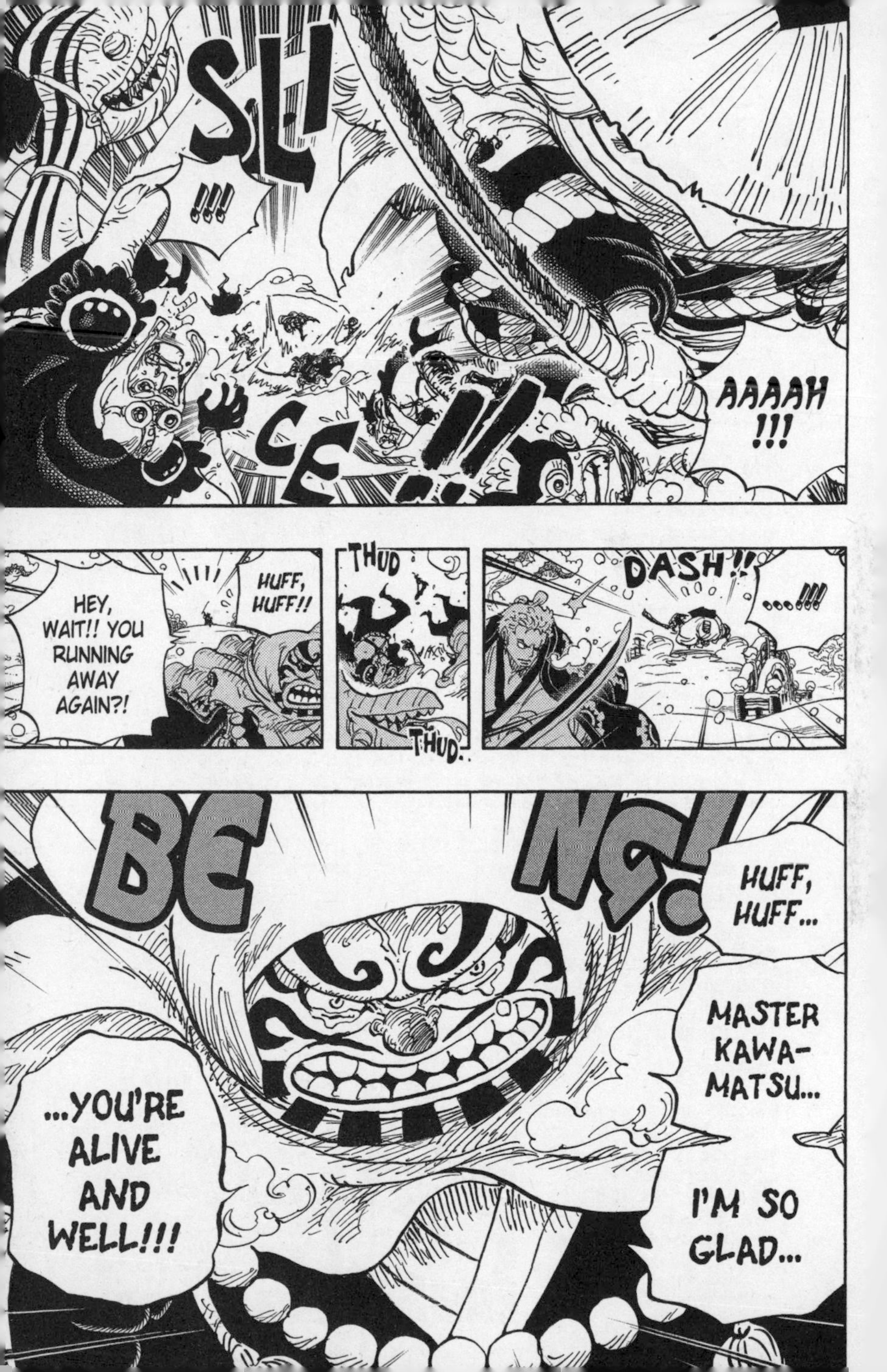
SLI
!!!
AAAAH !!!
CE...
DASH!!
...!!!
THUD
THUD..
HUFF, HUFF!!
HEY, WAIT!! YOU RUNNING AWAY AGAIN?!
BENG!
HUFF, HUFF...
MASTER KAWA-MATSU...
I'M SO GLAD...
...YOU'RE ALIVE AND WELL!!!

エス
ビー
エス
質問コーナー

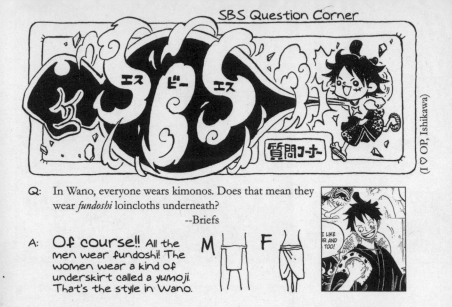

(I ♡ OP, Ishikawa)

Q: In Wano, everyone wears kimonos. Does that mean they wear *fundoshi* loincloths underneath?

--Briefs

I LIKE
OR AND
TOO!

A: Of course!! All the men wear fundoshi! The women wear a kind of underskirt called a *yumoji*. That's the style in Wano.

M
F

Q: Do you still look at every single postcard and piece of fan mail you get, Oda Sensei?

--Suemitsu

A: I read them all! Of course I do! In fact, I've never discarded a single piece, in 22 years (*laughs*). It's way too much to keep at home, so I rent out a place to keep the letters I've already read and have them sent there. It's at "bust through the floor" levels of weight! Thank you, everyone!! You've sent all your honest feelings, so of course I can't throw them away.

Q: Odacchi! I just realized something! Hyogoro has flaming-style hair, just like the komainu and koma deer, and so on… So he must be a "koma human"!!!

--420 Land

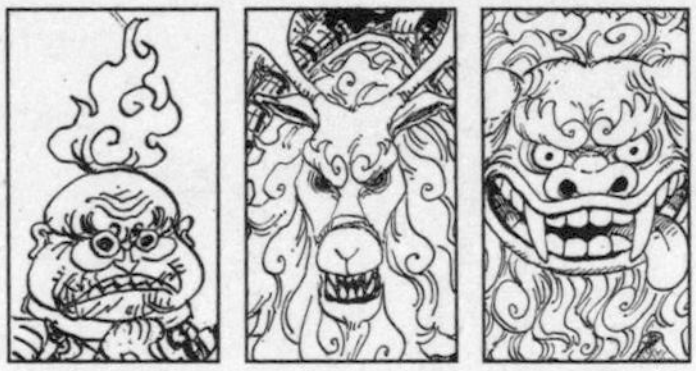

A: Oh! So that's the answer...! In that case, he's a koma human.

Q: Is the light Imu will erase from history…me?

SWI-
SWI-
SWI-
SWI
SH!!
HAVE YOU DECIDED UPON ANOTHER LIGHT...
...TO BE ERASED FROM HISTORY?
SIMPLY STATE ...
...THE NAME YOU WISH STRICKEN!!

A: I wouldn't worry about that. Live your life as you see fit. And that goes for all of you!! Have a great life! The SBS is over now!! See you next volume!!!

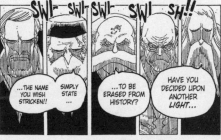

Chapter 953:
ONCE A FOX

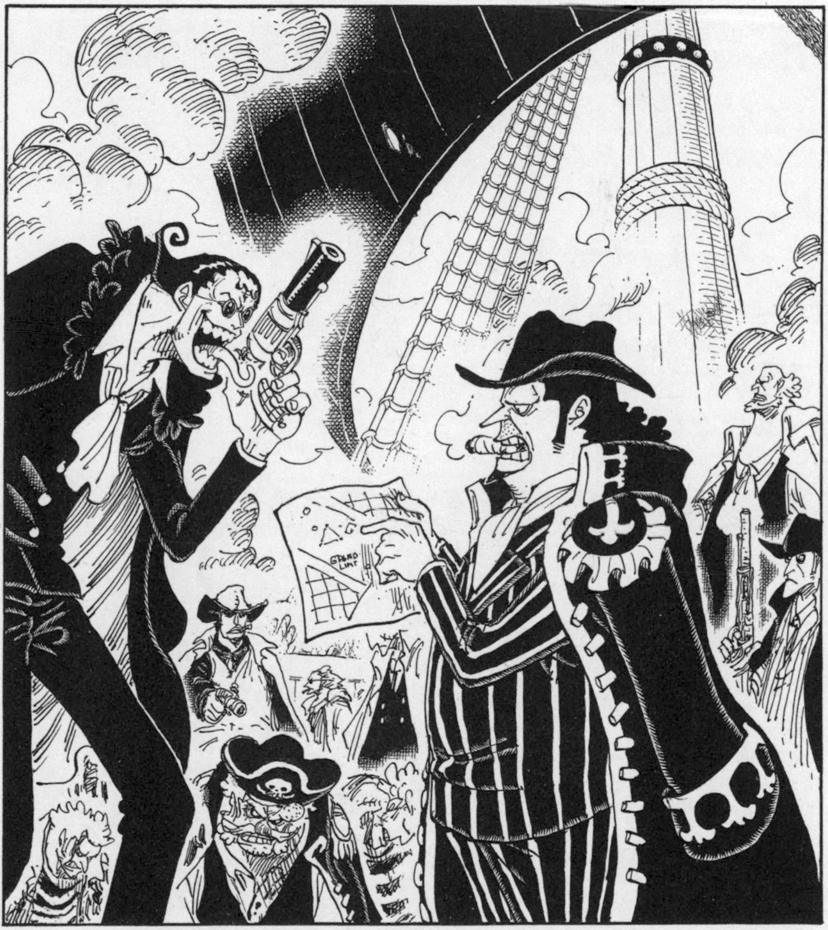

GANG BEGE'S OH MY FAMILY, VOL. 4:
"ENEMY SHIP SEIZED!! OFF TO THRILLER BARK"

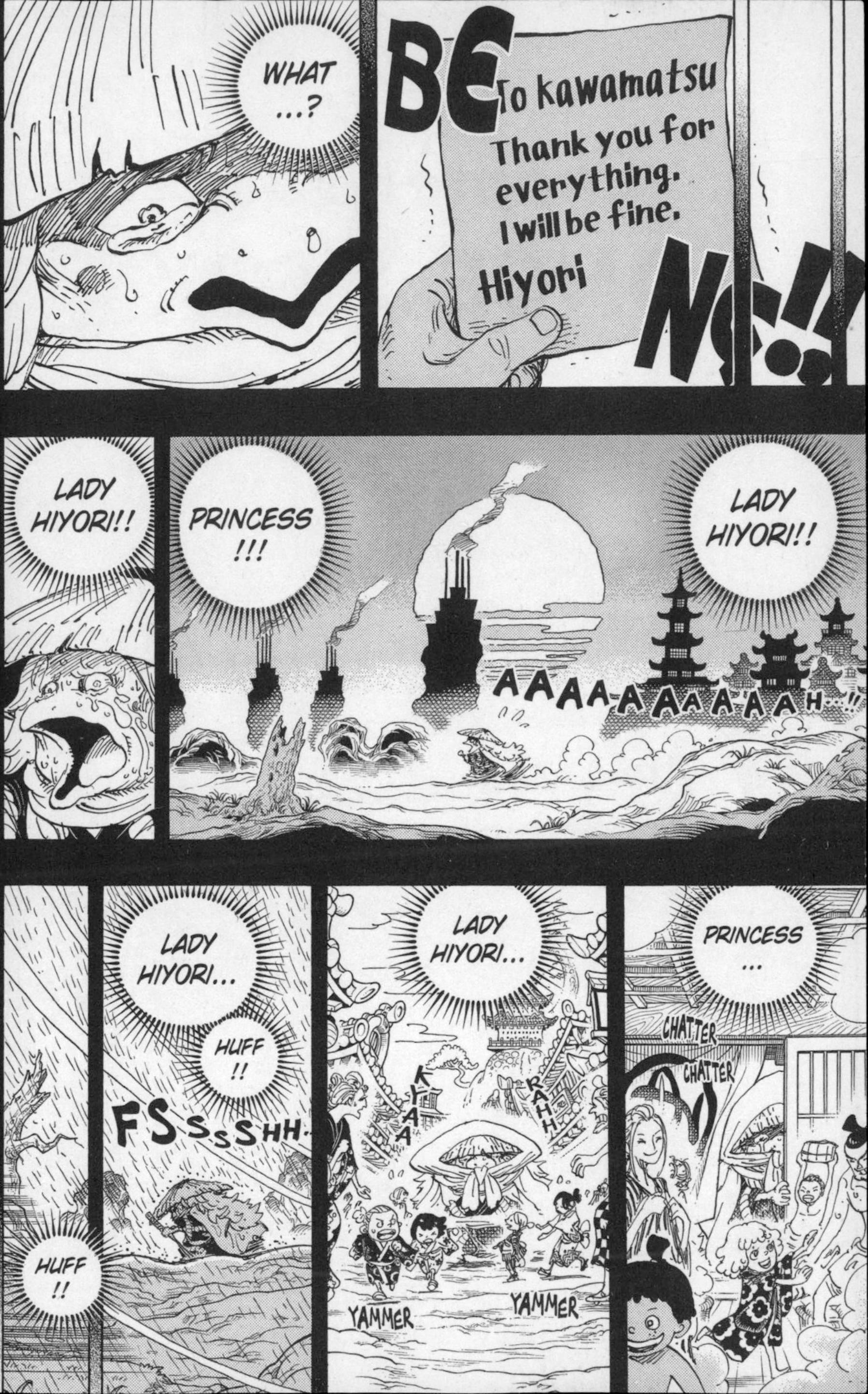
BE
To kawamatsu
Thank you for
everything.
I will be fine.
Hiyori
WHAT ...?
LADY HIYORI!!
PRINCESS !!!
AAAAAAAAAAAH...!!
LADY HIYORI!!
PRINCESS ...
CHATTER
CHATTER
LADY HIYORI...
KYAA
RAHH
YAMMER
YAMMER
LADY HIYORI...
HUFF !!
FSSSSHH
HUFF !!

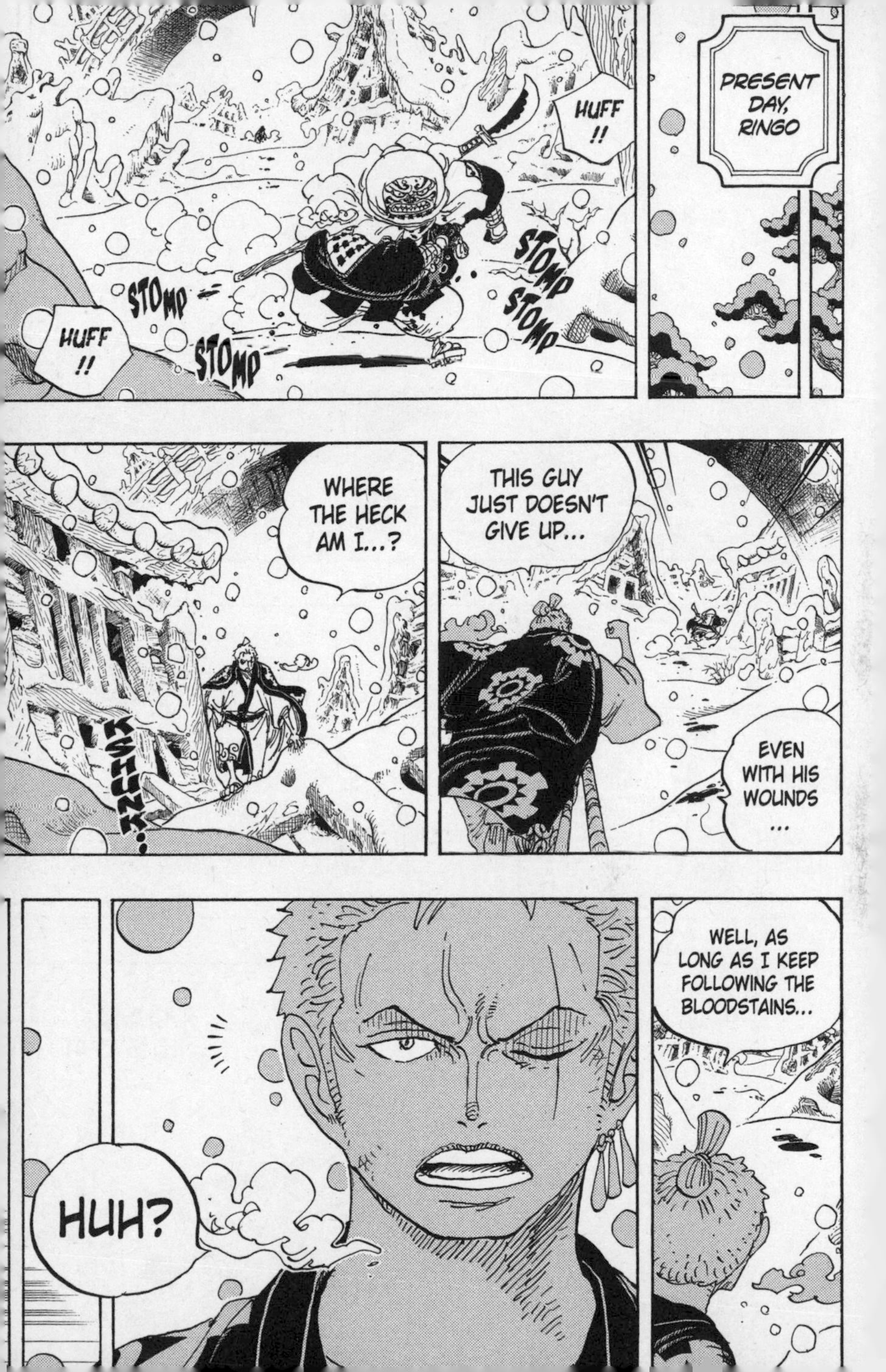
PRESENT DAY, RINGO
HUFF !!
STOMP STOMP
STOMP
STOMP
HUFF !!
STOMP
THIS GUY JUST DOESN'T GIVE UP...
EVEN WITH HIS WOUNDS ...
WHERE THE HECK AM I...?
KSHUNK...
WELL, AS LONG AS I KEEP FOLLOWING THE BLOODSTAINS...
HUH?

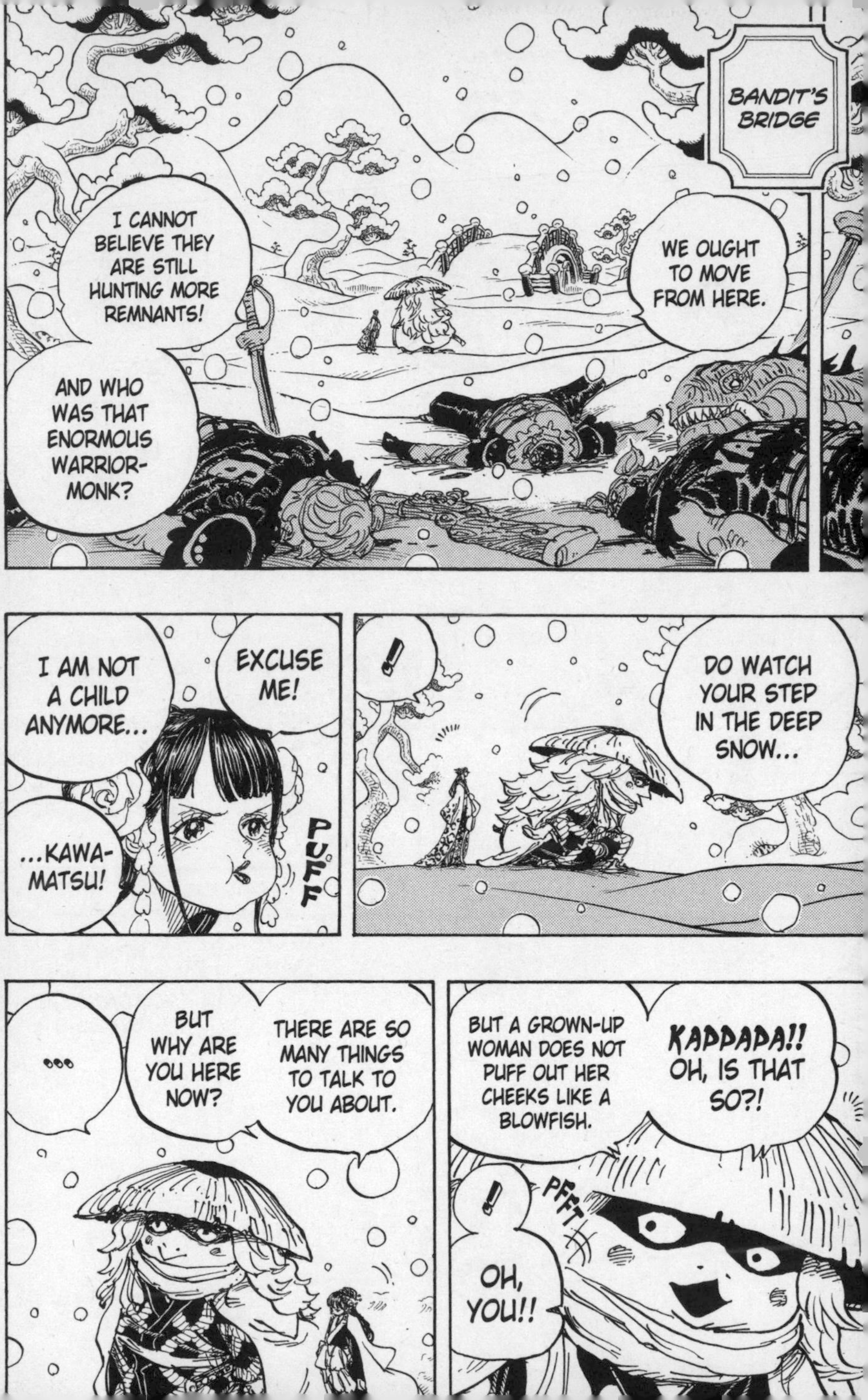
BANDIT'S BRIDGE
WE OUGHT TO MOVE FROM HERE.
I CANNOT BELIEVE THEY ARE STILL HUNTING MORE REMNANTS!
AND WHO WAS THAT ENORMOUS WARRIOR-MONK?
DO WATCH YOUR STEP IN THE DEEP SNOW...
!
EXCUSE ME!
I AM NOT A CHILD ANYMORE...
...KAWA-MATSU!
PUFF
KAPPAPA!! OH, IS THAT SO?!
BUT A GROWN-UP WOMAN DOES NOT PUFF OUT HER CHEEKS LIKE A BLOWFISH.
PFFT
!
OH, YOU!!
THERE ARE SO MANY THINGS TO TALK TO YOU ABOUT.
BUT WHY ARE YOU HERE NOW?
...

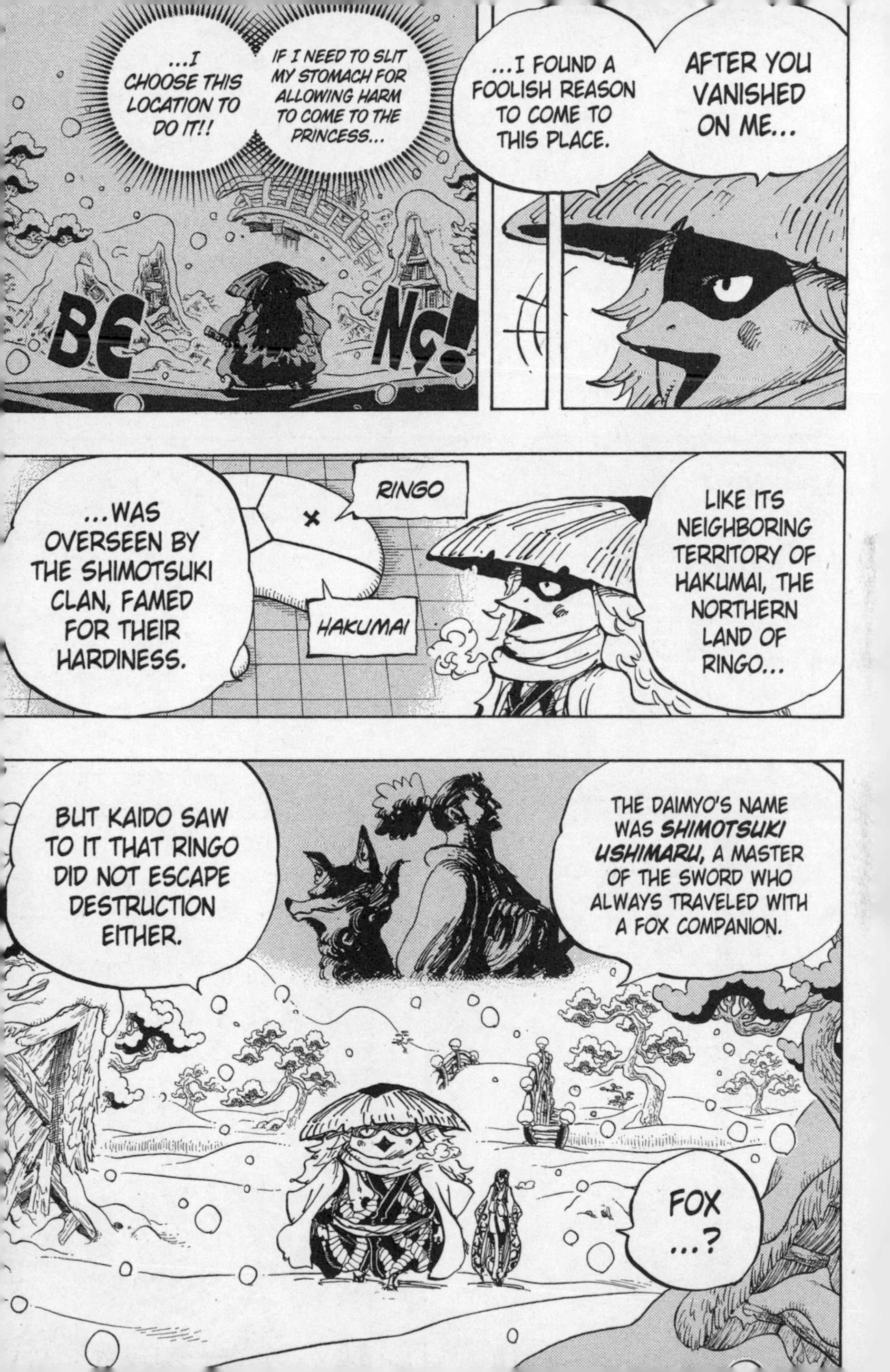
AFTER YOU VANISHED ON ME...
...I FOUND A FOOLISH REASON TO COME TO THIS PLACE.
IF I NEED TO SLIT MY STOMACH FOR ALLOWING HARM TO COME TO THE PRINCESS...
...I CHOOSE THIS LOCATION TO DO IT!!
BE NG!
LIKE ITS NEIGHBORING TERRITORY OF HAKUMAI, THE NORTHERN LAND OF RINGO...
RINGO
HAKUMAI
...WAS OVERSEEN BY THE SHIMOTSUKI CLAN, FAMED FOR THEIR HARDINESS.
THE DAIMYO'S NAME WAS *SHIMOTSUKI USHIMARU*, A MASTER OF THE SWORD WHO ALWAYS TRAVELED WITH A FOX COMPANION.
BUT KAIDO SAW TO IT THAT RINGO DID NOT ESCAPE DESTRUCTION EITHER.
FOX ...?

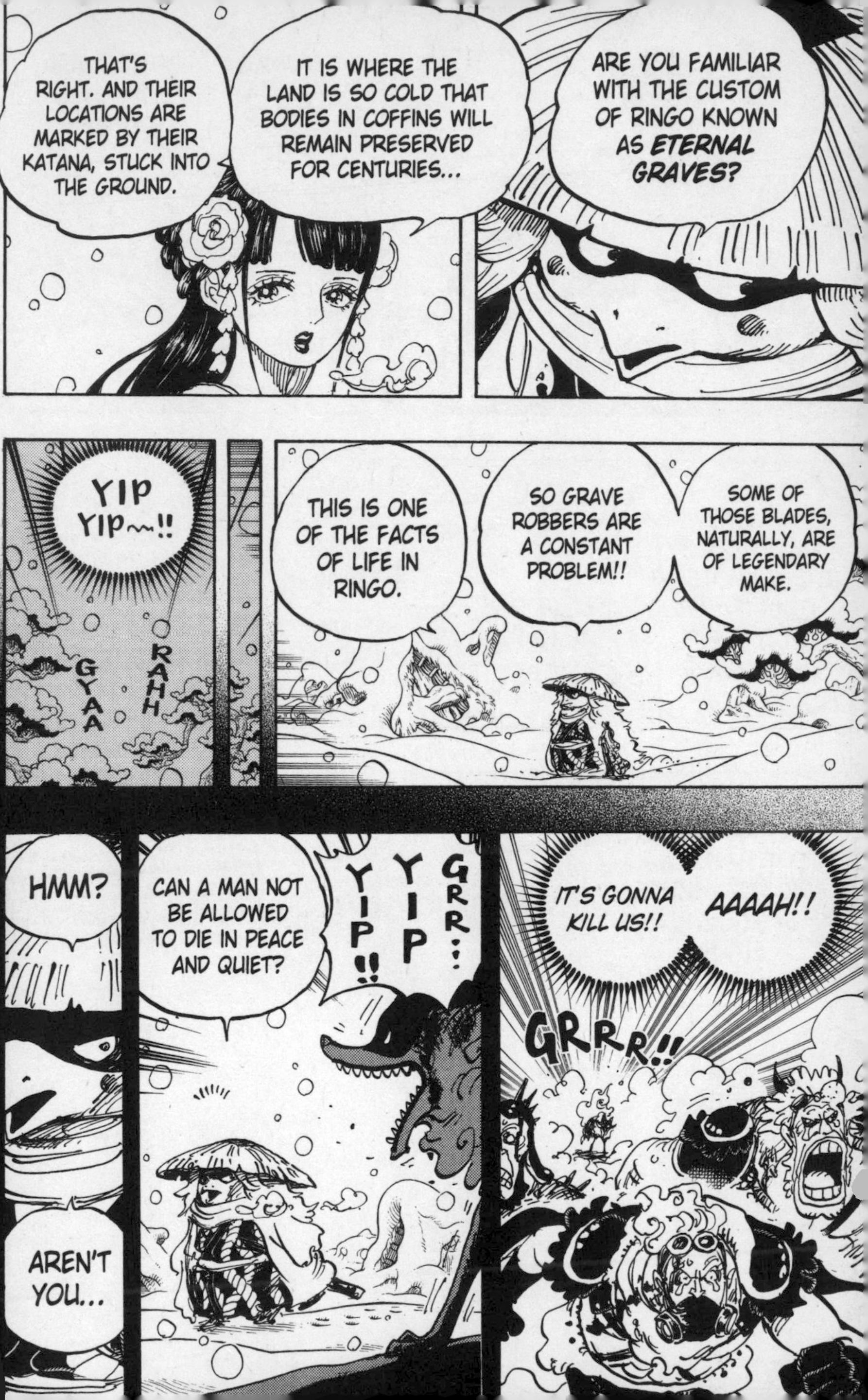
ARE YOU FAMILIAR WITH THE CUSTOM OF RINGO KNOWN AS ***ETERNAL GRAVES?***
IT IS WHERE THE LAND IS SO COLD THAT BODIES IN COFFINS WILL REMAIN PRESERVED FOR CENTURIES...
THAT'S RIGHT. AND THEIR LOCATIONS ARE MARKED BY THEIR KATANA, STUCK INTO THE GROUND.
SOME OF THOSE BLADES, NATURALLY, ARE OF LEGENDARY MAKE.
SO GRAVE ROBBERS ARE A CONSTANT PROBLEM!!
THIS IS ONE OF THE FACTS OF LIFE IN RINGO.
YIP YIP~~!!
RAHH
GYAA
AAAAH!!
IT'S GONNA KILL US!!
GRRR!!
GRR..!
YIP
YIP!!
CAN A MAN NOT BE ALLOWED TO DIE IN PEACE AND QUIET?
HMM?
AREN'T YOU...

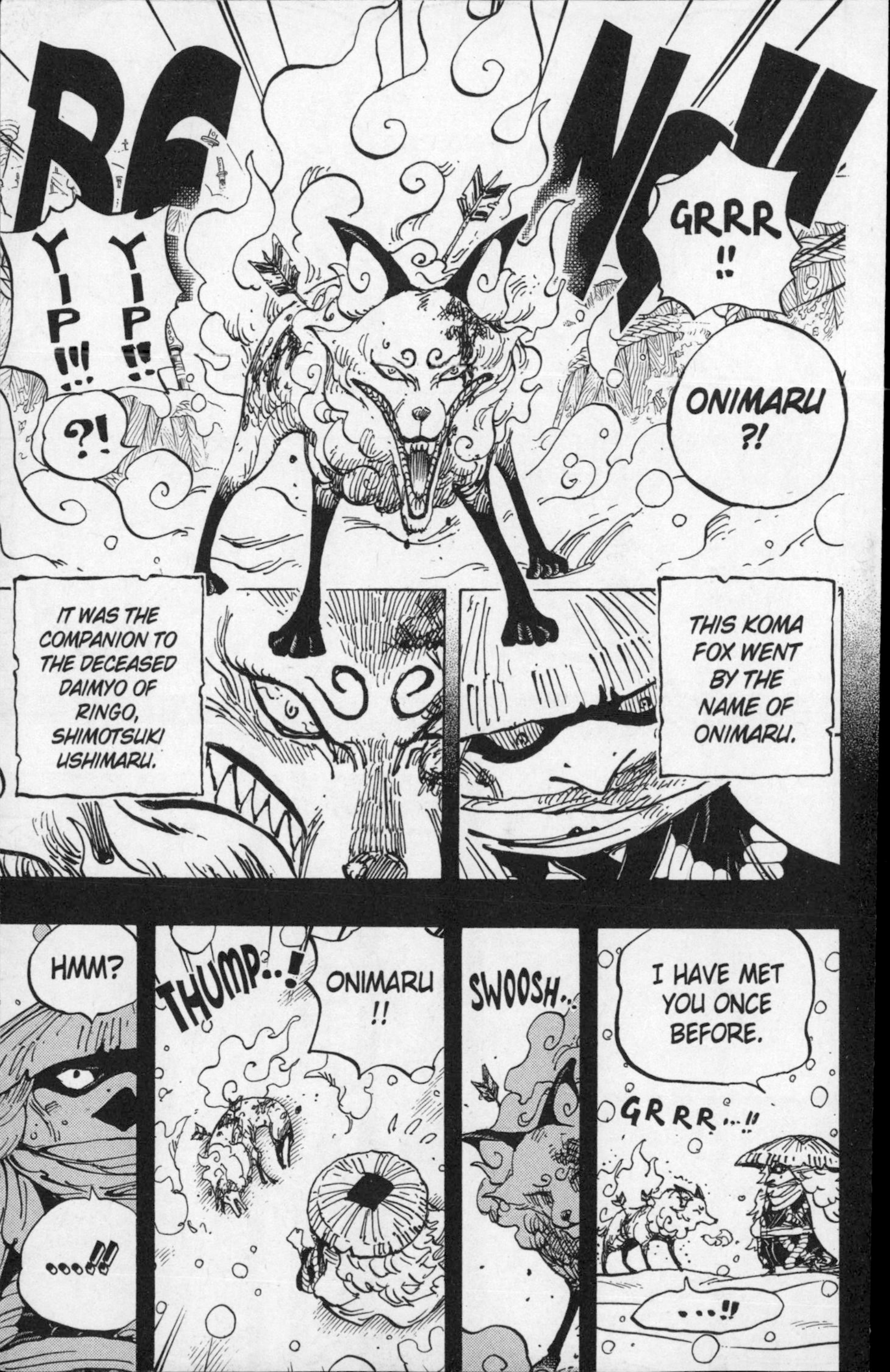
GRRR!!
ONIMARU?!
YIP!!!
YIP!!
?!
THIS KOMA FOX WENT BY THE NAME OF ONIMARU.
IT WAS THE COMPANION TO THE DECEASED DAIMYO OF RINGO, SHIMOTSUKI USHIMARU.
I HAVE MET YOU ONCE BEFORE.
GRRR...!!
...!!
SWOOSH..
ONIMARU!!
THUMP..!
HMM?
...!!

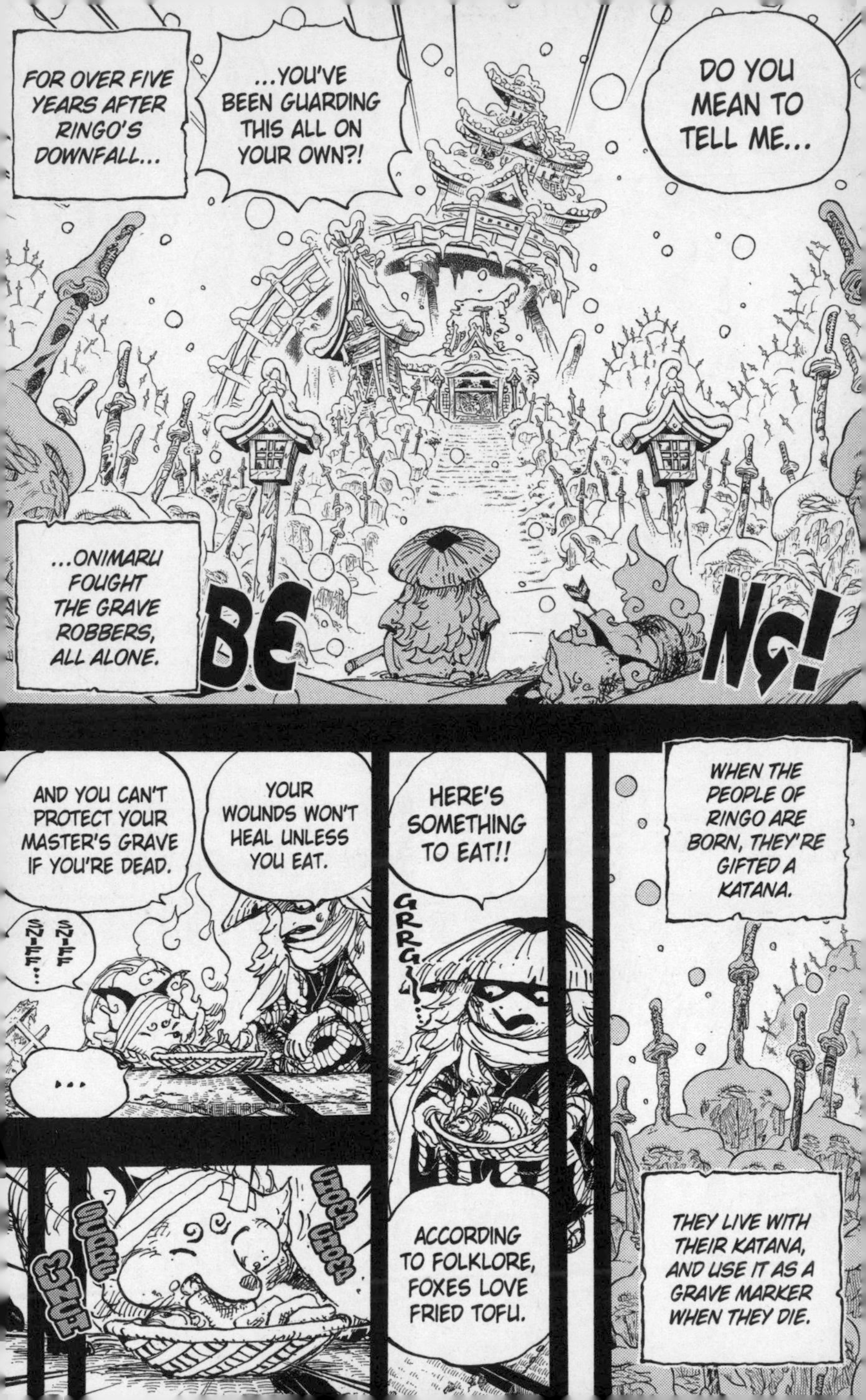
DO YOU MEAN TO TELL ME...
...YOU'VE BEEN GUARDING THIS ALL ON YOUR OWN?!
FOR OVER FIVE YEARS AFTER RINGO'S DOWNFALL...
...ONIMARU FOUGHT THE GRAVE ROBBERS, ALL ALONE.
WHEN THE PEOPLE OF RINGO ARE BORN, THEY'RE GIFTED A KATANA.
THEY LIVE WITH THEIR KATANA, AND USE IT AS A GRAVE MARKER WHEN THEY DIE.
HERE'S SOMETHING TO EAT!!
GRRR...
ACCORDING TO FOLKLORE, FOXES LOVE FRIED TOFU.
YOUR WOUNDS WON'T HEAL UNLESS YOU EAT.
AND YOU CAN'T PROTECT YOUR MASTER'S GRAVE IF YOU'RE DEAD.
SNIFF SNIFF...
...

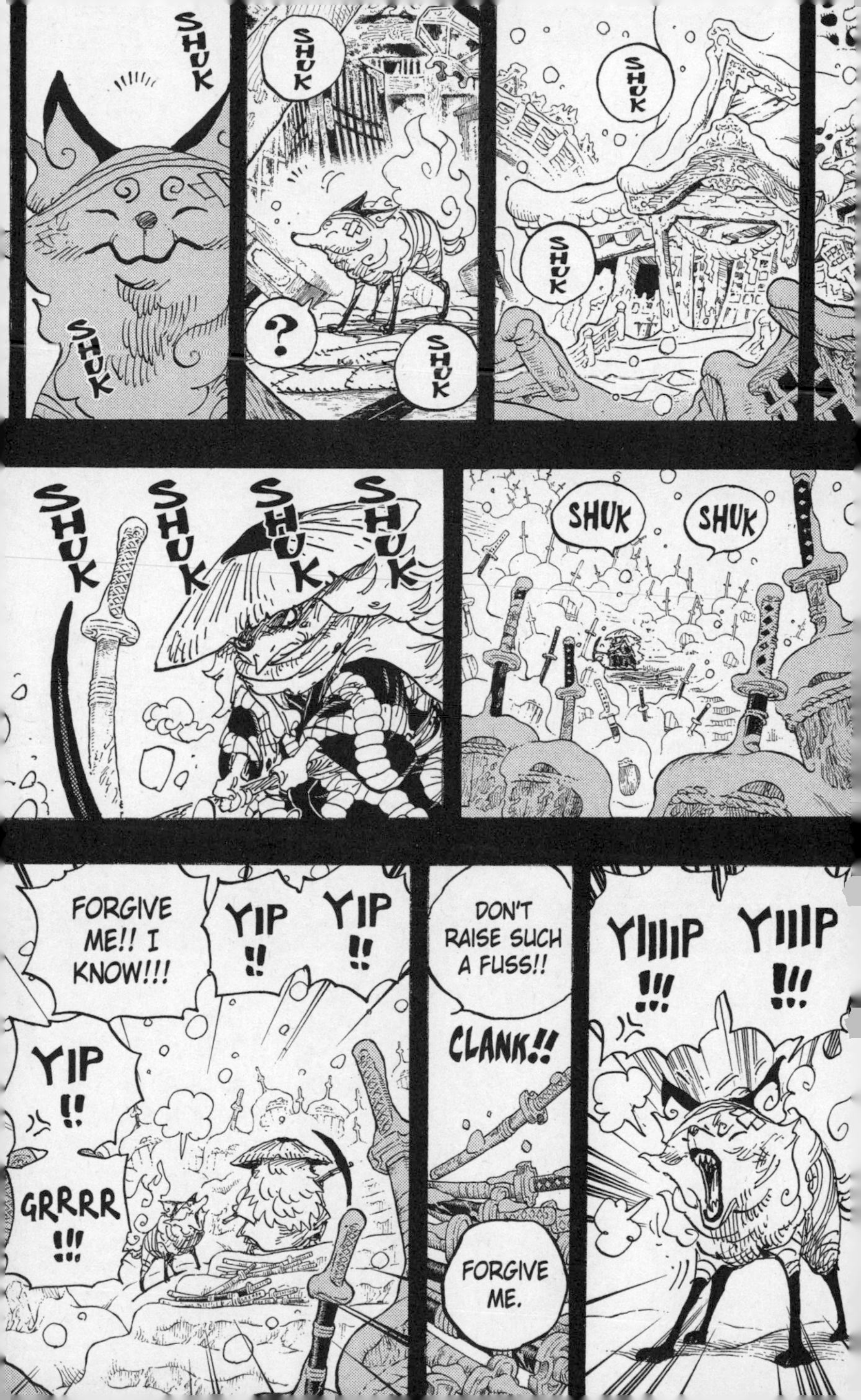
SHUK
SHUK
SHUK
?
SHUK
SHUK
SHUK
SHUK
SHUK
SHUK
SHUK
SHUK
SHUK
YIIIIP!!!
YIIIIP!!!
DON'T RAISE SUCH A FUSS!!
CLANK!!
FORGIVE ME.
YIP!!
YIP!!
FORGIVE ME!! I KNOW!!!
YIP!!
GRRRR!!!

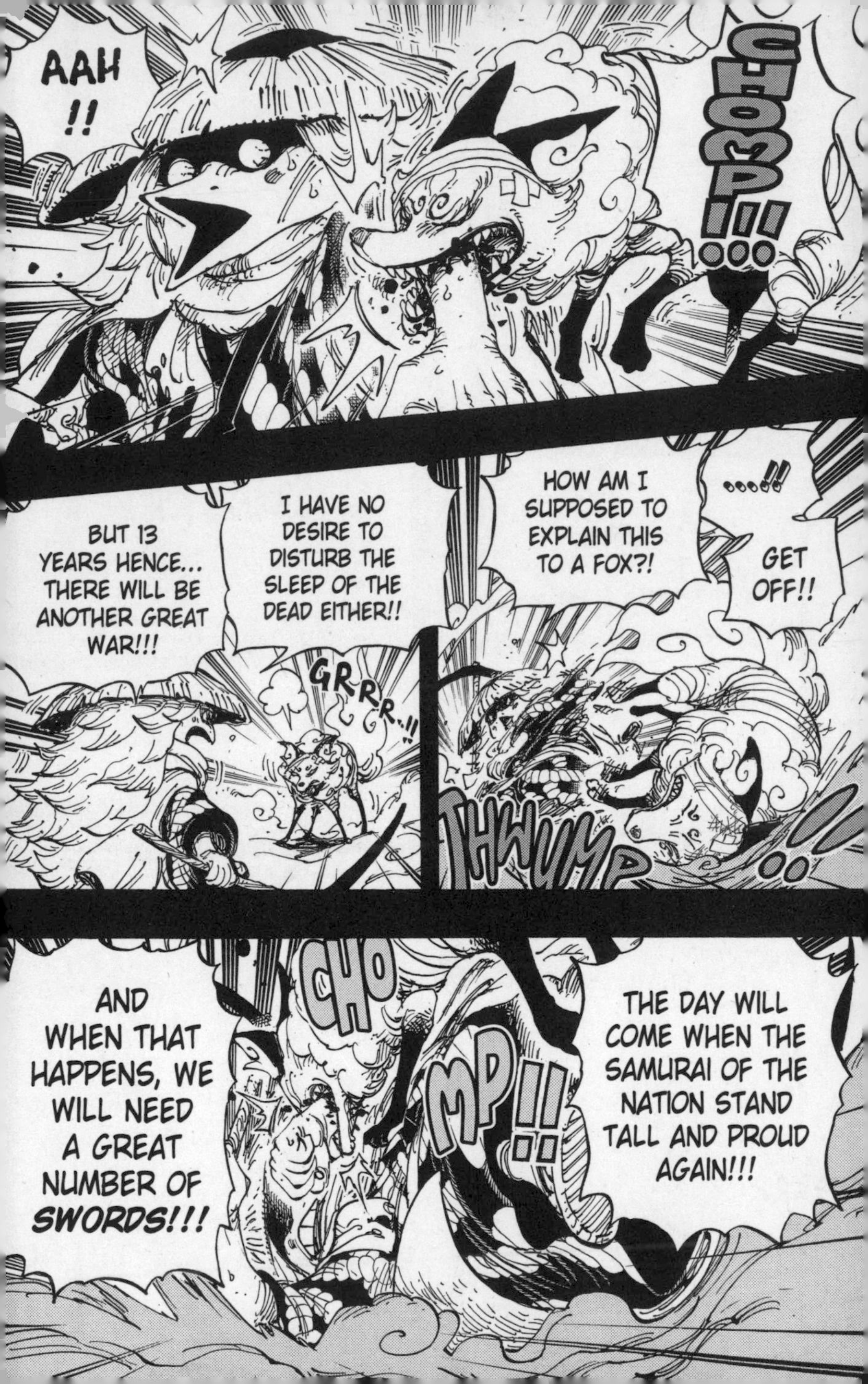
CHOMP!!...
AAH !!
...!!
GET OFF!!
HOW AM I SUPPOSED TO EXPLAIN THIS TO A FOX?!
THWUMP!!..
I HAVE NO DESIRE TO DISTURB THE SLEEP OF THE DEAD EITHER!!
BUT 13 YEARS HENCE... THERE WILL BE ANOTHER GREAT WAR!!!
GRRRR..!!
THE DAY WILL COME WHEN THE SAMURAI OF THE NATION STAND TALL AND PROUD AGAIN!!!
CHOMP!!
AND WHEN THAT HAPPENS, WE WILL NEED A GREAT NUMBER OF SWORDS!!!

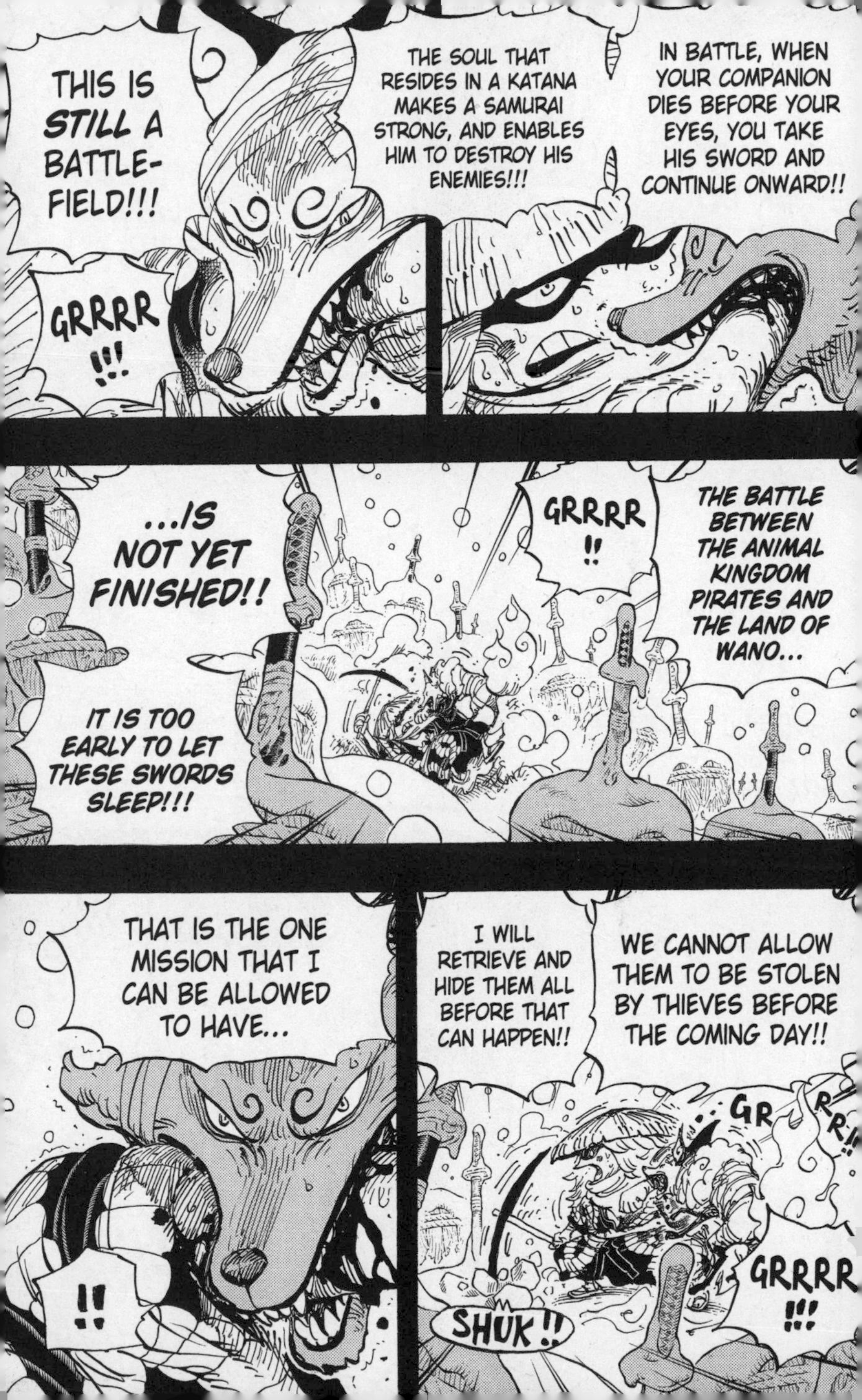
IN BATTLE, WHEN YOUR COMPANION DIES BEFORE YOUR EYES, YOU TAKE HIS SWORD AND CONTINUE ONWARD!!
THE SOUL THAT RESIDES IN A KATANA MAKES A SAMURAI STRONG, AND ENABLES HIM TO DESTROY HIS ENEMIES!!!
THIS IS STILL A BATTLE-FIELD!!!
GRRRR !!!
THE BATTLE BETWEEN THE ANIMAL KINGDOM PIRATES AND THE LAND OF WANO...
GRRRR !!
...IS NOT YET FINISHED!!
IT IS TOO EARLY TO LET THESE SWORDS SLEEP!!!
WE CANNOT ALLOW THEM TO BE STOLEN BY THIEVES BEFORE THE COMING DAY!!
I WILL RETRIEVE AND HIDE THEM ALL BEFORE THAT CAN HAPPEN!!
GR RRR!!
GRRRR !!!
SHUK!!
THAT IS THE ONE MISSION THAT I CAN BE ALLOWED TO HAVE...
!!

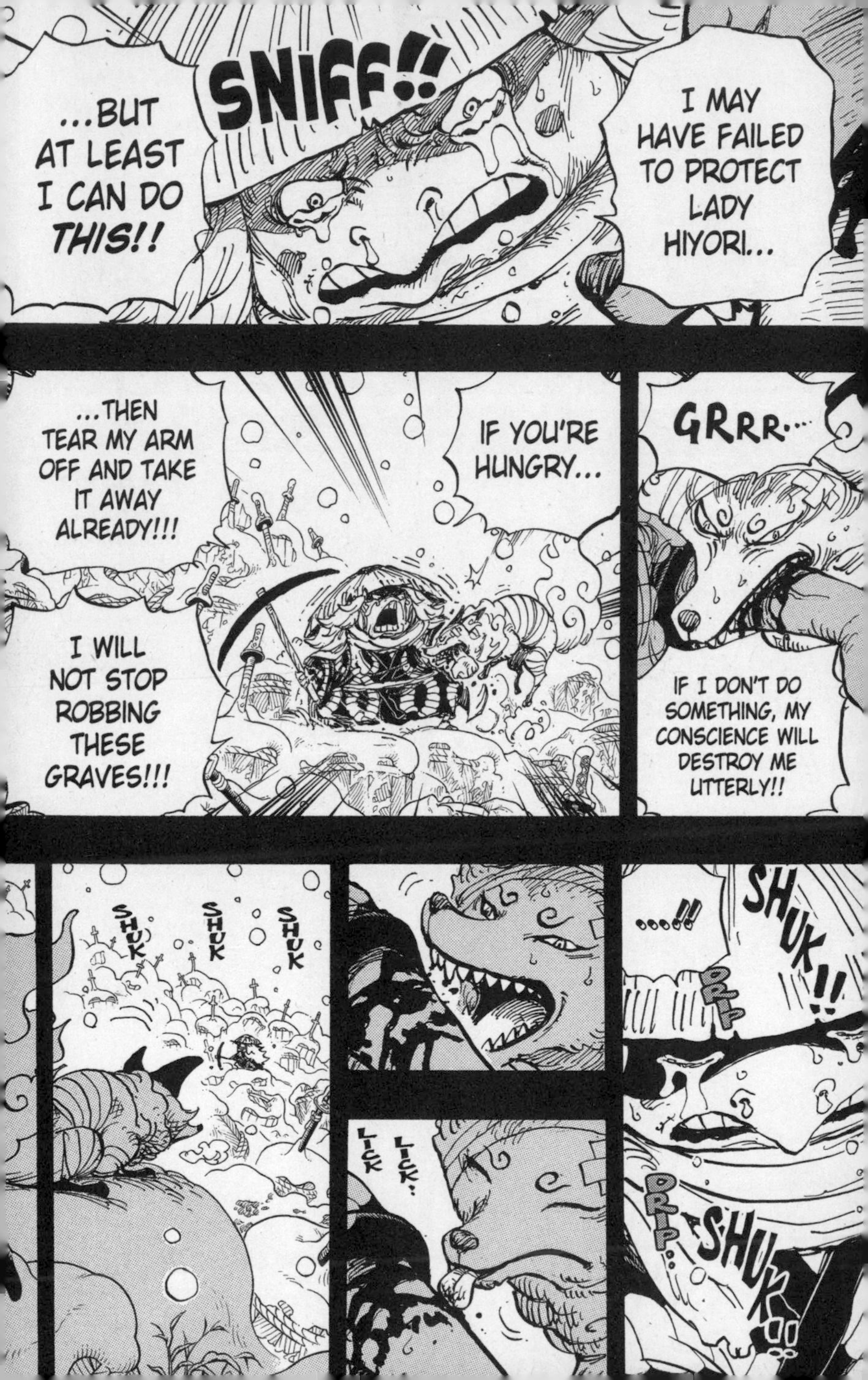
I MAY HAVE FAILED TO PROTECT LADY HIYORI...
SNIFF!!
...BUT AT LEAST I CAN DO THIS!!
GRRR...
IF I DON'T DO SOMETHING, MY CONSCIENCE WILL DESTROY ME UTTERLY!!
IF YOU'RE HUNGRY...
...THEN TEAR MY ARM OFF AND TAKE IT AWAY ALREADY!!!
I WILL NOT STOP ROBBING THESE GRAVES!!!
....!!
SHUK!!
DRIP
DRIP...
SHUK...
LICK LICK
SHUK
SHUK
SHUK

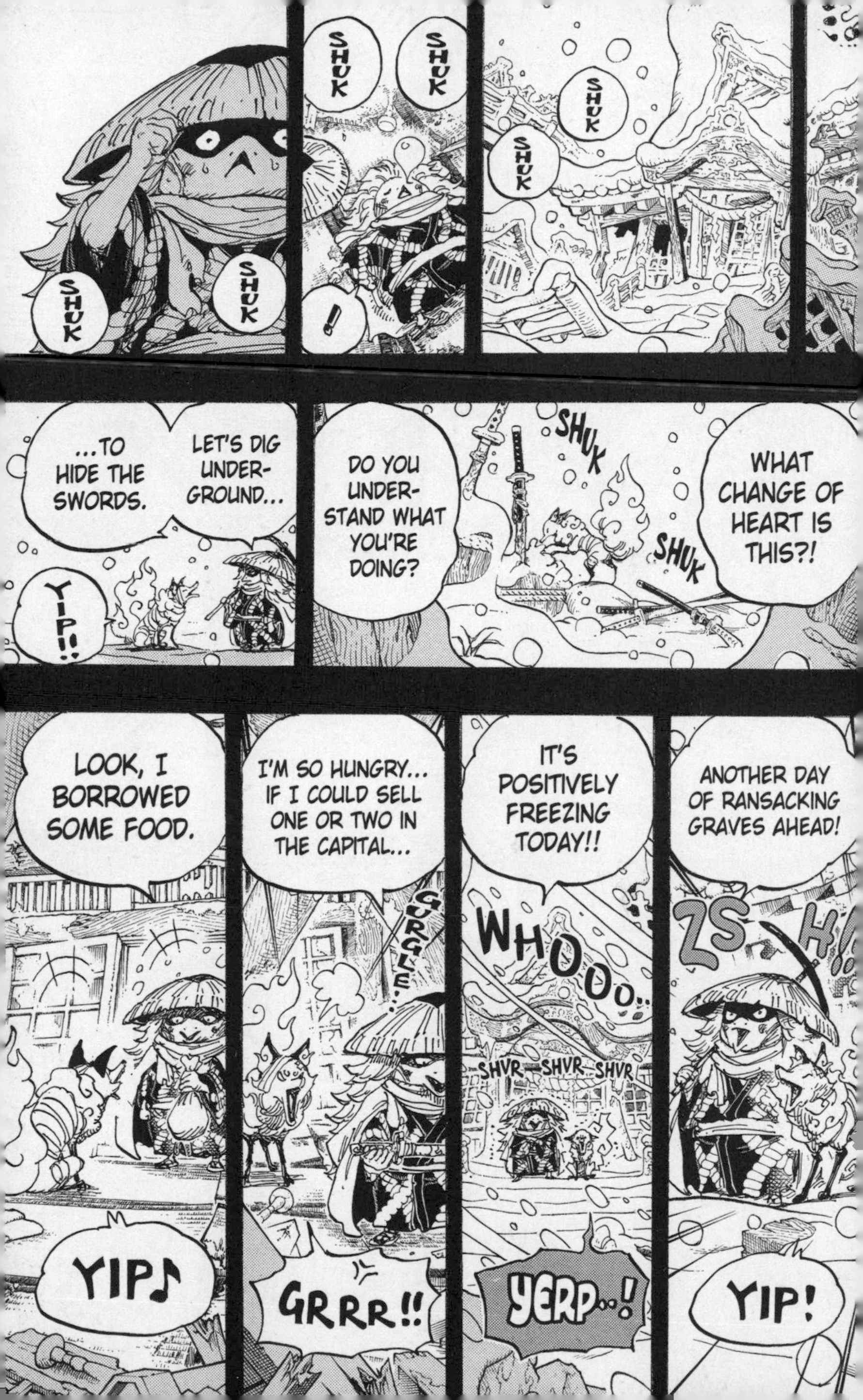
SHUK
SHUK
SHUK
SHUK
!
SHUK
SHUK
WHAT CHANGE OF HEART IS THIS?!
SHUK
SHUK
DO YOU UNDERSTAND WHAT YOU'RE DOING?
LET'S DIG UNDERGROUND...
...TO HIDE THE SWORDS.
YIP!!
ANOTHER DAY OF RANSACKING GRAVES AHEAD!
ZSH!!
YIP!
IT'S POSITIVELY FREEZING TODAY!!
WHOOOO..
SHVR SHVR SHVR
YERP..!
I'M SO HUNGRY... IF I COULD SELL ONE OR TWO IN THE CAPITAL...
GURGLE..
GRRR!!
LOOK, I BORROWED SOME FOOD.
YIP♪

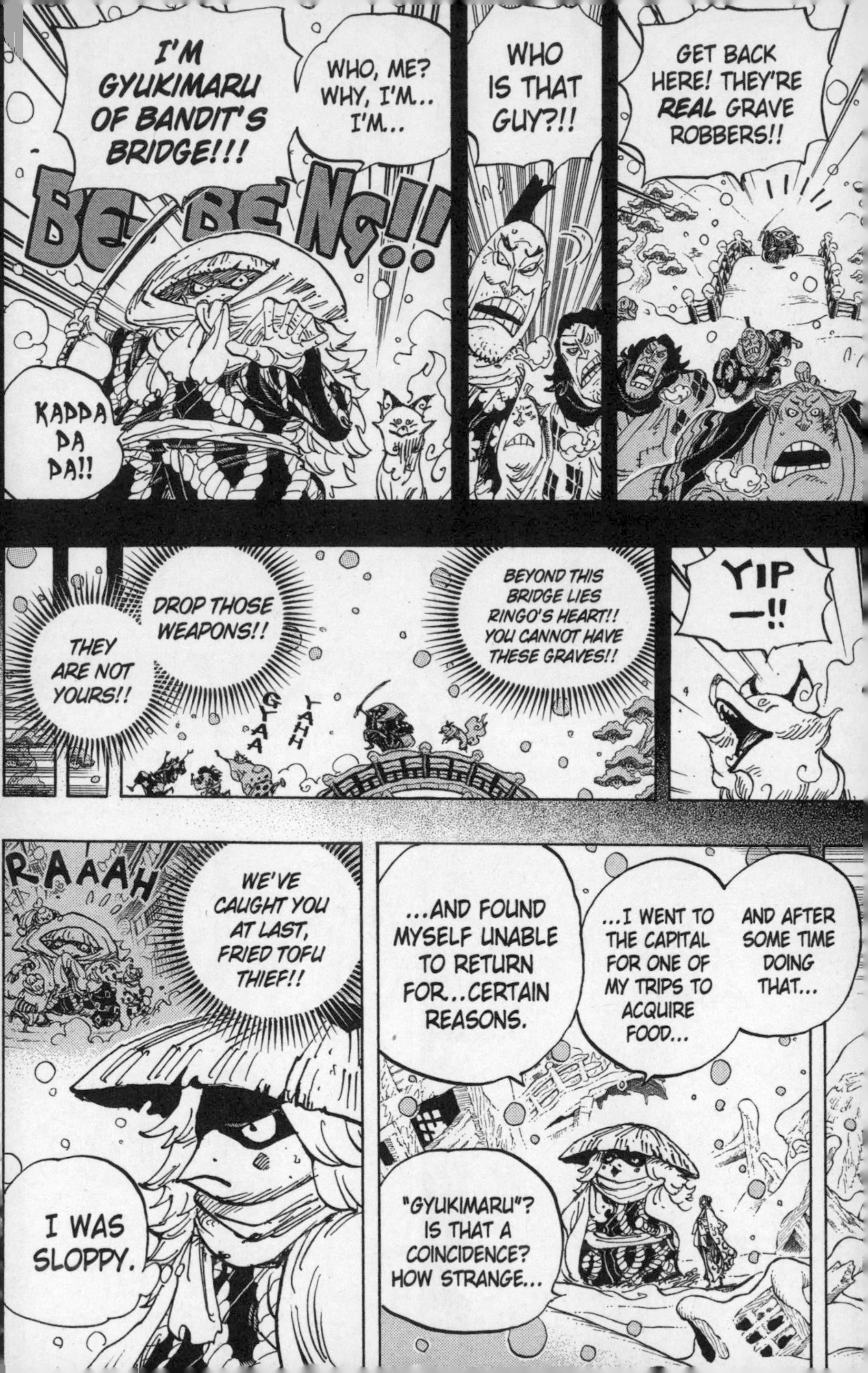

GET BACK HERE! THEY'RE REAL GRAVE ROBBERS!!
WHO IS THAT GUY?!!
WHO, ME? WHY, I'M... I'M...
I'M GYUKIMARU OF BANDIT'S BRIDGE!!!
BE BE NG!!
KAPPA PA PA!!
YIP—!!
BEYOND THIS BRIDGE LIES RINGO'S HEART!! YOU CANNOT HAVE THESE GRAVES!!
DROP THOSE WEAPONS!!
THEY ARE NOT YOURS!!
YAHH
GYAA
AND AFTER SOME TIME DOING THAT...
...I WENT TO THE CAPITAL FOR ONE OF MY TRIPS TO ACQUIRE FOOD...
...AND FOUND MYSELF UNABLE TO RETURN FOR...CERTAIN REASONS.
"GYUKIMARU"? IS THAT A COINCIDENCE? HOW STRANGE...
RAAAH
WE'VE CAUGHT YOU AT LAST, FRIED TOFU THIEF!!
I WAS SLOPPY.

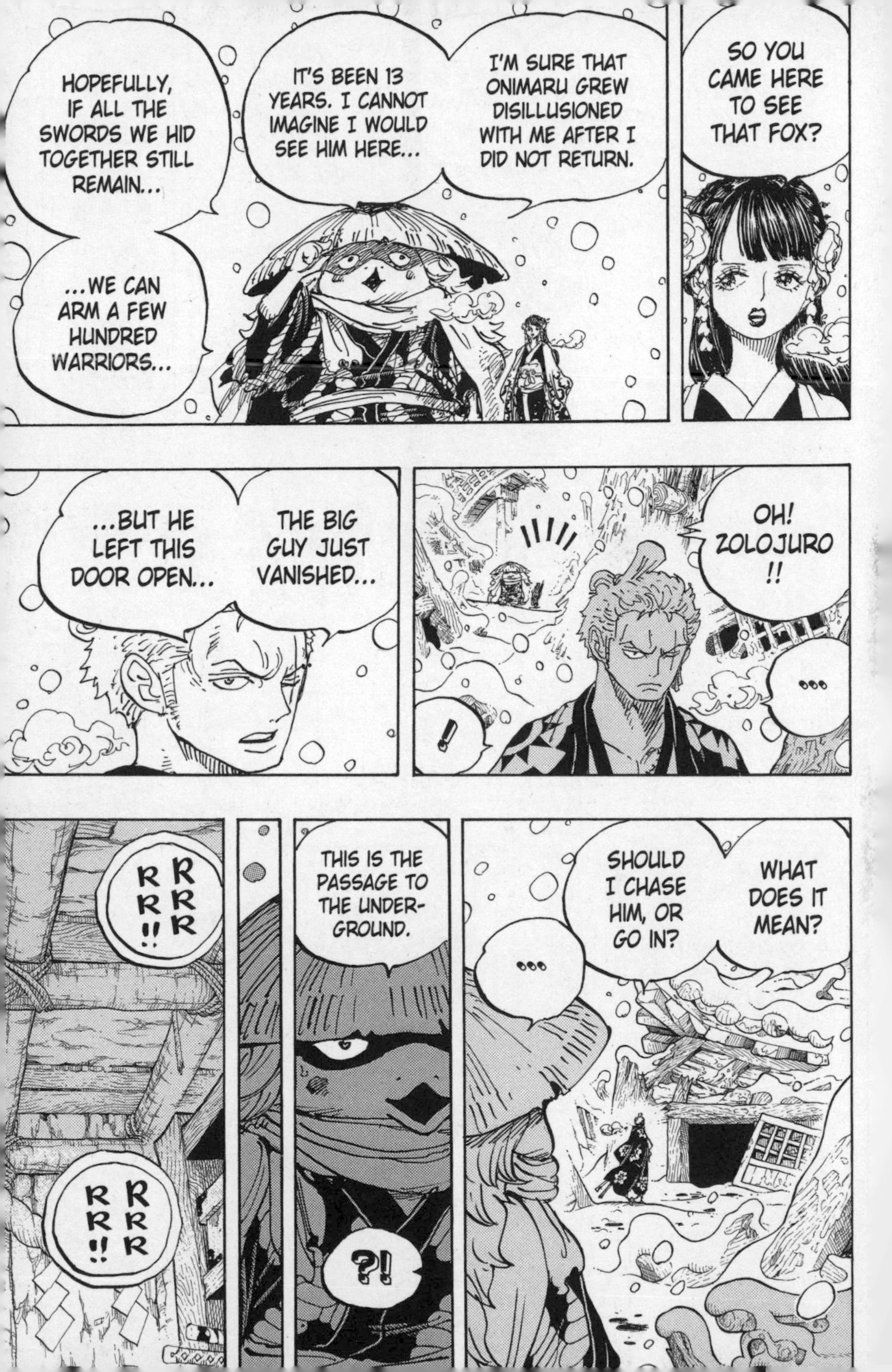
SO YOU CAME HERE TO SEE THAT FOX?
I'M SURE THAT ONIMARU GREW DISILLUSIONED WITH ME AFTER I DID NOT RETURN.
IT'S BEEN 13 YEARS. I CANNOT IMAGINE I WOULD SEE HIM HERE...
HOPEFULLY, IF ALL THE SWORDS WE HID TOGETHER STILL REMAIN...
...WE CAN ARM A FEW HUNDRED WARRIORS...
OH! ZOLOJURO !!
...
!
THE BIG GUY JUST VANISHED...
...BUT HE LEFT THIS DOOR OPEN...
WHAT DOES IT MEAN?
SHOULD I CHASE HIM, OR GO IN?
...
THIS IS THE PASSAGE TO THE UNDER-GROUND.
?!
RRRRR!!
RRRRR!!

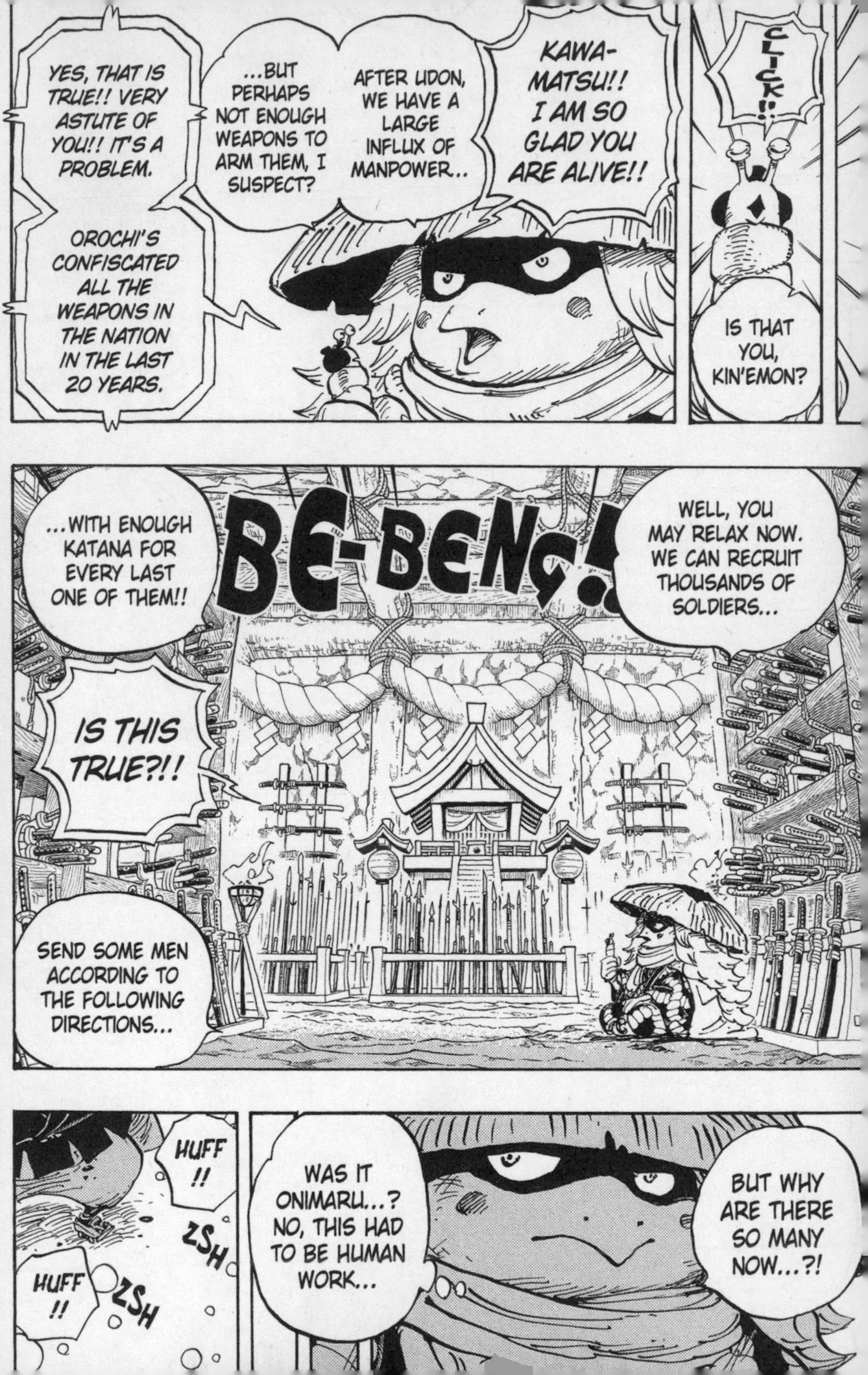
CLICK!!
IS THAT YOU, KIN'EMON?
KAWA-MATSU!! I AM SO GLAD YOU ARE ALIVE!!
AFTER UDON, WE HAVE A LARGE INFLUX OF MANPOWER...
...BUT PERHAPS NOT ENOUGH WEAPONS TO ARM THEM, I SUSPECT?
YES, THAT IS TRUE!! VERY ASTUTE OF YOU!! IT'S A PROBLEM.
OROCHI'S CONFISCATED ALL THE WEAPONS IN THE NATION IN THE LAST 20 YEARS.
WELL, YOU MAY RELAX NOW. WE CAN RECRUIT THOUSANDS OF SOLDIERS...
...WITH ENOUGH KATANA FOR EVERY LAST ONE OF THEM!!
BE-BENG!!
IS THIS TRUE?!!
SEND SOME MEN ACCORDING TO THE FOLLOWING DIRECTIONS...
BUT WHY ARE THERE SO MANY NOW...?!
WAS IT ONIMARU...? NO, THIS HAD TO BE HUMAN WORK...
HUFF !!
ZSH
HUFF !!
ZSH

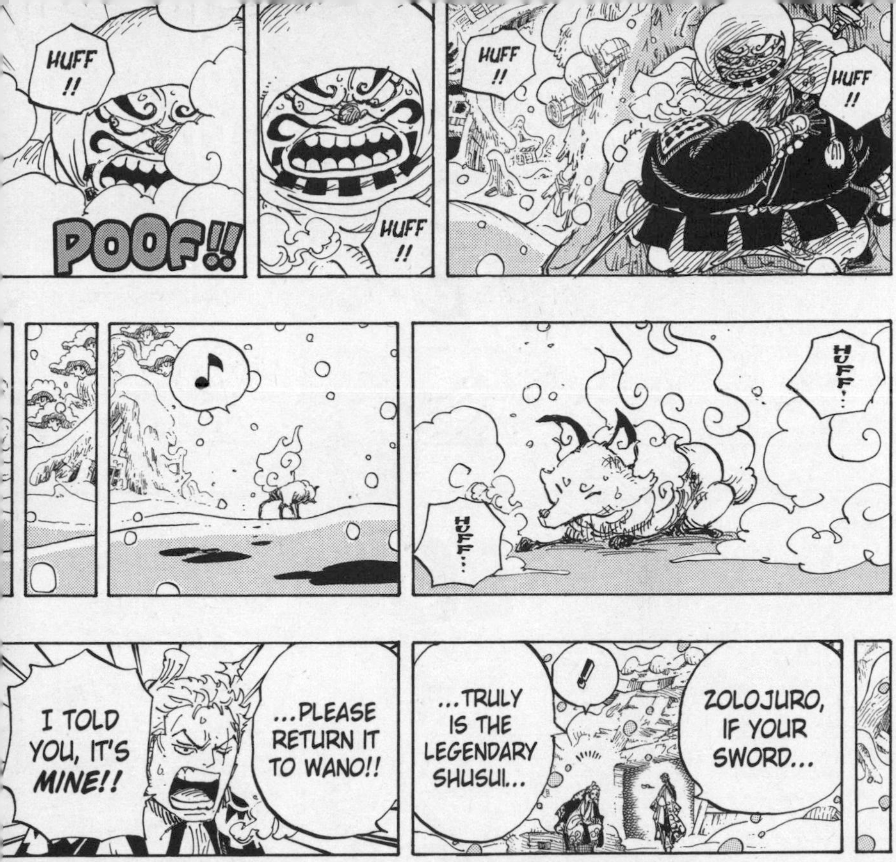
HUFF!!
HUFF!!
HUFF!!
HUFF!!
POOF!!
HUFF...
HUFF...
♪
ZOLOJURO, IF YOUR SWORD...
!
...TRULY IS THE LEGENDARY SHUSUI...
...PLEASE RETURN IT TO WANO!!
I TOLD YOU, IT'S *MINE!!*

TO BE CONTINUED IN *ONE PIECE*, VOL 95!

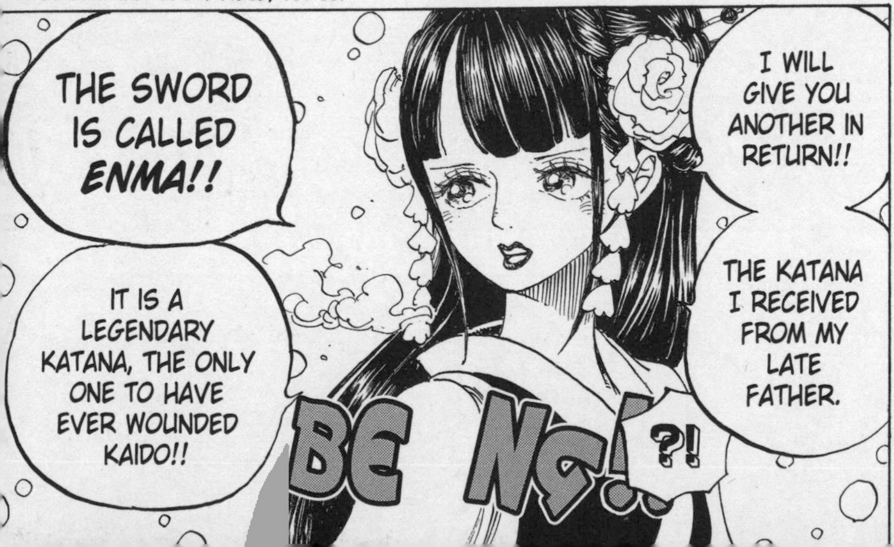
I WILL GIVE YOU ANOTHER IN RETURN!!
THE KATANA I RECEIVED FROM MY LATE FATHER.
THE SWORD IS CALLED *ENMA!!*
IT IS A LEGENDARY KATANA, THE ONLY ONE TO HAVE EVER WOUNDED KAIDO!!
?!
BE NG!

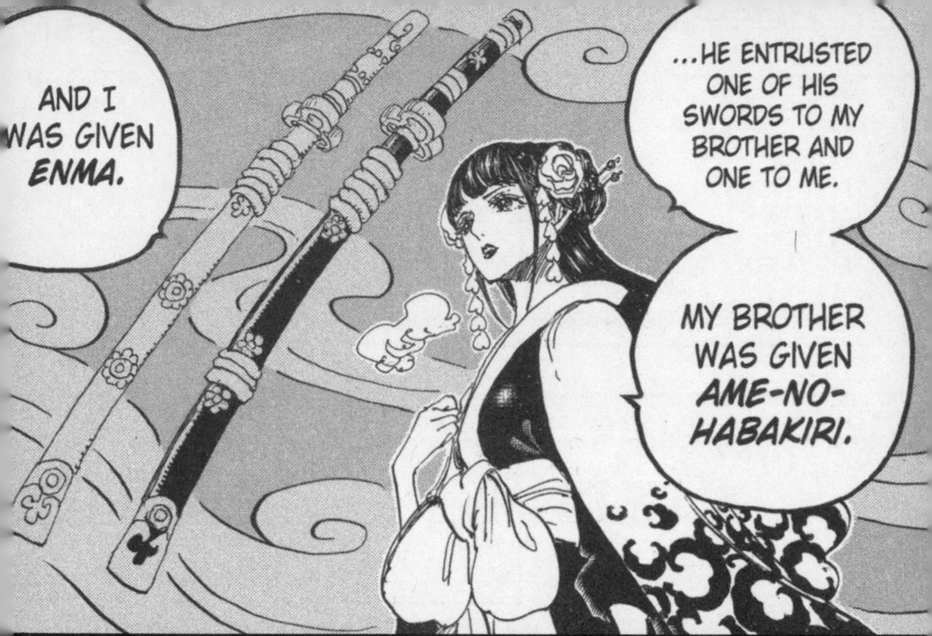
...HE ENTRUSTED ONE OF HIS SWORDS TO MY BROTHER AND ONE TO ME.
MY BROTHER WAS GIVEN *AME-NO-HABAKIRI.*
AND I WAS GIVEN *ENMA.*

As Kaido and Big Mom battle it out, the Straw Hats and their samurai allies continue to amass strength. They'll need ships, weapons and thousands of men. But will it be enough?

ON SALE DECEMBER 2020!

ONE PIECE VOL. 94
WANO PART 5

SHONEN JUMP Manga Edition

STORY AND ART BY EIICHIRO ODA

Translation/Stephen Paul
Touch-up Art & Lettering/Vanessa Satone
Design/Yukiko Whitley
Editor/Alexis Kirsch

Printed in the U.S.A.

Published by VIZ Media, LLC
P.O. Box 77010
San Francisco, CA 94107

10 9 8 7 6 5 4 3 2 1
First printing, August 2020

viz.com

shonenjump.com

DEMON SLAYER
KIMETSU NO YAIBA

Story and Art by
KOYOHARU GOTOUGE

In Taisho-era Japan, kindhearted Tanjiro Kamado makes a living selling charcoal. But his peaceful life is shattered when a demon slaughters his entire family. His little sister Nezuko is the only survivor, but she has been transformed into a demon herself! Tanjiro sets out on a dangerous journey to find a way to return his sister to normal and destroy the demon who ruined his life.

BORUTO
=NARUTO NEXT GENERATIONS=

CREATOR/SUPERVISOR **Masashi Kishimoto**
ART BY **Mikio Ikemoto** SCRIPT BY **Ukyo Kodachi**

A NEW GENERATION OF NINJA IS HERE!

Naruto was a young shinobi with an incorrigible knack for mischief. He achieved his dream to become the greatest ninja in his village, and now his face sits atop the Hokage monument. But this is not his story... A new generation of ninja is ready to take the stage, led by Naruto's own son, Boruto!

ASTRA
LOST IN SPACE

CAN EIGHT TEENAGERS FIND THEIR WAY HOME FROM 5,000 LIGHT-YEARS AWAY?

It's the year 2063, and interstellar space travel has become the norm. Eight students from Caird High School and one child set out on a routine planet camp excursion. While there, the students are mysteriously transported 5,000 light-years away to the middle of nowhere! Will they ever make it back home?!

ASTRA
LOST IN SPACE
Story and Art by KENTA SHINOHARA

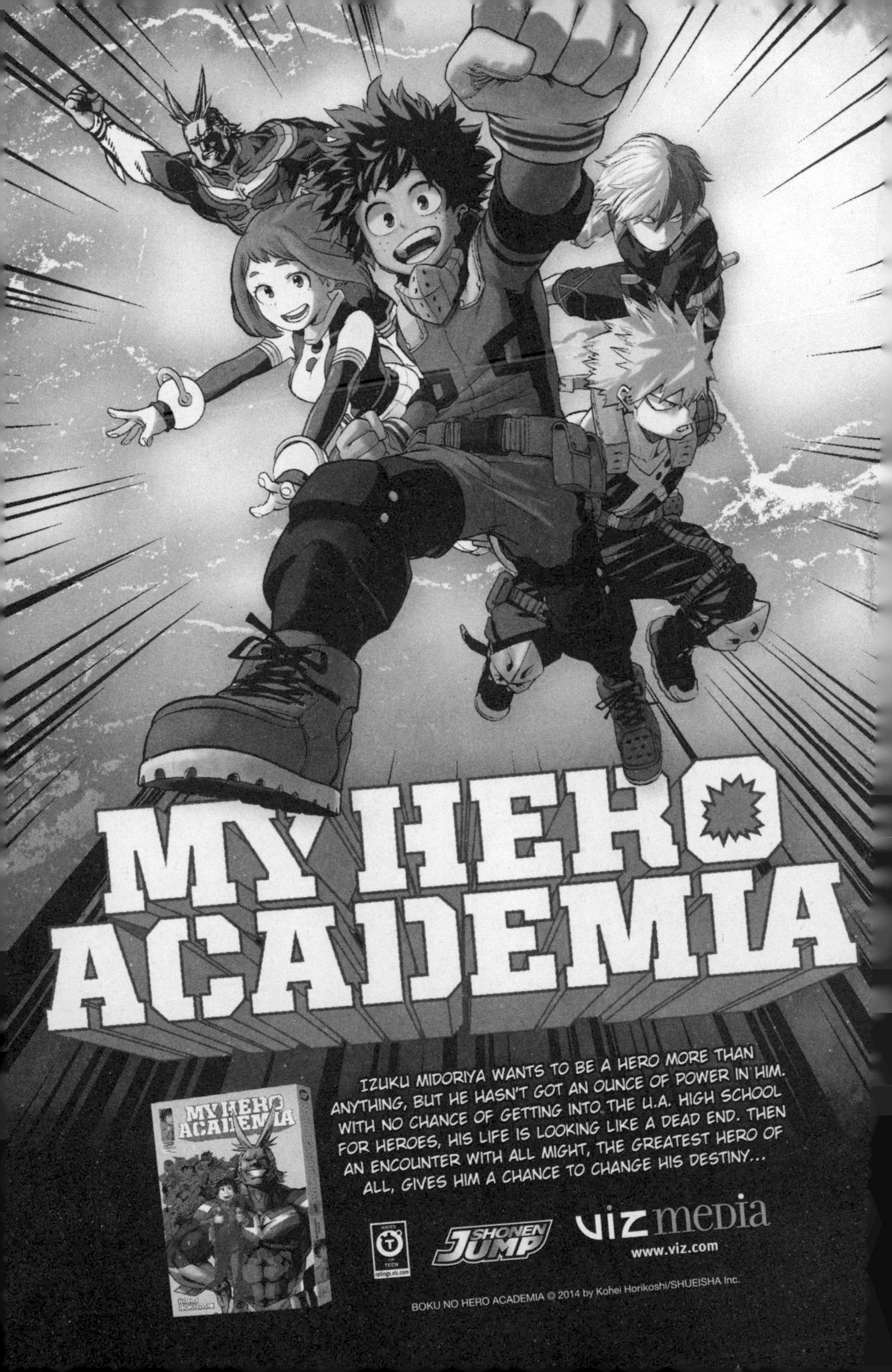
MY HERO ACADEMIA
IZUKU MIDORIYA WANTS TO BE A HERO MORE THAN ANYTHING, BUT HE HASN'T GOT AN OUNCE OF POWER IN HIM. WITH NO CHANCE OF GETTING INTO THE U.A. HIGH SCHOOL FOR HEROES, HIS LIFE IS LOOKING LIKE A DEAD END. THEN AN ENCOUNTER WITH ALL MIGHT, THE GREATEST HERO OF ALL, GIVES HIM A CHANCE TO CHANGE HIS DESTINY…
SHONEN JUMP
viz media
www.viz.com
BOKU NO HERO ACADEMIA © 2014 by Kohei Horikoshi/SHUEISHA Inc.

Dr. STONE

STORY BY
RIICHIRO INAGAKI

ART BY
BOICHI

One fateful day, all of humanity turned to stone. Many millennia later, Taiju frees himself from petrification and finds himself surrounded by statues. The situation looks grim—until he runs into his science-loving friend Senku! Together they plan to restart civilization with the power of science!

You're Reading in the Wrong Direction!!

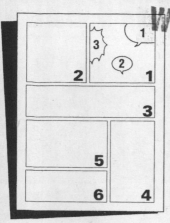

Whoops! Guess what? You're starting at the wrong end of the comic!

...It's true! In keeping with the original Japanese format, **One Piece** is meant to be read from right to left, starting in the upper-right corner.

Unlike English, which is read from left to right, Japanese is read from right to left, meaning that action, sound effects and word-balloon order are completely reversed...something which can make readers unfamiliar with Japanese feel pretty backwards themselves. For this reason, manga or Japanese comics published in the U.S. in English have sometimes been published "flopped"—that is, printed in exact reverse order, as though seen from the other side of the mirror.

By flipping pages, U.S. publishers can avoid confusing readers, but this process is not without its downside. For one thing, a character in a flopped manga series who once wore in the original Japanese version a T-shirt emblazoned with "M A Y" (as in "the merry month of") now wears one which reads "Y A M"! Additionally, many manga creators in Japan are themselves unhappy with the process, as some feel the mirror-imaging of their art skews their original intentions.

We are proud to bring you Eiichiro Oda's **One Piece** in the original unflopped format. For now, though, turn to the other side of the book and let the journey begin...!

—Editor